INTRODUCING AMERICA

Barbara Kreutz & Ellen Fleming

INTRODUCING
AMERICA

Eyre Methuen
London

We dedicate this book to our long-suffering
families who have contributed boundless
enthusiasm and knowledge to this venture,
and especially to I.W.K. without whom
it would all have been impossible.

First published in Great Britain in 1963
by Methuen & Co Ltd
Reprinted 1964
Paperback edition 1968
New revised and reset edition first published
in Great Britain in 1973 by Eyre Methuen Ltd
11 New Fetter Lane London EC4P 4EE
Copyright © 1963, 1973 by Barbara Kreutz and Ellen Fleming
Printed in Great Britain by
Cox & Wyman Ltd, Fakenham, Norfolk

SBN 413 29210 X hardback
SBN 413 30280 6 paperback

CONTENTS

ILLUSTRATIONS

Permission has kindly been given for use of photographs as follows:

Air Force Academy (Colorado), plate 10a; Associated Press Ltd,
plate 4a; David Barton, plate 14a; Camera Press Ltd (London),
plate 13b; J. Allan Cash Ltd (London), plates 5 and 8b; Mrs Ellen
Fleming, plate 13a; Free Lance Photographers Guild Inc (New
York), plates 11b, 12a, 12b and 16b; The New England Council
Inc, plate 2; Pritchard Wood & Partners, plate 3a; San Francisco
Convention and Visitors Bureau, plate 15; The United States
Department of Interior, plates 3b, 4b, 7, 8a, 11a and 16a; The
United States Information Service, plates 9 and 10b; The United
States Travel Service, plates 1, 6a and 14b; Wisconsin Natural
Resources Department (Madison, Wisconsin), plate 6b.

INTRODUCTION

America is different. It is not in the least like England, although many of its roots are English, and it is certainly not like any other European country, nor other places where Europeans have settled. Unless a traveller goes prepared to discover a foreign land, he will miss or misunderstand half of the United States. Many things are done differently in America, and one must not assume that this is a sign of inadequacy or a lack of sophistication. Different challenges evoke different responses; what was esteemed a virtue in Boston, Lincolnshire, could very well prove a liability in Boston, Massachusetts.

Americans are either mad idealists or ruthless pragmatists, depending on how you look at them. You may agree with Compton Mackenzie and Mrs Trollope that it was appalling effrontery for nineteenth-century Americans to have called their totally uncivilized frontier outposts 'Athens' and 'Paris' and 'New Berlin'. Or you may be moved by the dream behind the deed. In any case, Americans are different, sometimes to an infuriating degree.

America is also enormous. Into the single state of Texas one could fit the British Isles, Norway, Belgium and Portugal, and still have room in the corner for Andorra and Lichtenstein. The wagon trains bound for California in the nineteenth century started from rallying points in Missouri, already a third of the way across the continent, and yet it still took them four months for the journey, crossing a mountain range vaster than the Alps, and trackless deserts. It takes considerably longer to go from New York to California by train than from Copenhagen to Athens.

This book is therefore selective. We have tried to include the most interesting places in the United States, but we have had to by-pass many regions as well as several entire states. Our choice of areas on which to concentrate was determined by several major considerations. We wanted to give the best possible sampling of the various distinct sections of the country and to note the places which best convey the flavour of each. We have also thought it useful to aim for a certain geographic coherence within each region, suggesting hypothetical routes and places to see along those routes. This has meant that some interesting corners of the country have had to be omitted; unfortunately it has also meant that we could do nothing with Alaska or Hawaii, which are simply too far removed from the rest of the nation. Finally, we have tried to concentrate on places and regions which would fit into an ideal trip, and we thus devote a considerable amount of space to rural and wilderness explorations. The principal cities of the United States certainly deserve attention, but one of America's true glories is her great outdoors.

We mention only a few restaurants and places to stay: only those which we find in some way unique. For that sort of information, there are several comprehensive food-and-lodging guides already available, and there are also excellent, locally written good-food guides for cities like New York, Washington, D.C., and San Francisco. Obviously we have tried to be accurate with opening hours and days, but we do warn that these can change overnight. Museums in particular seem to be constantly experimenting with new hours; it is well to check locally, or by telephone, before going a long distance to see a particular collection. Further, all prices we mention are correct as of 1972; as these too constantly change, we provide them only as an indication of a price range one should expect. Finally, we apologize for frequently using 'America' and 'American' as synonymous with the United States, but there is simply no practical substitute.

Many people on both sides of the Atlantic have generously given time and energy to helping with this book. We cannot hope to mention them all, but we are particularly indebted to the following: John and Ticker Ballard; David and Lydia Barton; Lois Raeder Elias of the New York Convention and Visitors Bureau; Anne Fleming; Shirley Hibbard; Josephine Killhour of the Philadelphia Visitors Center; Mary Lawson; Dorothy Longaker; Richard P. Longaker; John N. McCormick and Pat

Droste of the International Center in New York City; Don and
Nicky MacInnes; Helen Marshall; Grant Midgely of the National
Park Service; Beverley E. Miller, Doreen Willis and Roger
Jarman of the United States Travel Service; George and Olive
Pierce; Polly Porter; Nathalie Rooney of IVIS in Washington,
D.C.; Landon and Charlotte Warner; Peg Watrous; Mary
Hewes Wharton; Jim Wilson of the Bureau of Indian Affairs.
And to Arletta Renneberg, who coped with the chaos of the
manuscript and patiently endured constant changes, we owe very
special gratitude.

July, 1972

1 · GENERAL INFORMATION

There have always been objections to visiting the United States. It is too far away, or too big once one gets there; too expensive or, lately, too violent. We can't make it any closer to Europe or Asia, although charter flights and off-season bargain fares today make the distance less costly. We can't make it any smaller, although we can and do suggest sections of the country one might combine in a trip for a good over-all view. We do know from our own experience that it need not be too expensive to see the U.S.A. If one chooses to stay only in the leading hotels of the largest cities, it will certainly not be cheap, but we are against that in any case.

The matter of violence, however, is a more difficult objection to counter. Unquestionably, the combination of racial tensions and increased drug addiction has created serious problems in some of the major cities. Yet it would be foolish to harbour exaggerated fears. For example, there are some sections of New York City we would no longer want to wander around in at night or alone, but these are not the 'tourist' sections anyway, and hundreds of thousands of foreign visitors (not to mention American tourists) still happily trudge around New York City every year. We will therefore suggest a few sensible precautions in the New York City chapter, but beyond that we refuse to fuss, and you should not.

CLIMATE

The tremendous size of the country means that there is no such thing as 'the American climate' either literally or figuratively.

New Mexico is as unlike Connecticut as Denmark is unlike Greece. The weather in the northeastern quarter of the United States is forbiddingly known to geographers as 'Manchurian-Appalachian', but in Florida and southern California it is subtropical.

Probably the pleasantest times to go to the United States are autumn and spring. October is clear and crisp almost everywhere, the hills and valleys a riot of red and gold. The maple trees in the Northeast and the upper Great Lakes region, the cottonwood and the aspen in the Rockies, produce a wonderful burst of colour. Spring is lovely too: late March and April in the South, and late April and May in the North. Then it is flowering time for dogwood and redbud across the central part of the country, azaleas in the Carolinas and Virginia, wild lilac and many other roadside flowers in California, and in the Southwest the desert bursts into spectacular bloom. Moreover, it is then less crowded almost everywhere than in the summer, when American tourists are out in force too.

Summer is usually hot throughout most of the continental United States; sometimes uncomfortably hot even in the northern half, and especially hot in the South and in the lower parts of the Southwest. But with air-conditioning everywhere, even an American heat-wave no longer seems too bad, and with care in the choice of destination, the usually dependable sunshine becomes a great boon. Summer is the season to sample the American seacoast with its marvellous beaches, to explore the Rockies, or the high country of northern Arizona and northern New Mexico with its Spanish and Indian culture still very much in evidence.

In winter, on the other hand, the northern half of the United States can be positively Siberian. One would go then to the Rockies only for skiing, and should be prepared everywhere in the North for the possibility of deep snow or bitter winds, or both.

What clothing to take to the United States thus depends entirely on the time of year. For winter in the northern parts, one certainly wants a heavy coat and women might want boots, but since all buildings are centrally heated, often excessively so, the rest of one's clothing should be light-weight. For summer, one should pack the sort of clothes one would then take to Rome or Sidney (or plan to buy them in the States, where summer clothes are attractive and not expensive). But remember that in high-altitude country, even in mid-summer, it can get freezing cold when the sun goes down. Moreover, in San Francisco and the Pacific Northwest, or in Maine, even summer days can sometimes be damp and chilly. Thus one should never go to the States, even in July and August, without something warm to put on top. And since air conditioning can often go to frigid extremes, women will want a cardigan or light wrap for the evening, even in Miami.

In mid-winter, to be sure of hot weather one must go to southern Florida, the California desert or southern Arizona. However, as late as November and as early as March, it is sometimes swimming weather in New Orleans, coastal Georgia, southern California, southern Texas. And since many of the more elaborate American motels now have indoor pools, one might want a bathing suit even in Minnesota in January!

THE STATES UNITED

The geographical and cultural complexity of the United States is compounded by the fact that there are fifty of them. They are joined in a federation under the Constitution, but they remain in many ways quite separate entities, and most of the laws which affect everyday life are state rather than national laws. This means that after you are admitted by the United States immigration officer and cleared by the United States customs man, you will have little further contact with federal officials. Aliens who must register their whereabouts every year do so at the post office, the only branch of the federal government readily at hand.

It is the individual states who decide how fast one may drive, and when, where, and at what age one can buy a drink. State legislatures determine what constitutes a crime and how it will be punished. Moreover, states vary greatly in the rigour of their law-enforcement. Connecticut, for example, is especially stern with drivers who break the speed limit, and while hitch-hiking is nominally illegal in most states, some are particularly hard on offenders.

Patterns of taxation also vary from state to state. Thus petrol for your car is likely to fluctuate in price (by 2 or 3 cents a gallon) as you go from one state to another. You will also discover that most states add a sales tax to all purchases and services, something to remember when you are considering a purchase. (Incidentally, that sum added to your restaurant or hotel bill is almost never a service charge, but this sales tax; one encounters 'service compris' in the States only at a few resort hotels.)

Of course it would be ridiculous to suggest that nothing is centralized or nationally controlled in the United States. Congress and the national government steadily exercise more influence locally through the technique of granting federal money to states and cities only under specified conditions. Moreover, Congress can and does legislate on all manner of issues which concern the national welfare as a whole, or which simply affect more than one state. And, finally, the federal government does interfere with state laws and procedures when there is adjudged to be some contravention of rights guaranteed by the Constitution; on these grounds, the Supreme Court forbade racial segregation in the schools, even though the operation of schools has always been left to the individual states and schools are run by local school boards.

PUBLIC TRANSPORT

Perhaps because of the great size of the country, most forms of public transport in the United States are inadequate by European standards. You can get from one large city to another without a car, and it is relatively simple to get about within the larger cities. But the moment you head for a small town not on any direct route between major cities, you are likely to run into difficulties. Moreover, many of the smaller cities lack adequate city bus systems, so once there you must either have a car or take a taxi.

A common American solution to this problem is to fly to the major town of a region, and then hire a car. There are a great many airlines in the United States, large and small, and between them they fly to almost every corner of the country. One can hardly cross the country for pennies on a plane; the distances, after all, are enormous. But mile for mile, plane fares in America compare very favourably with those in Europe, and there are 'family plans' and 'youth fares' (22 and under) which can cut flying costs substantially. Moreover, most of the airlines currently offer substantial discounts to foreign visitors, provided they buy their tickets before they enter the country or, in some cases, within 30 days after their arrival. The various plans change a bit from year to year, but one now gives as much as 50 per cent off the regular fare, and another currently offers unlimited travel on certain airlines for 21 days for $150 adult fare. Bear in mind, too, that while one may need to buy these specially discounted air tickets or vouchers in advance, it is usually not necessary to have the tickets written up in exact detail at the same time. In fact it is often preferable to wait until one reaches the United States to decide what precise scheduling one wants.

Except for commuter service to and from the large cities, passenger train service in the States is now severely reduced. Furthermore, it takes a long time to cross America by train: three full days from New York to California, changing trains at Chicago. And, with sleeping accommodations, it is generally more expensive than flying. For some people it nonetheless remains a splendid way to see the country, and so we will note that the passenger railroad service has been unified into a single, federally-subsidized system called Amtrak, and any Amtrak station can give information and arrange reservations on any passenger train. We should also note that the trains along the 'eastern corridor', from Boston to Washington, D.C., are not bad, and there is even one crack service, the Metroliner, an extra-fare train (several trips a day, reservations required) which runs from New York City to Washington, D.C., via Philadelphia and Baltimore, and costs about half as much as the comparable plane fare.

A popular alternative is offered by the long-distance buses, operated mainly by Greyhound and Continental Trailways, throughout the United States and Canada. Their fares usually come to between half and two-thirds the cost of comparable plane fares. However, like the airlines, these major bus firms have discount plans for foreign visitors: currently, $99 for 21 days' unlimited travel, or longer time-periods for proportionately more. (In general one must purchase these special bus tickets before one enters the United States or Canada. However, foreign students and visiting research scholars or lecturers can arrange for them after they've arrived; any Greyhound terminal or the International Sales Department of Continental Trailways, Dallas, Texas, can supply details.) The buses are clean and comfortable. We would not want to cross the country non-stop by bus, but for journeys of six or eight hours, we have found these buses quite all right.

Note, too, that you can ship an unaccompanied suitcase quite inexpensively by Greyhound bus. For example, to send a 35-pound case 1,000 miles currently costs $8.80.

There are also two major sightseeing bus firms which do tours of the principal cities and in some instances also trips into the surrounding country: Gray Line (not to be confused with Greyhound) and American Sightseeing. The latter currently offers foreign visitors a discount.

TRAVELLING BY CAR

If you want to see the best of America, you must limit your time in the cities and get out into the country. And the simplest way to do this is to have a car.

To rent a car in the U.S. one need only be 21 and have an acceptable credit card or money for a deposit. The two biggest car-rental firms are Hertz and Avis. Both offer foreign visitors a discount on car rentals, and each also has various plans open to everyone whereby one can rent a car for a set number of days for a considerably reduced rental. Anyone contemplating a trip to the United States ought certainly to check with the nearest United States Travel Service (USTS) office to discover what bargain car-rental plans are currently in effect.

There are also many 'budget' car rental firms. Some are more truly 'budget' than others; we have had good luck with Airways. These budget firms offer fewer services; for example, they do not have reservation desks at airports, nor can one usually rent one of their cars in one town and leave it in another, as one can with Hertz (often without even paying any extra charge). These budget firms are worth considering if one only wants a car for a day or so locally, so long as one makes sure the rental-plan includes adequate insurance protection. For longer rentals, however, the Hertz no-mileage-charge plan is usually much the best bargain. On long trips it is the mileage charge which mounts up most alarmingly, and you should always note carefully the mileage rates before you hire a car.

Visitors planning a rather extended stay in the United States might consider buying a second-hand car and selling it again at the end. This has worked well for many people, but one ought to plan on an initial investment of perhaps $600, and of course there are always risks in buying a used car. One should make sure the dealer has a good reputation, and it certainly helps if one knows enough about cars to tell good from bad.

To drive in the U.S., theoretically you need only a valid driving licence from your own country (with the exception of a very few countries), but an International Driving Permit in addition is a good idea. All petrol stations supply regional maps free of charge. But it can be useful to have an all-inclusive road atlas as well, and we can recommend either the large *Rand McNally Road Atlas* (widely available in the United States and Canada) or the compact *Falk Road Atlas for the U.S.A.* (published in Western Germany and available here and there in the U.S.). The latter, incidentally, also includes an exceptionally detailed street map of Manhattan.

We strongly urge anyone who contemplates driving in the States to get from the USTS their 'driver's kit'. It includes a badge for the car which identifies one as a foreign visitor deserving special courtesy, as well as all kinds of useful information about American traffic laws and driving practices. USTS can also advise about insurance and registration for anyone planning to buy a car.

If you belong to an automobile club in your own country, you should plan to get in touch with the American Automobile Association, known as the AAA or 'Triple A'. There are AAA offices all over the United States. As a reciprocal courtesy, they will supply you with AAA Tour Books and maps for the regions you plan to visit, and they can also help with general travel information and arrangements. (The AAA Tour Books are very good, covering 'what to see' in every section of the country in considerable detail and listing hotels and motels as well; we only wish they included more medium-priced accommodations.) If you will be doing a lot of driving, in your own car, you perhaps ought actually to join the AAA, so that you can also use their emergency road service. Non-residents of the United States can get a 'membership-at-large' for $20 for one year; such memberships can be instantly arranged at any AAA office, but only after arrival in the States.

The great turnpikes and 'thruways' of the northeastern section of the country are well worth their tolls because they save so much driving time in that most populous part of the country. Elsewhere in the United States, the super-highways are mainly free. But we do feel there is something sterile about seeing a nation only from its super-highways, by-passing all the towns, and we would hope that all travellers would sample a few true back-roads as well. One can find astonishingly unspoiled country that way, even in some of the most densely populated sections.

Observe the speed limits everywhere, and when driving on a multi-lane highway, take care to keep to your lane and to change lanes only after signalling. Try to avoid going in or out of the major cities on the freeways at rush hours. Never pass a yellow school bus when it is stopped to let children out, even if you're coming from the opposite direction; you yourself must just stop too. If you plan to drive across the desert in mid-summer, carry extra water or consider driving at night and spending the day at some nice motel with a swimming pool and air conditioning. Finally, particularly at motels in or at the edge of large cities, don't leave tempting valuables or luggage in the car overnight, even if the car is locked. We ourselves have never had a car rifled (except in a European city which shall be nameless) but we know people who have.

FOOD

In addition to proper restaurants, there are two indigenous sorts of inexpensive eating places in the United States: the drive-in and the drugstore. Drive-ins are what their name implies: you drive in, either pick up a hamburger or something similar at the counter, or order it to be brought to you, and then eat in the car. The McDonalds hamburger chain is perhaps the quintessential American drive-in, and one we're rather partial to. The American drugstore probably needs no introduction; it has supplanted the old-fashioned 'general store' as the purveyor of everything to everybody. It is likely to be open from 8 in the morning until 9 or 10 at night. Most drugstores have counters where sandwiches and often entire meals are served, although their gastronomic specialty traditionally was and still is the milk-shake, the malt, the ice-cream soda and the ice-cream sundae. While we have certainly never had a drugstore meal worthy of Michelin, we have had many which were perfectly adequate.

The very mixed ethnic heritage of the American people is reflected in American eating habits and eating places. Thus the tremendous influx of southern Italians and Sicilians, which peaked around the turn of the last century, has led to the enormous popularity of pizza and 'pizza parlours', and also (especially in the Northeast) to the 'Italian' or 'hero' sandwich or 'submarine' or 'grinder' (the name varies with the locality). This last is a sandwich, sometimes hot, sometimes cold, of sausage and tomatoes and peppers tucked inside an Italian bread-roll. Good ones are spectacularly good. And, as a result of another influx from the other direction, you are likely to find moderately-priced Chinese restaurants almost everywhere in America. (The Chinese originally came into the country to work in the mines of the West and on the railroads, and many later migrated eastwards.)

Ordinary restaurants vary tremendously in the United States, both in price and quality, and it must be admitted that some very expensive ones serve miserable food by international standards. Conversely, some very simple ones do very well, especially with regional or local ethnic specialities. The one sort of restaurant you'll find everywhere is the 'steak place'; it won't be cheap, but the steaks will probably be good. Otherwise, like everything else, restaurants tend to be more expensive in the East, particularly in the major cities, than in the West or South. It is hard to generalize accurately about food costs, however, and the best we can do is to say that in our experience travelling across the country it is perfectly easy to average $8 to $9 a day for meals, eating very well, so long as one has a continental breakfast and does not insist on a large meal at both midday and night. By subsisting largely on hamburgers and pizza and the like, one can of course eat for much less. And one can certainly spend more, especially in the cities, if price is no object!

A cautionary note or two: breakfast is almost never included in the price of an American hotel room, and even a continental breakfast in a hotel can be quite expensive if you have it brought to your room. (In America, even where *things* are cheap, *services* are very dear.) In cities like New York, American travellers anxious to economize with breakfast will sometimes avoid even the 'coffee shop' in their hotel and go out instead, to a nearby drugstore or luncheonette. We should also warn that in small towns restaurants often stop serving dinner as early as eight o'clock at night.

As you will discover, ordinary American families eat out far more than their European counterparts do. Thus if you want to know where to eat in Kalamazoo or Kansas City, just ask your taxi driver or the policeman on the corner.

– AND LODGING

Very few hotels or motels in the United States have a distinct personality of their own. From coast to coast you will find the same Gideon Bible, the same 'sanitized' tumbler in a transparent paper bag, the same imitation Dufy on the wall. Nor do standards in comfort vary markedly, except that the newer the hotel or motel, the more likely it is to have hermetically-sealed windows and year-round air-conditioning. The beds are always good, but if you want a second blanket or two pillows, you will usually have to ask. In general we therefore favour economizing on lodgings in the United States, or at least we save our splurges for the few hotels here and there which really warrant it.

USTS can supply hotel lists for the principal cities, or one can write to the Convention and Visitors Bureau of each city. We found it possible for two people to stay comfortably in New York City or Washington, D.C., or San Francisco for about $18 a night (a double room with bath), but one must choose a bit carefully in order to accomplish this and still be in a convenient section of the city. The big, well-known hotels will cost considerably more.

Driving through the country, one finds that in some areas motel rates go up and down according to the season. Thus while one might easily find a double room with bath in Florida or the Southwest, at a motel with a swimming pool, for an average of $14 a night 'off-season' the price was likely to be half again as high during the high season. In other, less 'seasonal' parts of the country, $16 was generally ample for a comfortable double room at a motel, all year round (unless one stopped at one of the elaborate 'motor hotels' which now ring the big cities).

We should perhaps qualify the prices we have given for motels by saying a bit more about the institution of the motel itself. Motels began as a cheaper and less formal substitute for hotels, but over the years more and more lavish ones have been built, until some are now grander than most hotels, with indoor and outdoor swimming pools, saunas, colour television sets in each room, and so forth. Anyone driving through the United States should surely try to sample one of these, stopping early for the night and staying late the next morning in order to get one's money's worth. But this sort of motel costs more than the rates we have indicated; 'our' sort will probably have only one small swimming pool, and only black-and-white television! Obviously, one can stop even more cheaply than that, and travellers must simply develop an eye for the inexpensive motel. A hint: the farther from a 'thruway' or super-highway the motel is, the farther off the beaten track, the less expensive the motel is likely to be.

There are two other possible ways to stop for the night at a reduced cost. One is to go into the nearest town and look for houses displaying signs saying 'Tourists' or 'Overnight Guests'; there will be pink-fringed lampshades and a chatty landlady, but the room will probably be both cheap and clean. The other is to go into the nearest town, if it is a comparatively small one, and see if there is a hotel still in operation. Competition from motels has driven many small-town hotels out of business; those that hang on tend to offer bargain prices.

Again, a final note of caution: the most expensive way to travel in America is alone. The rate for one person in a hotel or motel room is only slightly lower than that for two, as a rule, and at motels in particular, which characteristically have two enormous double beds in each room, a third or fourth person can usually stay for only $1 or $2 more apiece. And there are no really comprehensive guides to hotels and motels in the United States. We have already noted that the AAA Tour Books tend to list only the more expensive places. There are also the Mobil Guides, a series of regional guides published by the Mobiloil Company (and available at Mobil petrol stations and in bookshops). They list somewhat less costly lodgings, and seem to us to be quite reliable in their evaluations of hotels and restaurants, but they are neither infallible nor all-inclusive.

MONEY AND BANKING

Credit cards are widely used in the United States, to enable goods and services to be obtained on account, so that the traveller need not carry large sums of money about with him. The cards can be used instead of cash for almost everything. Intending visitors should inquire at travel agencies and banks in their own countries about firms issuing credit cards which they can use in America. For example, we have found that any big place which takes the Bank Americard will usually also accept its British cousin, the Barclaycard.

Banks in the United States usually open at 9 a.m. and shut at 2 or 2.30 p.m., from Monday to Friday. Banks in the larger cities will change foreign currency, or give dollars for travellers cheques in foreign currency, but if you are planning to use travellers cheques here and there across the country, it is absolutely necessary to have dollar cheques, and American Express cheques are the most preferable. Travellers should also be very sure to have some American money when they arrive in the United States, since changing facilities are not available at all airports at all times, and one cannot pay for anything with foreign currency.

Banks and shops and post offices in the United States shut on New Year's Day; on the last Monday in May (Memorial Day); on July 4 (Independence Day); on Labor Day (the first Monday in September); on Thanksgiving Day (the fourth Thursday in November); and on Christmas Day. In some states, other holidays are observed as well.

TELEPHONES, TELEGRAMS, AND LETTERS

Telegrams are sent at Western Union offices, not at a post office. And you may well need to send telegrams, or telephone 'long-distance', for letters move rather slowly in America, again perhaps because of the enormous size of the country.

Public telephones are known as 'pay-phones', and are commonly found on street corners, in drugstores, at petrol stations. The telephone service is very good in the United States, and every 'phone booth' gives careful directions to the user. But you must be sure not to confuse the alphabetical 'O' with the numerical 'o' on the dial. One can make long-distance calls 'collect'; the person at the other end pays. But if one makes a long-distance call at one's own expense from a pay-phone, it is important to remember that in the States the operator does not always signal when you've used up all the money you will have deposited at the start of the call (for three minutes). Thus you should either time yourself carefully, or be prepared for the operator to ring back at the end and ask for more money. Remember too that long-distance calls are much cheaper at night and on weekends.

One invaluable adjunct of the American telephone system is the 'Yellow Pages', a directory to services and shops. In large cities, the Yellow Pages are bound separately; in smaller towns they are to be found at the back of the ordinary directory.

In every American city or town, there will be only one 'main' post office, but in the larger cities there are innumerable 'postal sub-stations' or 'branch post offices'. Finding one of these will save you from having to patronize the ubiquitous 'stamp machines', where one has to pay extra for stamps.

In a crisis, anywhere, simply dial 'O' for Operator, and tell her what's wrong.

TIPPING

New York City is far and away the most tip-hungry part of America, as well as the most expensive in every other way. But everywhere in America, tipping is expected to some extent, for waiters, porters and so on. On the other hand, one never tips at petrol stations, and one neither pays for theatre programmes nor tips the usher. Furthermore, it is no longer usual to tip the chambermaid in a hotel, unless one has stayed a long time or asked for special service. In restaurants and bars, and at barbershops and the hairdressers, one leaves 15 per cent. Only in New York City will you be expected to leave a tip at the 'lunch counter' of a luncheonette or drug store; in other parts of the country this is optional, but nowhere should it be less than 10¢ (a dime). A nickel (5¢) is never an adequate tip for any service. Give taxi drivers in New York City 10–15 per cent of the fare or a minimum tip of 25¢ (being a quarter of a dollar, 25¢ is called a quarter). In other cities the tip can be less, and one does not tip the drivers of airport limousines. The boy who carries your suitcase up to your room will expect approximately 50¢ a case in the big cities, 25¢ a case in the smaller towns. The same applies to the porter who carries your suitcase at an airport or a railway station. Give 25¢ to the hotel doorman who ushers you into a taxi (and 50¢ if he's had to work to get you one). Twenty-five cents will also do for the 'washroom' attendant or the girl who checks your coat; 25¢ is the standard tip for any small service.

NATIVE CUSTOMS AND CHARACTERISTICS

Electric fittings are standard all over the United States; the current is generally 110–115 volt, 60-cycle A.C. Cigarettes and tobacco are sold at drugstores, and cigarettes alone are widely available in vending machines everywhere, including petrol stations. Many things are pleasantly cheap in the United States, but men's haircuts definitely are not.

American terminology differs in innumerable instances from British. For example, in the United States, the ground floor is the 'first floor'; a return ticket is a 'round-trip' ticket; the lift is an 'elevator'. 'Broiled' meat is what the British call grilled, and chips are 'French fries'; biscuits are 'cookies'. One buys petrol at 'gas stations'.

There are four time-zones across the country, each an hour behind the next: Eastern, Central, Mountain, Pacific. With the exception of Hawaii, Arizona, Indiana and Michigan, all of the United States observe Daylight Saving Time in summer.

Americans often give street directions in terms of 'blocks': 'go four blocks east and then turn left', or 'it's at the end of the block'. A block is one square of the grid which in most American cities provides the street-pattern; hence 'four blocks east' means 'east to the fourth turning'. Within each American block, you will usually find the odd-numbered buildings (for example, 1701–1799) on one side of the street, even-numbered (1700–1798) on the other. But the visitor should remember that streets in American cities can be terribly long; when someone gives you a street address, it's as well to ask what the nearest cross-street is.

Laundry and dry-cleaning services are relatively inexpensive, good, and quick in the United States. In most cities, you can get something washed or cleaned in the course of a day, if necessary. Travellers driving through the country rejoice in the fact that most towns have laundromats which are often open until late at night.

There are almost no public lavatories as such in the United States, and those which do exist are almost universally grubby and to be avoided. Instead one repairs to a hotel, to a department store, or to a petrol station, and the operative word is 'ladies' room' or 'men's room'; in the United States the cloakroom is merely where one leaves one's coat.

BASIC ECONOMICS

We have already mentioned several ways in which one can economize while seeing America: through taking advantage of discounts available to foreign visitors, for example, and through adopting such American customs as a drugstore meal or a pizza or a hot sandwich for lunch or supper. Economics will also figure in some of our regional chapters. But there are other general ways to save money too.

Renting a car, for example, can work out to be quite an inexpensive way of travelling if there are four people involved. And even with only two people, one can often save money by having a car, since one can thus seek out those less expensive lodgings. Furthermore, American families travelling long distances by car almost always carry basic picnic supplies, including an insulated bag or a cheap styrofoam picnic hamper to keep things cold. (In it, we keep a jar or a double plastic bag full of ice cubes to act as the refrigerant, and at night we replenish the ice cubes supply; ice cubes are dispensed free at every motel.) With our own families, we also carry along an inexpensive electric 'hot pot' with which to boil water. Thus equipped, one can do a continental breakfast cheaply and easily in the motel room, and then picnic at lunch as well. Neither acquiring the basic supplies nor the daily food-buying is a problem, for nowadays one finds super-markets and shopping centres on the edge of virtually all American cities and towns, usually open at night until 9 o'clock and almost always including shops which sell things like electric 'hot pots' and picnic hampers at bargain prices. (A big drugstore or a 'discount store' will do.) One could buy all the basic equipment for $10, and proceed to save a good deal of money in the course of several days' trip. Most states have designated picnic stops along their highways, or one can find a nearby state park on the map and turn off to picnic there.

Particularly in Florida, many motels advertise 'efficiencies': rooms not only with the normal beds and bath but also with tiny kitchenettes attached. 'Efficiencies' often seem to cost no more than ordinary motel rooms, yet make it possible to live much more cheaply.

Particularly for visitors travelling in the western part of the United States, in the warmer months, camping can be not only a great money-saver but also great fun. We will say more about it later.

One way to enconomize on good food in the larger American cities is to act counter to American custom and have one's main meal at midday. The better restaurants in New York or Chicago or San Francisco almost always charge more at night.

Many hotels in the United States give discounts on room rates to foreign visitors. In Philadelphia, for example, almost every hotel now does this. It is worth trying for the discount every time, and trying hard; not all clerks will be familiar with the scheme, so it sometimes takes a fair amount of prodding. Moreover, some of the big hotel chains, like Sheraton, sometimes offer special weekend rates.

We will be making many more references to the splendid National Parks, but here we must note the happy fact that foreign visitors need not pay entrance fees to go into any area administered by the National Park Service. (If one camps there, however, one must still pay the 'user fee' for camping.)

Youth hostels are rather few and far between in the United States, but there are probably enough of them in good places to warrant hostellers bringing their international hostelling card. However, it should be noted that there is *no* youth hostel in New York City, although the American Youth Hostels headquarters there (20 West 17th Street) can sometimes help hostellers find fairly cheap hotel rooms. They can also supply hostel directories.

Museums which charge admission (not all do) usually offer special student rates. Anyone in that category ought to carry an International Student Card.

Getting down to the ultimate in money-saving, we should re-emphasize the fact that hitch-hiking is illegal almost everywhere in the United States. Moreoever, the law is especially severely enforced in some of the southern and western states. The legal definition of hitch-hiking does vary from state to state, so that in some areas one can 'hitch a ride' without risk of arrest so long as one stays on the curbing and does not stand in the road. But even this is not legal along the thruways and the big interstate highways, or the entrances thereto, so the whole picture becomes somewhat complicated, and we are very reluctant to advocate hitch-hiking for anyone not conversant with the various state laws and the ingenious techniques developed by generations of American undergraduates. We must also warn that it is absolutely not safe for girls alone, or even for girls in pairs; grisly things have happened time and again to girls on the road.

Foreign students trying to get across the United States cheaply can sometimes find a free night's lodging by going to the Student Union of any large American university and asking around. They may even hear there how to get free lodging on the West Coast by looking up the 'Jesus people', but that takes us out of our depth!

One final warning: it is strictly illegal for anyone who has entered the United States on a visitor's visa to take a job, and this is rather closely checked.

TRAVELLING MADE EASY

Fifteen years ago, prospective visitors to the United States found it very hard to get accurate travel information before going, and found the situation only slightly better once they'd arrived. However, we have recently tested the United States Travel Service, the official tourist information agency, and we think it's very good, although a more modest operation than its European counterparts. Currently, there are USTS offices in London (22 Sackville Street); Sydney (37 Pitt Street); Toronto (P.O. Box 363 or Toronto-Dominion Centre); Paris (123 Avenue Charles de Gaulle, 92 Neuilly); Tokyo (Kokusai Building; 12, 3-chome Marunouchi, Chiyoda-ku); Mexico City (Plaza de los Ferrocarriles, 3, or c/o American Embassy); Frankfurt (Boersenstrasse, 1); and Buenos Aires (Florida 683–4°, '36' or c/o American Embassy).

USTS can supply all the standard sorts of travel information one would expect, including vital facts about all currently operative discounts and special bargains for foreign visitors. And they have also developed several ingenious plans to make travel in the United States more pleasant for outsiders. Perhaps the most ingenious is the magic telephone number (800–255–3050, and ask for the Visit U.S.A. desk), which can be dialled toll-free from anywhere in the United States, connecting the visitor with a universal problem-solver. If you lose your passport, or need to know the nearest bank which will change rubles, or are simply lost in Iowa, you just dial the number. What's more, the people at the other end of the line can speak French, German, Spanish, and Japanese, as well as English. (USTS can also supply lists of hotels with a multilingual staff.)

Another good USTS idea, perhaps borrowed from the Danes, is 'Meet Americans at Home'. In some 70 cities all across the country, there are people willing, even eager, to entertain foreign visitors for an evening. All one need do is ring up the local organizer and allow a day or two; an effort will be made to match hosts and guests according to their interests or professions.

Unfortunately, USTS has no offices within the United States themselves (although the headquarters is at the Department of

Commerce in Washington, D.C., and one can write to them there). One should therefore amass all necessary brochures and information before starting one's trip. But within the United States, each major city does have a Convention and Visitors Bureau (sometimes simply 'Visitors Bureau') and we have found most of these to be excellent sources for local information. In the appropriate chapters, we'll mention those we personally know to be particularly good (but this must not be taken to imply criticism of the many we have simply never tested).

There are also International Visitors Centers (again, the name differs from place to place) in several cities. Some of these, like the International Center in New York City, are largely concerned with people who have come to the United States for a period of months or even years, such as foreign students or teachers, foreigners taking part in training programs, and so forth. Others, like IVIS in Washington, D.C., are primarily organized to help transient foreign tourists, who may only want to know how and where to see the sights. We'll mention each of these centres, too, in the appropriate chapters. They are splendid organizations, largely staffed by public-spirited volunteers.

The big-city Visitors Bureaux and International Visitors Centers are 'walk-in' places, although one can of course write ahead to them too. One can also write to the individual states' departments for tourism. Almost every one is called something different, but a lettter addressed to the 'Department of Commerce and Tourism' at the capital city of any given state would almost surely end at the proper desk. Two cautions are necessary, however. You should ask for an airmail reply, since surface mail overseas takes forever. And be prepared too for the fact that some of these organizations are appallingly slow in responding to inquiries.

– AND HAZARDS

A late-Victorian guidebook solemnly declares that 'Manhattan' is an Indian word meaning 'the place where everybody gets drunk'. The Indians perhaps were looking ahead to the day when unsuspecting foreigners would discover only too late that whisky in America is often 100-proof and that the dry martini there is likely to be at least four parts gin to one part vermouth, and even more potent because it is chilled. But drink can also be a problem in the United States for quite a different reason. Nation-wide Prohibition ended in 1933, but some few states still will not allow wine or spirits to be sold in public places; some will allow it to be sold by the bottle, in shops, but not by the glass; and even in 'wet' states there will be certain 'dry' towns, without bars or liquor stores, or you may encounter Sunday closings. In such cities as New York or Boston or Chicago or San Francisco you will not find any of these complications, but if you venture into the agricultural states west of the Mississippi or into the South (areas where the nonconformist and Calvinist influence is great), be warned. If you will be desolate without a drink in the evening, you had better carry your own bottle with you into the hinterland.

In America, 'inn' and even 'tavern' do not always imply drink. They are merely designations that seem to Americans to have a pleasant, traditional ring to them, and anyone starting up a country restaurant is likely to call it 'The-Something-Inn'. It may not be licensed, it may not have rooms for stopping overnight. It will probably have good food with a regional flavour; home-made hot breads in the South, good fish chowder in New England, and so on. The same sort of warning applies to 'tearooms' which, if they do tea at all, will do it only incidentally. The inclusion of 'tea' in the name of an eating place is merely to impart a homely quaintness; again, you will probably get a good regional meal, but the place may well be closed at tea-time!

On city buses you will in most cities be expected to board the bus at the front and pay the driver the exact fare; he may not be allowed to give change. Thus you would be well advised always to carry a good supply of coins. It will be useful in any case for the many vending machines you will encounter. You are usually meant to leave the bus by the rear door; sometimes to open that door you must step down on the inner step.

Anyone who plans to picnic or walk in the country should learn to recognize poison ivy (*toxicodendron radicans*). It is most often found east of the Mississippi, in woods, on banks, and along fences. It is trifoliate, and characteristically the stem of the centre leaf is longer than the stems of the other two. The leaves are reddish in autumn and spring, shiny and green in summer. It is not to be confused with Virginia creeper, a much more common and perfectly harmless plant whose leaves grow in groups of five instead of three. People vary in their sensitivity to poison ivy, but it may cause a severe and long-lasting irritation wherever it comes into contact with the skin. A pharmacist can give you preparations to ease the discomfort; serious cases are best seen by a doctor.

Particularly at dusk in the summer, mosquitoes become a plague in many parts of America. You can, however, buy various sorts of mosquito-repellent, which are quite effective, and indispensable on summer evening picnics or for camping.

If you like to know about all possible hazards, you can bear in mind that there are only four sorts of poisonous snakes in America: the coral snake, found only in the South; the water moccasin or cottonmouth (which lives along the rivers but is very shy); the copperhead; and the rattlesnake. Most Americans live and die without ever seeing a poisonous snake, and it is not a danger one should worry about. Some natives of the Southwest say that one should never walk through the desert without high boots because of the rattlesnakes; others, equally experienced, say that this is ridiculous and that they have walked hundreds of miles in isolated country without ever seeing one.

This brings us logically to the subject of medical treatment in the United States. You must not believe all you hear about the astronomic charges of doctors in America. Nevertheless, specialists are expensive and hospital fees very high, and it would be wise for anyone going to America to take out a health and accident insurance policy.

There are two American holidays which all prospective travellers should be especially warned about: the Fourth of July weekend, and the Labor Day weekend. Depending on whether July 4th comes toward the end of the week or the beginning, the weekend nearest it is likely to be stretched forward or back to encompass it, thus making a virtual holiday out of the hapless day in between. (This also happens with Thanksgiving, which is always a Thursday.) Banks and shops won't be closed on that in-between day, but the people you want to see may well be gone. Even more important for the traveller is the fact that on the Fourth of July weekend and the Labor Day weekend, Americans themselves rush to the seashore or the mountains, and accommodations everywhere but in the deserted cities may be hard to find. Right after the Labor Day weekend, however, most Americans head for home, and the rest of September is thus an especially good time to visit the United States, with good weather and no crowds.

A special sort of hazard is the tourist trap. With its love of extravagant advertising, the United States seems to have an unlimited supply of signs proclaiming the eighth wonder of the world just around the next bend. You must recognize these lures for what they are and not succumb – unless, that is, you really want to see 'the longest unnavigable river in the world' (it's the James River in South Dakota) or alligator-wrestling. The sad part is that one may become so cynical about much touted 'sights' that one is likely to turn back short of the Grand Canyon. (It is told of P. T. Barnum, the great circus impresario, that he once had difficulty getting the crowds to leave his Museum of Marvels so that new crowds could be admitted. Knowing his fellow Americans, he put up a sign over the exit reading TO THE EGRESS. The people poured out, ever eager for a new attraction.) As a rule of thumb, we would suggest that the more an attraction is advertised along the roadside, the less likely it is to be worth seeing.

Finally, if you are taking a long bus trip in the United States it is important to make sure your luggage is put on the same bus, so that it will arrive at your destination at the same time you do. And if you are making a plane trip which involves changing planes, it is well to carry on to the plane some sort of overnight case which can fit under your seat, so that you won't be too seriously inconvenienced if your luggage is temporarily delayed en route.

THE GREAT OUTDOORS

The National Parks are one of the great glories of the United States. The original concept was the preservation of the finest wilderness areas in the face of encroaching civilization, and this is still a primary function. The Parks are kept as nearly as possible in their natural state. But since the Parks are completely open to everyone, with only a few restrictions (no shooting the animals, no camping or fires except in designated areas), more and more people have flocked to them and some Parks began to suffer from over-use. The Park Service is trying in several ways to solve the problem; one development is an increasing restriction on the use of private cars within the Parks, coupled with ingenious forms of public park-transport. And the number and area of the National Parks (and of their lesser siblings, National Monuments, National Recreation Areas, National Seashores) is being rapidly expanded.

More new ones will no doubt have been established by the time this book is out. Some of the lesser siblings, incidentally, are almost as magnificent as the more famous Parks, but they tend to be smaller in area and to offer only minimal camping facilities, if that.

Since everyone knows about the Parks, wilderness purists tend to scorn them and go themselves to more remote areas. But we have found that even in so popular a Park as Grand Teton in mid-summer, one need certainly not be smothered in people so long as one picks a camping site some distance from the car-parks or goes for a hike well away from the roads. In other words, the National Parks are what you make of them, and it seems foolish to disregard the fact that, by design, they encompass extraordinarily beautiful country. However, in July and August, one ought to try to avoid the most crowded ones: Great Smoky, Yosemite, Yellowstone, and the South Rim of the Grand Canyon.

There are four ways to stay at most National Parks. One can set up one's tent, or come in a 'camper' (a sort of van with living quarters built-in, now enormously popular in the West, and rentable in many places; consult USTS). Or one can stay in a cabin or sometimes in considerable luxury, in a lodge or hotel. These last vary in quality and price from Park to Park, for while the Park Service itself maintains the Parks and mans the Visitors Centers, and Park Rangers conduct trail-walks and so forth, the lodges and whatever food facilities there are (and even some tours within some Parks) are privately operated.

To decide which Park to visit, a prospective traveller might get the USTS brochure, *The Great Outdoors of the U.S.A.*, which describes them all, with pictures. (We found the map in the 1971 edition quite inaccurate in part, but we understand that is being corrected.) Then one should write to the Superintendent of the particular Park for the Park's informational brochure. (These are excellent, and will be sent overseas, airmail, on request.) There is also an excellent *National Park Guide* published by Rand McNally, which is packed with vital and illuminating information about each National Park and Monument, including good descriptions of the sorts of accommodation.

At many of the western Parks, staying in a cabin can provide a reasonable compromise between genuine camping and luxuriating at the lodge; it requires no equipment but is primitive enough to seem proper for the surroundings. And one can make reservations for the cabins, as one also can for rooms at the lodges, whereas all camping sites are available only on a first-come, first-served basis, with a limit on the number of days one can occupy a site.

For those who might want to camp, but lack equipment, tents and so forth can be hired in many of the towns near the big western Parks, or in cities like Denver. (The USTS can supply information.) And one can, of course, camp in many places in the West in addition to the National Parks. There are many splendid state parks (established by the individual states), National Forests, and privately-owned camping areas. In fact knowledgeable campers now much prefer the National Forests, since they have fewer and less crowded campsites with more of a wilderness flavour. USTS has another brochure describing all sorts of camping and wilderness possibilities, and listing sources for more information about each.

Or we can recommend simply staying at a ranch; there are 'dude ranches' everywhere in the West. Some are real working ranches, with a few dudes and a great many cattle; others have very few cattle and a great many dudes. The prettiest ranches, in the most beautiful situations, are often the least 'genuine', if it is cowboys and cows you seek; most of the big cattle spreads are on the open plains, far from the mountains. Dude or 'guest' ranches in the scenic areas may offer extra treats like pack trips into the mountains, whereas simple working ranches may provide no entertainment for their dudes other than letting them tag along after the cowboys and try their hand at ranch work. Ranches thus can vary greatly in their prices. Currently rates seem to run from $10 to $22 a day per person, all-in, with heated swimming pools at one end of the spectrum and not even indoor plumbing at the other.

In addition to the established dude ranches, which rarely accept people for less than a week, there are all kinds of lodges and quasi-dude ranches in the West which will take people just for a night or two and furnish horses as well.

The Dude Ranchers Association, Billings, Montana, can supply lists of member-ranches throughout the West. But there are also two paperback guidebooks which we heartily recommend for anyone interested in any aspect of the American outdoors. One is the *Farm and Ranch Vacation Guide*, which has good descriptive listings not only of Western ranches which take guests (in Canada too), but also of farms in the East and Midwest. It also now includes an 'Adventure Trip Supplement', listing pack trips, 'float' trips (on some of the more spectacular Western rivers), canoe, hiking, and jeep trips into wilderness areas; some of these are rugged, some relatively tame. The same people now also have a separate and more comprehensive *Adventure Trip Guide*, entirely devoted to exotic or specialized trips. If one is hungry for something like ballooning, or bird-watching, or travelling by covered wagon or under sail on an old windjammer, the *Adventure Trip Guide* is the one to get (and it includes the canoeing and hiking and float trips as well). Via boat mail (which can take 6 weeks or more), the *Farm and Ranch Guide* currently costs $3 U.S. to anywhere outside the States; the *Adventure Trip Guide* is $3·50. For airmail, add $0·75 more for Europe and South America, or $1 more for Asia, Africa, Australia and New Zealand. To order, write Farm & Ranch Vacations, Inc., 36 East 57 Street, New York, N.Y., 10022.

One final note: places where one is likely to stay a week or more, like ranches and resort hotels, usually quote rates 'American plan'. That means all meals are included in the price; 'European plan' means that the price covers only the room.

PERSONAL OPINION

People with special interests may not need suggestions about where to go, although we might urge anyone with a specific professional interest to get in touch, before the trip, with the appropriate American organization. American hospitals, city planners, community centres and so forth, welcome visitors with similar professional concerns, but this is best arranged in advance. The appropriate American organization can facilitate this as well as suggest the best places to visit.

And for those who would welcome suggestions, we will give our own personal view about what would constitute an ideal trip to the United States. We will assume that all travellers inevitably begin and end with a major American city, and since each of the largest cities has a distinct personality of its own, that is fine. Everyone ideally ought to see New York and San Francisco and Washington, D.C., and Chicago and New Orleans. But the United States, almost half a continent, is more than the sum of

her cities, and we therefore strongly feel that visitors should see
more than urban America. If you go to the United States on
business and are therefore centred in a city, at least try for a day
or two outside of it. Hire a car, and set off!

But if you can possibly manage it, spend only part of your visit
in cities, and the rest exploring the other America. Unless you
have lots of time, of course, seeing the other America will
involve careful planning and some hard choices. Contrary to the
happy illusion of many European visitors, the Grand Canyon and
Niagara Falls are not a mere day's trip apart, at least not by car.
Thus you will have to decide what you want most to see. If you
crave the wide open spaces of the traditional cowboy country,
you must look to the area generally east of the Rockies but well
to the west of the Mississippi. If you like your country arranged
on a more manageable scale, and steeped in history and tradition,
you had better choose the East Coast, north or south. The West
Coast can supply both great cities and remote wilderness areas;
California, for example, offers more dramatic contrasts in topo-
graphy and climate than any other single state.

If you are driving through the United States, and have the
time, we are in favour of choosing routes along the outer edges
of the coasts, or along the great rivers (the Ohio, the Mississippi,
the Missouri). We are also advocates of islands.

If we had only one week to spend away from the major population centres, and did not want to spend too much of it behind the
wheel of a car, we would, for the summer, choose from amongst
the following: a week travelling through the Southwest, from
the Grand Canyon to Santa Fe; a week on a New England
island; a week in and around any of the western National Parks
or on a ranch in comparable country; a week travelling from the
northwestern corner of the country down to California. For
spring, we would choose a trip down the Blue Ridge Parkway
through Virginia and North Carolina and then along the Carolina
and Georgia coast, or we would go to the western deserts. In the
autumn, we would drive through the Adirondacks ('upstate'
New York) or western New England for the blazing red and gold
of its autumn foliage. For a winter trip, we would either go where
the cold and snow is at its best, to Vermont or to Aspen, Colorado;
or we would escape to the Florida Keys and the Everglades, or
to California or the desert country of southern Arizona. If it were
the Christmas season, on the Dickensian theory that Christmases

past are always the best, we would head for Williamsburg and the candlelit past of America.

And wherever we were going, we would take good binoculars. One wants them for the wonderful clear distances of the country west of the Mississippi, and everywhere for the unusual animals and birds.

2 · NEW YORK CITY

Anchored to the very edge of the continent, with the international flavour of all great ports, New York City is hardly a typical American city. Certainly it influences the rest of the country; it is the financial centre and the publishing centre and the pre-eminent theatre and art and radio and television centre. But it is not nearly so much the centre of everything as New Yorkers like to think, or as London is the centre of England and Paris the centre of France. The country is simply too big for that; you cannot dismiss San Francisco, for instance, as simply a 'provincial' city.

Yet in one respect New York City is indeed quintessential America. In the days when travellers came to New York by ship, the first thing they saw silhouetted against the breathtaking sky-line of Manhattan was the Statue of Liberty, standing on an island in the harbour. Every American schoolchild used to memorize the verse inscribed at the base of the statue:

> Give me your tired, your poor,
> Your huddled masses yearning to breathe free,
> The wretched refuse of your teeming shore,
> Send these, the homeless, the tempest-tossed to me;
> I lift my lamp beside the golden door.

It was a good introduction to New York and to the rest of the country, for it served to remind everyone of the diverse elements which have gone into the making of the United States. Despite the language and the common law, less than a third of the blood flowing through American veins today is British; the first

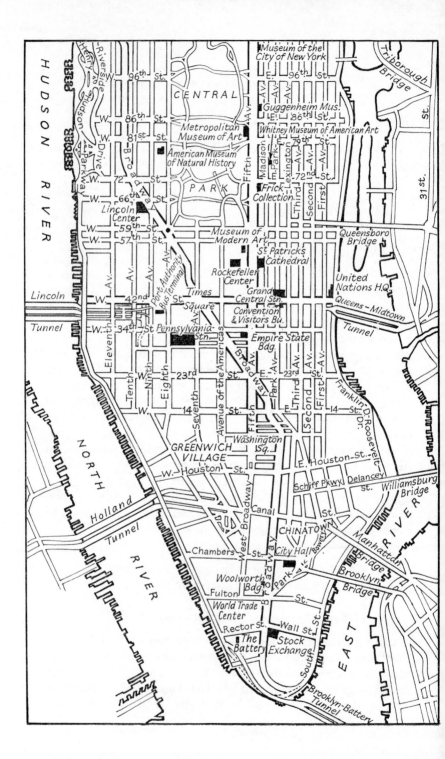

Americans, after all, were the American Indians, and the English were not even the first European settlers. The Spanish were in Florida and the American Southwest before the first English settlers came to the Atlantic coast, and the Spanish heritage is still evident in the architecture and the atmosphere of Texas, Arizona, New Mexico, and California. The French were busy too, leaving marked traces in the way of French place-names in widely scattered sections of the country; even today, pockets of French-speaking people remain in the bayou country west of New Orleans and in those parts of New England which border on French Canada. It was the Dutch who first settled New York City and the Hudson River valley. Pennsylvania began as an English Quaker settlement, but in the early eighteenth century countless pious German farmers were also attracted to the rich Pennsylvania countryside. And the Negro: the first recorded slave ship reached Virginia in 1619. By 1776, there were perhaps half a million blacks in the United States, and even after the importation of slaves was made illegal in 1807, 'blackbirders' continued to smuggle them in.

Of even greater importance, numerically, was the great wave of immigration in the nineteenth century. The first to come then were the Irish, who began to cross over in large numbers at the time of the Potato Famine (1845–6). Next came a new wave of Germans (including German Jews), particularly as a result of the social and political upheavals of 1848 in Europe; many of these immigrants were men of considerable education who soon exerted a marked influence on the cities in which they settled. Scandinavians too began to immigrate. Most of them headed for what are today the states of Minnesota and Wisconsin, Iowa and Nebraska and the Dakotas; rich farming country now, but only vast lonely plains then. After the American Civil War (1861–5), the great swell of immigration from southern and eastern Europe rolled in, until in the years before World War I, 2,500 immigrants a day were entering the United States: Italians and Sicilians, Greeks and Slavs and Croats; Jews from Poland and Russia; and, on the West Coast, Chinese.

The lot of the immigrants varied tremendously. Yet no matter how grim things were, there was the sustaining hope that life could at least be better here for their children, and by and large the next generation did achieve the sort of success and security they could never have dreamed of in the 'old country'.

You must remember all this as you travel through the United States. You can never hope to understand the country unless you are conscious of all the racial and cultural diversities it encompasses. And you must particularly bear it in mind in New York City, for New York City has continued to lure the poor and the desperate. The 'immigrants' today are mainly Puerto Ricans, exchanging their own over-populated island for the equally over-populated island of Manhattan, and black refugees from the American South, where agricultural mechanization has rendered much of the rural population superfluous. These newcomers must now vie with the sons and grandsons of the earlier immigrants for a slice of the pie (as the American phrase has it) and this is the source of much of the tension in New York City today. But it is not a condition new to New York, and painful though some of the side-effects may be, it is well to remember that New York City has weathered these tensions in the past, and owes to all her immigrants much of her richness and excitement.

Since New York City can be a bewildering place to visit for the first time, we suggest easing into it gradually. On your first day, you might well begin with an orientation session, going to the top of the Empire State Building to see how it all looks from above. (The new World Trade Center towers are taller than the Empire State Building, but they are not as ideally situated for orientation purposes.) There are two special observation areas, one on the 86th floor and one on the 102nd; the tickets are not cheap, but unless you are very hard pressed it is worth the money.

From above, it is easy to see the five boroughs which together make up New York City: Queens, Brooklyn, The Bronx, Richmond, and Manhattan. Manhattan Island, which the canny Dutch bought from the Indians in 1624 for the equivalent of $24, is what most people have in mind when they talk about New York City. It is indeed an island, with the Hudson River on the west, the East River on the east, the harbour to the south, and Spuyten Duyvil Creek some five miles beyond Central Park to the north. Queens and Brooklyn lie east of Manhattan, side by side on the western edge of Long Island. The borough of Richmond is really Staten Island, in the harbour beyond the Statue of Liberty. The Bronx is the only part of New York City actually on the mainland; beyond it stretch Westchester County and the way to New England.

The bridges connect Manhattan not only with the state of New Jersey, but also with three of the other metropolitan boroughs; before the bridges, there were only ferries. The Brooklyn Bridge was the first to be built, the first great suspension bridge in the world (1883), impressive even today; from the Brooklyn end, in Brooklyn Heights, one has the most famous view of the Manhattan skyline. The George Washington Bridge (to New Jersey) is perhaps the most beautiful. The Triborough Bridge, as its name indicates, connects three boroughs: Manhattan, Queens and The Bronx. The new Verrazano-Narrows Bridge, longest suspension span in the world, connects Staten Island and Brooklyn.

There are other links between Manhattan and the surrounding area which you cannot see; the Lincoln and the Holland Tunnels go under the Hudson River to New Jersey south of the George Washington Bridge. The Brooklyn-Battery Tunnel connects Brooklyn with lower Manhattan, and the Queens-Midtown Tunnel runs from Queens to Manhattan near the United Nations.

Looking north, you can see Central Park, its southern edge fringed by the most expensive shops and hotels in the city. To the east of it lies the most expensive residential section. Near the south-west corner is Lincoln Center with its new Metropolitan Opera House, two theatres, a concert hall, a museum-library and a school for the performing arts, in a great complex of contemporary buildings designed by America's leading architects. Away to the north, at the top of Central Park, is Harlem, originally a separate Dutch village, now America's most celebrated black community.

Fifth Avenue runs along the east side of Central Park, and then continues south until it ends at Washington Square. The other main north–south streets are also 'avenues', beginning with First Avenue near the East River. The cross-streets (when you go from east to west or vice versa it is called going 'cross-town') are also numerically designated but are called 'streets', beginning with First Street just a bit below Washington Square and continuing north until one finally reaches 220th Street at the uppermost tip of Manhattan. One speaks of east or west in Manhattan in relation to Fifth Avenue. 'Uptown' is north, 'downtown' south.

Now look south, at the tip of Manhattan Island, the one area in which the streets are not arranged according to the tidy grid system characteristic of the rest of the city. That is where New

York City began, where the first Dutch settlers had their houses and farms. As in London, the financial district has remained in the oldest part; Wall Street was once an actual wall, separating the tiny Dutch settlement from the wilderness to the north. The village in those days was called New Amsterdam. It was controlled by the Dutch West India Company from 1626 until 1664, when the last Dutch governor, the irascible Peter Stuyvesant, watched in helpless rage as the townspeople surrendered to the British without firing a shot. The British forces had been dispatched by the future James II, then Duke of York, to whom Charles II had graciously granted a sizeable chunk of America, including land the British did not really own. Apparently the New Amsterdam burghers felt that any new ruler was bound to be preferable to the interfering, domineering Stuyvesant, but today the proudest old New York families are those, like the Roosevelts, who can trace their ancestry back to the original Dutch settlers.

The spectacular twin towers of the new World Trade Center, designed by Minoru Yamasaki with Emery Roth and Sons, demark the north-west edge of the financial district. As you look towards them you will see a bit nearer to you the Woolworth Building, first of New York's great skyscrapers, built in 1913. East of it, near the Brooklyn Bridge, is City Hall Park with its city government buildings, and just to the north of that lies Chinatown.

On the same side but a bit farther 'uptown' is the Bowery, in the mid-nineteenth century the roaring centre of the theatre and music-hall district, but latterly only the bleak last refuge of down-and-outers. In the beginning it had been an Indian trail, and later acquired its name as the path leading to Peter Stuyvesant's farm (*bouwerij*). To the east of the Bowery lies what is known as the Lower East Side. As fashionable New York moved north in the early nineteenth century, the immigrants poured into this part of Manhattan. The Irish and the Germans now have vanished from there almost without a trace. But the Italian section and the Jewish section and the Polish section are still there, even if partially buried under a new wave of immigrants, this time Puerto Ricans.

To the west of the Bowery, as you look south from the Empire State Building, you can see Greenwich Village centred around Washington Square, where Fifth Avenue ends. In the novels of

Henry James, this was the heart of fashionable New York; today it can be loosely described as New York's Left Bank, combining a little bit of everything.

Once you have your bearings, you can descend from the heights and plunge into the city. But we have one more preparatory stop to recommend. Walk north up Fifth Avenue from the Empire State Building, past such landmarks as the New York Public Library and Lord and Taylor's tantalizing department store, and turn east on 42nd Street. At 90 East 42nd Street is the New York Convention and Visitors Bureau, a superb tourist information centre open 365 days a year. Their basic visitors' kit includes invaluable maps and guides and listings of everything going on in the city at the moment, and in addition they are happy to cater for special interests. Their information is particularly useful for anyone anxious to see the best of New York at the least possible cost, and their staff is friendly, multi-lingual, and supremely knowledgeable. There is another, smaller information centre at Times Square, but the Convention and Visitors Bureau is unique.

Either of these information centres can tell you about sightseeing tours of the city. Most visitors particularly enjoy taking one of the boats which circumnavigate Manhattan. But we would also like to recommend our two favourite New York tours. One is Penny's Sightseeing Tour of Harlem, run by a splendid black lady who knows Harlem intimately and takes her groups not only to see the standard tourist sights in that part of Manhattan but also to churches and community centres. The other is 'Discover New York', a choice of three tours emphasizing various aspects of New York City life and history, operated under the aegis of the Municipal Art Society; these tours are limited to twelve people, go in a smart Mercedes mini-bus, and include a picnic with wine along the way. Either or both will provide you with a view of New York City that most visitors never get.

Once you have gone to the top of the Empire State Building, stopped at the Convention and Visitors Bureau, and perhaps signed up for a tour, you will want to see some parts of the city in more detail. One important 'sight' on any visitor's list is the United Nations complex; you could take a bus 'cross-town' to it, from the Convention and Visitors Bureau.

Everything about the United Nations is interesting, including the architecture, and there are excellent guided tours from the

General Assembly Building. The tours last about forty-five minutes, and a new tour begins every few minutes; the guides are recruited from all member nations. You can also apply at the admissions desk in the General Assembly Building for seats to watch the United Nations at work. If the Security Council or the General Assembly is in session, there may be a queue; seats are usually more readily available in the public galleries of various U.N. committees and commissions. There is a cafeteria on the lower floor of the General Assembly Buildings, too: an inexpensive place to lunch. And one of the best places to shop in all of New York City is the United Nations Gift Shop, on the lower floor of the General Assembly Building, near the cafeteria.

Before you leave the neighbourhood of the United Nations, you might walk back west along 42nd Street to see the Ford Foundation building, one of New York's most interesting new architectural sights. Designed by Kevin Roche with John Dinkeloo and Associates, it is a stunning combination of architecture and space, with tropical plants growing skywards within its soaring glass-walled office block.

Or one might leave the U.N. for another day, and go instead 'uptown' to New York's richest museum district. The Frick, the Whitney, the Metropolitan, and the Guggenheim are all within walking distance of each other (if you have stout shoes and stamina to match) between 70th Street and 89th Street, on or near Fifth Avenue. The Metropolitan is the most prestigious museum of art in the United States, with an exceedingly rich, all-embracing and international collection. The Metropolitan also has a pleasant and inexpensive place to lunch, in its Fountain Court, and now even a licensed bar to succour the weary connoisseur. In addition, it has a multiplicity of museum shops; indeed, when you first come into the Metropolitan it may seem more like Bartholomew Fair than a museum. But since they get no public money for their support, museums in the United States are trying all sorts of new ventures these days to keep afloat.

The Whitney Museum is nearby, on Madison Avenue; it is New York's pre-eminent collection of twentieth-century American art, housed in a handsome new building by Marcel Breuer, and boasting the only lifts in the world one would not mind getting stuck in. The Whitney too has a cafeteria, but it is more expensive and less varied in its choices. A better 'buy' at the Whitney is the *avant-garde* movies it offers, free with the admission to the collection. We might also note that near the Whitney on Madison Avenue are many of New York's most elegant art-sales galleries, where the elegant New Yorkers who live in this part of Manhattan can buy their Renoirs and Chagalls. Parke-Bernet, now a branch of London's Sotheby's, is on Madison Avenue along here too, and one can walk in and watch a sale in progress; it's a pleasant way to rest the feet. More to the point perhaps for most visitors is the fact that the principal office of the American Automobile Association is at 28 East 78th Street, just around the corner from Parke-Bernet; if you belong to an automobile club in your own country and plan to be using a car in the United States, you might want to stop in.

The Guggenheim Museum, north of the Metropolitan Museum on Fifth Avenue, was Frank Lloyd Wright's last major project. Devoted to contemporary art of all sorts, it was opened in 1959, and while its collection is not as remarkable as others in New York City, it is well worth going to see for the sake of the building. Many people think it is more successful inside than out, so the interior should not be missed.

The Frick, also on Fifth Avenue but 'downtown' from the Metropolitan, is a private collection made public, and one of the most charming small museums anywhere. Henry Frick was of Pennsylvania Swiss–German stock; an associate of Andrew Carnegie, he made a fortune in coal and steel. On his death, he left his house and pictures to the public. The house itself was built in that period just before the First World War when American architects seemed at last able to combine the desired classical grandeur with beauty and utility; thus not only is the collection superb but the surroundings are delightful. In winter there are chamber music concerts at the Frick.

In the same general area as these four museums there is now a new attraction which, while certainly not a museum, is equally a treat for the eyes: the new Gimbels East department store, at the corner of 86th Street and Lexington Avenue. The old traditional Gimbels has long been a rival and neighbour of Macy's, notable for bargains. Gimbels East, on the other hand, is extravagantly sybaritic, from its marble exterior to its Rich Uncle boutique; you ought to take a look.

The Empire State Building and the United Nations or a museum or two is more than enough for one day, and the visitor will now be thinking about dinner. Meals in New York City can be more expensive than anywhere in the world or they can be very cheap indeed. In Chapter 1, we talked generally about how to eat cheaply, at hamburger places and drugstores and luncheonettes. New York City offers a wide choice of quick and inexpensive meals because of the diversity of its population; thus one can not only get pizza but also souvlaki and shishkebab, or at one of the many Zum-Zums around town, wurst and German beer. We can even recommend eating in the street, if you encounter a Sabrett's hot-dog vendor; complete with sauerkraut, onions, and mustard, a Sabrett's hot-dog is not to be scorned. For a more substantial meal, however, we suggest consulting the excellent free guide the Convention and Visitors Bureau can supply; it lists restaurants by area, with an indication of their prices. *Cue*, a weekly theatre and entertainment guide, has a similar list.

For things to do after dinner, we suggest you consult the entertainment listings and evaluations in *The New Yorker* or *New York*. *Cue* is good for movies and theatre, but not as helpful for jazz and discotheques and that sort of thing. *The Village Voice* is useful for the off-beat and the 'underground'. All of these are weekly publications, obtainable at any news-stand.

The theatre in New York is no longer neatly confined to the Broadway–Times Square area. The hit musical comedies and the plays with established stars are still mostly to be found there. But some of the most exciting theatrical productions are to be found these days 'off-Broadway', in the less expensive experimental theatres which are scattered all over the city, many of them in Greenwich Village. Nothing changes faster than the theatrical scene, but two of the most interesting off-Broadway developments in the early 1970s have been the growth of significant black theatre, with groups such as the Negro Ensemble Company, and the opening of the Public Theater under the direction of the inspired and indefatigable Joseph Papp. The Public Theater is really four theatres in one building, the lovely old Astor Library on Lafayette Place on the eastern edge of Greenwich Village; anything done there is almost sure to be worth seeing, but one of the four theatres, the Anspacher, in what was originally the reading room, is particularly handsome in itself. Joseph Papp is also the man who began Shakespeare in Central Park in the summer, and that too is well worth seeing.

You might also consider an evening at Lincoln Center, which variously offers in its splendid new buildings the Metropolitan

Opera, the New York Philharmonic, theatrical repertory, and George Balanchine's superb New York City Ballet. Lincoln Center is worth seeing purely for its architecture too; if you aren't going there for a performance, consider simply going and taking the tour.

Or there is the sporting world. Americans are sports mad, and if the season is right you too might enjoy a hockey game or a basketball game at what someone has aptly described as an intergalactic sports palace, the new Madison Square Garden which has been built above Penn Station. Or, in summer, go to a baseball game, or football in the autumn; your chief problem will be getting tickets for the latter.

Even a visitor with only two days in New York will want to spend part of one day in the vicinity of Rockefeller Center. This great complex of buildings on Fifth Avenue somehow typifies New York, and its central plaza is a delightful place to sit on a fine day. There are restaurants on either side of the plaza, and in summer one can eat at tables out of doors. In winter the central court is flooded and frozen for skating, and there is no pleasanter place for a leisurely Sunday breakfast than in the English Grill at a table by the window from which one can watch the skaters. One more among the many restaurants in Rockefeller Center which should be particularly mentioned is the Rainbow Room, high up in the R.C.A. Building. It is a fairly expensive place to dine, but one can also go up there just for a drink before dinner, to enjoy the view. Rockefeller Center has a regular Observation Roof too and there are guided tours of the Center from nine in the morning to nine at night. Moreover, N.B.C., one of the three principal television and radio networks in America, has its headquarters in Rockefeller Center, and there are guided tours of the studios.

On the Sixth Avenue side of Rockefeller Center is Radio City Music Hall, the largest cinema in the world, once notable as well for its flamboyant but innocent stage spectacles; unhappily now the Rockettes have gone the way of other relics of the 30s. Directly across Fifth Avenue from the Rockefeller Center is St Patrick's Cathedral, the best-known and largest Roman Catholic church in the United States. And just north of Rockefeller Center is St Thomas' church, the most elegant Episcopal church in New York, superb imitation Gothic.

When you are at Rockefeller Center, Manhattan certainly looks very prosperous. As an 1885 *Englishman's Guide to the United States* observed, 'The sights along Fifth Avenue must impress upon visitors from the old world the marvellous strides in the refinements of civilization America is continually making.' With the exception of Lord and Taylor's at 38th Street, all the smartest large stores are on Fifth Avenue between Rockefeller Center and Central Park, and the cross-streets here, to the east of Fifth Avenue, have most of the expensive boutiques. The Plaza Hotel, the city's last real bastion of elegance, sits to the west of Fifth Avenue along 58th Street, where Fifth Avenue meets the Park.

Everyone ought to window-shop along Fifth Avenue, but you might also bear in mind that the Museum of Modern Art, New York's richest collection of modern painting, sculpture, photography, and design, is on 53rd Street just west of Fifth. In the summer one can have lunch or tea very pleasantly in the Museum garden, and every day there is a showing of some film classic in the Museum cinema.

The Museum of Contemporary Crafts is just past the Museum of Modern Art, and the American Folk Art Museum is a little farther on along 54th Street. Both of these new museums owe their existence to Rockefeller enthusiasms. Incidentally, good contemporary American crafts are for sale at the American Crafts Council Gallery, across the street from the Museum of Modern Art. And on 54th Street at the Avenue of the Americas (Sixth Avenue) is the Burlington House Mill, one of the city's most popular new free entertainments; one rides on a moving walkway past giant machines and rollers weaving, spinning, dyeing in a joyous psychedelic ballet.

Sometime during your stay in New York, perhaps after shopping along Fifth Avenue, walk east to Park Avenue. Here, on a street once famous only for the wealth of the people who lived there, are several of the most dramatic office buildings in America, including the Seagram building (Mies van der Rohe and Philip Johnson) at Park Avenue and 53rd Street, and at 54th Street, Lever House (Skidmore, Owings and Merrill). The Four Seasons, one of New York's most elaborate and expensive restaurants, is in the Seagram Building.

Beyond Park Avenue and Lexington Avenue comes Third Avenue, which has all sorts of smart little shops, from about 45th Street all the way uptown to about 67th. You may not want to make a special trip all the way over to Third Avenue just to walk along it, but you might have dinner one night in one of the good restaurants in that area.

Almost everyone who comes to New York wants to see Greenwich Village. One might choose to go down there in the evening, when the Village is at its liveliest; there are innumerable restaurants, mostly moderate in their prices and many exotic in their choice of foods. The Village is also still the best part of the city for many other sorts of night life, especially jazz. But one might also enjoy going to the Village in the daytime and simply wandering around looking at the wild array of shops selling Tibetan lamas' coats and beaded headbands and pottery and handmade jewellery. Almost all the shops are open at night too, but many are shut in the mornings and all day on Mondays.

The heart of the Village is Washington Square, and one can take a Fifth Avenue bus directly down to it. Washington Square was a potters' field and also the site of most public hangings at the time of the American Revolution. Later it was turned into a park and well-to-do New Yorkers began to build their houses around it, until by the 1880s there was no more elegant address than Washington Square. By the 1920s it had declined enough so that rents in the area were cheap, and struggling artists and writers, lured both by the low rents and the undeniable charm of the houses along these streets, began to move into the Village and give it the air it still has today.

One can still live cheaply in the Village, particularly in the East Village, east of the New York University buildings on the eastern edge of Washington Square. But it can also be an expensive and fashionable place to live, especially on Macdougal Alley, the smart mews behind Macdougal Street on the north-western edge of Washington Square, or on Washington Square Mews, its counterpart on the north-eastern side. The West Village too is now very smart, and if you want to see it and also get a sense of Village flavour in the 20s and 30s, you could go for lunch to the Waverly Inn, at 16 Bank Street, just off Waverly. It has good, inexpensive food that is American with a touch of the Old South: chicken pot pies, delicious breads and desserts. In the winter a fire burns in the fireplace, and there is a little garden open in summer. After lunch, you might stroll west along Bank Street to West 4th Street, and there turn south and wander back towards Washington Square. Perhaps the purest essence-of-Village is to be found in the streets just south-west of Washington Square: off-Broadway theatres and more shops.

Not far south of Greenwich Village proper is a district known as 'So-Ho' (pronounced 'Sow-How' because it means 'south of Houston', a street which New Yorkers perversely call 'Howston'). While one will find galleries in Greenwich Village, and fancier ones on the upper floors of buildings along 57th Street just east of Fifth Avenue, So-Ho is where one encounters the greatest range of *avant-garde* art in New York today. A good starting place for an exploration of this district, full of splendid old buildings, is the O. K. Harris gallery at 465 West Broadway. (West Broadway runs south from the middle of Washington Square, and is NOT to be confused with Broadway.) Just beyond O. K. Harris, at 420 West Broadway, there are five more galleries all under one roof in a very smart converted warehouse. At either of these places you can get a map showing the other galleries in the area, if you'd like to look further.

A trip to Greenwich Village will have taken you away from midtown Manhattan, but you should certainly make some other expeditions as well. We have already suggested Penny's Sightseeing Tour as the best way to see Harlem; on her tours one also gets a good over-view of 'uptown' New York on the way to Harlem and back, and most of her groups stop at the Jumel Mansion, the city's best surviving example of Revolutionary-era elegance. For another day you might consider going 'downtown', or even to one of the other boroughs.

The best way to get down to Wall Street, the heart of the financial district, is to take the subway (underground train). Once there, you will find, just east of Broadway, the New York Stock Exchange (different from the American Stock Exchange which handles less well-established stocks); it has a visitors' gallery. Almost opposite the New York Stock Exchange is the United States Treasury Building, at Wall and Broad Streets, on the site of Federal Hall. Federal Hall was the setting for the Stamp Act Congress, that first formal colonial protest gathering which antedated the Revolution by eleven years. Here too Washington was inaugurated, the Bill of Rights passed, and the Supreme Court organized. Now all that remains is a rather bleak little museum beneath the stately entrance to the Treasury Building.

Most of the city's principal banks have their head offices on or near Wall Street. In the United States you will notice that every city and town has its own independent banks, connected and controlled only through the government's Federal Reserve Banking system. The major New York City banks, however, exert an undeniable influence on banking policies throughout the country.

Facing Wall Street, on Broadway, is Trinity Church, a dark Victorian Gothic building now dwarfed by skyscrapers around it. There are of course hundreds of churches in New York City, but most of them are neither very old nor very new, and few have any marked architectural or historical significance. Trinity Church is one of the few which does warrant attention, both because of its situation and because of its historical associations. Many illustrious Americans lie buried in Trinity churchyard: Alexander Hamilton and Robert Fulton are probably the two whose names mean most today. Hamilton was the illegitimate son of a West Indies planter; he came to New York before the Revolution, married into one of the richest and most influential old Dutch families, and during the war made a splendid record as aide to General Washington. Brilliant and strong-willed, he put the young republic on its feet financially after the Revolution, but he made implacable enemies on both Left and Right, and in 1804 was killed in a duel with Aaron Burr. Robert Fulton, ten years younger, was America's most interesting and original scientist after his fellow-Pennsylvanian, Benjamin Franklin. As a young man he went to London to study portrait painting, and there he met the Duke of Bridgewater and James Watt and was induced to abandon art for engineering. At the turn of the century he was in Paris, experimenting in the Seine with his missile-firing submarine *Nautilus*; but no one was interested. Finally he devoted himself to the work for which he is remembered today, steam-driven boats, and in 1807 he saw his first steamboat, the *Clermont*, start scheduled runs on the Hudson River between New York City and Albany.

A dramatic new feature of the financial district is the World Trade Center complex with its twin towers, now the tallest buildings in New York. To get there from Wall Street walk north along Broadway to Liberty Street and there turn west. By 1974 the observation deck in the South Tower should be open, and a restaurant is planned for the top of the North Tower. But there is more to the World Trade Center than mere height, and some-time soon guided tours are scheduled to start; if all the plans materialize, it promises to be a fascinating place to visit.

If one goes east along Wall Street to South Street and then turns north, one soon comes to the Fulton Fish Market. If you like fish, you could walk over there for lunch at Sweet's; the food is simple but very good and the atmosphere hasn't changed in fifty years. Nearby along the water is the South Street Seaport, a little nautical museum with an old ferry, a schooner, and a square-rigger tied alongside.

From this general area one has a choice of three further explorations: on south to the Battery and a boat ride, across the river to Brooklyn Heights, or back to midtown Manhattan by way of City Hall and Chinatown.

If one opts for the Battery and a boat ride, one might walk to Battery Park in a slightly roundabout manner in order to pass Fraunces Tavern at the corner of Pearl Street and Broad Street. The most notable pre-Revolutionary building in this part of the city, this was first a house, built in 1719. In 1762 it became an inn, and during the Revolution, while British troops occupied New York, Black Sam Fraunces, the inn-keeper, made his hostelry the rebels' best listening-post in Manhattan. Perhaps it was for this reason that George Washington chose Fraunces Tavern for the gathering which constituted his formal farewell to his officers at the end of the Revolution. Fraunces Tavern today is still an eating place, but the interior of the building is much altered.

Battery Park is in every respect the beginning of Manhattan; it was here that Peter Minuit concluded his bargain with the Indians for the island in 1626. It is a pleasant place to sit and watch the ships, and it is also the embarkation point for the Statue of Liberty boats and the Staten Island ferries.

One assumes that the beauty of Manhattan is its superb functionalism, the purity of line of its tall buildings massed against the sky. But this is not all; the very situation of the city is striking, and since one is no longer likely to arrive in New York by sea, a boat trip across the harbour seems a good idea.

Boats leave for the Statue of Liberty every half-hour from nine to five in the summer, hourly nine to four in winter. The round trip takes about forty-five minutes; allow more time if you plan to get off and climb up into the statue and see the little museum.

Ferries for Staten Island also go frequently, and the ride there and back is one of New York's greatest bargains, only a nickel. Parts of Staten Island are still surprisingly rural, although the new Verrazano Bridge may soon change all that. One would need a car to explore thoroughly, but visitors on foot could simply wander a little way from the ferry dock and then take a bus to the Richmondtown Restoration: nice old buildings and a small historical museum, but somewhat limited in opening hours. Or if you fancy snakes, the reptile collection at the Staten Island Zoo is reputed to be one of the world's finest. At any rate, Staten Island might make a pleasant expedition for a Sunday.

To see another, more populous borough, you might take the subway (IRT line) from Wall Street to Brooklyn Heights, a wonderful old section of Brooklyn now rediscovered as a highly desirable place to live. All Brooklyn-bound IRT trains stop at Clark Street, the station for Brooklyn Heights. When you emerge into the street, look for the Brooklyn Bridge to the north, and walk towards it along Henry Street. You will come almost immediately to Pineapple Street, and there you can turn left and begin a serpentine trail which will show you a picturesque and peaceful corner of the city in the course of an hour's pleasant stroll.

13 Pineapple Street must be the most charming old wooden house still standing anywhere in the city, and with a delightful garden too. A little beyond it is the Esplanade, above the water; it is nice to sit on a bench here for a while, to look at Manhattan across the harbour and the boats coming and going. Then you can go south along the Esplanade to Pierrepont, and there turn left and then left again at Willow. Between Pierrepont and Clark on Willow are several particularly nice old houses. When you come to Orange Street, turn right and you will pass Plymouth Church, famous all over America in the nineteenth century. Its fiery minister was Henry Ward Beecher, of a distinguished New York family; his sister was Harriet Beecher Stowe, author of *Uncle Tom's Cabin*. One can get into the church by applying at the church office at 75 Hicks Street.

In Brooklyn Heights you are not far from a splendid, traditional restaurant, Gage and Tollner; it is delightfully Victorian and moderately-priced. But you could also make another worthwhile stop in Brooklyn by taking another subway train on to the Brooklyn Museum stop. The museum is a good one, with a fine collection of American paintings and furniture and decorative arts, and an excellent Near Eastern and Egyptian section, beautifully displayed. On the ground floor there is a cafeteria, one of the best museum shops we've ever seen, and a very good ethnological collection (Africa, people of the Pacific, Central and South America, American Indians). And next to the museum is the Brooklyn Botanic Garden, particularly lovely in spring when its spectacular magnolias, cherry trees, lilacs and azaleas follow each other in bloom. The Brooklyn Botanic Garden also publishes the most respected gardening pamphlets and guides in America; all gardeners should stop at the sales desk. For those who have a car, we might even note that there is ample parking behind the museum.

A third choice of routes from Wall Street is to go back up Broadway towards central Manhattan. On Broadway, between Fulton and Vesey Streets, is St Paul's Chapel of Trinity Church, built in 1764 by a pupil of James Gibbs, the architect of St Martin-in-the-Fields in London. It is the oldest church still standing in Manhattan; its parent, Trinity Church, represents an older foundation (1697) but the original building burned to the ground and the present Trinity Church only dates from 1846.

Just beyond St Paul's Chapel is City Hall Park, and on the other side of the park is City Hall itself. City Hall is not commonly found in a list of famous New York sights; it deserves more attention. Begun in 1803, it was designed by a Scots–American named McComb. It is a rather unusual combination of disparate styles and materials but beautifully proportioned and altogether charming. On the ground floor is the headquarters of New York's city government; the Mayor's offices are here. Since the Mayor of New York has one of the most arduous jobs in the United States, with New York City seemingly always in a state of crisis, the environs of the Mayor's office can be a fascinating place to loiter.

But the proper excuse for visiting City Hall is to see the state rooms on the floor above: the Governor's Rooms and the Council Chamber. The Governor's Rooms are at the head of the handsome circular staircase; the Governor of the State of New York uses these rooms on his official visits to the city. Most of the furniture was brought here from Federal Hall when that building was torn down: there are the desks of the first four Presidents of the United States, silver andirons cast by Paul Revere, and a splendid group of Trumbull portraits. Round the bend of the stairwell from the Governor's Rooms is the very handsome Council Chamber.

From City Hall it is only a short walk north-east up Park Row to Mulberry Street, and if you turn left there you will soon be in the centre of Chinatown, one of New York's most fascinating neighbourhoods. Mott and Pell and Bayard and Doyers are the principal streets; the entire area is quite small and one hardly needs precise directions for exploring it. There are a great many restaurants and tea parlours; every New Yorker has his own particular favourite and you must simply choose for yourself. They are almost all inexpensive and good. Cantonese cooking used to predominate, but there are now several places which specialize in Mandarin and Szechuan food. The one recommendation we might make is the Fung Wong Bakery at 30 Mott Street; surely every traveller needs black bean cakes to take back to the hotel room!

To get back to that hotel room from Chinatown, you can take a bus uptown along the Bowery and then First Avenue; tell the bus driver your ultimate destination and he can suggest where to get off and take a cross-town bus.

And having taken you this far, we will now leave you on your own. You must simply pick and choose amongst all the other fascinating things New York City has to offer. For example, one of our very favourite museums is the Museum of Natural History; if you think it is merely a lot of stuffed animals, you couldn't be more wrong. Their stuffed animals are superlative, to be sure, but we find even more exciting their anthropological exhibits, the extraordinary Man in Africa section, the Mexican and Central American section, and the total sensory experience of the new Peoples of the Pacific hall. If you're looking for presents to take home, you might also like to know that the museum shop here has a pretty fair selection of American-Indian-made silver jewellery. And as if the museum itself were not enough, the Hayden Planetarium is next door. There are three other museums too which we should at least mention, although they are each a considerable distance from midtown Manhattan: the Museum of the City of New York, a light-hearted revelation of the city's past; the Museum of the American Indian, which has the finest collection of its kind in the country (South and Central American as well as North American) and is now at last displaying it to advantage; and the Cloisters, parts of several medieval French and Spanish monastic buildings skilfully reassembled to house the Metropolitan Museum's medieval treasures and situated in a park on the heights of northernmost Manhattan overlooking the Hudson River. And finally there is the Morgan Library, one of New

York's real jewels; if its current exhibit tempts you at all, by all means go there.

Since visitors often feel at a loss on Sundays in a strange place, we might say something about what to do on a Sunday in New York. Some of the expeditions we have already mentioned would of course be fine for a Sunday; one might go to Brooklyn, or to Staten Island, or to Greenwich Village, or Chinatown. In fact if you were feeling really energetic, you could begin at Chinatown (very lively on Sundays), then walk east on Canal Street to Orchard Street, follow Orchard up through the Lower East Side district, which on Sundays is still full of Orthodox Jews peddling from push-carts just as it has been since the turn of the century, and finally wind your way in a north-westerly direction to Washington Square, where the Villagers are out in force on Sunday afternoons.

Or you could do what thousands of New Yorkers do on Sundays: go to Central Park. You may have heard that Central Park is a dangerous place these days, and this can be very true of the northern end (above the Metropolitan Museum) even in the daytime and of all but the best lighted and most heavily frequented parts of the entire Park at night. But if you stick to the paths and the parts of the Park with other people around, you need not worry about the southern end in the daytime, and on Sundays this part of the Park is so full of people that any would-be mugger or purse-snatcher would have a hard time finding operating room. One can rent a bicycle, or a row-boat for the lake, or simply stroll and look at the people. The Zoo is a pleasant section to head for; on weekdays New York's most elegant babies are to be found in the neighborhood of the Zoo, with their nannies or their elegant young mothers, but on Sundays you will probably find a more mixed and egalitarian crowd there. For another sort of crowd, you might wander to the Bethesda Fountain, to observe what is called New York's greatest freak show. There is a pleasant open-air restaurant near the Bethesda Fountain too, open for lunch and dinner in the warmer weather.

This book does not pretend to be an exhaustive good-food-guide, but we do try to mention restaurants when their situation is in some way unique. In this connection we should therefore say something about two popular places to eat or drink on high. One is the Top of the Sixes, at the top of 666 Fifth Avenue; it is medium-expensive, and vital to book a table near the window.

A popular place for lunch, or a drink in the early evening (it does not serve dinner), is the Copter Club, at the top of the Pan-Am Building; again, it is wise to book for lunch, which has a prix fixe of approximately $5.

Finally, we must say a word about a splendid organization which any foreign visitor in New York City for a matter of months should certainly join: the International Center. Run on a shoestring, largely by unpaid volunteers, it performs countless useful services for foreigners in what can be a rather bewildering city. There are organized activities and films and lectures of all sorts, skiing trips and tours to places of interest outside New York, and sometimes even free tickets for members to concerts and plays. One can get advice about schools and living quarters, or arrange invitations to American homes. Altogether it is a most valuable place to be in contact with, and the staff is friendly and sensible and wise in the ways of the city. If you will be in New York City for some time, go to 745 Seventh Avenue and see for yourself.

SPECIAL KNOWLEDGE

If you are coming to New York by air, you will probably find it best to take an airport coach in to the city terminal. But if there are as many as three of you, it should cost no more to take a **taxi** straight from the airport to your hotel. Moreover, you might ask the driver how much more the fare would be if he took you by way of the Triborough Bridge, for the view. (If you do take a taxi from the airport, ask the fare in advance anyway, or be sure the meter is running.) In the city, bear in mind that taxi drivers will no longer give change for a bill larger than $5; and also that taking a taxi through the cross-town traffic in midtown Manhattan is usually slower than walking.

On **buses** in New York City, as in most American cities now, you must have the exact fare to put into the fare-box as you enter. And if you plan to **take subway trains** frequently, be sure to keep a few subway tokens on hand at all times since at some stations there will be no one to give change on weekends and at night. (Subway tokens can be used on buses too.) It is best to avoid the subways at rush hours (8–9.30 a.m. and 4–6.30 p.m.); compared to London or Moscow, the New York subway system is poorly marked and dirty at best, and at rush hours it is quite incredible. For midday travelling, however, the subways certainly provide the most sensible way to go long distances, and the station guards are helpful. Don't, however, make the mistake of taking an 'express' train when only a 'local' will stop at your destination.

The subways are one of the places one is now warned to avoid late at night, particularly if one is alone. And generally, if you want to avoid even **the possibility of trouble**, don't wander away from the central part of the city at night alone. The most frequented and touristed areas are fine; if you want to go farther afield, travel in a group. Since the source of most of the trouble is desperate narcotics addicts needing money, you should also observe the precautions wise anywhere to preclude the possibility of a disastrous robbery; don't carry a lot of money about with you, and keep your hotel room locked at all times, with the bolt or chain-lock on as well when you go to bed at night.

You can write ahead to the Convention and Visitors Bureau for their comprehensive hotels list and visitors kit. They are also an excellent source of information for fascinating **free things to do** in the city; especially in the summer New York offers all kinds of tempting free entertainment, including **open-air concerts** and **operas** and **plays**. The **New York Public Library** offers a surprisingly rich and diverse program of bargain entertainment, too. It is also well to ask everywhere about possible **foreign-visitors discounts**. And **students** with student cards can often get reduced admissions at museums.

An extremely good all-purpose map-guide to New York City, including bus and subway routes, theatres and museums, is the Ballantine *New York in Maps*. Anyone who will be in New York more than a few days might also consider buying *The New York Times Guide to Dining Out* (available in paperback) or *The Underground Gourmet*. The best comprehensive guide to the city is Kate Simon's *New York: Places and Pleasures* (also available in paperback). And the Sunday edition of the *New York Times* has an excellent entertainment section.

To get **tickets to theatres or concerts**, the simplest procedure is to call 644–4400 and ask where you'll find the Ticketron office nearest you; the Ticketron fee per ticket is only about 50¢. But there is also the glorious institution known as 'twofers'; plays which are not selling to capacity, often hits which have been running a long time, sometimes sell tickets two-for-the-price-of-one. You will find 'twofers' on sale in all sorts of unlikely places like drugstores and delicatessens; the Convention and Visitors Bureau has them too.

The better **supper clubs** and **jazz clubs** almost always impose either a 'cover' or a 'minimum' charge. A cover charge is an additional sum added on the cost of your drinks or food, like an admission charge but paid at the end. With a minimum charge, the total bill must equal the minimum per person times the number of people at your table. Some establishments have minimums which apply only to drinks; in other places any food you order is counted in too. Any place which has a minimum or cover charge must so indicate on a notice at each table.

Especially if you are contemplating going some distance to get to a particular **museum**, telephone ahead to make sure the hours haven't just been changed. Museums seem constantly to alter their opening and closing arrangements.

And, finally, don't believe anyone who tells you you can do New York on $5 a day. There are a surprising number of real bargains in New York, and on the whole it is certainly no more expensive than any other major city around the world. But it is almost impossible to find really cheap lodgings there, with not even a youth hostel.

SHOPPING

ALEXANDERS, 731 Lexington Avenue. The inexpensive department store with bargains for the discerning eye.

B. ALTMAN & CO., Fifth Avenue at 34th Street. Good department store.

AMERICAN CRAFTS COUNCIL GALLERY, 44 West 53rd Street. Contempory American crafts. Tuesday to Saturday 10–5.30.

AMERICAN INDIAN ARTS CENTER, 1051 Third Avenue, near 62nd Street. Superb Indian and Eskimo artefacts.

ANTIQUES CENTER OF AMERICA, 415 East 53rd Street. Covered antique market of small booths. Expensive Americana. Closed Friday.

BERGDORF GOODMAN, 57th to 58th Streets. Good and expensive.

BLOOMINGDALE'S, Lexington Avenue at 59th Street. A large store with boutiques which specializes in decorative houseware. The showrooms on the 6th floor are changed four or five times a year.

BROOKS BROTHERS, Madison Avenue at 44th Street. Distinguished men's and boys' clothing.

GIMBELS, 33rd Street and Broadway. A large, inexpensive department store.

SAM GOODY, THE RECORD SHOP, 250 West 49th Street. A large selection of records; daily bargains.

KORVETTES, Fifth Avenue at 47th Street. One of the biggest and best of the 'discount' shops; many daily bargains.

LORD AND TAYLOR, Fifth Avenue at 38th Street. Good for everyday town and country wear and accessories. Large price range.

MACY'S, 34th Street and Broadway. A giant department store. Macy's *Traveler's Guide* gives the European equivalents of American sizes, measurements and prices. They also sell electrical equipment for use with European voltages.

OHRBACH'S, 5 West 34th Street. High fashions at low prices.

THE RECORD HUNTER, FIFTH AVENUE, 507 Fifth Avenue between 42nd and 43rd Streets. Records of every kind. Daily bargains are advertised in the morning papers.

SAKS FIFTH AVENUE, Fifth Avenue at 49th Street. Similar to Lord and Taylor; good for lingerie.

F. A. O. SCHWARTZ, Fifth Avenue at 58th Street. New York's best toy shop.

TIFFANY'S, 725 Fifth Avenue. Here one can walk amongst fabulous jewellery and feel rich.

UNITED NATIONS GIFT CENTER, 46th Street and First Avenue. Daily 9.30–5.30. Sells handicrafts from all over the world.

WOMEN'S EXCHANGE, 54th Street and Madison Avenue. Upstairs handmade things (the quilting is particularly beautiful) and delicious fudge. Lunch downstairs.

In addition to those mentioned there are little speciality shops with handmade crafts, leather goods, toys and jewellery in Bleeker's Street in Greenwich Village and Greenwich Avenue west of Sixth Avenue. Also between 57th and 67th Streets along Third Avenue there are more sophisticated boutiques and antique shops.

NEW YORK CITY CONVENTION AND VISITORS BUREAU, 90 East 42nd Street, New York, N.Y. 10017. Telephone 687-1300. Daily 9-6.

TIMES SQUARE INFORMATION CENTER, Times Square. Monday to Saturday 10-8, Sunday 10-6.

AMERICAN AUTOMOBILE ASSOCIATION, 78th Street and Madison Avenue.

AMERICAN MUSEUM OF NATURAL HISTORY, Central Park West at 79th Street. Weekdays 10-5, Sunday and Holidays 1-5. Closed Thanksgiving and 25 December.

BROOKLYN BOTANIC GARDEN, Eastern Parkway and Washington Avenue, Brooklyn. 1 May to 31 October, Monday to Friday 9-6, Saturday, Sunday and holidays 10-6; 1 November to 30 April, Monday to Friday 9-4.30, Saturday, Sunday and holidays 10-4.30. Free.

BROOKLYN MUSEUM, Eastern Parkway at Washington Avenue, Brooklyn. Monday and Tuesday 1-9, Wednesday to Saturday 10-5, Sunday 10-6. Some sections closed additional mornings. For further information telephone 638-5000.

BURLINGTON HOUSE MILL, Avenue of the Americas at 54th Street. Tuesday to Saturday 10-7. Free.

CIRCLE LINE BOAT TRIPS, Pier 85, West 43rd Street. End of March to end of October, 3-hour boat trips around Manhattan. Many trips daily, starting at 9.45.

CITY HALL, City Hall Park at Broadway and Fulton Street. Governor's Room, Monday to Friday 10-3. Free.

THE CLOISTERS, Fort Tryon Park. Tuesday to Saturday 10-5; Sunday and holidays 1-5.

DISCOVER NEW YORK, 41 East 56th Street. Telephone 472-1415. Daily 4-hour tours, beginning at 10. Three different itineraries.

FRICK COLLECTION, 1 East 70th Street. 1 September to 31 May, Tuesday to Saturday 10-6, Sunday 1-6; 1 June to 31 August, Thursday, Friday and Saturday 10-6, Wednesday and Sunday 1-6. Children under 10 not admitted. Free.

GUGGENHEIM MUSEUM, Fifth Avenue at 89th Street. Tuesday to Saturday 10-6; Sunday and holidays 12-6; Tuesday also 6-9 when it is free. Closed 4 July and 25 December.

HAYDEN PLANETARIUM, 81st Street and Central Park West. Monday to Friday 2 and 3.30, Saturday and Sunday on the hour from 1-5, Saturday also at 11. Additional presentations 1 July to 30 September.

HUDSON RIVER DAYLINE, Pier 81 West 41st Street. End of March to end of October 3-hour boat trips around Manhattan. Several trips daily.

THE INTERNATIONAL CENTER, 745 Seventh Avenue. Telephone 245-4131. Monday, Wednesday and Thursday 9.30-8, Tuesday and Friday 9.30-10, Sunday 4-10. For all sorts of helpful information and hospitality for long-term international visitors.

LINCOLN CENTER FOR THE PERFORMING ARTS, 62nd to 66th Streets between Columbus and Amsterdam Avenues. Guided 1¼-hour tours start from the Philharmonic Hall, on Broadway and 65th Street, daily 10-5 at frequent intervals.

METROPOLITAN MUSEUM OF ART, Central Park, Fifth Avenue at 82nd

Street. Tuesday and Friday 10–9, Wednesday, Thursday and Saturday 10–5, Sunday and holidays 11–5.

MORGAN LIBRARY, 29 East 36th Street. Weekdays 9.30–5.

MUSEUM OF AMERICAN FOLK ART, 49 West 53rd Street, Tuesday to Sunday 10.30–5.30. Closed August, 25 December and 1 January. Also closed 4 times a year to set up new exhibitions. For further information, telephone 581–2474.

MUSEUM OF THE AMERICAN INDIAN, Broadway at 155th Street. The best, most comprehensive collection anywhere of Indian culture, both North and South American. Tuesday to Sunday 1–5. Closed August and holidays.

MUSEUM OF THE CITY OF NEW YORK, Fifth Avenue and 103rd Street. Tuesday to Saturday 10–5, Sunday and holidays 1–5. Open Monday if a holiday, then closed Tuesday. Free. Walking tours of New York City mid-April to mid-October alternate Sundays 2.30. For further information telephone 534–1672.

MUSEUM OF CONTEMPORARY CRAFTS, 20 West 53rd Street. Monday to Saturday 11–6, Sunday 1–6.

MUSEUM OF MODERN ART, 11 West 53rd Street, Monday 12–7, Tuesday to Saturday 11–6, Sunday 12–6, Thursday open till 9. Closed 25 December. Classic films shown daily.

NEW YORK STOCK EXCHANGE, 20 Broad Street. Tours Monday to Friday 10–3.30.

PENNY'S SIGHTSEEING TOUR OF HARLEM, 303 West 42nd Street. Telephone 247–2860 for information and reservations.

RICHMONDTOWN RESTORATION, on Staten Island. Some of the restored buildings are open Sunday 2–6. They will be open more frequently in the future. For information write to the Director, Richmondtown Restoration, Richmondtown, Staten Island, New York.

ROCKEFELLER CENTER, Fifth Avenue between 48th and 52nd Streets. Tours, daily, lasting 1 hour, start from the R.C.A. Building and leave every 20 minutes.

SOUTH STREET SEAPORT MUSEUM, 16 Fulton Street. Daily 12–6. Closed Thanksgiving and 25 December. Pier open 1 June to 30 September, 12–9.

STATEN ISLAND ZOO, in Barret Park, West Brighton. Tuesday to Sunday 10–4.

STATUE OF LIBERTY NATIONAL MONUMENT, 15 November to 15 March boats leave hourly 10–4; 15 March to 15 November 9–4. 1 April to 30 September, additional sailing. A return trip takes 45 minutes; allow another hour if you plan to go up into the Statue.

UNITED NATIONS, First Avenue between 42nd Street and 48th Street. Frequent guided tours daily 9–4.45. Closed 1 January and 25 December. Tickets for the General Assembly and other sessions are not bookable, but are distributed free, 30 minutes before the start of a meeting and thereafter additional tickets are handed out as seats become available.

WHITNEY MUSEUM OF AMERICAN ART, 945 Madison Avenue at 75th Street. Weekdays 11–6, Tuesdays to 10, Sunday 12–6.

WORLD TRADE CENTER, tour information available from the Convention and Visitors Bureau.

3 · SUBURBIA, EXURBIA, AND THE MIDDLE ATLANTIC REGION

It is said that only the very rich and the very poor live in Manhattan these days; everyone else commutes. Some commute only to one of the other boroughs, but many go farther: east to the 'dormitory towns' of Long Island, west across the river into New Jersey, or, if a bit richer, up along the Hudson River or north into Westchester County or even Connecticut. The commuter country closest to New York City is 'suburbia', towns which have mushroomed since the Second World War until they now tend to merge one into the other. There are some expensive sections here, but mostly this is middle-income territory. The commuter regions farther from the city constitute 'exurbia', upper-income territory, where the stockbrokers and the advertising agency tycoons play at country living.

We will begin this chapter with a few suggestions for day trips one might make from New York City into some of these areas, and then we will talk about those parts of the Middle Atlantic states which are a bit farther afield: 'upstate' New York, and New Jersey, and then Pennsylvania, with Philadelphia its major centre.

The end of Long Island nearest to New York City is probably best left unexplored unless you have a sociological interest in American suburbia or a friend there to visit. But along Long Island's north shore, at Oyster Bay, one can see Sagamore Hill, the rambling family home of Theodore Roosevelt, President of the United States just before the First World War and a cousin of Franklin Delano Roosevelt. Crammed with mementoes of his fiercely active life, and delightfully situated with a view of Long

2. The Green, Lexington, Massachusetts

1 *overleaf*. The Brooklyn Bridge with the twin towers of the World Trade
Center complex in the background

Island Sound, it would give you an idea of what Long Island was like before the population explosion, when it was chiefly a summer retreat for affluent New York City families. And just beyond Oyster Bay are three little towns which have been there since before the American Revolution: Cold Spring Harbor, Stony Brook, and Setauket. At Stony Brook there is the delightful open-air Carriage House Museum, with every sort of horse-drawn vehicle and several little nineteenth-century buildings and shops. Setauket has some nice old houses, and a church built in 1729 and known as the Caroline Church because George II's queen helped to endow it. If you have a car and a good map to thread your way there on the parkways, this region could provide a pleasant excursion from New York City. You might also include the Old Westbury Gardens, a handsome Long Island estate now open to the public.

If you have more time, the best Long Island excursion undoubtedly is to East Hampton and Sag Harbor and Montauk at the very end. Montauk is a port, the base for fishing trips out into the Atlantic. East Hampton is a charming old village with many good colonial-period houses around its green; it has become, as the guidebooks say, a 'fashionable summer colony', but in the most attractive possible way. Moreover, a good many successful artists and writers now live at East Hampton year-round, making it an interesting place to visit even out-of-season. There are various public beaches along this part of Long Island too, but the Atlantic surf here can be very rough and there is frequently a strong undertow. Many people therefore prefer to do their swimming in the bay at Sag Harbor, and Sag Harbor is well worth seeing in any case. An old whaling town, it still has a special flavour and also a fine little whaling museum.

You would want to stay overnight if you were to venture all the way to the eastern end of Long Island, and while one can get to East Hampton by fast train, without a car you would be limited to that one place. There is, however, one Long Island expedition one can make without a car which would be ideal for anyone interested in hot sun and a swim and a glimpse of the way great masses of Long Islanders spend their summers. On summer mornings, there are buses from the Port of New York Authority bus terminal which go directly to Jones Beach, the most remarkable and justly popular public beach in America. On a weekend it is unbearably crowded, and it is scarcely deserted even on

c

weekdays, but we still recommend it. One can hire bathing suits and towels if necessary, there is a giant salt water pool as well as the ocean to swim in, and changing huts and food facilities and 'life guards' sitting on high perches to watch out for swimmers in trouble. Altogether, it is an American scene one should not miss, so long as one bears in mind that the sun hereabouts can give a very nasty burn; it may seem unlikely, but New York City is in the same latitude as Naples and Istanbul.

Many of New York City's most affluent commuters live in Connecticut, and we will not discuss Connecticut here since it is one of the New England states and thus belongs in Chapter 4. But we can at least say that any invitation to that commuter region should certainly be accepted; it is handsome country, with well-groomed, attractive towns. And we also suggest that anyone driving to this portion of Connecticut take the Merritt Parkway rather than the New England Thruway. The parkways leading in that direction are nicely landscaped and pleasant to drive along, except at the rush hours, when all roads are likely to be clogged.

Perhaps the best single expedition one can make from New York City in one day with a car is along the Hudson River. In the seventeenth century, the lands along the Hudson all the way to Albany belonged to a mere handful of Dutch overlords. They adhered to the continental system of inheritance, however, and with each succeeding generation their estates became more fragmented. Some of them also supported the losing side in the Revolution and thus lost their lands entirely. But the memory of the Dutch lives on in this part of the country, and two of the old Dutch estates on the east bank of the Hudson have been restored and are now open to the public: Philipsburg, in North Tarrytown, and Van Cortlandt Manor, a few miles farther north. In each case what remains is only a fraction of the original estate, but the houses and some of the outbuildings are there, and the restoration-standard, supported by Rockefeller grants, is as high as that of Williamsburg.

To get there from New York City, it is best to take the Henry Hudson Parkway up the west side of Manhattan, cross the river on the George Washington Bridge, follow the Palisades Parkway to Route 9W and the signs for the Tappan Zee Bridge, and then cross the Tappan Zee back to the eastern bank of the Hudson to go north through Tarrytown on Route 9. Philipsburg is two miles north of the bridge. It is the simpler of these two Dutch restorations but thoroughly delightful, with its gristmill still grinding corn, an operation fascinating to watch. Philipsburg also serves as the headquarters and information centre for these restorations, and so it is logical to begin there and see the film which gives something of the history of the two manors.

The entire complex is called Sleepy Hollow Restorations, in honour of Washington Irving, the early nineteenth-century American author who based many of his tales, including 'The Legend of Sleepy Hollow' and 'Rip van Winkle', on the Dutch folklore of this region. His house, Sunnyside, forms part of the complex. But unless you have a particular interest in Washington Irving, we suggest not trying to see Sunnyside but simply going on north, after Philipsburg, to see van Cortlandt Manor with its handsome house and ferry buildings. It would take an hour apiece to see each place properly, and one could happily spend even more time; yet we cannot choose between them. Each is a delight, and quite different; Philipsburg is restored to its early eighteenth-century condition and Van Cortlandt more nearly represents the end of that century and is therefore more substantial, even elegant. One warning, though: be sure to get good directions at Philipsburg for finding Van Cortlandt or you might miss the turn-off for it as you drive north on Route 9. Ask, too, about the old Dutch church which you will pass just after you leave Philipsburg. It is a simple little stone building but well worth noticing.

Going north on Route 9 from Van Cortlandt, you will come quite soon to the town of Peekskill. In order to see another splendid and totally different restoration, you should turn west on the far side of Peekskill on to Route 202, towards the Bear Mountain Bridge; then instead of crossing the bridge, turn north again just short of it, on to Route 9D. About eight miles along on Route 9D, just beyond Garrison, you will come to the entrance to Boscobel. This is one of the loveliest late eighteenth-century Adam-style houses in America. It is set high above the Hudson, is beautifully furnished, and has fine gardens. Two nights a week in summer there is a Sound and Light program as well.

If by now you have not had too much of Route 9 with its endless traffic and roadside billboards, and if there is still time, you can go on after Boscobel to two more interesting places, Franklin Roosevelt's house at Hyde Park, and the Vanderbilt Mansion a few miles farther north. The rambling Roosevelt house has no particular architectural or decorative distinction, merely a thoroughly lived-in look, but one guides oneself through it with the aid of a tape-recording made shortly before her death by Eleanor Roosevelt, President Roosevelt's remarkable wife, and this makes one's visit wonderfully evocative. The Library and Museum on the grounds are also worth visiting. If you take advantage of the combined admission ticket to go on to the mock-Renaissance Vanderbilt Mansion, you will see quite another side of American life. Personally, we found the Vanderbilt Mansion rather disappointing inside, but its situation and grounds are lovely, and one is permitted to picnic in a grove of trees overlooking the river.

Even if one arrived at Philipsburg as it opened in the morning, we must admit it is unlikely one could fit into one day all the stops we have suggested for this trip up the Hudson. In any case, at whatever point you begin to flag, we suggest returning to New York City along the west bank of the river, and staying as close to the river as possible. Below Newburgh this means taking the old Storm King Highway (Route 218), a winding road cut into the cliffs above the river, which leads one past the United States Military Academy at West Point, the American Sandhurst. One can visit the Academy, and one gets a lovely view of the Hudson from its grounds. Just south of it is Bear Mountain State Park, a wonderful place to ramble on a nice day. And on south another fifteen miles or so is the town of Nyack, the centre of an affluent exurbanite region and full of tantalizing antique shops which are open even on Sundays. After Nyack, one would head for the Palisades Parkway back to New York City.

One can also make a day-long trip up the Hudson River on an excursion boat. In the summer the Hudson River Day Line offers cruises up the river, leaving New York City at 10 in the morning and returning at 7 that night. One can stay on the boat all the way to Poughkeepsie and back, or disembark at either Bear Mountain State Park or West Point for half a day at either of those places. It's a very pleasant trip. Gray Line also runs day-long coach tours from New York City to the Roosevelt and Vanderbilt homes at Hyde Park, stopping at West Point and Bear Mountain Park en route.

The region within commuting distance of New York City, or within easy reach on a day-long excursion, is just a small part of the area of the state of New York. Hyde Park is only half-way along the Hudson to Albany, the state capital, and north of Albany the Adirondack Mountains stretch for nearly two hundred miles to the Canadian border. Much of the Adirondacks is true wilderness, woods and lakes punctuated only by a scattering of summer resorts and ski areas. In the heat of a New York City summer, the cool Adirondacks have always seemed very tempting, and New Yorkers have been flocking there for a century now. When taking the waters was all the rage, Saratoga Springs in the Adirondacks was the most elegant spa in America, 'the summer residence of the most refined circles of American society'. After the First World War, Saratoga began to decline, and the grandest of the old summer hotels have now all been torn down, but its August race meeting, and its yearling sale, still go on, still attracting the cognoscenti of the horse world. And more recently a new lure has been added; in July and August, the Saratoga Arts Festival now presents the New York City Ballet and the Philadelphia Orchestra.

About seventy-five miles north of Saratoga is Fort Ticonderoga, so handsomely situated on Lake George that one would enjoy going there even without a particular interest in its history. Yet the fort was a crucial bastion in its day. Taken from the French by the British General Amherst in 1759, it was captured during the Revolution by the Americans under Benedict Arnold, and then retaken for the British by General Burgoyne; each side regarded it as vital to their success. Today it is restored to its original state, but one somehow feels very unwarlike wandering about its ramparts in that idyllic setting.

West of Albany, the Dutch place names are intermingled with Indian names, and anyone who studies a local map will also notice that within a fifty-mile radius of Albany there is a Johnstown, a Fort Johnson, and a Johnsonville. This was Mohawk Indian country, and in the eighteenth century the greatest name in the Mohawk valley was that of Sir William Johnson. One always hears about men on the frontier who failed to understand the Indians, who tricked them and mistreated them; it is a pity that so few people have heard of this one remarkable exception. No other official of the Crown was ever so loved and trusted by the Indians as Johnson, and he in turn loved and defended his Mohawks. In time, he even took a Mohawk wife, the sister of a Mohawk leader called Joseph Brant; she was known as 'the brown Lady Johnson' to distinguish her from her paler predecessor.

Sir William's success in keeping the Mohawks pro-British is clearly one reason why he is so little known in the United States. Guided by Sir William's son, John, the Mohawks remained fiercely loyal to the Crown during the Revolution. In fact they took so many American scalps that the Johnson name became anathema in the region, and Sir John was forced to flee to Canada together with many of his Mohawk supporters.

For many years Sir William Johnson had lived at Fort Johnson, in a small stone house which is now the local museum. Later he had a manor house built for himself and his half-Mohawk family; called Johnson Hall, the house can still be seen in Johnstown. Most of the outbuildings are gone, and in some ways it is disappointing to visit, set as it is today in a tame park at the edge of a commonplace town. Yet what an anomaly it must once have seemed, neat and Georgian here in the wilderness, with Indians encamped in the grounds.

A two-hour drive west of Albany is Cooperstown, a pretty little town in rolling country on a pleasant lake with boating and a public bathing beach. Cooperstown is best known to Americans for its Baseball Hall of Fame, but it has many other attractions, including the delightful Farmers' Museum, run by the New York State Historical Society.

The first building of the Farmers' Museum contains a comprehensive collection of early farming tools and machinery which enthralls modern farmers. Beyond this lies an open-air museum which is a reconstructed village of the New York State of a hundred and fifty years ago. It is not as extensive as Old Sturbridge Village in Massachusetts, but in some ways it is even more fun because of the enthusiasm with which the mock-inhabitants of the Cooperstown village play their nineteenth-century roles.

The headquarters of the Historical Society is at Fenimore House, across the road from the Farmers' Museum on the site of

James Fenimore Cooper's house; the Cooper family, the leading landowners of the region, gave their name to the town. At Fenimore House today one can see a charming collection of itinerant paintings and other examples of early American folk art.

The Baseball Hall of Fame, with memorials to all the great players of the past, is in Cooperstown because baseball began here; the first playing field was laid out in 1839 by one Abner Doubleday, a Cooperstown schoolmaster bent on devising a new sport for his boys. In the tourist season, multitudes of eager fathers can be seen propelling their sons from one exhibit to the next in the Hall of Fame, lecturing and admonishing.

About a hundred miles west of Cooperstown are the lovely Finger Lakes. One of the largest is Lake Cayuga, with Cornell University on the heights at its southern end. At the foot of Seneca Lake is the beautiful Watkins Glen, now part of a state park. South of Watkins Glen is the town of Elmira, where Mark Twain lived for many years after his marriage; he and his wife are buried there, and one can visit his old studio, built in the shape of a Mississippi river boat pilot house. West of Elmira is Corning, where the Corning Glass Company turns out every kind of glass, from Steuben, the most expensive decorative glass made in America, to dishes for cooking and giant lenses for observatories. The Corning Glass Center includes a splendid collection of ancient and modern glass, and there are also demonstrations and films to entertain and enlighten visitors.

Visitors to New York City sometimes arrive with the vague notion that Niagara Falls is just beyond the suburbs; actually it is more than four hundred miles away. It is easy to reach, however, and by car the quickest way is along the New York State Thruway. This follows the old route of the Erie Canal, which was cut through the state of New York from Buffalo to Albany in the 1820s, opening up a vast new area to trade and settlement. In its day, the Erie Canal was a momentous development; it made New York City the most important port on the east coast of North America. Once the railways spread, however, the Erie Canal became less significant, and today it has almost disappeared; it has been blocked off, built over, and in some places combined with a newer canal. Yet here and there one can still find a stretch of it, all overgrown and sluggish, going through some sleepy little town like Canestota which once resounded to the cries of the canal boatmen.

There are several big industrial towns along the Thruway which owed their beginnings to the Erie Canal. The most interesting is probably Rochester, the Eastman Kodak headquarters. You can tour the Kodak works, and in George Eastman House there is an excellent museum of photography and photographic processes. Eastman generosity founded the Eastman School of Music in Rochester, too; it is one of the two or three best music schools in the country. In the late spring, Highland Park is famous for its lilacs; and there is also a pleasant example of Greek Revival architecture in Rochester: the Campbell-Whittlesey House.

Beyond Rochester, not far from Buffalo, anyone consulting a map may exclaim excitedly that there is an Indian reservation just north of the Thruway and another one nearer Niagara Falls. Actually, however, there is nothing to see. There are Indians, to be sure, but they dress like every other American, and live simply on small, scattered farms. Their most colourful characteristic is not visible as you drive through the reservation lands: many New York Indians have made a speciality of high construction work, on bridges and skyscrapers.

Buffalo has a fine art gallery, the Albright-Knox. Otherwise it is a big industrial city, best avoided; one can by-pass it and go directly to the chief attraction in this part of America, Niagara Falls.

Niagara Falls belongs both to Canada and the United States, and since the view from the Canadian side is superior one should certainly go to the Niagara Falls prepared to cross the border. For aliens, this usually means only that you must be sure to have your passport and visa with you. People crossing the border are also sometimes asked to show proof that they have some right to the car they are driving.

There is always a carnival atmosphere at Niagara Falls in the summer tourist season, and one is importuned on every side to take this or that guided tour and to stop at this or that motel or hotel. Niagara Falls has always been part circus and part natural wonder. In the nineteenth century the most respectable people gathered here to see the incredible Blondin pirouette above the Falls on his tightrope, or to watch someone go over the Falls in a barrel. Niagara Falls had so much of everything, in fact, that it became a mecca for couples on their honeymoon. Sophisticated

Americans now roar with laughter at the idea of going to Niagara Falls on a wedding trip, but many newly married couples still do go there.

The Maid of the Mist boat trip to the foot of the Canadian Falls is traditional and exciting, and can be done from either side. On the American side one can also descend the cliff and take a guided walk in oilskins under the Falls. For that matter, one can walk from the Canadian to the American side on the Rainbow Bridge; signs point the way for 'Pedestrians to the United States'. On summer nights the Falls are illuminated with coloured lights, and in the winter they are spectacular in quite another way, with ice and freezing mist and blessedly few tourists.

The St Lawrence Seaway and the vast Niagara power project have resulted in new things to see in the vicinity of Niagara Falls: various aspects of the power project, and the Welland Locks on the Seaway. Anyone interested in these developments should go first to the Power Authority Exhibit Building in Niagara Falls.

For a totally different sort of outing, there is also Fort Niagara, on the shores of Lake Ontario. It is an eighteenth-century outpost, now colourfully restored and complete even to soldiers in period uniform.

The state of New Jersey is immediately west of New York City. It has a flat, sandy coastline dotted with summer resorts and fine beaches, several ugly industrial towns at the end nearest Manhattan, and a great market-garden region in the centre. Northwestern New Jersey is different again, with rolling hills and old farmhouses, and if one were driving from New York City to Philadelphia and could afford to give a day to the trip, one might plot one's route along the edge of this pleasant country and go through Princeton and Bucks County.

Princeton is a pretty old town with a venerable university which was a hotbed of Revolutionary radicalism and Presbyterian fire in the eighteenth century. By the 1920s, however, the old religious fervour had faded, and Princeton had come to epitomize the ultimate in undergraduate sophistication; it was no accident that the young F. Scott Fitzgerald chose Princeton. Today, slightly more sober and still a distinguished university, it is a pleasant place to visit, and undergraduates lead walking tours. The oldest part of the university is along Nassau Street;

Nassau Hall, the oldest building, was finished in 1754. On Library Place in the town there are several handsome old houses, too, including Morven, built in 1709 and now the official residence of the Governor of the state of New Jersey.

One could simply make Princeton the focal point of a day trip from New York City; it is easy to get there and back by bus. But if you have a car, or are in Princeton en route to Philadelphia, you might enjoy driving out of the town on Stockton Street in the direction of Lawrenceville. This was the Post Road at the time of the Revolution; on it you will pass an estate called Drumthwacket, with a very old lodge (1696) hidden in the trees, and a more recent and more visible house (1830). Just before the old stone bridge, beyond Drumthwacket, you should turn left, and just across Mercer Street on the left is the old Quaker Meeting House. In 1777, the American army under General Washington won an important battle here, defeating British troops under the command of Cornwallis. Many of the soldiers from both sides lie buried near the Quaker Meeting House and in the grounds of Drumthwacket.

North-west of Princeton, along the Delaware River which forms the boundary between New Jersey and Pennsylvania, is the little town of New Hope, the unofficial capital of the Bucks County region. While on weekends the whole of Bucks County sometimes seems likely to sink between the weight of its visitors, on any weekday we would certainly recommend spending a little time there, going along the lovely Delaware River and exploring some of the back roads. Particularly in the spring, this is beautiful country, with many pleasant little towns and villages, and fine old stone houses of a sort characteristic only of this eastern end of Pennsylvania. New Hope has a celebrated summer theatre, and from New Hope one can also do mule barge trips along the old Delaware canal or ride for a few miles on an old steam train. But since the quaintness of New Hope itself is now almost smothered in antique shops and craft shops and restaurants, we suggest that anyone wanting to spend the night might stay instead in a quieter place along the Delaware like Lumberville or Washington Crossing. There, as throughout this region, there are attractive, albeit moderately expensive, old inns.

From New Hope, it is only an hour's drive into Philadelphia. In the good old days of vaudeville (the American music hall) it was always easy to raise a laugh at the expense of Philadelphia, reputedly the stodgiest city in the entire United States. (W. C. Fields once said he'd like on his gravestone 'On the whole, I'd rather be in Philadelphia'.) The reputation was derived mainly from the fact that Philadelphia was forced by Pennsylvania state law to restrict severely the sale of spirits, banning the sale entirely on Sundays. In the early nineteenth century, too, Mrs Trollope found the Philadelphia upper classes 'most polished in manner', but noted that chains were stretched across the streets on the Sabbath to prevent the use of carriages.

Today, however, one can carouse in Philadelphia as easily as anywhere else, and it is also a lovely city, totally unlike either New York or Washington, D.C., and full of pleasant things to do and see. We think it would therefore be a particularly good choice for someone, perhaps in New York on business, who wanted to see another side of America yet had only two or three days to spare.

Philadelphia is Pennsylvania's largest city. At the time of the American Revolution it was the largest city in all the American colonies, second only to London among the English-speaking cities of the world, and very elegant and cosmopolitan according to most trans-Atlantic visitors. It had been established in 1682 by William Penn as the centre of his Quaker settlement in the New World, and the industrious Quakers had quickly made the region prosperous.

Quakers and Quaker influences are still surprisingly strong in Philadelphia, even though there is now a strong admixture of many other ethnic and racial elements as well. One is very conscious of the Quakers when one drives through the more affluent residential sections of the city and sees a Quaker Meeting House at the core of each, and the solid, handsome, but seldom ostentatious houses of Philadelphia's old families and her upper middle class. Moreover, perhaps influenced by the Quaker tradition of service and responsibility to the community, the wealthy families of Philadelphia have been very generous over the years in their support of parks and public gardens and museums and good music. Thus Fairmount Park is not only the largest but also surely the most attractive city park in America, encompassing thousands of acres of beautiful and unspoiled country. And Philadelphia's museums and her symphony orchestra are among the finest in America. More recently, Philadelphia has become notable too for having done the most successful job of urban renewal of any American city.

One should begin one's visit to Philadelphia at Penn Center, just east of the wonderful mock-French-Renaissance City Hall with William Penn watching over his city from its top. In the centre of the square, part of the impressive new Penn Center complex, is the Visitors Center, one of the best city tourist information bureaux in America. In addition to the standard brochures about standard tourist sights, the Philadelphia Visitors Center will supply information about renting bicycles for a leisurely exploration of Fairmount Park, or give you a map for a self-guided walking tour of Society Hill, a delightfully renovated old residential section just south of Independence Hall, the city's historic core.

Once armed with brochures and maps, one should take the mid-city loop bus to what is formally known as Independence National Historic Park, although actually it is simply a group of disparate buildings significant for their association with the beginnings of the United States of America. In Carpenters Hall, for example, the First Continental Congress met in 1774 to discuss what steps the various American colonies might take to force the British government to relax some of its demands. Two years later, in one of the handsome pine-panelled rooms of Independence Hall, the colonial representatives to the Second Continental Congress signed the Declaration of Independence. The American Revolution had formally begun. The Constitutional Convention later met here too, to hammer out the laws which were to govern the new federated nation, and in Congress Hall the new Congress of the United States met from 1790 to 1800, until it moved to the newly created capital of Washington, D.C. There are many buildings in this area which are well worth seeing, and if one has not already been supplied with a map and guide at the Visitors Center, in the summer there is an information kiosk near Independence Hall.

One might, for example, go see the Betsy Ross house on Arch Street, where the first American flag is supposed to have been made out of strips of petticoat and flannel; it is especially charming because so minute. Just around the corner, off Second Street, is Elfreth's Alley, a narrow cobbled street with attractive small Georgian houses. And on Second Street is Christ Church, built in the second quarter of the eighteenth century and very little altered since. It still has its wine-glass pulpit and the original pews, one with George Washington's name on it; many of the delegates to the Continental Congresses worshipped at this church during the long months they were in Philadelphia.

In and around this section, and especially in the Society Hill area just to the south, there are many fine old houses, several of which are now open to the public. The Hill-Keith-Physick House and the Powel House are particularly attractive, but we would hope that you would also simply stroll through Society Hill with the Visitors Center walking-tour guide in hand, observing the commendable blend of old and new, and ending perhaps with some ale and a sandwich at the old Head House Tavern.

We have said that Philadelphia's museums are exceptional. The most imposing, looming like a massive Greek temple over the Schuylkill River and the edge of Fairmount Park, is the Philadelphia Museum of Art. Its collection is as impressive as its exterior suggests. (And it is not only the exterior of the museum which is in the classic Greek style; below it on the bank of the Schuylkill are the old waterworks, a gloriously fanciful array of little Greek temples, built in the nineteenth century.) But our own favourite Philadelphia museums are the University Museum, the Barnes Foundation collection, the Franklin Institute, and the Pennsylvania Academy of Fine Arts.

The latter two are peculiarly Philadelphian. Benjamin Franklin was one of the most remarkable Americans of the eighteenth century. Born in Boston, he moved as a young man to Philadelphia where he soon became celebrated as a writer and printer-publisher of uncommon originality. In the years before the Revolution, his writings on natural science and political economy and his scientific experiments made him famous abroad as well, and he was given honorary degrees by both Oxford and St Andrews and elected to both the Royal Society and the French Academy of Sciences. As agent of several of the colonies, he spent many months in London before the Revolution, trying to arrange compromise solutions for the Anglo–American disputes, but when compromise proved impossible and the Revolution broke out, despite his age and his many English friends he turned his energies to work tirelessly for the fragile new American con-federation. During the Revolution he was mainly in France, advancing the American cause as envoy there; the French loved him, perhaps most of all for his wit, and when he died, in 1790, the French assembly went into mourning for three days. The imaginative museum of science which bears his name is surely just the memorial he would have wanted.

The Academy of Fine Arts is the oldest public art gallery in the country. It has a notable collection of American art, especially portraits, from pre-Revolutionary days to the twentieth century, which seems particularly appropriate since Philadelphia for generations produced more good painters than any other American city, well represented both here and at the Museum of Art. One of her best artists was Thomas Eakins, who painted Philadelphians and Philadelphia life at the turn of the century; it is a sign of the continuity one senses everywhere in Philadelphia that one can still see oarsmen sculling on the Schuylkill just as Eakins painted them.

The University Museum is an adjunct of the University of Pennsylvania, one of America's oldest and finest privately-supported universities. It is the most exciting archeological museum we know, with an extremely good collection brilliantly exhibited. The University of Pennsylvania is perhaps most famous archaeologically for its work in the Near East and the collection reflects this emphasis, but there are also splendid sections devoted to North and South America and Polynesia. In addition, there is a pleasanter than average cafeteria, and the very best museum shop we have seen, with fine Navajo jewellery, African artefacts, and even a selection of small archaeological finds to buy. One can get to the University easily by bus or subway train from Penn Center and we urge all visitors to Philadelphia to do so.

The Barnes Foundation is not so easy to get to. In the first place, it is open only three days a week and then only by reservation. In the second place, it is not in central Philadelphia but in Merion. But one can get there by bus (the Visitors Center can advise you) and if you can possibly manage it, go. It is an extraordinary collection of chiefly Impressionist and Post-impressionist paintings, collected by one extraordinary man and hung massed together, room after dark room, in a manner defying all contemporary rules of museumship. Everything about the place sounds off-putting and yet the final effect is absolutely wonderful.

We have left until last the final glory of Philadelphia, Fairmount Park. In the summer there are concerts in the Park, at Robin Hood Dell. There is a charming Japanese house and garden. And there are also six notable colonial-period houses in the Park, any one of which would be rewarding to visit. Mount Pleasant is the best known; built in 1761, it is a handsome, formal house, obviously reflecting the best architectural taste of its day. Woodford has the most interesting furniture. Cedar Grove, built in 1746, is homely and endearing; all its contents are original, the accumulation of one family over two hundred years. Sweetbriar is notable for its unity of style; it is pure Adam, built in 1797. Lemon Hill is one of the most attractive of them all, but open to the public only once or twice a month. One can get to Sweetbriar and to Strawberry Mansion by bus. (Inquire at the Visitors Center.) For the others it is necessary to have a car. There are also tours of the houses under the auspices of the Philadelphia Museum of Art, but the arrangements for these tours seem to vary from year to year. If a tour is available, we certainly suggest taking it, for Philadelphia has a rich heritage of distinctive architectural and decorative styles and it is nice to be intelligently guided through this.

Finally, to see the very best of Fairmount Park one should find a way to get to its heart, where the Wissahickon Creek runs through the deep, wooded Wissahickon Valley past the venerable Valley Green Inn. Theoretically, you could hire a horse or a bicycle and ride here, or in winter skate along the frozen creek. But in any case we can think of nothing pleasanter than lunch at the Valley Green Inn.

Going south-west from Philadelphia, one soon crosses from Pennsylvania into the small state of Delaware. Delaware actually began as a Swedish settlement, but for more than a century now it has been dominated by the Du Pont family. The centre of the Du Pont industrial empire is Wilmington, the capital of Delaware, and between Wilmington and Philadelphia there are three note-worthy examples of Du Pont munificence. One is Longwood Gardens, which many think the finest gardens in America. Long-wood has an ornamental lake, fountains and formal gardens, delightful natural sections, an enormous conservatory, and even an outdoor theatre where there are concerts of all sorts in summer. It is only thirty miles south-west of Philadelphia to Longwood, and about eight miles to the south-east of Longwood is another magnificent Du Pont foundation, Winterthur. Winterthur also has fine gardens, but it is chiefly famous for its collection of American furniture and silver and decorative styles, the finest of its kind in the United States. Experts and decorators and dealers come to do research at Winterthur, which has almost two hundred rooms, each one furnished in the style characteristic of some particular period or region in America during the seventeenth, eighteenth, or nineteenth century. There are no rope barriers but you must be accompanied by one of the guides, and to see the entire collection one normally must write to Winterthur well in advance for reservations. However, in late April and May this stricture is relaxed, and there is then a sort of open season on Winterthur, with a reduced admission charge. Moreover, at any time of the year there are ten rooms at the Reception Center which one can see without a reservation. Finally, along the Brandywine Creek not far from Winterthur there is the delightful little Hagley Museum, with working models of the first Du Pont mills and echoes of some of the other early activities in this region too. The whole thing is unpretentious but extremely well done, and the situation is charming: a wooded park, with a few of the old mill buildings still standing along the river.

Longwood, Winterthur, and the Hagley might seem enough for one day, but just south of Wilmington on the Delaware River there is one more place which would well repay a visit: the pretty little town of New Castle. Built around a green, it still boasts a fine array of Dutch and English colonial-period houses, brick pavements and cobbled streets. The Strand, along the river, is especially attractive. In the old days the ferry came across the Delaware River to New Castle; now that traffic flows instead across a bridge to the north, New Castle seems blissfully forgotten. One could stop and see it in the course of a day trip from Philadelphia, or one might diverge to spend a pleasant hour or two there if one were driving from New York to Washington, D.C.

Visitors whose interest in the American Revolution has been whetted by the Independence Hall section of Philadelphia might like to take a trip out of the city to Valley Forge. Gray Line runs coach tours there, or it is an easy drive in a car. The colonial army camped at Valley Forge during the bleakest winter of the Revolution, in 1777-8. The first enthusiasm had worn off, the war was going badly for the Americans, enlistments had expired and thousands of General Washington's soldiers simply took their rifles and went home. For those who remained there was no warm clothing and little food. At Valley Forge they built rude huts and waited, in the snow and cold. Actually this was the turning point of the war, for in the spring word came that the French government was sending troops to help the Americans fight the British; until then only a few individual Frenchmen like Lafayette had been in the field with Washington's forces. This new assistance was to make all the difference, but if the ragged American army had not held together at Valley Forge, no amount of French aid could have turned the tide. Thus Valley Forge is the great landmark of the Revolution, the most popular shrine. One can still see the encampment almost as it was that winter, with the little huts and the farmhouse which General Washington used as his headquarters.

Or one might make an expedition to the west of Philadelphia, into the Pennsylvania Dutch country. Many of the early Pennsylvania colonists were German and others came from Holland or the German-speaking part of Switzerland; together, they all came to be known as 'Pennsylvania Dutch'. The Quakers welcomed their industriousness, and most of these settlers were quickly absorbed into the mainstream of Pennsylvania life. But some of these settlers, members of strict religious sects, had fled to America in order to preserve their faith intact and their practices undisturbed; in Pennsylvania they continued determined to keep apart from the rest of the world. The most important of these groups were the Mennonites, and a kindred sect, the Amish. Today, when someone mentions 'the Pennsylvania Dutch', he is probably referring to the Amish, 'the plain people'; the Amish are the most extreme of the surviving groups. Amish men have beards and wear broad-brimmed black hats and black suits or blue working clothes; the women wear close-fitting caps and long dresses, and the children are dressed in small versions of the adult costume. The Amish are pious, hardworking farmers, and they frown on all but the most wholesome pleasures. Moreover they eschew machinery and will not own cars or have telephones. They have sometimes come into conflict with the state over schooling for the children, and over their refusal to take part in any government activity; they will not serve on juries or join the army. But usually they manage to be left alone, and there are today about 50,000 Amish and strict Mennonites combined; they are best known in Pennsylvania but many of them also live in sections of Ohio and Indiana.

The centre of the Amish country today is the nice old town of Lancaster, and on any back road in this region you are likely to encounter an Amish farmer with his horse and buggy. Or if you go into Lancaster on Tuesday, Friday or Saturday, market days, you will find Amish and Mennonite farm wives selling their produce in the market stalls. Their vegetables and home-made bread and sausage and jam are delicious. (There are several different marketplaces; ask in Lancaster where the market is that day.) Lancaster itself is a lovely place, too, especially attractive in the section bounded by Orange and Lime and Chestnut and Shippen Streets. You might like to spend a night in the Pennsylvania Dutch country and one can stay inexpensively at Lancaster in a 'tourist home'. The Pennsylvania Dutch Tourist Bureau, which has its headquarters in Lancaster but also an information centre at the Hempstead Road interchange of Route 30 east of Lancaster, could advise you about other accommodations. (Incidentally, it was here in Lancaster in 1879 that F. W. Woolworth opened his very first 'five and ten cents store'.)

All of the Pennsylvania Dutch country has become a great tourist attraction and one must pick one's way a bit carefully among the advertised sights and stops. But for a glorious Pennsylvania Dutch meal, complete with shoo-fly pie, we can recommend the Plain and Fancy Farm and Dining Room, along Route 340 nine miles east of Lancaster, near the village of Bird-in-Hand. It is certainly touristy, but the food is wonderful and great value for the price. And if you'd like to know more about the Amish, go to the Amish Farm and Home five miles east of Lancaster on Route 30, near Paradise. This is not a tourist trap but a genuinely interesting place, run by people sympathetic to the Amish and anxious to explain their customs and beliefs.

The Pennsylvania State Historical Commission administers two properties within range of Lancaster which one might like to include in a visit to this region. One is the Pennsylvania Farm Museum, a little open-air museum illustrating various facets of rural American life in the nineteenth century. It is along Route 222 on the way north from Lancaster to Ephrata. The other is Cornwall Furnace, a small ironworks which operated from 1742 until 1883; the mines nearby are still being worked and the original miners' cottages are still being lived in, but the old furnace and foundry are now preserved as an illustration of mid-nineteenth-century technology. In this connection, we must also mention the Hopewell Village National Historic Site, an even more extensive preservation of an early ironworks complex. At Hopewell Village, the National Park Service has managed to preserve the entire original site, nearly a thousand acres, complete with the ironmaster's house and many other outbuildings. It is about ten miles north-east of the Morgantown exit of the Pennsylvania Turnpike, on Route 23, and could thus be seen on the way to or from the Lancaster region.

And at Ephrata, just off Route 222 which leads from the Pennsylvania Turnpike to Lancaster, there is another especially interesting place to visit, the Ephrata Cloister. Founded by German Seventh Day Baptists in the early eighteenth century as a community of strictly celibate men and women, the Cloister community rapidly became celebrated not only for its piety and good works but also for its superb choral singing, for the books produced by the Cloister press, and for a special sort of caligraphy known as *frakturschriften*. Unfortunately, during the Revolution a typhus epidemic sadly reduced the numbers of the community and in the nineteenth century it dwindled further, to eventual dissolution. But its buildings now are owned by the state and open to the public as a particularly good example of those Utopian religious communities which were so numerous in America in the eighteenth and nineteenth centuries. It is a fascinating place, set in lovely country, and we heartily recommend it.

East of Lancaster via York is Gettysburg, the scene of the most famous battle of the American Civil War. Under the brilliant leadership of Robert E. Lee, the Confederate armies had one success after another in the first years of the war, and by 1863 they were penetrating deep into Northern territory. At Gettysburg, however, the tide turned; the battle lasted three days, with more men engaged on either side than in any other encounter of the war, and at the end the Confederates were forced to retreat back into Virginia. Both sides had suffered appalling losses. A few months later, Abraham Lincoln gave his brief and beautiful 'Gettysburg address' at the dedication of a memorial there. The National Park Service now administers the battlefield area, and the Park Visitors Center can provide maps for a self-guided tour around the battlefield, or even, for a fee, furnish a licensed personal guide. And opposite the graveyard in the privately-run Gettysburg National Museum, a huge map dotted with electric lights illustrates the three-day battle while a recorded voice gives a running account.

It is pleasant to drive to Gettysburg on minor roads through the Pennsylvania Dutch region, but most people going there from Philadelphia take the Pennsylvania Turnpike. Built for the most part in the 1930s, this turnpike was the first great superhighway in the United States. It is still in many ways the most impressive. In the eastern part of the state it winds through rolling country dotted with fieldstone houses and farms. Then not far beyond the Gettysburg turning, the Turnpike goes through its first tunnel. There are six or seven tunnels in all, as the Turnpike pierces the Allegheny Mountains. The superb engineering rather softens the effect of these mountains, which used to seem a formidable barrier when one had to twist and climb for a hundred miles. This part of the Turnpike is very pleasant; the mountains are heavily wooded, with a blue cast to them except in the autumn when they are flaming red and gold.

The entire Allegheny region, extending well down into West Virginia, is coal-mining country. In the beginning many of the miners were Welsh and Scotch and Cornish, as some of the place-names indicate: Carnwath and Grampian, Crum Lynne, Treverton, Trevose. But in time many of these first miners made enough money to leave the hard life of the mines, or else moved on to the mining regions of the West. There were new recruits then from among the thousands of Central European immigrants who came to the United States in the years before the First World War, and the Allegheny coal fields became one of the great melting-pot areas. In this region arose many of the first great American labour leaders.

The heart of this area is Pittsburgh, which was Fort Pitt in the days before the American Revolution; it was then the key outpost on the western edge of British territory in America. The advantages of the site are obvious. Pittsburgh lies in a narrow valley at the confluence of the Ohio, the Monongahela, and the Allegheny rivers. You come down round a steep hill, and suddenly there before you is the iron and steel capital of America.

Pittsburgh was once one of the ugliest industrial cities in the United States, but it is now one of the most impressive. A few years ago, when industrial blight seemed about to devour it completely, the leading citizens decided that dreadfulness had gone far enough. Today, in a section which was formerly one of the worst in the city, where the Monongahela and the Allegheny come together to squeeze the heart of Pittsburgh into a point, there is now the Golden Triangle, a group of striking modern office buildings set around a little park. There is a wonderful view of the Golden Triangle at night from the top of Mount Washington at the edge of the city; one might go just for a drink to Le Mont or The Tin Angel, two expensive restaurants up on the heights.

SPECIAL KNOWLEDGE

In deciding which of the regions described in this chapter to visit, one should take **the time of year** into consideration. The Adirondacks and 'upstate' New York are at their most beautiful in the autumn; the foliage is spectacular and the air clear and crisp. Spring is certainly the very best time to go to the Philadelphia region, or to drive from New York City to Washington, D.C., with side-trips to some of the places in the Philadelphia region. Many of the gardens are particularly rich in azaleas, and the dogwood and other flowering trees and shrubs along the way are lovely. In summer, Philadelphia and the country around it sometimes wilt beneath oppressive, sticky heat, whereas New York State is seldom so bad. In winter, on the other hand, 'upstate' New York usually gets more snow than any other section of the United States, and driving there then might present problems.

Philadelphia seems particularly kindly disposed to foreign visitors. At the moment, at least, almost all her hotels offer them special (and substantial) discounts; one can write to the Visitors Center for a list. Most large American cities have a 'Meet Americans at Home' program; we would be particularly inclined to sample it in Philadelphia, and one could inquire about that at the Visitors Center. For people staying some time in Philadelphia, there is also a special Center for International Visitors. Youth hostellers should note that Philadelphia's hostel is a fine old house in Fairmount Park, Chamounix. And anyone in Philadelphia without a car might like to know that Gray Line offers trips to Valley Forge, to Gettysburg, and to the Pennsylvania Dutch country.

Like New England, this mid-Atlantic region is particularly rich in many seasonal entertainments such as **music festivals** and **summer theatres**. For example, both Chautauqua, at the western end of New York State, and Glens Falls in the Adirondacks, have summer opera festivals. Visitors should inquire locally, or simply keep their eyes open for notices, to see what might be going on.

Don't forget that the eastern edge of New York State borders New England, and therefore a trip to the Adirondacks could also easily include Vermont, or the Berkshires of Massachusetts, or north-western Connecticut. See Chapter 4. And while we have had to draw an arbitrary line between the region south of Philadelphia and the region north of Washington, D.C., in actual fact these two areas merge one into the other almost imperceptibly, and any visitor planning a trip to the former should also see Chapter 5 for the latter.

Buffalo, New York State
BUFFALO FINE ART ACADEMY, Allbright-Knox Art Gallery, 1285 Elmwood Avenue. Tuesday to Saturday 10–5, Sunday and holidays 12–5. Closed 1 January, Thanksgiving and 25 December.

Cooperstown, New York State
FARMERS' MUSEUM, 1 May to 31 October, daily 9–6; 1 November to 30 April, Tuesday to Saturday 9–5, Sunday and Monday afternoons.
FENIMORE HOUSE, opposite the Farmers' Museum. July and August, daily 9–9; May, June, September and October, daily 9–6; November to April, daily 9–5.
NATIONAL BASEBALL MUSEUM, Main Street. 1 May to 31 October, daily 9–9; 1 November to 30 April, daily 9–5.

Corning, New York State
CORNING GLASS CENTER, 1 November to 31 May, Tuesday to Sunday 9.30–5; June, September and October, daily 9.30–5; July and August, daily 8.30–5. Closed 1 January, Thanksgiving and 25 December.

Cornwall Furnace, Pennsylvania, off U.S. Route 322, south of Lebanon.
Mid-May to mid-October, Monday to Saturday 8.30–5, Sunday 1–5; mid-October to mid-May, Monday to Saturday 9–4.30, Sunday 1–4.30.

Elmira, New York State
MARK TWAIN'S STUDIO, Elmira College campus. 1 July to 1 September, daily 1–4.30; other times by appointment. Free.

Ephrata, Pennsylvania
EPHRATA CLOISTER, at the junction of U.S. Routes 322 and 222. Summer, Monday to Saturday, 8.30–4.30, Sunday 1–4.30; winter, Monday to Saturday 9–4.30, Sunday 1–4.30. Closed holidays.

Fort Ticonderoga, New York State
Mid-May to 30 June and 1 September to mid-October, daily 8–6; 1 July to 31 August, daily 8–7.

Garrison, New York State
BOSCOBEL, eight miles north of Bear Mountain Bridge on State Route 9D. 1 April to 31 October, Wednesday to Monday 9.30–5; March, November and December, Wednesday to Monday 9.30–4. Closed January, February, Thanksgiving and 25 December.

Gettysburg, Pennsylvania
GETTYSBURG NATIONAL MILITARY PARK. Mid-June to Labor Day, daily 9–9; rest of the year, 9–5 (or until 6 during Daylight Saving Time).
GETTYSBURG NATIONAL MUSEUM, on U.S. Route 15. Winter, daily 9–5; spring and autumn, daily 8.30–7.30; summer, daily 8–8.45.

Hopewell Village, Pennsylvania (National Historic Site)

10 miles north-east of Morgantown exit of Pennsylvania Turnpike on State Route 23. 1 March to 31 October, daily 9–6; 1 November to 30 April, daily 8–5. Closed 1 January and 25 December. Free.

Hudson River, New York State

GRAY LINE TOURS, 900 8th Avenue between 53rd and 54th Streets, New York City. Telephone 765–1600. West Point, Hyde Park, Vanderbilt House, Bear Mountain tour lasts 10 hours. Mid-May to mid-October, Tuesday, Thursday and Saturday, departs at 8.30.

HUDSON RIVER DAY LINE, Pier 81, end of West 41st Street, New York City. Telephone 270–3131. End of May to mid-September, tours to Bear Mountain and West Point leave at 10 a.m. and last 9 hours. Weekends, extended return boat trip from West Point to Poughkeepsie (non-stop).

Hyde Park, New York State

FRANKLIN D. ROOSEVELT HOUSE, LIBRARY AND MUSEUM, 2 miles south of Hyde Park on U.S. Route 9. Daily 9–5. Closed 1 January and 25 December. House closed Monday and Tuesday between Labor Day and Easter.

VANDERBILT HOUSE, north of Hyde Park on U.S. Route 9. Easter to Thanksgiving, daily 9–5; Thanksgiving to Easter, Wednesday to Sunday, 9–5. Closed 1 January and 25 December.

Johnstown, New York State

JOHNSON HALL, Hall Avenue. Tuesday to Saturday 9–5, Sunday 1–5. Free.

Jones Beach, Long Island

In summer, buses leave New York City from the Port Authority terminal at 41st Street and 8th Avenue at Gate 46, Monday to Saturday continuously between 9 and 9.30 a.m., Sunday between 9 and 10 a.m., returning from the beach at 5. Fare $1.50 each way.

Lancaster, Pennsylvania

VISITORS OFFICIAL INFORMATION CENTER, U.S. Route 30 at Hempstead Road interchange. Telephone (717) 393–9705.

AMISH FARM AND HOME, 5 miles east of Lancaster on State Route 30, just beyond Paradise.

PLAIN AND FANCY FARM AND DINING ROOM, 9½ miles east of Lancaster on State Route 340. Farm hours Tuesday to Saturday 8.30–8; Dining Room, Tuesday to Saturday 11.30–8. Closed 25 December.

PENNSYLVANIA FARM MUSEUM, 3 miles north off U.S. Route 222. Mid-May to mid-October, Monday to Saturday 8.30–5, Sunday 1–5; mid-October to mid-May, Monday to Saturday 9.40–4.30, Sunday 12–4.30.

New Hope, Pennsylvania

MULE BARGE TRIPS leave from New Street above State Route 32. During April and from Labor Day to 1 November, Wednesday, Saturday and Sunday; 1 May to Labor Day, Tuesday to Sunday at 1, 3, 4.30 and 6.

THE NEW HOPE AND IVYLAND RAILROAD, west on U.S. Route 202. 4 July to 30 August, daily; 1 April to 4 July and 1 September to 30 November, weekends and holidays only.

Niagara Falls, New York State

MAID OF THE MIST BOAT RIDE, late May to early October, daily 9.45–5, July and August to 7. Trips leave every 20 minutes.

Old Fort Niagara, New York State

North of Youngstown in Fort Niagara State Park. 1 July to Labor Day, daily 9 until dusk; Labor Day to 30 June, 9–4.30. Closed 1 January, Thanksgiving and 25 December.

Old Westbury, New York State

OLD WESTBURY GARDENS, Old Westbury Road between Long Island Expressway and Jericho Turnpike. Early May to last Sunday in August, Wednesday to Sunday and holidays 10–5.

Oyster Bay, Long Island

SAGAMORE HILL (Theodore Roosevelt's house), 3 miles west of Oyster Bay. Daily 9–5.

Philadelphia, Pennsylvania

VISITORS CENTER, Kennedy Plaza, Penn Center. Daily 8.45–5, summer weekdays until 9. Branch kiosk at Independence Hall open in the summer, daily 9–5. Closed 25 December.

'MEET AMERICANS AT HOME.' For information inquire at Visitors Center.

BARNES FOUNDATION, Latch's Lane and Lapsley Road, Merion. Friday and Saturday 9.30–4.30, Sunday 1–4.30. Closed July, August and holidays. Advanced reservation necessary but can sometimes be done last minute by phone (215) 667–0290.

BETSY ROSS HOUSE, 239 Arch Street. Daily 9.30–5.15. Closed 25 December. Free.

CARPENTERS' HALL, 320 Chestnut Street. Daily 10–4.

CHRIST CHURCH, 2nd Street, between Arch Street and Market Street. Daily 9–5. Sunday services at 9 and 11, open 1–5.

FAIRMOUNT PARK HOUSES. For information about tours telephone 765–0500.

CEDAR GROVE. Daily 10–5. Closed holidays.

LEMON HILL. Summer, second and fourth Sunday 1–4: winter, Thursday 11–3.

MOUNT PLEASANT. Daily 10–5. Closed holidays.

SWEETBRIAR. Monday to Saturday 10.30–5. Closed July.

WOODFORD. Tuesday to Sunday 1–4. Closed August and holidays.

FRANKLIN INSTITUTE. Benjamin Franklin Parkway at 20th Street. Monday to Saturday 10–5; Sunday 2–5. Closed 1 January, Labor Day, Thanksgiving and 25 December.

HILL-KEITH-PHYSICK HOUSE, 4th and Delancey Streets. Tuesday to Saturday 10–4, Sunday 1–4.

INDEPENDENCE HALL, Chestnut Street between 5th and 6th Streets. Daily 9–5. Free.

PHILADELPHIA MUSEUM OF ART, end of Benjamin Franklin Parkway in Fairmount Park. Daily 9–5. Closed holidays. Free on Monday.

POWEL HOUSE, 244 South 3rd Street. Tuesday to Sunday 10–5 (winter until 4).

UNIVERSITY MUSEUM, 33rd and Spruce Streets. Tuesday to Saturday 10–5. Closed holidays. Free.

Princeton, New Jersey

By bus from New York on Suburban Transit Line. Buses leave Port Authority every half-hour from 6 a.m. to midnight.

MORVEN, Stockton Street at Library Place. Tuesday 2–4 by appointment. Closed July, August and December.

PRINCETON UNIVERSITY. Apply to Stanhope Hall for free Campus Guide Service; Monday to Saturday 9–5, Sunday 1–5. Telephone 452–3603.

Rochester, New York State

CAMPBELL-WHITTLESEY HOUSE, 123 South Fitzhugh Street at Troup Street. Tuesday to Saturday 10–5, Sunday 1–4.

GEORGE EASTMAN HOUSE (museum of photography), 900 East Avenue. Tuesday to Sunday 10–5. Free.

Sag Harbor, Long Island

SUFFOLK COUNTY WHALING MUSEUM, Main Street. 30 May to 12 October, Monday to Saturday 10–5, Sunday 2–5.

Setauket, Long Island

CAROLINE CHURCH, Main Street at Setauket Green. Daily 9–5.

Stony Brook, Long Island

SUFFOLK MUSEUM, Christian Avenue, north end of village green. 15 March to 20 December, Wednesday to Sunday 10–5.30.

CARRIAGE HOUSE OF THE SUFFOLK MUSEUM, State Route 25A (south). 1 April to 15 November, daily 10–5.

Tarrytown, New York State

SLEEPY HOLLOW RESTORATIONS

PHILIPSBURG MANOR, in North Tarrytown on U.S. Route 9. 1 April to 15 November, daily 10–5; 16 November to 31 March, Monday to Friday 12–5, Saturday and Sunday 10–5.

SUNNYSIDE, south of Tarrytown; West Sunnyside Lane off U.S. Route 9, 1 mile south of Tappan Zee Bridge. Opening hours same as Philipsburg.

VAN CORTLANDT, south of Croton-on-Hudson, on U.S. Route 9. Opening hours same as Philipsburg.

Valley Forge, Pennsylvania

STATE PARK near Valley Forge. Daily 9–5.

West Point, New York State

VISITORS INFORMATION CENTER, near the Thayer Gate, open mid-April to mid-November, Monday to Saturday 9–5, Sunday and holidays 11–5. Parades: early September to November and May, usually 3 times a week. Telephone (914) 938–3507.

Wilmington, Delaware

HAGLEY MUSEUM, Barley Mill Road. Tuesday to Saturday, 9.30–4.30, Sunday 1–5. Closed holidays. Free.

LONGWOOD GARDENS, 13 miles north of Wilmington. Daily 8 until sunset. Conservatories, daily 11–5. Free.

WINTERTHUR MUSEUM, 6 miles north-west of Wilmington on State Route 52. Advance reservations must be obtained from Reservations Office, Winterthur Museum, Winterthur, Delaware 19735. Tours Tuesday to Saturday 9.30–3.30. They are split into 2 with 1 hour for lunch. 10 rooms in Reception Area 9.30–4 without reservations. Children under 16 not admitted to Main Museum. For 6 weeks beginning mid-April, Tuesday to Saturday 9.30–4, a selection of rooms in the Main Museum and the 10 rooms in the Reception Area may be visited without reservation. Gardens, mid-April for 6 weeks and during October, Tuesday to Saturday 10–4.

4 · NEW ENGLAND

The New England states are Connecticut, Rhode Island, Massachusetts, Maine, Vermont, and New Hampshire. Clustered together in the north-eastern corner of the country, these six states are linked historically as well. The first European settlements were made along the coast in the seventeenth century by close-knit groups of English Dissenters, and splinter groups from these first settlements later colonized the interior. Sharing thus a homogeneous tradition, the New England states have continued to form a cohesive block.

Today, the population of New England contains a notable ethnic diversity. Boston in the eighteenth century had attracted a few French Huguenot families like the Reveres and the Faneuils; the proximity to French Canada has since brought a steady stream of Catholic French Canadians into New England, and one is especially conscious of this in Maine, where many of the place-names are French too. By the time of the American Revolution, New England also had a sizeable number of free Negroes, one of whom became the first Revolutionary-era 'martyr'. (His name was Crispus Attucks and he was the first man shot in what Americans call the 'Boston Massacre', in 1770.) New England's black population has grown since then on that solid base. In the nineteenth century, an enormous number of Irish Catholics also came to settle in New England. A large percentage of the present-day population of Boston is thus of Irish descent; the Kennedy family is the most celebrated example. Later in the nineteenth century great numbers of Italians and Portuguese came too, the latter mostly to settle in the ports and work on the fishing boats.

And from Poland and the countries of central Europe, immigrants came to find work in the New England mill towns.

Tangible evidence of this ethnic diversity is to be found in the variety of foods one is offered these days in New England. The traditional specialities, Boston brown bread, baked beans, Indian pudding, Rhode Island jonny cakes and maple sugar, lobsters and clams, are still to be found, but so now are pizzas and Portuguese sausage and a wealth of other exotic delights. Travelling through New England, one should sample the traditional specialities in traditional New England inns, but one should also sample such newer gastronomic treats as 'grinders', Italian sandwiches on crusty bread rolls.

If the New England of today is infinitely more complex than seventeenth-century New England, nonetheless it still resembles old England far more than any other section of the United States. Boston often reminds visitors of London, and New Englanders as a whole have always prided themselves on embodying those virtues which one associates with rural England of the eighteenth century: independence, industrious self-reliance, and thrift. Even the proud emphasis on New England's key role in the American Revolution is a manifestation of this English connection, for the New England Revolutionary leaders first insisted only that a free-born Briton in the colonies must enjoy the same rights and privileges he would have had back in England.

Perhaps because of its innate conservatism, New England has preserved more of its eighteenth- and early nineteenth-century architecture than any other part of America. Thus today tourists flock to New England to try to recapture the past, thinking to find in the simple, graceful lines of a white clap-board New England church on a village green the reflection of a purer and simpler society. And New England is eager to help; nowhere in the United States will you find more concern with the preservation of ancient monuments. The result is that you must exercise discretion unless you really want to spend all your time in New England in solemn contemplation of bed-warmers, butter-churns and mildewed samplers. However, the best of the old houses open to the public are charming. And time spent at the museum villages of Shelburne, Deerfield, Mystic, or Sturbridge is time very well-spent.

Boston, the capital of the state of Massachusetts, is the heart of

New England. It was founded in 1630, but to understand Boston one must begin outside the city limits and farther back in time: in 1620, to be exact. In that year one hundred 'pilgrims' embarked for the New World in the *Mayflower*. All of them were English, most of them were Separatists, and some of them had recently tried living as refugees in Holland. Their new venture was financed partly by religious sympathizers, and partly by disinterested speculators who hoped only for a good return on their money.

From our superior vantage point, it is hard to see how anyone could have thought that anything but trouble could come from letting the fractious, dissenting Separatists go off to settle the New World for England; it was sweeping gunpowder under the rug. But the attempts to settle the Virginia territory with more orthodox colonists had not been particularly successful; perhaps by 1620 England was grateful for any would-be settlers foolhardy enough to brave the voyage and the Indians and the American climate. In any event, the Pilgrims obtained land grants in the Virginia territory, and they set sail, ill-provisioned, ill-prepared for what lay ahead, but never lacking in courage and always sustained by their sense of righteousness.

Storms and haphazard navigation brought them ashore far to the north of the Virginia territory, but it was already mid-December so they decided they had better stay where they were. And stay they did, even though less than half of them survived that first grim winter. They had sailed from Plymouth in England; they named their landing place Plymouth, too, perhaps because the two harbours do bear a superficial resemblance to each other in shape.

Realizing that they were outside the jurisdiction of the Virginia colony, the Pilgrim leaders drew up a rudimentary code on board the ship and insisted that everyone sign it before dis-embarking; it came to be known as 'the Mayflower Compact'. So there was an independent government of sorts from the very beginning; you might say that the American Revolution really began in 1620.

Ten years after the Pilgrims reached Plymouth, a much larger group of Puritans, almost a thousand strong, landed twenty miles farther up Massachusetts Bay. As they approached their new world, their leader, John Winthrop, sat himself down in the cabin of the *Arabella* and wrote a few words which three hundred years later still keep their proud ring:

'. . . wee must consider that wee shall be as a citty upon a hill. The eies of all people are upon us soe that if wee shall deale falsely with our God in this worke wee have undertaken wee shall be made a story and a by-word through the world.'

Under a charter which gave them fishing and trading rights and allowed them to organize local government as they saw fit, they founded Boston and several smaller towns nearby; eventually the Plymouth group allied themselves with them. In the years ahead, almost all the other settlements in New England came into being as off-shoots of this Massachusetts Bay Colony, with Boston as its centre. Some of these new settlements were patterned after the parent colony, but others were organized quite differently, by Massachusetts Bay rebels and outcasts. There were a good many of these. For the Massachusetts Bay Colony was a rigid theocracy, administered much like Calvin's Geneva. If you were one of God's elect, and worked hard, you could expect to prosper; should adversity overtake you, the community would care for you and your family. If, however, you were a late-comer, you would have to prove your conformity, your obedience, before you had any hope of acceptance. And if ever you dared to disagree with the elders of the church, you could expect persecution, exile, even death.

> Now let's drink a toast to old Boston
> The home of the bean and the cod
> Where the Cabots speak only to Lowells
> And the Lowells speak only to God.

The Cabots and the Lowells may feel that this little verse is over-quoted, but there in four lines one does have at least part of the essence of Boston; first, homely, seafaring, colonial Boston, then the image of the 'proper-Bostonian' of the nineteenth century as the ultimate in stiff-necked American aristocracy, and last, but never least in Boston, God.

Obviously, then, the proper place to begin a visit to Boston is at the site of its first church, where Tremont and Park Streets cross at the edge of Boston Common. Boston is almost unique among large cities in still having its common, which is now at the centre of the city. It gives the city a quaint and friendly air, totally different from both the sleek impersonality of New York and the stateliness of Washington.

Where the first church once stood, there is now a newer building, the Park Street Church. Built in 1810, it was a centre of anti-slavery sentiment in the years before the Civil War when most of New England's leading citizens were fervent Abolitionists. (It seems peculiarly fitting that Massachusetts in the 1960s elected a black United States Senator, Edward Brooke.) Today the Park Street Church is a leading example of the independent and evangelical sort of church so common in the United States; a church with no governing body other than its own vestry, and with a minister who attracts crowds through the power of his preaching.

The Park Street Church is also the official starting point for the Freedom Trail, a suggested sign-posted walking tour which leads past Boston's most important historic sights. To follow the Freedom Trail in its entirety might involve too large a dose of rather repetitious American history. But one should surely do at least some of it. From the Park Street Church, the Trail leads on a few feet along Tremont Street to the Old Granary Burial Ground. Several of the leading Revolutionary figures lie here, including John Hancock (who was the first to sign the Declaration of Independence, writing his name large 'so the King can read it without his spectacles') and Paul Revere. But perhaps the most famous grave is that of Mother Goose: Mrs Isaac Goose, she was, and she died in Boston in 1690; the rhymes she had recited to her children and grandchildren were collected and printed by her son.

A few steps farther on along Tremont Street is King's Chapel. The present building was finished in the middle of the eighteenth century. It was designed by Peter Harrison, one of the most celebrated architects of colonial New England; there is more of his work in Newport, Rhode Island, and Christ Church on the Common in Cambridge is his. The original church, built in 1688, had been the first Church of England, or Episcopal, church in the Massachusetts Bay Colony, and as such it was bitterly resented by most of the colonists. After the Revolution, King's Chapel was rededicated as the first Unitarian Church in America. Wherever you go in New England, if you seek the oldest church, look for the Congregational Church; but the second oldest will very likely be Unitarian. The strictness of the Congregational Church (originally Puritan or Separatist) did not suit everyone, and Unitarianism won many adherents.

King's Chapel gave evidence of recurrent friction in New England over religious matters. As the colonists became more ambitious in their trading and fishing ventures, they also grew less tolerant of commercial restrictions imposed from London. The only thing which kept relations comparatively polite was the fact that Britain's problems in Europe kept her from paying much attention to the American colonies. Left to their own devices, the settlers prospered; particularly in New England, they simply circumvented those restrictions they found annoying. Then, in about 1760, England took cognizance of the fact that her American children were somewhat undisciplined, and she also noted that they were quite big and strong enough to be of considerable help to their mother, so the struggle over stamp duties and taxes and import and export quotas began. It was really too late now for firmness, which only aroused stubborn hostility and open defiance, but succeeding British governments persisted in trying. Only a few British leaders (Pitt, Charles James Fox, Burke) seemed to comprehend the seriousness and the complexity of the situation, and their advice was disregarded.

For thirty years before the Revolution, a Boston radical named Sam Adams had been speaking and writing against 'English tyranny'. The well-to-do merchants who by now controlled Boston affairs paid scant attention to Adams and his 'rabble' until about 1760. Then, enraged first over the Writs of Assistance (unreasonable searching of ships, they thought), and later over the Stamp Acts (unreasonable duties imposed), many of them began to listen more sympathetically. The most important of the new converts was John Hancock, scion of one of the richest shipping families, and with him to several of Sam Adams's meetings came a distant cousin of Sam's, one John Adams, a studious, respectable young lawyer. If one adds the engraver and silversmith Paul Revere to this list, one has the four Revolutionary leaders from Boston whose names are best known today. Together they represented that cross-section of class and interest which, united, made success possible.

Everyone should see at least one of the buildings which figured so prominently in the struggles leading up to the Revolution, and the Freedom Trail markers lead on to one of the best, the Old South Meeting House. The Congregational ministers were among the most ardent revolutionaries, dreading any extension of royal power for fear of Church-of-England control.

3a. The White House, Washington, with the Washington Monument and the Jefferson Memorial in the background

3b. Independence Hall, Philadelphia

4a *left*. Eighteenth-century houses on the Chesapeake and Ohio Canal in Georgetown, Washington, D.C.

4b *above*. The Saugus Ironworks, Massachusetts

So the Congregational meeting houses, and especially this one, welcomed mass meetings of the aroused citizenry. In 1773, the Boston Tea Party began here, at the end of a protest meeting chaired by John Adams which had failed to move the Governor from his determination to enforce the tax on tea and to compel the unloading of two controversial shipments waiting in the harbour. Disguised as Indians, a large group of respectable Boston citizens proceeded to the ships and threw all the casks of tea overboard.

One can continue on the Freedom Trail and see the charming little Old State House, and Faneuil Hall, the market house which sheltered many a patriotic meeting and is still the centre of the market district. Two of the Boston restaurants most familiar to tourists are there, both with good local seafood: the Durgin Park and the Union Oyster House. Nearby one can also see the new Government Center, a striking blending of new building with old surroundings.

Or this might be the moment to head for one of the most interesting sights in Boston, the frigate U.S.S. *Constitution*, known as 'Old Ironsides'. You can get there by underground train on the M.B.T.A., the Boston public transport system, going to the Navy Yard stop in the Charlestown section of Boston. The U.S.S. *Constitution* is the oldest fighting ship still afloat anywhere in the world; she was launched in 1797 and saw action in the war of 1812. She is now docked at the Navy Yard, where the Navy looks after her, and she is fun to visit.

Paul Revere's house and the Old North Church are in a section of Boston which is just across the Charles River from the Navy Yard. You can walk there from the Common; they are at the end of the Freedom Trail. But it is a fairly long walk and not a particularly attractive one; we would suggest a taxi.

Paul Revere is most famous today for having ridden out to Lexington and Concord one night in 1775 to warn the leaders there that the British troops were on the march. The next day 'the shot heard round the world' was fired, in Lexington, and, although no one yet realized it, the Revolution had begun. But in his own day Paul Revere was far better known as a silversmith; he was a fine one, and his silver is much sought after today. His house, which is open to the public, was built about 1680, and is an interesting example of simple domestic architecture in eighteenth-century Boston.

D

The Old North Church is the oldest church still standing in Boston (1723). In its steeple hung the lanterns which gave Paul Revere the signal to ride. The church and the house are in what is now one of Boston's principal Italian districts; you can sit in the little park behind the church and eat an Italian ice and watch the elderly Italians arguing over their checker boards.

But Boston has another, more recent past which also bears investigation: nineteenth-century Boston, the Boston of Henry James's novels, the Boston where the Lowells spoke only to Cabots. There is no more pleasant walk in Boston than a stroll across the Common to the handsome 'new' State House and then down Beacon Street, that symbol of the world of the Boston brahmin. The Athenaeum, a private library and holy of holies, is just along to the right when one reaches the north-west corner of the Common, and downhill from the State House lie the old proper-Bostonian town houses, in an area known as Beacon Hill. (The name comes from the fact that there was once an actual beacon at the top, a signal light made of rushes, ready to be fired whenever Indians threatened or some dramatic event needed advertising.) Here at the corner is the Saint-Gaudens memorial to the young Union Civil War officer Colonel Shaw and his Negro troops; one is reminded that the Boston brahmin was after all descended from John Winthrop, and was not likely to 'deale falsely' with either God or Man.

If you walk down Beacon Street from the State House, you should glance at the windows of number 39 and number 40. Some of the old panes are a lovely shade of mauve, from an ancient impurity in the glass. And we suggest turning right off Beacon Street on to Spruce Street and then Willow, to get to Louisberg Square, the heart of the Beacon Hill district. It is reminiscent of a Georgian square in London, but more plain, more Puritan.

If you go south-west from Beacon Hill across the Common and then across the adjacent Public Gardens, where children like to ride in the swan boats, you come to the area of the most fashionable shops and hotels: 'Back Bay Boston'. In the midst of it, where Boylston Street meets Huntington Avenue, is Trinity Church, that incredible mass of Victorian Romanesque. Southwest of Trinity Church is the Prudential Center, financed by the Prudential Insurance Company, with shops and housing and office buildings and an auditorium, all in one enormous plaza.

For a fine view over Boston, one can go to the 'top of the Pru' for a drink or a meal, or simply a look round from its Skywalk. On the far side of the Prudential Center are those landmarks of the Christian Science Church, the Mother Church, and the Christian Science Publishing House. The latter is responsible for one of the best newspapers in America, the independent *Christian Science Monitor*; there are tours of both the church and the newspaper plant.

On Huntington Avenue two streets beyond the Prudential Center is Symphony Hall; the Boston Symphony is one of the finest orchestras in America. Farther on along Huntington is the Museum of Fine Arts, and nearby, on the Fenway, is the Isabella Stewart Gardner Museum. You can take an M.B.T.A. bus from Copley Square (Trinity Church) out Huntington Avenue to get to these museums, but it should be noted that the Gardner Museum is only open in the afternoon and both museums are shut on Mondays.

The Gardner is a reconstructed Venetian palazzo, built as a town house for one Isabella Stewart Gardner at the turn of the century. Eccentric, beautiful, rich, and not-quite-accepted, she amassed a remarkable collection of art with the aid and advice of the young Bernard Berenson. Like the Frick in New York, this gallery is relatively small, but charmingly personal and rich in treasures.

The Museum of Fine Arts is many times the size of the Gardner; it is second only to the Metropolitan Museum in New York in the range and importance of its collection. And in addition to European and Graeco–Roman and Oriental sections, it has several excellent purely American treasures: Paul Revere silver, some fine examples of the work of Winslow Homer, and a series of rooms of early American furniture and décor. The Museum of Fine Arts has profited from centuries of collecting on the part of discriminating Bostonians.

There is one other collection which should be mentioned for the benefit of those particularly interested in early-American architecture and artefacts. The Society for the Preservation of New England Antiquities, at its headquarters in the handsome old Harrison-Gray-Otis House at 141 Cambridge Street, has a good collection of china and glass, pewter, toys, ingenious displays illustrating early American building styles, and the like.

For those interested, the city also has a fine new Science

Museum along the Charles River, and a splendid Aquarium on the harbour near the site of the Boston Tea Party.

Boston would not be Boston without Cambridge. Cambridge is a separate city, not a borough of Boston, but it is just across the Charles River, a few minutes' ride on an M.B.T.A. train to Harvard Square. The eminence of Cambridge began with the founding of Harvard College there in 1636. The oldest university in America, it was founded by the Puritans to train teachers and preachers for the Massachusetts Bay Colony. Most of the Puritan leaders had been Cambridge-educated in England, and so the college town was called Cambridge: the college itself was named for one of those Cambridge men, the young John Harvard, late of Emmanuel College, who had died after a few years' preaching in the Massachusetts Bay Colony and left what money and books he had to the new school. Harvard grew and prospered; it became more liberal, and attracted young men from the other colonies, and later from all the other states. In a frontier society, the lure of such a university town was overpowering for certain kinds of men, and Cambridge reached its zenith in the nineteenth century, when Longfellow lived there, and James Russell Lowell, and many men and women whose fame has dwindled, like Margaret Fuller, 'the female thinker'.

To recapture this past, it is pleasant to walk from the clamour and confusion of Harvard Square up Brattle Street to Longfellow's house, which is in a particularly nice section of Cambridge. The first two or three blocks of the walk take one past Cambridge's best shops, including The Window Shop, which is not only a shop but also a restaurant and a Harvard and Cambridge institution. After one passes the Loeb Drama Center, in the next block, the precincts of Radcliffe begin on the right-hand side of the street; once a separate women's college, Radcliffe has now been absorbed by Harvard. After you've seen the Longfellow house, you might ask to be directed back to Harvard Square in the roundabout way which would take you past the striking new Radcliffe library.

It is also pleasant to walk around Harvard itself. Or if one fancies a tour, Harvard undergraduates lead tours in the summer.

Massachusetts Hall in New Yard is the oldest Harvard building still standing (1720). Opposite it, University Hall (1815) was designed by Charles Bulfinch, who was also responsible for the central portion of the 'new' State House in Boston. The statue of

John Harvard here is the work of Daniel Chester French, better known for the statues of Lincoln in the Lincoln Memorial in Washington and in Parliament Square in London. But one should see more of Harvard than this. One might go to the Fogg Art Museum and look too at its neighbour, the Carpenter Visual Arts Center, the first le Corbusier building in America. Then you might walk down Boylston Street to Memorial Drive along the river and go east past Eliot House and John Winthrop House to Plympton Street, where you can turn north again and wind your way back towards Harvard Square. The river is particularly pleasant along here, with boating, and walks and bicycle paths along the banks.

The Harvard 'houses', Eliot and Winthrop and Lowell and all the others, are only for sleeping and eating; like most American universities, Harvard groups all its undergraduates together in one vast 'college of arts and sciences'. In the United States, there are usually separate colleges within a university only for those embarking on purely technical careers or learning to be teachers, and for those doing postgraduate studies.

But a technical college is not always part of a larger university, and one of the most prestigious independent technical colleges is the Massachusetts Institute of Technology. Sheltering a veritable pride of Nobel prizewinners, it too is in Cambridge, where Massachusetts Avenue crosses the river. There are tours of M.I.T. which include a look at its synchrotron and at the lovely little chapel and the Kresge Auditorium, both designed by Eero Saarinen. (Or one can of course simply see the latter two on one's own.)

For anyone who may have two or three days in Boston and wants to make a trip out of the city, one possibility is a journey to Lexington and Concord. Concord is only twenty miles or so; Lexington is even nearer, in the same direction. There are organized bus tours which include them both.

If you have been to the Old North Church in Boston, you will have heard of the midnight ride of Paul Revere and you will remember that it took him to Lexington. In Lexington you can see the Hancock-Clarke house, his first stop that night in 1775. Expecting trouble, John Hancock and Sam Adams were staying here, out of Boston, out of sight; Paul Revere came to warn them that eight hundred British troops were heading that way. Today the house is interesting to fervent patriots for its historical associations, but it is also interesting simply as a good example of a plain colonial-Massachusetts dwelling house. Equally interesting is the old Buckman Tavern where seventy-odd Minutemen, the local militia, gathered later that night. The Tavern is at the edge of the green, where the militia met the troops the next day and gave way before them after several men on each side had been killed.

The British troops marched on from Lexington to Concord, where there was rumoured to be a large cache of rebel arms. At Concord Bridge they met the Concord Minutemen, who, rather surprisingly, forced them to retreat.

Concord, however, has associations over and above the Revolutionary ones. This is where the Little Women grew up; this is where Louisa May Alcott lived. And Nathaniel Hawthorne lived here, and Henry David Thoreau, and Ralph Waldo Emerson, whose Transcendentalist movement was pure Concord. Cambridge was an intellectual centre in the early nineteenth century, but Cambridge was too complacent to suit everyone; the iconoclasts gathered in Concord.

Louisa May Alcott's father, Bronson Alcott, was an educator, a philosopher, and an altogether endearing man, who was at one time far more widely known than his daughter. He abhorred violence and he had complete faith in the perfectibility of human nature. The fact that he seldom succeeded in supporting his family embittered neither his family nor his friends, who rallied round with unfailing affection.

There are two houses in Concord in which the Alcotts lived: Wayside, and Orchard House, next door to each other on the Lexington Road. Of the two, only Orchard House is now open to the public. The Alcotts moved from Wayside into Orchard House in 1848, when Louisa May was sixteen; Hawthorne then moved into Wayside. Emerson, 'the American Carlyle', in that day the most famous of all the Concord figures, lived on the other side of Concord, near the North Bridge; his house too is open to the public. Thoreau lived on Main Street, and a mile or so to the south of Concord is Walden Pond, where Thoreau spent two winters in the woods in a hut he built himself. *Walden*, the book which resulted from that experience, is an American classic.

Many of Bronson Alcott's Concord friends had also been involved with him in either the Brook Farm or the Fruitlands experiments in communal living and a return to a simple, agricultural life. Hawthorne, who spent one miserable winter at Brook Farm, complained that after a day in the fields or with the cows he was too tired to think or write clearly. Others eventually grew impatient with the sacrifices demanded: one must not wear wool, because it was unfair to sheep, or use oil lamps, because they were unfair to whales. And then the amateur farmers found that they were ill-equipped for competition with the rest of the world, and the accounts suffered. So both Brook Farm and Fruitlands in turn languished and died. Fruitlands, however, can still be seen, in a lovely setting some twenty miles beyond Lexington and Concord. It is not as it was in Bronson Alcott's day; it has been turned into an open-air museum, with several unrelated buildings scattered down a rolling green hill-side. But it is still a pleasant place to visit. In addition to the Alcott house there is a small American Indian museum, an excellent collection of early American paintings, and a Shaker house. For Fruitlands is at Harvard, Massachusetts (not to be confused with Harvard University at Cambridge), and Harvard had one of the most important Shaker colonies. Many of the Shaker buildings can still be seen, on the other side of Harvard village, and there is a Shaker burial ground there too, the grave markers looking like rows of lollipops stuck in the ground. None of these Shaker houses is open to the public, however; one must be content with visiting the one transported complete to Fruitlands.

The Shakers were one of those strange sects which seemed to flower in the New World. They combined an insistence on simplicity in dress and daily life with religious services which culminated in spontaneous ecstatic dancing, so they were known as 'shaking Quakers', and soon simply 'Shakers'. Strictly celibate, they nonetheless built mixed communities, with separate dormitories for men and women. They flourished principally in the nineteenth century, although a few elderly Shakers are still living in one of the seventeen original settlements, at Sabbathday Lake near Poland Spring in Maine. What has made them celebrated today is the fact that their insistence on simplicity in all things led to a unique Shaker style in building and cabinet-making; simple, functional Shaker furniture is now tremendously sought after.

If you have time on the way back to Boston, you might brave the industrial town of Waltham to see Gore Place, considered the finest Federal-period country house in New England. (The Federal period in American architecture and decoration roughly corresponds in date to that of the Regency period in England.) We are not architectural historians, but we would agree that Gore Place is one of the loveliest houses we know, elegant yet also warm and livable, and set in fine grounds.

Lexington, and more particularly Concord and Fruitlands, lie well inland from Boston, in a pleasantly rural part of New England. Another good day's trip from Boston is along the more populous North Shore, to Marblehead and Salem, and the pretty villages beyond Beverly, and Gloucester and Rockport, and Ipswich. En route one could detour to Saugus to see America's first ironworks, which began operations in the mid-seventeenth century. The great forge hammer, the water wheels and the bellows have been restored to working order.

Marblehead is one of those towns considered tremendously picturesque, with rather too many people and cameras around on a summer afternoon, but it is deservedly popular. The Jeremiah Lee House, at 161 Washington Street, is one of the best colonial-period houses in New England.

Salem too has some fine houses open to the public, most notably two side by side on Essex Street, the Pingree House (Samuel McIntire) at number 128 and the Crowninshield-Bentley House at number 126. But in Salem one should also go to Derby Wharf, for towards the end of the eighteenth century Salem became the leading American port for the China trade. Sending ships to China and the East Indies like latter-day Venetians, the merchants of Salem made her for a time one of the wealthiest towns in the New World. And to help local ship captains, a young Salem man, Nathaniel Bowditch, in 1802 put together the classic *Practical Navigator*. The old Customs House (where the young Nathaniel Hawthorne had a post) is still there on Derby Street, and near it is Derby House, built in 1762 by Salem's first great merchant prince, Elias Derby. One can see some fascinating relics of this China trade in the local Peabody Museum, on Essex Street. But few traces now remain of that earlier dread Salem of the witch-craft trials, when in 1692 the good citizens did to death twenty men and women before sanity prevailed. One can, however, visit that great Salem tourist attraction, the House of Seven Gables, supposedly the inspiration for Hawthorne's novel of the same name in which the witch trials cast a shadow. And recently an enterprising entrepreneur has opened a Witch-trial Museum, where recorded voices read from the trial records as various displays and living tableaux light up. It is very effective.

Beyond Salem, Route 127 leads north-east along the shore through a whole series of pretty places like Pride's Crossing and Manchester until it reaches Gloucester. Gloucester was the fishing port in Kipling's *Captains Courageous*, and it still has Portuguese fishermen and considerable character. It also has Beauport, a house-cum-museum with what is quite rightly characterized as 'an extraordinary and fascinating assembly of period rooms', the individual expression of one man, who left it at his death to the Preservation Society.

Rockport is out on Cape Ann, beyond Gloucester. Like Provincetown at the tip of Cape Cod, it attracts artists and also the sort of people who come to stare at artists; it is suitably picturesque.

There is a nice beach which one can reach by back-tracking from Gloucester, or by going due north from Salem: Crane's Beach. And in the neighbouring town of Ipswich is still another fine old house, the seventeenth-century John Whipple House at 53 Main Street. The two most popular public beaches near Boston are Revere Beach on the north and Nantasket Beach on the south; one can even reach Nantasket Beach by boat, from Boston harbour. But these two beaches are crowded and noisy, completely unlike the peaceful stretch of sand at Crane's Beach.

Driving from New York City to Boston, one has a choice of two main routes, both with super-highways all the way (and turnpike tolls to pay for much of the distance). One of these routes is Interstate 95 the entire distance from New York to Boston; it goes along the coast through Connecticut and then swings up through Rhode Island. The other route involves taking Interstate 95 only as far as New Haven in Connecticut, there shifting to Interstate 91 to Hartford, and then from Hartford taking Interstate 86 to the Massachusetts Turnpike (Interstate 90) which leads on to Boston. While this second route may sound complicated, it is actually not; one by-passes the cities and need worry only about being sufficiently alert at the inter-changes. And it is more direct and thus usually quicker, although it does also get heavier traffic.

There are of course variations one can play on these two main routes too, as any good map will show. One might, for example, take Interstate 684 out of New York City in order then to swing through the exurbanite country of upper western Connecticut, of which the town of Litchfield is the chief jewel. Or in the summer one can drive from New York City to the end of Long Island and then take a car-ferry from Orient Point to New London, Connecticut; the AAA can supply schedules. However, we will assume that most of our readers will elect one or the other of the two main routes.

As far as New Haven, Connecticut, the two routes are one and the same, marked the 'New England Thruway'; one passes through a mixture of suburbia and industrial towns. On the outskirts of Bridgeport, an unprepossessing industrial town, is Stratford, where the American Shakespeare Festival is held every summer. The productions here vary in quality; the Stratford Festival in Canada is usually better over-all. But the theatre, a reproduction of the Globe, is delightful, its pennants waving in the breeze from Long Island Sound.

New Haven is best known as the seat of Yale University, founded in 1701 by Connecticut Puritans and today one of America's most prestigious universities. It got its name from Elihu Yale, a rather sour old man who made a fortune in the East India trade and seems to have given £560 to help the new college mainly to spite Harvard, which he thought had grown entirely too liberal. Few people have bought immortality so cheaply, and, as he would have wished, Yale has always considered itself Harvard's particular rival.

Visitors who have admired the Georgian symmetry of Harvard may at first find Yale ugly; many of its main buildings are Victorian Gothic, and the surrounding town is industrial and lacking in charm. But Yale nonetheless makes for a very interesting stop; it has some superb modern buildings and a very fine art gallery. Moreover, if one is driving from New York City, it is at New Haven that one first begins to get a sense of New England. There, on the old village green which the university borders, stand three handsome old churches side by side. North Church (also called United Church) is the loveliest, but behind Center Church (1814) one should note the grave of one of the men who presided at the trial and condemnation of Charles I. He and two others of the regicides fled to Connecticut after the Restoration and were hidden for several years in and around New Haven. A plaque on the rear wall of the church commemorates all three. We might

also point out that the Grove Street Cemetery, north of the green
along Prospect Street, has the graves of several of those New
England inventors who made New Haven and Connecticut
bywords for Yankee ingenuity. Buried there are Eli Whitney,
who invented the cotton gin and the Winchester rifle and was
among the first to experiment with interchangeable parts and the
assembly line; Samuel F. B. Morse, who developed the first
practical telegraph; and Charles Goodyear, who first patented the
vulcanizing process for rubber.

In this same direction are two of Yale's most remarkable
contemporary buildings: on Prospect Street beyond the cemetery
is the Ingalls Ice-hockey Rink, designed by Eero Saarinen, and
at the corner of High and Wall Streets is a building which may
just be the most beautiful and successful contemporary building
in the United States, the Beinecke Rare Book and Manuscript
Library, designed by Gordon Bunshaft of Skidmore, Owings,
and Merrill. One must go into it and walk around. From the
Beinecke one can then go south-west along High Street to reach
the Yale University Art Gallery, and one should not miss this
either. It is one of the finest museums in the country; not particularly big, but with each collection extraordinarily good of its
kind. Its holdings in early American painting and silver are especially fine: its Revolutionary-era Trumbull portraits for example,
and fine New York Dutch silver as well as the more usual Anglo–
American. Equally splendid are its Rabinowitz and Jarves
collections of Renaissance painting. At the Art Gallery, one is
also near the new college designed for Yale by Eero Saarinen,
and you should see this too. It may or may not be successful, but
it is at least a very interesting try at solving the problem of how
to blend new with old.

For those taking the shorter route to Boston via Hartford, we
have one other suggested stop along the way: Old Sturbridge
Village in Massachusetts, near the intersection of Interstates 86
and 90. After Colonial Williamsburg in Virginia, Old Sturbridge
Village is the most elaborate museum-town in the United States.
But compared to Williamsburg, Sturbridge re-creates a much
simpler life; New England after all was strongly Puritan. Then
too Sturbridge is a much more artificial reconstruction. The
restored section of Williamsburg is a recreation of what was
once actually there, with many of the original buildings still
standing on their original sites; Sturbridge, however, is a village

that never was, with appropriate old buildings brought from all over New England to be reconstructed here in a village setting. But Sturbridge is great fun, and well worth the entrance fee if you can spend at least two or three hours there. It has suitably picturesque eating places as part of the complex, and there are also many inns and motels nearby where one can spend the night.

For travellers taking Interstate 95 all the way to Boston, we suggest turning off the highway again soon after New Haven, to see Guilford and Madison, two attractive small New England towns. Guilford has an unusually large number of colonial-period houses centred around its old green. Follow the markers south of the green, to the Whitfield House, an early (1639) stone house which one may visit. Notice also, just to the east of the First Congregational Church on the green, the delightful Victorian house, and beyond it across the street an earlier house with exceptionally fine detail in its decorative mouldings.

Madison is only three or four miles east of Guilford, along the old Boston Post Road (U.S. Route 1). Like Guilford, it increases its population considerably in summer; many of its charming old houses are now used chiefly as summer retreats for affluent city dwellers from New York City and New Haven and Hartford. In Madison there is a fine Congregational Church on the green. And along the main road, just east of the green at the corner of Academy Street, stands a dark, unpainted wooden house, almost hidden behind overgrown trees and shrubbery; known as the Graves House, it is remarkable for being a virtually unaltered seventeenth-century frame house.

Unless you want to stop at Hammonasset, a fine state beach, you should return to Route 95 after seeing Madison. The country-side will get steadily more rural as you go along; indeed both of these main routes will surely surprise the visitor who has been led to believe that the eastern regions of the United States are now 'megalopolis', a densely populated urban sprawl. Both go for much of their distance through rolling, wooded country with scarcely a sign of human habitation.

Approaching the city of New London, site of the United States Coast Guard Academy and also the United States Navy's chief North Atlantic submarine base, you will want to keep to the coast on Interstate 95 and not be inadvertently swept off to the north with the Connecticut Turnpike. Shortly after you pass New

London, you will see signs for Mystic Seaport. For anyone interested in the sea and seafaring, we recommend spending two or three hours at this reconstruction of a nineteenth-century New England port town. Except on a terribly crowded August day, it is fun to stroll about here, observing the various nautical craftsmen playing at plying their trade, and going over the old ships moored along the quay. One of these ships is the last surviving nineteenth-century American wooden whaling ship. The more studious can investigate such special exhibits as Mystic's fine collection of navigational instruments.

A few miles farther along the coast from Mystic is Stonington, one of New England's prettiest little towns. It was a bustling port in 1800; Nelson's Captain Hardy bombarded it in the war of 1812. Today it is peaceful and relatively unspoiled; one might eat at the seafood restaurant on the harbour or browse in an antique shop.

Returning to Interstate 95, this will take you through Providence, the capital of the state of Rhode Island and the second largest city in New England. Providence was founded in 1636 by Roger Williams, who had been banished from the Massachusetts Bay Colony because he would not acknowledge the authority of the church in civil matters and he also objected to land being forcibly taken from the Indians. With genuine religious freedom and good relations with the Rhode Island Indians, Providence flourished. It seemed particularly to attract Quakers, and in that ironic manner so characteristic of New England, kindly Quaker shipowners proceeded to amass fortunes in the rum and slave trade. This in turn encouraged good craftsmen to settle in Providence, and in the nineteenth century, when other New England seaports fell upon hard times, Providence shifted almost effortlessly to manufacturing, which is still her mainstay. There are some fine colonial-period houses in the heart of Providence, and if you are willing to tangle with city traffic, you might go see the museum of the Rhode Island School of Design (which has a much more wide-ranging collection than the name suggests), and the John Brown House. But in your preoccupation with the relics of Providence's past, don't omit to notice how much of Providence's present-day character is due to the Italians and Portuguese who came in great numbers at the turn of the century.

Even the stop at Providence may be more than most travellers bound for Boston will have time for. But if the purpose of your trip is to see the best of New England, we would like to suggest making an even wider detour and going for a day or two to Newport, Rhode Island. To get there from Mystic one simply follows Route 1 to the turn-off for the Jamestown Bridge which leads one in turn to the Newport Bridge; together they span Narragansett Bay. If one were coming instead from Interstate 95, one would take State Route 138 east to the Jamestown Bridge.

Just east of Usquepaugh, Route 138 passes the site of the Great Swamp Fight, the most important battle in that bitter conflict between colonists and Indians which was known as King Philip's War. King Philip was the son of Massassoit, one of the Pilgrim's first Indian friends, but Philip himself had come to realize that the white settlements meant eventual disaster for his people, and when he succeeded his father as chief of the Narragansetts he tried to unite all the various New England Indian tribes in order to wipe out the colonists once and for all. From the beginning, all the New England settlements except those in Rhode Island had had trouble with the Indians, and the whites had usually retaliated by persuading one Indian tribe to help them attack the other; most frequently, Uncas' Mohicans were the settlers' allies. But now Philip of the Narragansetts persuaded his fellow chiefs to make common cause, and from 1675 to 1677 the united Indians waged a kind of sustained warfare which they were never to repeat. In those two years about nine hundred men on each side were killed, and that meant one out of every ten men among the colonists. Many whites were taken prisoner, too, and many Indians captured and sold as slaves. More than half of all the towns in New England were destroyed; even Providence was burned. But in the end Philip himself was betrayed by another Indian and killed, and a pathetic remnant of these tribes made their way to the Ohio territory.

Route 138 leads on through Kingston, a pretty village which is also the seat of the University of Rhode Island, and then to the Jamestown Bridge and across Conanicut Island to Newport Bridge. One used to be able to make the final stage of the journey to Newport on a ferry, which was certainly the proper way to approach a town so intimately connected with the sea. Now, unhappily, one must settle for bridges all the way. But one should still head first for Newport's waterfront, and the route there will take you along Thames Street through a section full of eighteenth-century houses, many recently refurbished.

The waterfront section of Newport is exceptionally rich in colonial-period buildings, including some of considerable architectural interest. The best way to see them is to stop at the foot of Washington Square, near the old Brick Market, and go to the Newport County Chamber of Commerce visitors information office at 93 Thames Street. There you can get a walking-tour guide and then set off on foot. You should see the Touro Synagogue, the Redwood Library and Trinity Church, our very favourite church in New England. The Touro Synagogue is the oldest American synagogue still standing and one of the finest buildings of the eighteenth-century America architect, Peter Harrison. Its interior is particularly lovely. Peter Harrison also designed the Redwood Library, up the hill from the synagogue, on Bellevue Avenue; it was the first private subscription library in America. You should walk in to see its interior too. You might also enjoy eating at the White Horse Tavern and simply wandering about looking at the houses.

In the middle of the eighteenth century, Newport was the most sophisticated town in New England. Not hampered by any narrow Puritanism, it attracted a varied group of remarkable men, from Isaac Touro, an aristocratic Portuguese Jew, to Bishop Berkeley, the Anglo–Irish metaphysician, who lived here for three years while trying to organize a missionary college in the New World. Berkeley's first two children were born here; the second is buried in Trinity Churchyard. His house, Whitehall, is still standing and open to the public, in the country just east of the town.

Whitehall is one of the two old Newport houses one really must see; the other is the Hunter House, which is splendidly furnished with what is called block-front furniture, mostly the work of those renowned Newport cabinet-making families, the Goddards and the Townsends. The Hunter House is in the old waterfront section. You can buy combination tickets, at a considerable saving, which will admit you to Whitehall and the Hunter House and also to the Breakers, that incredible Vanderbilt house which is the most palatial of all the late nineteenth-century 'summer cottages'.

At the Hunter House one learns that five thousand French troops under Rochambeau landed at Newport to aid the American cause during the Revolution; this army, which included among its officers Marie Antoinette's Count Fersen, stayed in and near

Newport for nearly a year. But despite the French, Newport was ruined during the war. For three years it was occupied by British troops; trade collapsed and never recovered. Those who could, fled, never to return, and Newport lay neglected and poor. It revived, however, in the middle of the nineteenth century. First, wealthy Southerners discovered it as a pleasant summer resort they could reach on coastal steamers from Charleston or Savannah. Then after the Civil War the new Northern millionaires took it over and it became a byword in America for extravagant splendour and social distinction. Today, crowds file through the Breakers, the Vanderbilt mansion, and gasp as the guides reel off the cost of every doorknob; it is fun to make the tour. The Breakers stables are delightful in quite a different way, with the mahogany horse-boxes still sanded and ready, the tack all oiled, and a variety of carriages lined up waiting to be driven.

The most elaborate houses, such as The Elms and Marble House, are along Bellevue Avenue near the Breakers. But every-one should also take the nine-mile Ocean Drive, not only to see the houses along it (splendid in a different manner) but also to see the surf pounding on the rocks and, in June, the wild roses bloom-ing all along the way.

And if you are in Newport at the end of July or the beginning of August, there is an added delight. For a two-week period, the Newport Music Festival presents concerts of classical music of the Romantic period. There are daytime as well as evening performances, and they are all given in one or the other of Newport's most elegant Gilded Age mansions. One can stroll around the grounds during the interval, sipping champagne. The combination of superb music and all that atmosphere is irresistible.

Driving to see Newport's Gilded Age mansions, one passes a cluster of smart shops along Bellevue Avenue. Here in the Casino block there is a tennis club which harbours the National Tennis Hall of Fame and its tennis memorabilia. Just to the rear of the Casino is the park where the Newport Jazz Festival began. Unhappily, the Jazz Festival now seems unlikely to be held at Newport any longer.

Not the least of Newport's attractions are its superb beaches. The smartest private beach club is Bailey's Beach (more formally, the Spouting Rock Association beach) on Ocean Drive. The public beaches are in the direction of Whitehall, east of the town.

Surfers prefer First Beach; Second Beach, a bit farther along, is somewhat quieter.

Newport is also one of the great sailing centres of America. The America's Cup races are held off Newport, many trans-Atlantic races start or finish here, and throughout the summer Narragansett Bay is full of boats of all sorts. And not only pleasure boats; Newport is a Naval base too. The waterfront bars and restaurants along Thames Street have a richly varied clientele of sailors off destroyers, affluent yachtsmen, and guitar-playing folksingers attracted originally to Newport in the days of the Jazz and Folk Festivals. Some of the bars are rowdier than others; some parts of Thames Street are becoming too deliberately quaint. For clam chowder or a good sandwich and beer in a place which seems just the proper mixture, we recommend the pub section of the Black Pearl.

Driving from Newport north to Boston, one should take Route 114, and about ten miles north of Newport, look for a small signpost along the road indicating a left turn for the Portsmouth Priory. A Roman Catholic boys' school, the Portsmouth Priory has a chapel and some other buildings designed by Pietro Belluschi. We think the chapel one of the most beautiful contemporary church buildings in America, and fortunately no one seems to object to quiet visitors going in to see it.

To get from there to Boston, one heads for Route 24, which takes one past Fall River on a super-highway. Fall River was the setting for America's most celebrated nineteenth-century murder case, involving Lizzie Borden, but someone speeding through it today will only notice that it is an old mill town. Many of the great textile mill buildings here and in other parts of New England are now derelict, the owners having moved operations south in search of cheaper labour.

Americans on holiday in New England go to Newport and to the other places we have mentioned, but they also go to Cape Cod and the islands of Martha's Vineyard and Nantucket, and to the Berkshires and the states of Vermont and New Hampshire and Maine.

Cape Cod has several pleasant little towns, and the more remote section of its south coast, a wild stretch of sand dunes and salt marsh, is now a protected National Seashore. But the Cape a casual visitor is most likely to see is depressingly overcrowded in the summer. This is true too of Plymouth, on the way from Boston to the Cape, where there is a reconstruction of the original Pilgrim settlement. But Plymouth has the *Mayflower II* docked there as well, and it may just be worth braving the crowds to see it. A replica of the original *Mayflower*, it was built in England and sailed over in 1957 during commemorative celebrations. It is unbelievably small; one shudders at the thought of the pilgrims' voyage.

Going to Cape Cod, one could detour to see New Bedford, the whaling town which *Moby Dick*'s Captain Ahab sailed from. The Seamen's Bethel is still there, and New Bedford also has a splendid whaling museum where one can happily spend an hour or two.

People who have gone for years to Martha's Vineyard and Nantucket complain that these islands are now overcrowded. Yet for a newcomer they still have great charm. Martha's Vineyard is closer to the mainland, larger, and more populous. It has several centres: Edgartown for the smart sailing crowd; Vineyard Haven, equally fashionable but quieter; Menemsha, a fishing village and artists' colony; and Oak Bluffs, disdained by most Vineyard regulars as too full of people off the day-boats, but worth seeing. Oak Bluff was once a thriving Methodist camp-meeting centre, and the camp-meeting ground is a delight with its hundreds of little cottages elaborately trimmed with fancy Victorian fretwork. At Gay Head on the Vineyard there still remain a few of the original Indians, whose forefathers often sailed with the newer settlers on whaling boats.

The island of Nantucket, like Martha's Vineyard, can be reached by boat from Wood's Hole on the Cape, or by plane from New York or Boston on days when the fog holds off. Like the Vineyard, Nantucket has fine sailing and swimming, but its particular charm is that it was once the most important whaling centre of them all. Nantucket ships, in fact, went everywhere, and not only after whales: the tea at the Boston Tea Party was thrown off a Nantucket boat, and the first ship to appear in English waters flying the new American colours after the Revolution was from there.

Today the whaling captains' houses with their silver door-knockers and the golden eagles over the fanlights are still ranged along the cobblestoned Main Street, and the memory of whale is everywhere. Two or three people still do and sell scrimshaw work, that intricate decorative carving on whalebone which whalers used to do to while away the long months at sea. Nantucket has capitalized on its past with more than usual grace. Almost everyone on the island in the summer either owns or hires a bicycle, to ride to the beach, or out across the moors to the wild south coast, or to Siasconset, a village on the east coast with tiny old fishermen's houses called 'warted cottages'. It takes time to get to Nantucket, but there are few pleasanter spots for a New England holiday.

The Berkshires, those sparsely settled wooded hills of western Massachusetts, have a nostalgic nineteenth-century air about them. The views are lovely; particularly in the autumn when the leaves have just turned, there are few drives in America more exhilarating than the Berkshire Trail, Route 9 from Northampton to Pittsfield, or the old Mohawk Trail, Route 2 from Williamstown to Greenfield and on towards Boston. The only trouble is that thousands of people are now thoroughly aware of this, and cars can sometimes be bumper-to-bumper in October.

Tanglewood, the most famous summer music festival in the United States, is in the Berkshires near Lenox. The Boston Symphony is its cornerstone, but there is also chamber music and opera; the season extends through most of July and August. You need not book seats if you are willing to sit on the grass, as hundreds of people do; it takes place out of doors. Accommodation, however, can present a more serious problem at the height of the season.

Nearby Lenox is eclectic: the Lenox Art Center has jazz concerts and folk-singing and *avant-garde* theatre and art exhibitions and showings of classic films throughout July and August. And at Lee there is the Jacob's Pillow Dance Festival which includes both classic ballet and modern dance.

In this same part of Massachusetts is Amherst, a college town where Emily Dickinson, that remarkable nineteenth-century poet, spent her secluded life, and where Robert Frost, equally remarkable in twentieth-century American poetry, lived for many years. Smith College, at nearby Northampton, has an excellent art gallery. (And at Williamstown, another college town in the north-west corner of the state, there is still another excellent art gallery, the Clark Art Institute.)

North-west of Amherst is the town of Deerfield, and on

its outskirts there is another historic open-air museum, Historic Deerfield. Historic Deerfield stretches along a single street: almost all of its houses have been there since the eighteenth century, but craft shops and an inn are now intermingled with the rest to simulate the Deerfield which literally rose from the ashes after a disastrous Indian raid in 1704. Deerfield is charming, its houses scrupulously restored and furnished. Our only regret is that one must see all the interiors on guided tours. (Our ideal colonial house is the Hunter House at Newport, where one can wander at will.)

There is also a restored Shaker colony in the Berkshires, Hancock Shaker Village, on Route 20 a few miles west of Pittsfield. It is worth the trip simply to see the ingenious round barn, but in addition one can sense here better than at any other Shaker centre the peculiar charm of the Shaker world.

North and north-east of the Berkshires lie Vermont and New Hampshire: skiing country, because they are mountainous, but equally popular in summer, and delightful and less crowded in the autumn. In New Hampshire, the attraction is the White Mountains, in Vermont the Green Mountains. Both areas have any number of large and small hotels and resorts. The White Mountains are particularly good for hiking; at intervals along the trails there are excellent hostels maintained by the Appalachian Mountain Club. At the centre of the region is Mount Washington, only 6,000 feet high but one of the most treacherous climbing mountains in the world; the weather station there once recorded winds at 231 miles an hour.

Our own preference is for Vermont, in part because it allows no billboards along its roads. Vermont is full of picturesque little villages and towns, and the more one can take back roads, the more one will be enchanted with Vermont. One pleasant town to stop at for the night is Manchester, and another is Woodstock. But we would urge that no one leave Vermont without going to Shelburne, near Burlington in the northern part of the State, and thus not far from Montreal in Canada. Shelburne contains our very favourite open-air museum, and usually one of the least crowded. While it roughly assumes the form of a village, it is really much more than a re-creation of old village life. It has some fine eighteenth- and early-nineteenth-century houses, but it also has an old Lake Champlain side-wheeler, and magnificent collec-

tions of all kinds of American folk art, from gaily painted hat-
boxes to patchwork quilts.

'Down east' from Boston is Maine, and any sailor who has had to
beat his way back to Boston after skimming up the Maine coast
can tell you why what looks 'up' should be called 'down'; the
prevailing winds blow relentlessly towards Nova Scotia. But any
sailor will also tell you that there is no lovelier coast in the United
States than the pine-fringed, rock-bound coast of Maine with its
profusion of bays and inlets and islands.

Inland Maine, rugged, heavily wooded, dotted with lakes, is
fine fishing and shooting country, very like parts of Canada. Indeed
parts of inland Maine seem very like the rural areas of French-
speaking Canada, with French more nearly the native tongue than
English. We regret we haven't space to describe inland Maine;
the section west of the Maine Turnpike between Portland and
Waterville has many ardent summer devotees.

Coastal Maine, like Vermont and New Hampshire, is mostly
pure 'Yankee'. One still finds here the archtypical monosyllabic
New Englander. But in the summer one also finds 'the summer
complaint', the annual influx of Americans from more harried
parts of America, seeking in the Maine woods and on Maine
waters the tranquility denied them the rest of the year. Many of
Maine's summer people retreat to private islands whose joys the
casual visitor can never hope to share. But if one penetrates
Maine far enough, one can sample at least some of its special
delights.

On the whole, the farther one goes along the coast of Maine,
the nicer it gets. We are thus inclined to recommend not stopping
short of Portland, but instead simply taking the Maine Turnpike
and by-passing the coastal region nearest Boston. Yet we must
admit that there is something to be said for the region around
Kennebunkport. For one thing, Route 35 from Kennebunk to
Kennebunkport is lined with wonderful houses, mostly in the
nineteenth-century style now called 'carpenters Gothic', which
makes them resemble fantastically decorated wedding cakes.
Many of them also have barns or carriage houses attached to the
main house by an enclosed walk-way, a bit of Yankee ingenuity
which makes brilliant sense for the American winter but which
seems not to have been taken up anywhere else but New England.

Portland is Maine's chief seaport. The Victoria Mansion there is another wonderful example of nineteenth-century decorative extravagance. And from Portland one can also do boat tours to the islands of Casco Bay, a delightful expedition on a nice summer's day and one that makes very clear the charm of Maine.

From Portland, we recommend Interstate 95 on to Brunswick, where Bowdoin College, founded in 1794, is a handsome example of that peculiarly American institution, the small but excellent private 'liberal arts college', a sort of mini-university. After Brunswick, one should continue on along the coast on Route 1. At Wiscasset, the Nickels-Sortwell House is a particularly good Federal-period house. And anyone with time for an all-day expedition to one of the choicest Maine islands should leave Route 1 after Wiscasset to go to Boothbay Harbor. Boothbay Harbor is a flourishing summer resort, with expensive shops and a summer theatre and rather too many tourists for our Maine tastes. But it is also an embarkation point for day-trips to Monhegan Island, and Monhegan we do strongly recommend. It stands nine miles off the coast, has the highest cliffs in New England, and a small, hardy resident population of lobstermen. Many artists summer on Monhegan, for reasons obvious once one has seen it, but its isolation seems sure to keep it from ever becoming over-crowded. Go if you can.

Route 1 continues on along the coast from Wiscasset. It by-passes Damariscotta, but one might like none the less to go into that attractive little fishing port, for a meal or some browsing in antique shops. Antique shops in Maine are good sources for nineteenth-century American folk art. But present-day Maine has also attracted many good contemporary artists and craftsmen, and the best shop we know for a representative sampling of Maine crafts is off the main road about twenty miles beyond Damariscotta, in the village of South Thomaston. It's called the Old Spalding House shop, and it's worth the effort necessary to find South Thomaston.

Rockland and Camden, on along the coast, are both popular summer sailing centres. At Searsport, the Penobscot Nautical Museum warrants a stop. And then at Ellsworth one can turn off for Bar Habor and the Acadia National Park, which is centred around Mount Desert. This is a fine region to explore; walking along the trails on Mount Desert one has splendid views, and below Mount Desert there is the only proper fjord on the East Coast, with Northeast Harbor (a very smart summer place) at its head.

From this point on, the coast of Maine becomes steadily more rugged and stark: fewer trees, more rocky open moor. For us, it has tremendous character; the closer one gets to the Canadian border, the more we like it. But not everyone shares our view, and so we will simply conclude by saying that at Columbia Falls there is a particularly lovely Federal-period house, the Ruggles House. Perhaps the fact that it stands here, in this poor and windswept country so unlike the lushness of southern New England, makes it seem even more special.

SPECIAL KNOWLEDGE

Except in its cities, New England seldom gets unbearably hot in the **summer**. Indeed Americans go to its mountains and its seacoast to escape the heat, and those who go to Maine sometimes find themselves longing for a really hot day. (One can sometimes spend an entire week along the Maine coast in thick fog.) **Autumn** is the loveliest New England season; **spring** there is all too brief, and **winter** in New England means steady cold and considerable snow.

We have found **food and lodging** in New England to be generally moderate in cost. Most of the picturesque old inns and summer hotels do charge more than middling motels, but you should try at least one nonetheless, and then economize if you must the next night. A guide which lists a choice selection of inns, especially in New England, is *Country Inns and Back Roads*, available for $2.95 from the Berkshire Traveller Press in Stockbridge, Massachusetts. We ourselves can also recommend the Island Inn on Monhegan Island in Maine, and, for the Berkshires, the Red Lion Inn at Stockbridge.

New England is famous for its **seafood**, especially lobsters and clams. If possible, have the lobsters boiled and the clams steamed. The simpler their preparation, the more delicious they are; New England's cooks aren't bad, but New England isn't France.

Anyone in Boston in the winter should check to see what the Theater Company of Boston is currently staging, and whether Sarah Caldwell's Opera Company of Boston has a production on. The latter is the most innovative and interesting opera company in the United States.

On the whole, it would be difficult to see the best of New England without a car. Surely, however, one could go car-less to the island of Nantucket and still enjoy it. At Newport, which one can get to by bus from New York City or Boston, one could manage almost everything but the beaches on foot, and it would be simple enough to take a taxi to the beach. And, finally, one can fly by small plane from Boston to Rockland, Maine, and take a taxi from Rockland to Port Clyde for the boat to Monhegan. Monhegan, only a mile and a half long, has no cars and no need of them.

For an energetic New England holiday, one might get in touch with the Appalachian Mountain Club and try a long hike through the White Mountains of New Hampshire. The Club offers week-long guided treks as well as maps and guides and the use of its hostels for independent hiking. Or you can sail for a week on a windjammer (a large schooner). A choice of **windjammer cruises**, costing about $150 a week all-in, go out of Camden and Rockland in Maine; for about $190 a week one can sail out of Vineyard Haven (Martha's Vineyard) or Mystic, Connecticut. The New England Council (see listings) can supply details. These cruises drop anchor each night at a different harbour, which in Maine is likely to be far more tranquil and secluded than the more popular harbours between Vineyard Haven and Mystic.

The best brief book about the American Revolution is Edward S. Morgan's *The Birth of the Republic*. It is a paperback, and one ought to be able to get it at any university bookshop, in New Haven, for example, or Cambridge. Or, to observe the Revolution through the eyes of its participants, buy the paperback *The American Revolution 1763–1783*, a fascinating collection of documents and interchanges edited by Richard B. Morris.

Tourist Information for all parts of New England
THE NEW ENGLAND COUNCIL, 1032 Statler Building, Boston; also New England Vacation Center at Rockefeller Center, New York City, where tourist information and useful brochures are available.

Amherst, Massachusetts
EMILY DICKINSON HOUSE. Tours, with prior reservations, from the secretary of Amherst College, telephone (413) 542–2321. Tuesday 3–5.

Appalachian Mountain Club
5 Joy Street, Boston, for information on hiking and hostels, especially in the White Mountains of New Hampshire.

Boston, Massachusetts
CONVENTION AND VISITORS BUREAU, 125 High Street, Boston.

AQUARIUM, Central Wharf on Atlantic Avenue. Monday to Friday 9–5, Saturday and Sunday 10–6. Closed 1 January, Thanksgiving and 25 December.

ISABELLA STEWART GARDNER MUSEUM, 280 The Fenway. 1 July to 31 August, Tuesday to Saturday 1–5.30; 1 September to 30 June, Tuesday 1–9.30, Wednesday to Sunday 1–5.30. Closed holidays. Free.

KING'S CHAPEL, Tremont and School Streets. Daily 10–4.

MUSEUM OF FINE ARTS, Huntington Avenue and The Fenway. Tuesday 10–9, free after 5, Wednesday to Sunday 10–5. Closed holidays.

OLD NORTH CHURCH, 198 Salem Street. Daily 9–4.

OLD SOUTH MEETING HOUSE, Washington and Milk Streets. 1 June to 30 September, Monday to Friday 9–5, Saturday 9–4. Rest of the year Monday to Saturday 9–4. Closed 1 January, Thanksgiving and 25 December.

OLD STATE HOUSE, Washington and State Streets. Monday to Saturday 9–4. Closed 1 January, Thanksgiving and 25 December. Free.

PARK STREET CHURCH, Park and Tremont Streets. Monday to Friday 9–4.30, Saturday 9–12.

PAUL REVERE HOUSE, 19–21 North Square. Monday to Saturday 9–3.45. Closed holidays.

SCIENCE MUSEUM, at Science Park. Monday to Saturday 10–5, Sunday 11–5, Friday evening until 10. Closed holidays.

SOCIETY FOR THE PRESERVATION OF NEW ENGLAND ANTIQUITIES, Harrison-Gray Otis House, 141 Cambridge Street, Boston. Monday to Friday 10–4. Closed holidays.

TRINITY CHURCH, Copley Square. Daily 8–5.

U.S.S. CONSTITUTION, in the U.S. Naval Shipyard across the Charles River at Wapping and Chelsea Streets, Charlestown. Daily 9.30–4. Free.

Brunswick, Maine

BOWDOIN COLLEGE. Guided tours Monday to Friday 9.15–4, Saturday and Sunday 9–12. Free.

Cambridge Massachusetts

HARVARD UNIVERSITY. Harvard Visitors Information Center, 1350 Massachusetts Avenue. During summer free tours leave the Information Center Monday to Saturday 4 times daily, Sundays and Labor Day twice daily.

FOGG ART MUSEUM, Quincy Street and Broadway. Monday to Saturday 9–5, Sunday, 2–5. Closed weekends in summer and holidays.

LONGFELLOW HOUSE, 105 Brattle Street. 1 May to 31 October, Monday to Friday 10–5, Saturday 12–5, Sunday 1–5; 1 November to 30 April, Monday to Friday 10–4, Saturday and Sunday 2–4.

MASSACHUSETTS INSTITUTE OF TECHNOLOGY, Massachusetts Avenue and Memorial Drive. Free guided tours leave the Admissions Office at 77 Massachusets Avenue, Monday to Friday at 10 and 2.

Columbia Falls, Maine

RUGGLES HOUSE, just off U.S. Route 1. 1 June to 15 October, Monday to Saturday 8.30–4.30, Sunday and holidays 10–4.

Concord, Massachusetts

ORCHARD HOUSE, east on Lexington Road. Early April to 31 October, Monday to Saturday 10–5, Sunday 2–6.

RALPH WALDO EMERSON HOUSE, Cambridge Turnpike and State Route 2A. 19 April to 30 November, Tuesday to Saturday and holidays 10–11.30 and 1.30–5.30, Sunday 2.30–5.30.

Deerfield, Massachusetts

HISTORIC DEERFIELD. 30 April to mid-November, Monday to Saturday 10–4, Sunday 1.30–4; 1 May to mid-November, Monday to Saturday 9.30–4.30, Sunday 1.30–4.30. Closed Thanksgiving and for 2 weeks over Christmas.

Gloucester, Massachusetts

BEAUPORT, Eastern Point Boulevard. Guided tours only. 1 June to 30 September, Monday to Friday at 2.30, 3.30 and 4.30. Closed holidays.

Guilford, Connecticut

WHITFIELD HOUSE, Whitfield Street. 1 April to 31 October, Wednesday to Sunday 11–5; 1 November to 31 March, Wednesday to Sunday 11–4.

Hancock, Massachusetts

HANCOCK SHAKER VILLAGE, 5 miles west of Pittsfield on U.S. Route 20. 1 June to 15 October, daily 9.30–5.

Harvard, Massachusetts

FRUITLANDS MUSEUMS, Prospect Hill Road, 2 miles west off State Route 110. 30 May to 30 September, Tuesday to Sunday 1–5, also Monday when a holiday.

Ipswich, Massachusetts

JOHN WHIPPLE HOUSE, South Village Green, State Route 1A. 15 April to 31 October, Tuesday to Saturday 10–5, Sunday 1–5.

Lenox, Massachusetts

TANGLEWOOD MUSIC FESTIVAL. For schedule, tickets and lists of accommodation, Festival Ticket Office, Tanglewood, Lenox, Massachusetts.

Lexington, Massachusetts

BUCKMAN TAVERN, on the Green. 19 April to 31 October, Monday to Saturday 10–5, Sundays 1–5. Closed holidays.

HANCOCK-CLARKE HOUSE, 35 Hancock Street. 19 April to 31 October, Monday to Saturday 10–5, Sunday 1–5. Closed holidays.

Marblehead, Massachusetts

JEREMIAH LEE HOUSE, 161 Washington Street. Mid-May to 12 October, Monday to Saturday 9.30–4.

Monhegan Island, Maine

Boats for Monhegan go from Boothbay Harbor and Port Clyde. The Boothbay Harbor boat is strictly a passenger excursion boat running from July to Labor Day, crossing in the morning and allowing 3 hours on the island before returning to the mainland. The Port Clyde boat is the morning mail boat, but during the high season it also makes an afternoon trip over and back. The trip takes about 1 hour from Port Clyde and a bit longer from Boothbay; reservations are unnecessary.

Mystic, Connecticut

MYSTIC SEAPORT, on State Route 27. Daily 9–5. Closed 1 January and 25 December.

Nantucket, Massachusetts

NANTUCKET INFORMATION SERVICE, 33 Federal Street. One can reach Nantucket by taking a bus to Woods Hole on Cape Cod, and then a ferry; or one can fly direct.

New Bedford, Massachusetts

THE SEAMEN'S BETHEL, 15 Johnny Cake Hill. I June to 31 December, daily 10–12 and 2–5; I January to 31 May, daily 10–12 and 2–4.

WHALING MUSEUM, 18 Johnny Cake Hill. I June to I October, Monday to Saturday 9–5, Sunday 1–5; 2 October to 31 May, Tuesday to Saturday 9–5, Sunday 1–5. Closed 1 January, Thanksgiving and 25 December.

New Haven, Connecticut

YALE UNIVERSITY. Guided tours start at Phelps Gateway on College Street. During the academic year, Monday to Friday at 10 and 2, Saturday at 11 and 2, Sunday at 1.30 and 3; during the holidays, Monday to Saturday at 9.15, 1.30 and 3, Sunday at 1.30 and 3. Free.

BEINECKE LIBRARY, High and Wall Streets. Monday to Friday, 8.30–4.45, Saturday 8.30–12.15 and 1.30–4.45, Sunday 2–4.45. Free.

YALE UNIVERSITY ART GALLERY, 1111 Chapel Street, between York and High Streets. Tuesday to Saturday 10–5, Sunday 2–5. Closed 1 January, Thanksgiving and 25 December.

Newport, Rhode Island

NEWPORT CHAMBER OF COMMERCE AND VISITORS BUREAU, 93 Thames Street at Washington Square. Free brochures and maps as well as the excellent *Newport: A Tour Guide* to buy.

THE BREAKERS. Along Shepard Avenue 2 streets east of Bellevue. Mid-April to 30 May, weekends and holidays 10–5; I June to 31 October daily 10–5; July and August until 10 except Sunday.

THE BREAKERS STABLE, Coggeshall Avenue between Victoria and Batemen Avenues. I July to Labor Day, daily 10–5.

THE ELMS, Bellevue Avenue. 15 April to 30 May, Saturday and Sunday 10–5; I June to 31 October, daily 10–5; July and August, Saturday until 10.

HUNTER HOUSE, 54 Washington Street. 30 May to I October daily 10–5; 2 October to 29 May by appointment; telephone 847–1000.

MARBLE HOUSE, Bellevue Avenue. Mid-April to 30 May, Saturday and Sunday 10–5; 31 May to mid-November, daily 10–5; July to mid-September, Friday till 9.

NEWPORT MUSIC FESTIVAL, 24 Bridge Street, or telephone 846–1133 or 846–1140.

OLD COLONY HOUSE, Washington Square. Sunday to Friday 9.30–4.30, Saturday 9.30–12. Free.

OLDPORT ASSOCIATION, 37 Touro Street, Washington Square (second floor). The co-ordinating office for the preservation of colonial Newport. June to October, architectural walking tours of colonial Newport are scheduled weekly.

TOURO SYNAGOGUE, 72 Touro Street. 29 June to Labor Day, Monday to Friday 10–5, Sunday 10–6; Labor Day to 25 June, Sunday 2–4. Open for services on Saturday.

TRINITY CHURCH, 141 Spring Street. 15 June to Labor Day, daily 10–5; rest of the year by appointment only.

VIKING PRINCESS, boat tours of the Bay, from the old ferry dock.

VIKING TOURS OF NEWPORT, 4 Bush Avenue. Tours of the town in shiny red coaches.

WHITEHALL, Berkeley Avenue, near Green End Avenue, Middletown. 1 July to Labor Day, daily 10–5.

Northampton, Massachusetts
SMITH COLLEGE MUSEUM OF ART, Elm Street. Monday to Saturday 9–5, Sunday 2–4; during the summer holidays, daily 2–4. Free.

Old Sturbridge Village, Massachusetts
At the junction of the Massachusetts Turnpike, U.S. Route 20 and State Route 131. 1 April to 31 October, daily 9.30–5.30; 1 December to 28 February, daily 10–4; March and November, daily 9.30–4.30. Closed 1 January and 25 December.

Plymouth, Massachusetts
MAYFLOWER II, moored at State Pier. 1 April to 16 June and 5 September to 21 October, Monday to Friday 9–5, Saturday and Sunday 9–6.30; 17 June to Labor Day 9–8.30; 22 October to 30 November 9–5.

PLIMOTH PLANTATION, 2 miles south, off State Route 3A. 1 April to 31 May and 1 November to 30 November, daily 10–4; 1 June to 16 June and 5 September to 31 October, daily 9–4; 17 June to Labor Day, daily 9–6; 1 April to 16 June and 5 September to 21 October, Saturday and Sunday till 5.

Portland, Maine
VICTORIA MANSION, Park and Danforth Streets. Mid-June to mid-October, Tuesday to Saturday 10.30–4.30.

Providence, Rhode Island
JOHN BROWN HOUSE, 52 Power Street. Tuesday to Friday 11–4, Saturday and Sunday 2–4. Closed holidays.

RHODE ISLAND SCHOOL OF DESIGN MUSEUM, 224 Benefit Street. Tuesday to Saturday 11–5, Sunday 2–5. Closed August and holidays.

Salem Massachusetts
CROWNINSHIELD-BENTLEY HOUSE, 126 Essex Street. 1 June to 15 October, Tuesday to Saturday 10–4, Sunday and holidays 10–4.30.

DERBY HOUSE, near Customs House, Derby Street. Guided tours daily 8.30–4.30. Closed 1 January, Thanksgiving and 25 December.

HOUSE OF SEVEN GABLES, 54 Turner Street. 1 July to Labour Day, daily 9.30–4.45 (including 3 houses in the grounds) and until 7.30, Gables only. Labor Day to 30 June (Gables only) 10–4.45. Closed 1 January, Thanksgiving and 25 December.

PEABODY MUSEUM, 161 Essex Street. 1 November to 28 February, Monday to Saturday 9–4, Sunday and holidays 2–5. 1 March to 31 October, Monday to Saturday 9–5, Sunday and holidays 2–5. Closed 1 January, Thanksgiving and 25 December.

PINGREE HOUSE, 128 Essex Street. Tuesday to Saturday 10–4. 1 June to 31 October, Sunday and holidays 2–4.30. Closed 4 July.

SALEM WITCH MUSEUM, 19½ Washington Square North. Summer daily 9–9.30; spring and autumn daily 9–5.

Saugus, Massachusetts

SAUGUS IRONWORKS, 224 Central Street. 1 April to 31 October, daily 9–5; 1 November to 31 March 9–4.

Searsport, Maine

PENOBSCOT NAUTICAL MUSEUM, on U.S. Route 1. 1 June to 30 September, Monday to Saturday 9–5, Sunday 1–5.

Shelburne, Vermont

SHELBURNE MUSEUM, 7 miles south of Burlington on U.S. Route 7. 15 May to 15 October, daily 9–5.

Waltham, Massachusetts

GORE PLACE, on U.S. Route 20. 15 April to 15 November, Tuesday to Saturday 10–5, Sunday 2–5.

Williamstown, Massachusetts

CLARK ART INSTITUTE, South Street. Tuesday to Sunday 10–5. Free.

Wiscasset, Maine

NICKELLS-SORTWELL HOUSE, Main and Federal Streets. 1 June to 30 September, Tuesday to Friday 11–5. Closed holidays.

5 · WASHINGTON, D.C., MARYLAND, AND VIRGINIA

The perfect entrance into Washington is by way of the Arlington Memorial Bridge from Virginia, on a night with a full moon. Crossing the bridge, you suddenly come upon the great classic white marble temple that is the Lincoln Memorial, dominating the park along the river's edge. Beyond it lies the White House and off to the right stretches the Mall, flanked by stately museums and government buildings. The entire city seems a ghostly and beautiful stage set, and some people would say that is exactly what Washington is, not a real city at all. Certainly it is not an ordinary city; it is nothing like those European capitals which are also the heart and soul of their countries.

Washington began as a compromise. New York would have liked to be the capital, or Philadelphia. But Alexander Hamilton, the first Secretary of the Treasury, needed to curry favour with the southern states to get their assent to his financial policies for the new republic. He hit upon offering the South the capital, and Virginia and Maryland agreed to donate the land. The entire seventy-square-mile-area is known as the District of Columbia.

A young French architect named Pierre l'Enfant was hired to plan the city; central Washington today is substantially as l'Enfant conceived it, with circles and broad avenues reminiscent of Napoleonic Paris. But the public buildings rose slowly; there were endless disagreements, and there was never enough money. Meanwhile, with no industry other than government, Washington remained a poor place in every sense of the word. The people who came there seldom thought of themselves as permanent residents,

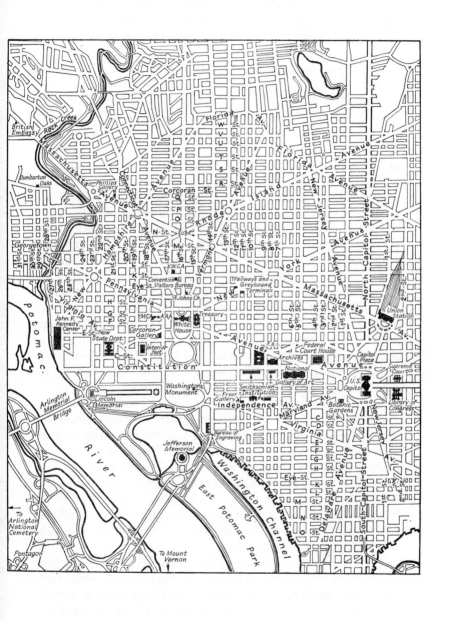

and the city suffered accordingly. Congress in those days was never in session for more than a few months of the year; instead of building fine houses, even the richer congressmen tended to leave their families at home and themselves stay in boarding houses. Only in comparatively recent years has this situation changed, and Washington still bears the scars of a century of neglect.

Moreover, Washington is an anomaly. The capital of a country founded upon the principles of self-government is governed not by its own elected representatives but by a committee of Congress. Resident Washingtonians have therefore been unable to take action against many of the problems which beset the city, and the poorer sections of Washington reflect this. Then too the more prosperous government people tend to live outside the District of Columbia, in the Maryland or Virginia suburbs, which drains wealth from the city, which creates more problems. Add the fact that almost everyone who works in Washington is working for one employer, the federal government, and you will understand why Washington is not like other cities. Yet you will, we think, like Washington. It is in many ways a very southern city, with the best sort of southern charm. And in addition, even its problems can be interesting to the visitor, since its citizenry, both black and white, seem currently to be involved in all sorts of unusual efforts to combat them. There are more different approaches to urban renewal being tried in Washington, for example, than anywhere else in America.

Because Washington was deliberately planned to look impressive, its chief public buildings are set at a considerable distance apart, with malls and wide avenues between. However, anyone can easily explore the central, governmental portion of the city through a judicious combination of walking and taking the Tourmobile, a minibus which circles from the Capitol to the White House to the Jefferson Memorial and around the Mall, and which one can use all day on one $2 ticket. Taxis are quite inexpensive in Washington too.

The visitor with only one day for sightseeing in Washington might try to see the White House, the Capitol itself where Congress sits, one of the Smithsonian Institution museums, and the Lincoln Memorial. Then in the evening it would be pleasant to finish with a leisurely stroll through Georgetown, the most inter-

5. Horse-hitching post in a street in New Orleans

6a. Plantation house, Dunleith, Natchez, Mississippi

6b. A Wisconsin farm near Green Bay

esting residential section of the District, and one which also boasts several attractive restaurants.

The White House is the appropriate place to begin any tour of Washington, since it is where the President lives. It is also the right place to start from a practical point of view, because it is only open to the public from ten to twelve in the morning, Tuesday to Saturday, and one needs to get there early to queue to get in.

The White House stands, all wings and porticoes, comfortably ensconced in a green park in the heart of the city. It was begun in 1792, burnt by the British troops in the war of 1812, and then rebuilt. It has been altered and added on to ever since. The public tour is a short one; you see only those state apartments which are used for official entertaining. Yet it is a tour well worth taking, especially since the restoration work which Mrs Kennedy began has made each room a collector's dream and an historian's delight.

Lafayette Square, facing the White House, has two fine Federal-period houses at its western edge: Blair House, where the government lodges visiting heads of state, and, on the next corner to the north, Dacatur House, now owned by the National Trust for Historic Preservation. Next to Blair House is one of Washington's newest and sprightliest museums, the Renwick. Part of the vast Smithsonian complex, of which we will say more later, the Renwick presents imaginative displays of American crafts and design in an elegant building which was erected in the early nineteenth century as Washington's first public art gallery.

St John's Church, facing the White House across Lafayette Square, is one of Washington's nicest old churches. When the President happens to be an Episcopalian, this is the President's church. The equestrian statue in the Square is of General Andrew Jackson, who first won fame as the victorious American leader in the battle of New Orleans in the War of 1812, that abortive renewal of hostilities with Great Britain which was part of the backwash of the Napoleonic Wars. Jackson, a great frontier figure, later became President. More than any other man, he was responsible for changing the pattern of American democracy from a sort of Athenian government-by-the-few to a popular government-by-the-many.

Leaving the White House, and going up Pennsylvania Avenue towards the Capitol, one passes buildings housing various government departments, all of them part of the executive branch,

E

which means under the jurisdiction of the President and one of his cabinet members or department heads. With the tri-partite balance-of-powers of the American political system, the President and the cabinet members are first of all administrators. Of course the President, as leader of his party, can also ask Congress to pass bills, to make changes in existing laws, and to appropriate money, but Congress may or may not prove agreeable. A strong President, exercising every bit of power the Constitution permits and every scrap of influence he has, can sometimes dominate Congress; a weak President may become merely the tool of Congress. Meanwhile, watching over both the legislative and the executive branches of the government is the judicial branch, the Supreme Court and the lower federal courts, there to see that neither Congress nor the President oversteps constitutional bounds. As one explores Washington, it is helpful to keep in mind this marked division of powers and roles in the government of the United States.

One of the largest government buildings on the right-hand side of Pennsylvania Avenue on the way to the Capitol is the Department of Justice. Just beyond it is the National Archives building, where the Declaration of Independence and the Constitution repose in glass cases. Beyond the National Archives building, Pennsylvania Avenue slices across Constitution Avenue, and here, back a few steps to the west along Constitution, is the National Gallery of Art. The nucleus of the collection here was amassed by the financier Andrew Mellon under the tutelage of Duveen, that flamboyant art dealer who was responsible for so many American acquisitions in the first half of this century. Following Mr Mellon's example, many other rich collectors who had also come under Duveen's influence left their pictures to the new National Gallery, and the Gallery is therefore particularly rich in works of the Italian Renaissance, including some magnificent ones. The National Gallery is one of the show-places of Washington, not to be missed.

Begun in 1793, the Capitol took seventy years to complete; meanwhile any architect in Europe or America with time on his hands would seem to have drifted to Washington to amuse himself changing the designs for the building. Recently it has again been altered, the east front pushed forward to make room for more offices. But one of the building's first authentically American details can still be seen in the north wing: the architect

Benjamin Latrobe's columns, some crowned with a design of tobacco leaves and others with capitals of Indian corn. There are guided tours of the Capitol, starting every few minutes all day long. They include a glance into the House and Senate chambers; if either of these is sitting, the tour will probably pause so that you can watch for a few moments.

You can also get passes to the gallery of the Senate by applying to the office of the Senate Sergeant-at-Arms; passes for the House gallery are available from the Doorkeeper's office on the House side of the Capitol. However, it is best to be prepared for disillusion. Only rarely does one hear the kind of challenging debate one might hope for in the parliament of so powerful a country, and there is nothing which corresponds to Question Time in the House of Commons. Indeed the Congress of the United States moves in mysterious ways and one must learn to understand it.

The Congress is divided into two parts, the House of Representatives and the Senate. The House of Representatives today has 435 members, elected every two years, and properly known as 'Congressmen'. According to the Constitution the Congressmen are apportioned according to population, one Congressman for every so many people, who may be widely scattered in a geographically vast rural district, or packed tight together in a geographically tiny city district. Nevada, for instance, has one Congressman for its 110,000 square miles; the state of Massachusetts, with an area less than one-twelfth the size of Nevada, has twelve Congressmen. There are, however, only two Senators for every state, large or small, and therefore the Senate now has an even one hundred members. When the republic was young and relatively small and there were far fewer Congressmen in the House of Representatives, a Congressman was every bit as eminent as a Senator. Today, however, almost all Congressmen secretly yearn to be Senators. Senators have to stand for election only every six years, and since there are only one hundred of them, each Senator is far better known than any Congressman can hope to be.

Yet even the Senate does not look impressive in session. The chamber itself is handsome, but there never seem to be many members there unless they are actually about to vote on a bill. Someone will be presiding, but it is more likely to be a Senator deputizing for the Vice-President than the Vice-President himself.

And someone will be speaking, but he is very likely to be speaking merely 'for the record', quite literally *The Congressional Record*, and in that event he will not mind that few of his colleagues are listening to him. He simply wants to be recorded as having supported or opposed some bill, so that in the next election campaign he can point to this support or opposition. In the United States, party discipline is not nearly so strong as it is in most democracies. This looser system seems to suit the size and complexity of America, but it means that each member of Congress must build his own individual record; he may well be elected quite irrespective of whether he is a Democrat or a Republican. (One must always except the South; still nursing the wounds of the Republican Reconstruction period after the Civil War, the Deep South still seldom elects anyone not labelled a Democrat. The result is that in the southern states both arch-conservatives and liberals belong to the Democratic party, which leads to considerable confusion in the halls of Congress.) Moreover, in America each member of Congress is considered in a very real sense to be the representative of his constituency. He must live in the area he represents in order to stand for election there, and he is regarded as a sort of delegate from, say, Iowa to the Congress of the States United. It is, after all, a federal system. As a result of this situation, meaningful debate seldom occurs on the Senate or House floor.

An increasing amount of the serious business of Congress has come to be transacted more privately, in the meeting of congressional committees. There are committees concerned with every aspect of government, from a Foreign Relations Committee to a Committee on Fisheries. The chairmanship of an important committee is a coveted office, which usually goes to that member of the majority party who has served longest on the committee. Committee hearings are usually open to the public. They may be held in the Capitol itself, or in one of the old or new Senate or House office buildings which are ranged around the Capitol. The morning newspaper, *The Washington Post*, lists 'today's Congressional hearings', giving the time and the place and indicating whether or not the meeting is open to the public. So long as it is not 'closed' or 'in executive session', you need only go to the right place, walk in and find a seat.

There is a cafeteria in the Capitol open to the public. There is also a little underground train which runs between the Capitol and the Senate Office Building; anyone may take it but it is particularly worth sampling when Congress is in session and the Senators and their aides are hurrying back and forth.

Opposite to the east entrance of the Capitol is the Library of Congress, with the Folger Library directly behind it. The Folger Library is a scholars' library, housing America's finest Shakespearean collection, other rare sixteenth- and seventeenth-century material, and a reconstruction of an Elizabethan theatre. The Library of Congress is a reference library for members of Congress; it is also the chief depository in the United States for books and printed matter, comparable in that respect to the British Museum, and it has many rare books and manuscripts of historical importance. One thing the casual visitor may find particularly interesting is the Library of Congress folk music collection, probably the most comprehensive in the world. The Library itself has sponsored and supervised countless recordings of folk music, not only American but also Asian, European and African. One can listen to the records there, and some of the most popular, particularly American folk ballads, have now been recorded in quantity and are for sale at the Library.

To the north, across East Capitol Street from the Library of Congress, is the Supreme Court Building. Visitors are admitted to the public gallery when the Court is sitting to hear arguments, which means two weeks of every month from October to April, Monday to Thursday from 10 to 2.30. It is not, however, a pyrotechnical display, but lawyer's law, with low-key intricate pleading.

On A Street about three blocks east of the Supreme Court building is another of Washington's new museums, and a wonderful one. It is the Museum of African Art, a superb collection in a handsome house which once belonged to the remarkable nineteenth-century black abolitionist orator and publisher, Frederick Douglass.

Stretching from the Capitol west to the Washington Monument is the Mall, with the buildings of the Smithsonian Institution on either side. Constitution Avenue borders the north side of the Mall, Independence Avenue the south. If one goes west along the Mall, the first Smithsonian building on the right is the National Gallery. When people talk of the Smithsonian, they are usually thinking of the science museums and the historical collections, but the National Gallery is also administered by the Smithsonian

Institution board of directors, and so is the zoo in Rock Creek Park.

After the National Gallery comes the Museum of Natural History and beyond it the Museum of History and Technology. On the opposite side of the Mall, along Independence Avenue, is the new Hirshhorn Museum, and then the Arts and Industries Building, the Air and Space Building, and the Freer Gallery. Dominating the whole array is the oldest Smithsonian building, a glorious turreted, crenellated edifice which now serves as headquarters.

All of this splendid display is the result of a gift from an Englishman who had never seen the United States. In 1829, one James Smithson died and left his entire fortune, £120,000, for the founding at Washington of 'an establishment for the increase and diffusion of knowledge among men'. He was the natural son of the first Duke of Northumberland and Elizabeth Hungerford Keate Macie, whom Smithson described as 'niece to the proud Duke of Somerset'. He himself never married. Educated at Pembroke College, Oxford, he became a considerable amateur chemist, and his bequest was clearly designed both to lend honour to his clouded name and to aid science. Moreover, although Smithson had never been to the United States, he was a man of marked republican sympathies.

The Smithsonian has assembled all the facts connected with its founding, and it makes for diverting reading. First there was a Dickensian three-year struggle in Chancery Court actually to get the money; we heave a great sigh of relief as Mr Richard Rush, the American emissary, finally boards the packet-boat at the London docks with his eleven cases of gold sovereigns. And then there was a nation-wide debate on exactly how the money should be used: for a university, or a library, or an art gallery, or an observatory, for agricultural experimentation or a zoological collection, to establish lectures on moral philosophy or to subsidize geographical exploration. In the end almost everyone won except those who wanted a university; the Smithsonian is a little of everything. But there is no doubt that it has accomplished precisely what James Smithson hoped: it has increased and diffused knowledge among men.

One can hardly expect to see all the Smithsonian museums in the course of a single visit to the city, and every visitor will have his own particular preferences. But we have found the Museums of Natural History and of History and Technology especially lively and interesting. One should not miss the mineralogy section in the former nor the rooms devoted to Americana in the latter. And since one can get very hungry absorbing all the knowledge the Smithsonian diffuses, it is worth noting that the Museum of History and Technology has an excellent cafeteria.

The elegant new Hirshhorn Museum and Sculpture Garden should be seen too. Its announced aim was to provide Washington with a significant collection of twentieth-century American painting, but it includes some notable contemporary European works as well, and its sculpture collection is international.

Between the Hirshhorn and the Capitol is the U.S. Botanic Garden, really a giant conservatory. We are partial to conservatories, and this one encompasses a particularly fine collection of tropical, sub-tropical, and desert plants.

At the western end of the Mall is the Washington Monument; visitors can have a splendid panorama of central Washington from the top of its slim shaft. The ornamental lake to the south-west of the Monument is ringed by Japanese cherry trees, a lovely mass of pink bloom in the spring. The Jefferson Memorial stands at the far side of this Tidal Basin. It is a particularly apt monument because it so perfectly captures Thomas Jefferson's own architectural style.

The Bureau of Engraving and Printing, where you can watch them make money and print postage stamps, is in the large building immediately to the south-east of the Washington Monument.

Across 17th Street from the Washington Monument is another park with a reflecting pool which forms the foreground for the Lincoln Memorial. It seems fitting that Lincoln's memorial should so dominate Washington, for the city might today be only an unimportant town on the border between two separate countries had it not been for Abraham Lincoln. Once the first flush of victory in the Revolution was over, once the leaders of the Revolutionary period were gone, the states tended to drift apart. Secession was talked of more than once, and not only by southerners. When the Civil War finally came, in the 1860s, it was more than a struggle over slavery and more than a contest between federal power and states' rights. It was, as Lincoln himself said, a battle to the death over the survival of the American system. And without him, the battle might well have been lost.

We trust that Lincoln, with his mordant wit, would not mind our moving on to cite him in quite another way. Some years ago, on being told about Lincoln's having been fatally shot during a performance at Ford's Theater, a member of the Washington diplomatic corps observed that Lincoln should have known better than to expect anything good from the theatre in Washington. And indeed until quite recently Washington exhibited all the symptoms of severe cultural malnutrition. Her museums enshrined the past well enough, but the present was sadly neglected: only second-rate music, theatre, dance, living art.

Today this is all changed, and the Kennedy Center for the Performing Arts is the most monumental but by no means the only symbol of the change. The new museums of which we have spoken are part of the picture. So is the refurbishing of Ford's Theater itself, which turns out to be a fine place to see a play after all. So is the Arena Theater, with its superlative repertory company and innovative productions. But it is undeniably the Kennedy Center which marks the change most dramatically, and if you can't get tickets to a performance in one of its mangificent theatres, at least go to see the building itself. Most evenings, its restaurants are crowded with theatregoers, but except on matinée days it's a good place to have lunch. (There's a restaurant to suit every purse.) The scale of the building may be too Babylonian; it seems rather to dwarf the spirit. But it is nonetheless the great new sight of Washington.

Washington is full of things to see. An impressive example of imaginative urban renewal is the Southwest district with its striking new commercial centre, L'Enfant Plaza. And we have mentioned only some of the art galleries; the Smithsonian complex also includes the Freer, with its unusual combination of Oriental art and late-nineteenth-century American painting, and, away from the others, in 'downtown' Washington, the Fine Arts and Portrait Galleries. The Fine Arts Gallery is a cheerful place, with children's art classes in amongst a fine sampling of two centuries of American art. Off in the embassy section of the city is the Phillips Collection, a superb small gallery which exhibits Impressionist, Post-impressionist, and more modern paintings perceptively collected over a lifetime by Mr and Mrs Duncan Phillips. And at Dumbarton Oaks, in Georgetown, in an attractive Federal-period house set in lovely grounds, you can see the Bliss collection of Byzantine treasures and pre-Columbian art.

Dumbarton Oaks, and the rustic and peaceful Dumbarton Oaks Park just beyond, are only two of the attractions in Georgetown,

Washington's most alluring residential district. Georgetown was already a small but pleasant little town at the end of the eighteenth-century, when the site for the capital was picked. By the end of the nineteenth century, however, its small neat Georgian houses had begun to be abandoned in favour of more lavish residences across the Potomac in the newer parts of the city. Then, happily, George-town was rediscovered in the period between the two World Wars, and today one must pay a small fortune for a Georgetown address.

No one can agree on any one 'best street' to see in Georgetown; you must simply wander. One of the most elegant eighteenth century houses is Tudor Place, at Q Street and 31st Street, very near Dumbarton Oaks. Wisconsin Avenue is Georgetown's main street, and most of the shops and restaurants are along there or on M Steet. The 3300 block of N Street is known as Cox's Row, and is reputed to be the finest row of Federal-period houses in America.

One special Georgetown attraction is a mule-drawn canal barge which does trips on the old Chesapeake and Ohio canal, on Saturdays and Sundays in the summer, starting from a dock at the foot of 30th Street. The trips take four hours, going through several locks, with a commentary by a Park Service historian en route.

In the spring, many of the houses and gardens in Georgetown are open for the benefit of various charities; other tours for charity include several of the Washington embassies. Anyone who is in Washington in the spring should make inquiries. And anyone who can, certainly ought to be in Washington in the spring. The summers are oppressively hot, the winters wet and cold, but Washington in the springtime is absolutely beautiful. People come from all over the country to see the cherry trees in blossom all around the Tidal Basin, but one should also see the masses of azaleas and spring flowers in Georgetown and in the Cleveland Heights section beyond it, where the impressive Washington Cathedral stands in lovely grounds.

The most popular trip out of the city is that to Mount Vernon, George Washington's house in Virginia. Built high on a bluff overlooking the Potomac River, it is a fine example of a colonial manor house, with the pillared front one associates with southern American plantation houses. For of course it was a plantation, not simply a house; this was once an enormous and profitable estate, and many of the outbuildings can still be seen, together with a handsome formal garden.

The Virginia Revolutionary leaders were by and large aristocrats. They imported their furniture, their wines, and their books from Europe, and frequently sent their sons back to England to be educated. Next to New England, Virginia was the most British in population of all the colonies, and Virginia had not even a religious difference to separate her from the mother country; the Church of England was the established and accepted church in Virginia. One can trace the American Revolution in New England back to the staunchly independent Puritan tradition, but in Virginia it is easier to trace it to Locke and Hume and Montesquieu, and all the other authors a well-read English gentleman might have been expected to know. George Washington was part of this aristocratic Virginia tradition, and Mount Vernon illustrates this.

Mount Vernon is open all the year round. In the summer it is possible to get there by boat; the trip takes about an hour each way. There are also several coach tours which go to Mount Vernon. Driving to Mount Vernon by car, one can easily include more of eighteenth-century Virginia. Woodlawn plantation, for instance, is only three or four miles away; originally part of the Mount Vernon estate, it belonged to Martha Washington's daughter and her husband. It is a handsome place too: red brick, and not painted over, which makes it more truly typical of Virginia colonial building than Mount Vernon. And then there is the Pohick Church, a charming colonial church with box pews. And Gunston Hall, another plantation house, this one designed by William Buckland, who was one of the most gifted colonial craftsmen-architects.

To reach any of these plantations, one goes through or near Alexandria, an old town now largely a dormitory for Washington. Both the Presbyterian Meeting House and Christ Church in Alexandria are interesting colonial churches, and anyone with the time to wander about in Alexandria will also see a great many handsome old houses, particularly in the area squared by the Potomac River and Queen, Washington, and Duke Streets.

Robert E. Lee's house, which he left, never to return, at the start of the Civil War, is within the grounds of the Arlington National Cemetery, only a city bus ride from the centre of Washington. Formally known as the Custis-Lee House, it is handsomely restored and open to the public.

Mount Vernon is the traditional expedition from Washington, but there are three other nearby places which anyone with access to a car ought to consider too. If you are interested in town planning, you will want to see Columbia, about twenty-five miles north-east of Washington, in Maryland. It is America's most ambitious 'new town', and visitors are very welcome; there is a central Exhibit Center at which one is meant to stop first. If you'd like to take a picnic and do some walking in particularly nice country, rich in birds and wild-flowers, you should go to Great Falls, on the Potomac River about twelve miles north-west of Washington. You can wander along past the old Chesapeake and Ohio canal locks here, and learn about the history of the canal in a little museum housed in the old Great Falls Tavern. (Ambitious hikers and bicyclers do the entire 184 miles of towpath along the canal; there are simple campgrounds along the way.) Or you could go ten miles west of Washington to Wolf Trap Farm Park for the Performing Arts; the unlikely name hides a summer music-and-ballet-and-opera festival. There are matinée and evening performances from mid-June to mid-September, and one can take a picnic and eat on the grass, or make reservations for the buffet supper.

For more information about any of these expeditions, or about anything else in the Washington area, we suggest you go to IVIS, the International Visitors Service Council, near the White House. Its office is staffed with cheerful, knowledgeable, multi-lingual volunteers who can provide answers to every possible sort of tourist question. They can also arrange for 'home hospitality', meeting an American family. And if you write ahead, IVIS will send a hotels list, noting which ones give special consideration to international visitors.

In the nineteenth century, when Washington was still raw and unfinished, the city of Baltimore, forty miles to the north-east in Maryland, was thought to be infinitely more attractive, combining southern gentility with an air of almost European culture. As the years passed, however, traffic and industry choked Baltimore, and today most travellers bound for Washington speed past it without stopping. Yet Baltimore still has its attractions. Both the Walters Art Gallery and the Baltimore Museum of Art have interesting collections; the latter is exceptionally strong in French painting of the nineteenth and twentieth centuries. For railway buffs, there is the B & O Transportation Museum, which is centred around the old Mount Clare Station, America's first railroad station. The old repair works and the roundhouse are still there, together with a unique assemblage of nineteenth-century rolling stock. Several major racing events take place at the Pimlico Racetrack during its spring and autumn meetings. Baltimore's football and baseball teams draw great crowds. And, to top it all, one can eat royally in Baltimore; the local crab, in particular, is irresistible.

Nearby Annapolis is interesting too, and easier to visit since it is comparatively small. It has been the capital of Maryland since 1694, and it has many handsome Georgian buildings. The most famous is the Hammond-Harwood House, the masterpiece of the colonial architect and craftsman, William Buckland. It and the United States Naval Academy, also at Annapolis, can be seen independently, or they can be included in guided walking tours conducted by Historic Annapolis, Inc., the organization largely responsible for preserving the best of old Annapolis.

Maryland began as a proprietary colony, granted in 1634 to Cecil Calvert, the second Lord Baltimore, as a place of refuge for English Catholics. The Calverts and a few other leading families continued to dominate Maryland well into the nineteenth century, and one still seems to sense this feudal tradition in the quiet hamlets of southern Maryland and in that portion of the state which lies across Chesapeake Bay and is known as the Eastern Shore. Fishing is a major source of income here, and there are many little fishing villages and also some small state parks. We have always wanted to see both Smith and Tangier, two small isolated islands in Chesapeake Bay. Still inhabited by descendants of the original English, Scotch–Irish and Cornish settlers, they can be reached only by ferry from Crisfield on the Eastern Shore.

There are seaside resorts along the Atlantic coast of Delaware and Maryland, but we find much more appealing the comparatively undeveloped Assateague Island National Seashore and the Chincoteague National Wildlife Refuge which adjoins it. Assateague Island is part of a chain of sandy barrier reefs which continues on south along the Atlantic coast to Point Lookout in North Carolina; we will be saying more about this in the next chapter. There is excellent surf fishing there, and one can swim off wonderful sand beaches; and in the marshy sections one can see sika deer and the wild Chincoteague ponies and snow geese and sea birds of many kinds.

About fifty miles north-west of Washington is Harper's Ferry. Here in 1859 the abolitionist John Brown led a raid attempting to free a group of slaves, and Robert E. Lee, then a colonel in the army of the United States, was the officer sent to capture Brown. John Brown's subsequent trial and hanging heightened the tensions which led to the outbreak of the Civil War a year and a half later. And Harper's Ferry is only the first of the countless Civil War landmarks in Virginia; no other state saw so much of the fighting. Bull Run, for example, is along the main road from Washington to the west; the sign pointing to Manassas National Battlefield Park suddenly brings alive that war so endlessly refought in novels and films. Manassas was the scene of two of the grimmest battles; this is where the little river called Bull Run ran red with blood for days. Chancellorsville and Spottsylvania and Wilderness, three more major battle sites, are close together west of the main Washington-to-Richmond road. And Appomattox Court House, where Lee's surrender to Grant ended it all, is in south-western Virginia, near Lynchburg.

Military historians delight in the Civil War. The issues were dramatic, the odds at the beginning seemingly even, the strategy and counter-strategy as engrossing as a chess game. Thus it is not only Americans who tour Virginia to see the battlefields. But Virginia was important long before the Civil War, and for her earlier history one goes to Williamsburg, and to Monticello at Charlottesville.

One can drive to Williamsburg on Interstate 95 as far as Richmond, which is the usual way, or take U.S. 17 beyond Fredericksburg, which leads in a leisurely fashion through a much less frequented part of the state, the old flat plantation country along the Rappahannock. One could even swing across and down through the Eastern Shore, stopping at Assateague and then taking the remarkable Chesapeake Bay Bridge and Tunnel across to Norfolk; the tolls on this route would be sizeable, however.

Buses and tours go to Williamsburg too, from Washington by way of Richmond, a handsome town with many fine colonial and Federal-period houses and a state capitol designed by Thomas

Jefferson. Its air of settled dignity notwithstanding, Richmond has had a fiery past. It was here, at a meeting in St John's Church, that Patrick Henry made the most inflammatory speech heard in the colonies before the Revolution, finishing with the words 'Give me liberty or give me death!' And during the Civil War, Richmond was the capital of the Confederacy.

Williamsburg, the most famous American effort to recapture the past, and the oldest and largest and still the best, is one of those places which one should not try to see in a hurry. To those who glance cursorily about for an hour or two, it may well seem disappointing. Admittedly it is in part a reconstruction, and there are people in costume. But somehow after a few hours it is as if you and they were together engaged in a cheerful conspiracy to step backwards in time.

Ideally, one should be housed at Williamsburg in one of the restored buildings along the gas-lit Duke of Gloucester Street, and there are a few rooms available in the Brick House Tavern and in nearby houses; the Williamsburg Inn makes reservations for them. The Inn itself and the Williamsburg Lodge are both on the edge of the restored area, and they are both very pleasant places to stay. However, while the prices at the Lodge seem on the average more moderate than at the Inn, the cheapest double room at either one is currently $20. Some of the motels near the town offer less expensive lodging. For any room, especially in the spring, one should try to book well ahead.

All visitors to Williamsburg should go first to the official Colonial Williamsburg Information Center. There one can obtain pamphlets listing the special attractions scheduled each day, and also find out about possible side-trips to Jamestown and Yorktown and the James River plantations. And, most important, the Information Center has continuous showings of a film about Williamsburg which everyone should see before setting off. It is a brief history very pleasantly done, and it makes everything much more meaningful.

Afterwards one can simply wander in and out of the various houses, and watch the wigmaker make wigs and the shoe-maker make shoes. The restored area is particularly charming at night, when there is only dim lighting along the streets; then you can sample real Virginia ham and other local delicacies in one of the eating places and stroll back to your rooms feeling very eighteenth century indeed.

Since Williamsburg was the capital of Virginia before the Revolution, the Governor's Palace and the old Capitol are the most important buildings to be seen in the restored section. At the other end of the town is the handsome College of William and Mary, the oldest university in America except Harvard.

No one who likes classic murders should miss the Wythe House. It is one of the most charming houses in Williamsburg, and George Wythe was a towering figure in colonial Virginia. After the Revolution he was formally appointed the first professor of law at the College of William and Mary, but before the Revolution, as teacher and mentor, he had already strongly influenced such Revolutionary leaders as Patrick Henry, George Mason, Thomas Jefferson, and the future first Chief Justice, John Marshall. When he was over eighty, but still vigorous and influential, Wythe was murdered, with arsenic in his breakfast coffee. For a year Virginia talked of little else. Surely his ne'er-do-well nephew must really have done it, although he was acquitted at the trial. But even more fascinating than the identity of the murderer was the mystery surrounding the motive. Did the nephew kill him in panic, to protect himself, or for gain? Was Michael Brown, the young freed slave, an accidental co-victim, or was he in fact the chief target? They sell a scholarly pamphlet at the Wythe House which discusses the murder in tantalizing detail. The entire affair seems to embody all the characteristics of eighteenth-century Williamsburg, including the deadly racial injustice on which this aristocratic society rested.

At the edge of the restored section is the Abby Aldrich Rockefeller Folk Art Museum. This is a charming collection, and since it is open in the evenings one can spend a pleasant hour or so there after supper.

From Williamsburg it is only a short drive to Jamestown, the scene of the first permanent white settlement in Virginia, in 1607. There is a small museum, and some of the original buildings have been reconstructed, along with the three tiny ships in which the settlers sailed across the Atlantic. This was a 'planted' colony, never as autonomous as those of Plymouth and Massachusetts Bay, and therefore not as interesting to many people. But everyone is familiar with one Jamestown legend: it was here that Captain John Smith went reconnoitring in the forest, only to be captured by Powhatan's Indian braves and then saved at the last moment from death at the stake through the intercession of

Pocohontas, Powhatan's daughter. Pocohontas later married another of the settlers, John Rolfe, and returned to England with him; she was presented at Court and had her portrait painted, but sickened and died towards the end of her first English winter.

In the opposite direction from Williamsburg, but just as near, is Yorktown. It was here that the British General Cornwallis surrendered to the American forces under Washington and their French allies led by Lafayette and Rochambeau. Although a peace treaty was not signed until two years later, Yorktown was to all intents and purposes the end of the Revolution. The battle-field with its redoubts and ridges is well marked; it seems intimate and peaceful today.

Not far from Williamsburg, along the James River, are three particularly fine plantation houses open to the public. Williamsburg was the capital of the Virginia colony because it was at the centre of the richest colonial development, and estates such as Carter's Grove and Shirley and Berkeley make one realize just how rich it was. Carter's Grove is the nearest to Williamsburg, on the Norfolk side; Shirley and Berkeley are both along the old river route to Richmond. The Colonial Williamsburg Information Center can supply further details.

On beyond Williamsburg to the south is the big naval centre of Norfolk and Newport News. In Hampton Roads, the waters offshore, the battle between the *Monitor* and the *Merrimac* took place during the Civil War: the first naval encounter involving ironclad ships.

Below Norfolk, at the North Carolina border, lies the Dismal Swamp. The South, with its heat and heavy rainfall, has several remarkable swamps: the Everglades, in Florida, is the most famous, and there is also the Okefenokee in Georgia. But the Great Dismal is a good swamp too, and a boat can be hired to take you through it into Lake Drummond in the centre. Few people seem to go there, and it is solitary and ghostly. They say that sounds are simply swallowed up in the Great Dismal, that one cannot hear someone fifty yards away should he shout for help. The most obvious difficulty for tourists, however, is not getting help in the swamp, but finding Wallaceton, the village where the boat can be hired. It consists of nothing more than two or three houses along the road, U.S. Route 17, and you are likely to cross the North Carolina border before you realize that that was

Wallaceton you passed. It is necessary to allow the better part of a day for the Dismal Swamp venture. It can take time to arrange for the boat, and the trip itself must be started early enough so that one comes back through the waterway before the locks suspend operations for the night.

Thomas Jefferson's name occurs over and over again, both in Washington and in Williamsburg. To see Monticello, his remarkable house, and the University of Virginia whose buildings he designed, you go west from Washington to Charlottesville. The main road from Washington, which passes Bull Run, runs for the first half of the distance along the southern fringe of the Virginia hunting country, whose centres are Middleburg and Leesburg. Charlottesville, farther on, is in the foothills of the Blue Ridge Mountains; the University of Virginia was founded there in 1819 as a recognition of the growing importance of western Virginia, with its Scotch–Irish and German settlers so unlike the wealthy aristocrats of the coastal region. Despite its founders' good intentions, however, the University of Virginia soon became a very aristocratic place indeed; only quite recently, with the admission of black students and women students, has its tone become slightly more egalitarian.

The main buildings, which Jefferson planned, are unique: typically Jeffersonian-Palladian-colonial. No university in America is more interesting architecturally. The complete eighteenth-century man, continually experimenting, inventing, talking, writing, Jefferson was the third President of the United States as well as Secretary of State in Washington's cabinet, but he asked that his epitaph include only two things: that he was the author of the Declaration of Independence, and that he was the architect of the University of Virginia. One must certainly see the University of Virginia, but even more memorable, perhaps because it is more personal, is Monticello.

This was Jefferson's own house, on a hill overlooking Charlottesville. The house is full of his labour-saving inventions, the garden is a record of his experiments, the whole estate reflects his interests and enthusiasms. Jefferson is the most attractive figure of the American Revolution, and certainly one of America's most brilliant Presidents. Like most thinking Virginians of his day, he deplored slavery and tried to write its end into the Constitution.

Ironically, his efforts failed not only because the rice planters of the Carolinas were opposed, but also because the pious New England shipowners were reluctant to give up their slave-trade profits. In almost every other respect, however, Jefferson's opinions eventually prevailed, and he did more to shape the course of American government than any other leader except Lincoln. His deftly-managed Louisiana Purchase opened the Mississippi Valley to American settlement, and the Lewis and Clark expedition, which he sponsored, presaged the extension of the United States all the way across the continent. Yet even more important for the future was his faith in a genuine democracy at a time when many Americans were not at all sure the people could really be trusted with such vast power. See Monticello, and delight in the flavour of the man.

Beyond Charlottesville are the Blue Ridge Mountains, and on the other side of the mountains is the Shenandoah Valley, as lovely as its name when the apple trees blossom in the spring. There is a splendid road, the Skyline Drive, which goes along the crest of the Blue Ridge through the Shenandoah National Park. In the spring people drive hundreds of miles to see the wild rhododendrons and azaleas in bloom along the Skyline Drive, and in the autumn the colours are exciting too. Bus tours come here from Washington. Like all National Parks, this area is kept in its natural state, with no houses or commercial enterprises allowed to intrude. There are picnic stops and camping places here, and you can see bears, and deer, and get some feeling of what the wilderness must have been like when the Virginia colonists first began working their way west through the mountains. 'Fruitfull Virginia', the Elizabethans called this land, and so she is, as fruitful today for tourists as ever she was for settlers.

SPECIAL KNOWLEDGE

Geographically, Washington, D.C., should be thought of as a giant circle with four quadrants and with the Capitol at the centre. Each quadrant is identified by initials: N.E., S.E., S.W., N.W. And since many of the major streets run a long way, it is extremely important with a **street address** to know not only the street number but also the quadrant initials. Tourists will spend most of their time in the north-west quadrant, but they should remain aware of the distinction.

In addition to IVIS, there are several other good sources for **tourist information** in Washington. There is a Convention and Visitors Bureau, and from May to September the Park Service maintains information kiosks on the Mall and in Lafayette Square. The Washington office of the AAA is invaluable for travel information, especially for expeditions by car to the places we have discussed. And there is also a tourist information desk at Union Station.

To get to Washington from New York City or Philadelphia or Baltimore, many people now favour taking the **Metroliner**, Amtrak's crack train. If you come by **plane**, you will probably take the airline coach in from the airport, but if by chance you are landing or leaving from Dulles Airport, do not under any circumstances think of taking a taxi. National Airport is quite close, and the taxi fare to it not bad, but Dulles is so far out of town that it can cost $15 or more to taxi there.

Otherwise **taxis** in Washington are quite reasonable. Be prepared, however, for the fact that each passenger pays. And on **buses** you must now have the exact fare; the driver will not give change.

For **theatre tickets**, there is a Ticketron service in Washington just as in New York City. For quick and inexpensive **meals**, Washington has innumerable cafeterias; those belonging to the Hot Shoppe chain seem fine. But Washington also has a tantalizing array of good restaurants, not all expensive. Georgetown has a great many interesting **shops**, although the trend there now is towards fewer antique shops and more shops selling Danish-modern cooking pots and Indian saris. The complex of shops called Canal Square, on M Street, is a good example of this new Georgetown; it also includes a very good bookshop, where one can buy, among other things, excellent walking guides of Georgetown, and guides to the best restaurants in Washington. The best example of the sort of shop one once went to Georgetown to browse in is Little Caledonia, on Wisconsin Avenue. We are always in favour of visitors going home with American Indian artefacts, and for that one can go to the Wooden Indian in Georgetown, or to the shop at the Museum of Natural History. The traditional Washington department store is Woodward and Lothrop, on F Street near Ford's Theater. And finally, if you'd like to see how affluent Washingtonians live, and if you had a car, you might enjoy going to the smart Chevy Chase Shopping Center, in one of Washington's most affluent suburbs.

In the spring, late March and April, when Washington is at its loveliest, it is also very crowded. Hordes of tourists, and great groups of school children, converge on the city. For that season in particular, one should be careful to book a **hotel room** well ahead.

Washington D.C.

THE CONVENTION AND VISITORS BUREAU, 1129 20th Street, N.W. (near the corner of Twentieth and K Streets).

IVIS (tourist information for international visitors), 801 19th Street, N.W. (near H Street and Pennsylvania Avenue).

AAA OFFICE, 1712 G Street, N.W.

AIR AND SPACE BUILDING, Independence Avenue, S.W. Daily 10–5.30. Closed 25 December. Free.

ARLINGTON NATIONAL CEMETERY, across the Potomac River over the Arlington Memorial Bridge. 1 April to 31 October, daily 8–7; 1 November to 31 March daily 8–5. President John F. Kennedy and his brother Robert Kennedy are both buried there, along with the Unknown Soldier from both World Wars and many other war dead, veterans and distinguished citizens.

ARTS AND INDUSTRIES BUILDINGS, Jefferson Drive and 9th Street, S.W. Daily 10–5.30. Closed 25 December. Free.

BUREAU OF ENGRAVING AND PRINTING, 14th and C Streets, S.W. Monday to Friday 8–2.30. Closed holidays. Free.

THE CAPITOL, centre of North, South and East Capitol Streets and The Mall on Capitol Hill. Daily 9–4.30, later if Congress is in session. Closed 1 January, Thanksgiving and 25 December. Tours, lasting 40 minutes, 9–3.55. Free.

DECATUR HOUSE, 748 Jackson Place. Daily 10–4. Closed 25 December.

DUMBARTON OAKS MUSEUM, 1703 32nd Street, N.W. Tuesday to Sunday 2–4.45. Closed 1 July to Labor Day and holidays.

DUMBARTON OAKS PARK. Entrance is via Lovers' Lane off R Street, between Avon Place and 31st Street. 1 April to 30 October, daily 9–5. Free.

FINE ARTS GALLERY (National Collection of Fine Arts), 8th and G Streets, N.W. Daily 10–5.30. Closed 25 December. Free.

FOLGER LIBRARY, 2nd and East Capitol Streets. Monday to Saturday 10–4.30; during the summer, Sunday 10–4.30. Closed holidays. Free.

FORD'S THEATER, 511 10th Street, N.W. Daily 9–5. Closed 25 December. The theatre is sometimes closed after midday for rehearsals. For general and ticket information, telephone 347–6260.

FREER GALLERY OF ART, Jefferson Drive and 12th Street, S.W. Daily 10–5.30. Closed 25 December. Free.

HIRSHHORN MUSEUM, Independence Avenue, S.W. Daily 10–5.30. Closed 25 December.

KENNEDY CENTER FOR THE PERFORMING ARTS, along the Potomac River near the Theodore Roosevelt Bridge. It is on D.C. Transit lines 80 and 81. On weekdays when the box office and restaurants are open, one can walk around the main part of the building and the foyers. The tour schedule varies; for further information, telephone 254–3674. Box Office open Monday to Friday 10–6; for ticket information telephone 254–3600.

LIBRARY OF CONGRESS, 1st Street and Independence Avenue. Monday to Saturday 9 a.m.–10 p.m. Sunday and most holidays 11.30–10.

MUSEUM OF AFRICAN ART, 316–318 A Street, N.E. Tuesday to Friday 11–5.30, Saturday and Sunday 12.30–5.30.

MUSEUM OF HISTORY AND TECHNOLOGY, Constitution Avenue between 12th and 14th Streets, N.W. 14 June to Labor Day, daily 10–9; Labor Day to 13 June, daily 10–5.30. Closed 25 December. Free.

MUSEUM OF NATURAL HISTORY, Constitution Avenue and 10th Street, N.W. Daily 10–5.30. Closed 25 December. Free.

NATIONAL ARCHIVES BUILDING, Constitution Avenue between 7th and 9th Streets, N.W. 1 March to 30 September, Monday to Saturday and holidays 9 a.m.–10 p.m., Sunday 1–10; 1 October to 30 April, Monday to Saturday and holidays 9–6, Sunday 1–6.

NATIONAL GALLERY OF ART, Constitution Avenue at 6th Street, N.W. 1 June to Labor Day, Monday to Saturday 10–9, Sunday 12–9; Labor Day to 31 May, Monday to Saturday 10–5, Sunday 12–9. Closed 1 January and 25 December.

NATIONAL PORTRAIT GALLERY (part of Fine Arts Gallery), 8th and G Streets, N.W. Daily 10–5.30. Closed 25 December. Free.

PHILLIPS COLLECTION, 1600–1612 21st Street at Q Street, N.W. Tuesday to Saturday 10–5, Sunday 2–7. Closed 4 July and 25 December. Free. Concerts are given 1 October to 31 May on Sundays at 5.

RENWICK GALLERY, 17th Street and Pennsylvania Avenue, N.W. Daily 10–5.30. Free.

ST JOHN'S CHURCH, 16th and H Streets, N.W. Daily 9–5.

SMITHSONIAN INSTITUTION, Smithsonian Institution Headquarters are on Jefferson Drive between 9th and 12th Streets. For information on galleries administered by the Smithsonian, telephone 628–4422. Special events are recorded daily on 737–8811. Administered by the Smithsonian are the Air and Space Building, Arts and Industries Buildings, Fine Arts Gallery, Freer Gallery of Art, Hirshhorn Museum, Museum of History and Technology, Museum of Natural History, National Gallery of Art, the National Portrait Gallery and the Renwick Gallery – see under separate listings.

SUPREME COURT, 1st Street and Maryland Avenue, N.E. Monday to Friday 9–4.30, Saturday 9–12. Closed holidays.

U.S. BOTANIC GARDEN, 1st Street and Maryland Avenue, S.W. Daily 9–4. Closed 1 January and 25 December. Free.

WASHINGTON MONUMENT, The Mall at 15th Street. Daily 9–5. Closed 25 December.

THE WHITE HOUSE, 1600 Pennsylvania Avenue. Tuesday to Saturday 10–12. Free.

Washington D.C.: Tours and Transport

CHESAPEAKE AND OHIO CANAL BOAT TRIPS. These leave from the foot of 30th Street, N.W. 1 May to 31 October, Saturday, Sunday and Monday departures at 10.15, 12.30 and 3. The trip takes 2½ hours. Reservations, which are essential, can only be made by purchase of tickets from Government Services Inc., 1135 21st Street, N.W., Monday to Friday 8–4. For information, telephone FE 7–8080.

D.C. TRANSIT has a 24-hour answering service giving information about public transport anywhere in the Washington area; telephone 832–4300. D.C. Transit also offers coach tours; for information, telephone 835–5100.

GRAY LINE, Washington House, 1010 Eye Street, N.W. Coach tours of Washington and district and also to the Skyline Drive, the Civil War Battlefields, Williamsburg (3 days) and even the Penn Dutch country (see Chapter 3). The trip to Mount Vernon can be done one way by coach and one way by boat from 3 April to 17 October. Free pick-up service from most hotels. For information, telephone (202) DI7–0600.

POTOMAC RIVER BOAT RIDES. Wilson Boat Line run trips from Washington to Mount Vernon. They leave the Wilson Boat Line Pier daily at 2, returning from Mount Vernon at 5.15; 22 May to Labor Day, additional departure daily at 9.30, returning at 12.15. For further information telephone 753–6036.

Near Washington

CHRIST CHURCH, Cameron and Washington Streets, Alexandria. Monday to Saturday 9–5, Sunday 2–5. Closed 1 January, Thanksgiving and 25 December.

CUSTIS-LEE HOUSE, Arlington. 1 April to Labor Day, daily 9.30–6; Labor Day to 31 March, daily 9.30–4.30. Closed 25 December.

GREAT FALLS, on the Potomac River 15 miles north-west of Washington. Parks are open 1 April to 31 May, daily 8.30–5.30; 1 June to 31 August, daily 8.30–9.30; 1 September to 31 March, daily 8–4.30. Great Falls Tavern is open 1 June to 31 August, daily 9.30–8. Sometimes open during the rest of the year.

GUNSTON HALL, State Route 242, 14 miles south of Alexandria. Daily 9.30–5. Closed 25 December.

MOUNT VERNON, George Washington Memorial Parkway, 16 miles south of Alexandria. 1 March to 30 September, daily 9–5; 1 October to 30 April, daily 9–4. For information on daily boat trips from Washington, see **Tours and Transport.**

POHICK CHURCH, U.S. Route 1, 2 miles south-west of Accotink. Open daily.

PRESBYTERIAN MEETING HOUSE, Fairfax Street, between Duke and Wolfe Streets, Alexandria. Monday to Friday 10–5, Saturday 9–12.

WOLF TRAP FARM PARK FOR THE PERFORMING ARTS, off State Route 7 on Trap Road. Mid-June to about the third week in September, daily 12–3 and 6.30–9. For reservations for the buffet supper, telephone 938–3800. Tickets obtainable from Ticketron or the AAA.

WOODLAWN, U.S. Route 1, 7½ miles south of Alexandria. Daily 9.30–4.30. Closed 25 December.

Neighbouring States
Annapolis, Maryland

HAMMOND-HARWOOD HOUSE, Maryland Avenue at King George Street. 1 March to 31 October, Tuesday to Saturday 10–5, Sunday 2–5; 1 November to 28 February, Tuesday to Saturday 10–4, Sunday 1–4, Closed 25 December.

HISTORIC ANNAPOLIS INC., 64 State Circle. Guided walking tours are available for groups of 3 or more people (for a minimum fee of $5). Reservations are required. For information, telephone 267–8149.

UNITED STATES NAVAL ACADEMY, Sands Road. Grounds are open daily 9–5. 1 June to 30 September, tours leave every half-hour; 1 October to 31 May every hour. No tours 1 January and 25 December.

Baltimore, Maryland

BALTIMORE MUSEUM OF ART, Art Museum Drive, near N. Charles and 31st Streets. 1 June to 30 September, Tuesday to Saturday 11–4, Sunday 2–5; 1 October to 31 May, Tuesday to Friday 11–5, Saturday 10.30–5, Sunday 1–5. Free.

B AND O TRANSPORTATION MUSEUM. Entrance is through the old Mount Clare Station at Pratt and Poppleton Streets. Wednesday to Sunday 10–4. Free.

WALTERS ART GALLERY, N. Charles and Center Streets. 1 September to 30 June, Monday 1–5, Tuesday to Saturday 11–5, Sunday 2–5; 1 July to 31 August, Monday 1–4, Tuesday to Saturday 11–4, Sunday 2–5. Free.

Charlottesville, Virginia

MONTICELLO, 3 miles south-east on State Route 53. 1 November to 28 February, daily 8–5, 1 March to 31 October, daily 9–4.30.

UNIVERSITY OF VIRGINIA. There is a hostess on duty at the Rotunda from Monday to Friday.

Dismal Swamp, Virginia and North Carolina

Wallaceton on U.S. Route 17 is where the canal starts up to Lake Drummond in the centre of the swamp. It is here that one can arrange a boat trip into the swamp.

James River Plantations

BERKELEY PLANTATION, Just south of State Route 5, 22 miles east of Richmond. Daily 8–5.

CARTER'S GROVE, on U.S. Route 60, 6 miles south-east of Williamsburg. 1 March to 30 November, daily 9–5.

SHIRLEY PLANTATION, on State Route 5, 20 miles east of Richmond. Daily 9–5. Closed 25 December.

Jamestown, Virginia

VISITOR CENTER, terminus of the Colonial Parkway. Open daily. Closed 25 December.

Smith and Tangier Islands, Maryland

For information about ferry service and accommodations, write to Captain Homer Windsor, Box 266, Crisfield, Maryland.

Williamsburg, Virginia

COLONIAL WILLIAMSBURG INFORMATION CENTER, Route 132, near Colonial Parkway. 1 July to 31 August, daily 8–10; 1 September to 30 June, daily 8.30–10. A second information centre at the Williamsburg Lodge is open 1 June to 31 August. For further information, write to the Colonial Williamsburg Foundation, P.O. Drawer C, Williamsburg, Va. 23185.

ABBY ALDRICH ROCKEFELLER FOLK ART MUSEUM, off South England Street, near the Williamsburg Inn. Monday to Saturday 10–9, Sunday 12–9.

EXHIBITION BUILDINGS AND CRAFT SHOPS open daily.

6 · THE SOUTH

The South does make one believe that geography is destiny. The soil and the climate in the lowlands of the South suited plantation-style agriculture, which led to slavery, which led to the Civil War and to all the problems which have plagued southerners, both black and white, ever since.

Yet even though most of the southern states were linked together on the Confederate side in the Civil War, they are by no means all alike. Geographically, economically, and in tone and tradition, the more mountainous regions of the central ridge are very different from the old plantation lowlands, and Florida is unlike either.

In this chapter, we will describe the Atlantic coastal route south from North Carolina to Georgia, and then we will move on to Florida. Next we will go to New Orleans and then up the Mississippi. And at the end of the chapter we will talk about the border states, Tennessee and Kentucky, and the Appalachian Mountains region which includes parts of many southern states.

Much of the coast from the southern border of Virginia all the way to Florida is marshland and sandy islands. This is most noticeable in North Carolina, where the upper coast is sparsely populated even today. Here lie the treacherous Outer Banks and Cape Hatteras, 'the graveyard of the Atlantic'. Over the years, the few people who settled along these sandy shoals acquired an evil reputation as wreckers, but this section had earned a bad name as early as 1590. In that year a ship arrived at Roanoke Island from England to provision a small colony planted by Sir Walter Raleigh in 1587, which had been the first English colony in

America. To their distress the sailors could find no trace of any of the colonists they had last seen three years before. There was simply nothing at all, except for the word 'croatoan' carved on a tree. Croatoan was the name given on some maps to a neighbouring island, and also to a local tribe of Indians. But the island yielded no clue, and the Indians were friendly but seemed not to understand the inquiries. To this day no more has ever been learned about the fate of those men, women, and children, including the first white child known to have been born in America.

In 1903, on a lonely flat stretch of these Outer Banks near a place called Kitty Hawk, very near the site of Raleigh's ill-fated settlement, the Wright brothers launched their first successful flight. Today this great stretch of beach is no longer lonely. In the summer, at least, the nearby resort town of Nags Head overflows with people. But southwards from Nags Head, for over a hundred miles, the sandy barrier reef stretches on. Much of it is now protected as the Cape Hatteras National Seashore; one can drive along it on State Route 12, and even in summer find miles of beautiful hard flat sand with no human being in sight.

The road ends at Ocracoke, where a ferry runs to the mainland. Inland hereabouts there were once great rice and indigo plantations, immensely profitable so long as there were slaves to provide free labour. It was a miserable existence for the slaves; even the sugar plantations of Louisiana and the West Indies were less dreaded. Mrs Trollope in the 1830s wrote of staying with a Virginia family who in her presence told a slave that he was to be sent to South Carolina. The man ran to the woodshed and hacked off his right hand with a hatchet; only that way could he avoid what he regarded as a sure sentence of death.

But towns throughout this region bear witness to the elegant life this plantation economy made possible for the landowners. The best example in North Carolina is New Bern, the old colonial capital, with its splendid Tryon Palace and the many fine smaller houses along its quiet streets. Farther down the coast, the culture of South Carolina had an added flavour because of French influence. Before any English settlers arrived, a group of French Protestants had made an abortive attempt to found a colony in South Carolina just below present-day Beaufort. And despite this initial failure, French Protestants continued to be drawn to this region, giving to the town of Charleston in particular a most cosmopolitan air. There is still an active Huguenot church in Charleston, and French names are common.

Charleston, and Savannah in Georgia, were the chief towns of this rich coastal low country, and they still are, each quite distinctive, each with its own partisans. Charleston is the more renowned as a tourist centre, and it is anxious to impress visitors with its past as the most aristocratic city in the South. (You may remember that Rhett Butler in *Gone with the Wind* had particular fascination for the ladies of Atlanta because he was not only a black sheep, but the black sheep of a Charleston family.)

Charleston was originally a walled city, one of the few in America, and it is therefore compact, with most of its finest houses close together on a few streets near the waterfront. The houses are delightful. Some of them, the town houses of the wealthy planters, are large and elegant, here pure English Georgian and there French, or romanticized with curves and ironwork. Still others are small row houses or converted carriage houses, painted every colour of the rainbow. Among the most distinctive are the houses which sit sidewise, one end on the street and the wide front facing the enclosed garden, with a two-story veranda the length of the front. And part of the charm of Charleston is the profusion of mews and alleys and hidden courtyards: Stoll's Alley is a good example. But what makes it all particularly lovely is the sub-tropical luxuriance, the flowering vines, the enchanting colours and scents everywhere: bougainvillea and jasmine and oleander and gardenia. And the mellow brick: Charleston is rich in lovely old brick and tile, much of it brought over as ship's ballast in the early days.

The best way to see Charleston is to walk, up Meeting Street and down Church Street, back and forth on Tradd Street, along East Bay. From Battery Park on the waterfront you can just glimpse the flag flying over Fort Sumter out at the mouth of the harbour. In 1861 the Civil War began when a detachment of South Carolinians fired on the federal garrison at Fort Sumter. You can take a boat trip out across the harbour to the restored Fort; the view of Charleston from the water is very nice indeed.

There are several churches in Charleston which lay claim to the visitor's attention, including St Michael's (1752), possibly designed by James Gibbs. Our own favourites are the First Baptist Church (1822), four-square and solid, with fat white pillars and box pews, and what is known as the Circular Congregational

Church (1892), a dark brown mock-Romanesque structure with an arena-style seating plan that prefigures the most *avant-garde* church designs of today.

The best time to go to Charleston is between mid-March and mid-April, when there are house and garden tours which include places normally closed to the public. Two of the three most famous Charleston-area gardens are also then at their very best: Magnolia Gardens and Cypress Gardens. Despite their names both of these gardens are loveliest in the azalea season, for this is superb azalea country, with the ideal climate and soil. Cypress Gardens is particularly exciting because it is really a swamp, with ink-black water and the dark cypress trees all hung with soft grey Spanish moss; you go through in a boat. When the brilliant colours of the azaleas are splashed against the sombre background, it is a sight one does not soon forget. The third of the famous gardens is Middleton Place, said to be the first elaborate formal garden in America. Like many eighteenth-century formal gardens, Middleton Place lacks flowers, but it does have flowering shrubs. Its chief glory is camellias, hundreds of camellias of every possible variety. These are at their best from Christmas to early February, but even at other times of the year Middleton Place is handsome because of its situation and the charm of its carefully contrived vistas.

While each of these gardens is actually part of an old plantation, the houses are neither particularly interesting nor open to the public. Many of the old plantation houses in this area were destroyed during the Civil War, and afterwards, when the once-proud planters were reduced to poverty, many other houses were simply abandoned to rot away. The few really old plantation houses left in South Carolina and Georgia are hard to find and seldom open to visitors. In Charleston itself, however, two handsome town houses are open to the public year-round. Our favourite is the Adam-style Nathaniel Russell House, which has a lovely oval sitting-room on its upper floor, and a free-flying staircase.

The Afro-American traditions of the Charleston region have always been particularly interesting to the collectors of folklore and folk music. George Gershwin's classic American folk opera, *Porgy and Bess*, was based on the Charleston stories of Dubose Heyward; the prototype of Catfish Row is now one of the smart sections of the town. Of even greater interest is the black world of the off-shore islands near Charleston. From the early nineteenth century, escaped slaves made their way to the marshes and pine woods of these islands, and after the Civil War many newly emancipated Negroes also settled there, well away from their former masters. Fishing and crabbing in the inlets, growing what crops they could, they eked out a meagre existence, sustained by their pride in independence and their fervent Christian belief in a better life to come. They spoke a dialect known as 'gullah', and sang spirituals of a very special quality. This gullah world is fast vanishing today; after the Second World War, whites began moving on to the islands, and bridges and causeways were built. The already difficult life of the gullah Negroes became in some ways even more difficult. So the young black people from these islands now tend to migrate north, and before long the gullah world will probably be known only through recordings in folk music collections. Meanwhile, any visitor who drives from Charleston out on to these islands, perhaps to one of the beaches, might look for what still remains of this world, the ramshackle cabins and the little gospel churches or 'praise halls', and mark them as evidence of an indomitable spirit in the face of adversity.

There are more 'gullah' islands on down the coast off Beaufort (here pronounced 'Bewfert'). On some of the larger islands hereabouts, long-staple cotton was once extensively grown: the highly valued 'sea island' cotton which in the nineteenth century supplanted rice as the chief crop of this region. Beaufort itself, once a busy port, now survives mainly as a winter resort. There are many handsome old houses near the waterfront, as well as a lovely Episcopalian church, St Helena's.

Savannah comes next, just across the state border, in Georgia. In part because of the manner of its founding, Savannah is very different from Charleston. The territory of the Carolinas had been granted by Charles II to eight of his courtiers; it was colonized as a proprietary financial venture. Georgia, however, began as a utopian experiment. In 1733, George II granted this territory to the philanthropist James Oglethorpe, who set about colonizing it with English debtors and the deserving poor, and with persecuted Protestants from the Continent. He appointed trustees to administer its government, and strict rules were laid down. There was to be no trade in rum, no matter how economically tempting, and no slavery; to fill specific English needs, the colonists were to plant hemp and grapevines, and mulberry trees for silk production. Like many an elaborate philanthropic scheme before and after, Oglethorpe's Georgia plan failed miserably; the trustee system and the regulations survived for only a scant twenty years.

Oglethorpe, however, had planned Savannah, the principal town, with great care and imagination; it was laid out with a symmetrical arrangement of open squares every other street. And today these squares remain Savannah's particular distinction, giving the city an air of genteel elegance unlike any other city in America. Ten years ago most of the handsome houses around these squares were slowly crumbling; indeed, ten years ago the entire city seemed to be slowly dying a romantic southern death. But a few stalwart citizens decided to fight death; they mobilized public sentiment, and Savannah began to restore and refurbish. Nowadays, as one walks through the old squares along the brick pavements, beneath the great live-oak trees and the magnificent magnolias grandiflora, one senses a new spirit abroad in the city.

You might begin an exploration of the old section of Savannah at the Chamber of Commerce information office along Factors Walk. One can get walking-tour maps here, and Factors Walk, the old cotton exchange, is in any case something one should see. From here do a zig-zag route, going first to Johnson Square and then left (east) along St Julian, to Reynolds Square, which will take you past Savannah's oldest surviving house, the Old Pink House (1771), now a restaurant. From Reynolds Square, go south to Oglethorpe Square, and there turn left (east) to see the Owens-Thomas House. Both it and Davenport House in the next square to the east (Colombia Square) should be seen. They are both particularly handsome early nineteenth-century houses, and each has distinctive features. One is Georgian in style, and the other a sort of planter's Regency. From Davenport House go south again, to Oglethorpe Avenue, which runs along one edge of the old Colonial Park Cemetery. If you turn right at Oglethorpe Avenue and walk west along the cemetery and then on for another two or three blocks, you will come to the Independent Presbyterian Church, a fine nineteenth-century copy of the original eighteenth-century church. All along the way on this walk you will have passed fine houses, many built of the pinky-grey brick characteristic of early Savannah building, and many trimmed with equally characteristic ornamental ironwork. You will have seen the best of Savannah, with one notable exception; you must also take a trip to the edge of the city to see the old Bonaventure graveyard with its extraordinary festoons of Spanish moss hanging from the live-oak trees.

There are several pleasant and atmospheric places to eat in Savannah, but for lodging there is nothing now but the usual run of modern hotels and motels. In this regard, Charleston does better by its visitors, with attractive guest houses and one fine old hotel in the old section.

Some few of the sea islands along the South Carolina and Georgia coast have been developed for tourists. There is, for example, a very attractive but also expensive resort development on Hilton Head, between Beaufort and Savannah. And off the southern Georgia coast, near Brunswick, three islands have been extensively developed. One of these, Jekyll Island, is now a state park, with all manner of recreational facilities in addition to a good beach. On nearby Sea Island there is an expensive resort hotel. And on St Simons, where the young John Wesley preached for a year as a missionary, there are some quite inexpensive motels.

Everything we have described thus far has been noticeably altered by man. Even the Cape Hatteras region, after all, has its highway. There are, however, a few places where one can still see this south-eastern coast of the United States essentially as it was before the white man arrived. This was a unique region, with an extraordinary variety of birds, and unusual animals, and a rich sub-tropical vegetation: palmettos and live-oaks, magnolias and holly, climbing vines and the omnipresent Spanish moss. One can see all this on Bull's Island, part of the Cape Romain National Wildlife Refuge just north of Charleston. It is deliberately kept somewhat inaccessible; there is only a boat three times a day, and there are no roads on the island, only a small information centre manned by a ranger, and fourteen miles of walking trails.

Inland, along the Georgia–Florida border, is the Okefenokee National Wildlife Refuge, which includes the major portion of the Okefenokee Swamp. 'Okefenokee' is a corruption of a Choctaw Indian word meaning 'trembling land', a reference to the swamp's floating brush-covered islands of peat. Much of the Okefenokee is a watery 'prairie' of bog and swamp grass, punctuated by floating islands and 'hammocks' or true islands. Here one can see a remarkable variety of aquatic plants, and also of birds, for the Okefenokee is on the Atlantic coastal migratory flyway. In the northern part of the swamp, one's boat goes through watery forests of towering cypress trees draped in Spanish moss; there

are alligators floating log-like along the way. Because it is so easy
to get lost in the Okefenokee, visitors are allowed to take boats
(motor boats or canoes) independently only into designated
sections of the swamp. Yet the Okefenokee is best seen on the
longest possible boat trip; the deeper one goes into the interior,
the more engrossing the experience. Thus we tend to favour
guided boat trips, but we strongly advise against going in by way
of Waycross and the 'Okefenokee Swamp Park', a thoroughly
commercial private enterprise at the northern end. The eastern
and western entrances are much to be preferred, from Folkston or
Fargo.

What does one say about Florida? One can say that great stretches
of once wild and beautiful seacoast have been so over-developed
that it is painful to see. But one must also grant that after a long
grey winter in some northern climate, Florida can seem paradise.
One can laugh (or cry) at the over-commercialism of Florida; you
are incessantly urged to see wax museums and miniature cathe-
drals with organs that really play and Leonardo's Last Supper
recreated full-size in mosaic and under-water ballets with girls
dressed as mermaids. Moreover, having destroyed much natural
beauty, Florida entrepreneurs are now simulating it; at Disney
World the delightful topiary animals turn out to be plastic. Yet
there are still glorious beaches where one can hunt for shells, and
there are the Everglades, and the Keys. Furthermore, it would be
foolish to imply that all the resort areas are unattractive. Many are
very tempting, even if virtually none now retain the splendid
simplicity a determined Florida visitor could still find as recently
as ten years ago.

St Augustine, at the northern end of the east coast, is the only
resort town in Florida with any real history. Founded in 1565,
forty years before the first permanent English settlement in
America, it was an important Spanish base during those three
hundred years when Spain held most of the southernmost sections
of what is now the United States. St Augustine talks a great deal
too much about being 'the oldest town'; actually much of the old
part is not very old at all. But the town has none the less preserved
a Spanish air in a way no other American town east of Santa Fe
has done. This may be partly due to the fact that long after the
Spanish occupation had ended, many Minorcans came to settle in
St Augustine. But there is also the fact that fragments of the city

wall are still to be seen, and the huge Spanish fort, el Castillo de San Marcos, still guards the harbour, and the central plaza still retains a languid Latin air. You can walk from the plaza south along narrow little Aviles Street to St Francis Street, where the Historical Society has the oldest house in St Augustine suitably furnished and open to the public; there is also a pretty little garden with marked specimens of native trees and shrubs, and a small museum. There are two amusing ways to see St Augustine without walking: one is to take the little trackless train that rumbles through the streets, and the other, the more traditional and delightful, is to hire a horse and carriage. The gaily decorated surreys with their be-plumed horses stand in the plaza and near the old fort; their drivers, elderly Negroes wearing battered top hats, importune you as you pass. St Augustine has a full quota of touristy attractions, yet for us it still also has considerable charm.

The northern end of Florida has a mild winter climate but not hot enough for swimming. Thus St Augustine is not one of the major beach resort towns, and although there are fine beaches all the way along to Daytona, this part of the coast has not been developed nearly as extensively as it is farther south. The next real 'tourist attraction' is more than a hundred miles south of St Augustine: the Kennedy Space Center near the Canaveral Peninsula. It may seem odd to describe the Space Center as a tourist attraction, but it certainly is one, and the authorities there have done a very good job of providing for the throngs of visitors who come. At the visitors' centre, one can start with an illuminating film and then examine actual Apollo and Gemini spacecraft, as well as many other space flight components. There are also bus tours through the launching area which include a look into such places as the flight crew training centre and the mammoth rocket assembly building. On Sundays (only) one can drive through on one's own, but that way you can't go into any of the working buildings.

Florida's greatest concentration of winter resorts begins another hundred miles farther south, around Palm Beach. From Palm Beach to Miami, there is virtually a solid line of hotels and motels along the coast. Palm Beach itself, traditionally very upper-crust, still retains much of its vaunted smartness; the shops along Worth Avenue prove that. Palm Beach has the advantage of having been developed comparatively early, at the turn of the century, when most of southern Florida was still a tropical wilder-

8a. The Virgelle Ferry, Missouri Breaks

7 *overleaf*. Spanish moss in the Great Cypress Swamp
near the Everglades National Park, Florida

8b. An American Egret (*left*) and a Roseate Spoonbill
in Everglades National Park, Florida

ness. The other, newer towns along here scarcely had time for individual character to evolve before they were assaulted by the enormous increase in Florida tourism which has taken place since the Second World War.

Miami and Miami Beach are the most celebrated examples of over-population and over-development. Miami Beach is now completely smothered in giant hotels, and Miami's only note-worthy asset these days is the influx of Cuban refugees who have given a fascinating new flavour to the city's nightlife and restaur-ants.

Ten years ago, we were very favourably impressed by the west coast of Florida; particularly at the southern end, there were still gloriously unspoiled areas. But the line of hotels and motels is creeping inexorably down the west coast too, and almost the only choice one has there now is between one resort town and another. Our own choice would be Sarasota, which is at least past the growing-pains stage. The white sand beaches of its off-shore keys may be the most beautiful beaches in all of Florida, and if you are up early in the morning after a high tide, you can find good shells along them. (The west coast of Florida is a rich hunting ground for shell collectors.) Furthermore, Sarasota really does have some worthwhile things to see. The Ringling Museum of Art, for example, founded by one of America's leading circus impres-sarios, is really very good. The building is an eccentric but attrac-tive Italianate villa, constructed of bits and pieces cannibalized from old buildings on either side of the Atlantic; it houses an interesting collection, especially strong in the baroque period. Also part of the complex is the lovely little Asolo Theater, an eighteenth-century theatre brought from Italy to be re-erected here; there are plays and concerts year-round at the Asolo. The Ringling Museum stands in handsome grounds; one can also go to the Sarasota Jungle Gardens, fifteen acres of tropical and sub-tropical plants, and suitably colourful birds. Then too there is Sarasota's new performing arts centre, Van Wezel Hall. Designed by the Taliesen Associates, Frank Floyd Wright's architectural heirs, it resembles nothing so much as a chambered nautilus. One might mention here too that Frank Lloyd Wright himself designed the buildings for Florida Southern College at Lakeland, not very far from Sarasota.

Since visitors to Florida are constantly bombarded with advertisements for various tourist attractions, we should perhaps single out those we have found worth a stop. We do like Marineland near St Augustine, and presumably the Seaquarium at Miami and the Theater of the Sea on the Keys are similar. Marineland is a great outdoor aquarium, where whales and sharks and exotic sea creatures are kept in glass-walled tanks which simulate an ocean environment; several times a day there are also pool-shows in which delightful trained porpoises do clever things. Another much-advertised attraction, Florida Cypress Gardens near Winter Haven, really does have some lovely vistas, and its water-ski show is fun to see.

The very best botanic garden in Florida, however, is the Fairchild Tropical Garden in the Coral Gables section of Miami; although it is supported in part by tourist admission fees, it is run by and for serious horticulturalists. It is a fascinating and beautiful place. Equally serious of purpose and equally fascinating in a very different way is the Corkscrew Swamp Sanctuary near Immokalee in south-western Florida. It is off the beaten path and slightly hard to find, but the two-mile walk one can do there on a boardwalk built into a virgin cypress swamp is well worth the trip.

The most popular tourist attraction in Florida these days is Disney World, opened in 1971 in central Florida. Disneyland in California is simply a particularly charming amusement park; Disney World is far more ambitious. At its core it does have a 'Magic Kingdom' which is almost an exact duplicate of Disneyland. But Disney World encompasses thousands of acres; there are two hotels now and more planned, camping facilities (in 'Fort Wilderness', of course!), a large lake, two golf courses, and a pet motel. Eventually it is even supposed to include an 'experimental prototype community of tomorrow', a new town, to be called 'Epcot'. We have mixed feelings about Disney World. It is certainly very pleasant to stay at one of its unusual 'theme' hotels and then ride across the lake to the Magic Kingdom on a paddlewheel steamboat. But the crowds there are often too much for the available facilities, too much even for the access roads, and the perpetually smiling young staff frequently seems unable to cope.

Inland Florida is not especially prepossessing: mile after mile of scrub pine and palm, with the roads bulldozed through in the least imaginative way possible. To be sure, in the central lakes region there are thousands of acres of orange groves, and the town of Ocala has now become a major centre for the raising of thoroughbred horses. But on the whole Florida is at its best along the coast, and its most unusual region is its southern extremity, with the Everglades and the Florida Keys.

The area known as the Everglades is tropical swampland: 'prairies' of sawgrass, watery mangrove jungles, and here and there open water. The chief portion of the Everglades is within Everglades National Park, which harbours alligators and crocodiles and manatees, rare varieties of egrets and herons, and the spectacular roseate spoonbill. The Park's main visitors complex is at Flamingo on the southern edge; it has a motel, a small museum with frequent naturalist lectures, restaurants, boat tours and boat rentals, and a campsite. There are also commercial boat trips into the Park from the town of Everglades on the northwestern edge, and the Park Service itself runs the Shark Valley Loop Trip, a fourteen-mile trip into the Park on a little tram-train, starting from a point about midway along the northern edge of the Park on the Tamiami Trail.

It seems to us that Everglades National Park needs to be approached in a special way (and probably not at all in summer, when the heat and the mosquitoes can be bad, and the bird and animal life is in any case more dispersed, less easy to spot). It is not like most of the other National Parks, not instantly dramatic. To appreciate fully its subtle ecological balance, one needs to spend a considerable amount of time there, and perhaps hire a canoe to penetrate the interior. The longer you are there, the more you will be impressed; there are marvels in the Everglades. But if you only have a half-day to spare, we suggest not going all the way to Flamingo. Two miles from the eastern entrance is the Royal Palm Interpretive Station, and one can take two short but interesting marked walks from there. Then you might go on another ten miles to the Pa-hay-okee overlook; these two stops combined would give you a good idea of the Everglades. Or you might simply go on the Shark Valley Loop Trip. On the other hand, we must admit that the greatest number of birds seem to be around Flamingo. And if you do have ample time, we are told that a trip by boat to Cape Sable should not be missed; boats go there from Flamingo.

Actually, driving along the Tamiami Trail on the northern edge of the Park one sees great numbers of egrets and herons and anhingas just along the highway. There are also straw-thatched Seminole Indian villages along the Tamiami Trail, and an Indian-owned restaurant at Miccosukee, near where the Shark Valley

Loop Trip begins. Along there too the Indians advertise rides through the swampland outside the Park on 'swamp buggies', flat-bottomed boats with giant propellers at the rear.

Florida Bay links the Everglades to the Florida Keys, that chain of islands which points from mainland Florida down towards Cuba. While the Keys may not look at all like the Everglades, especially those keys which have been heavily developed, in actual fact they have most of the same birds and much similar vegetation. The climate along the Keys, however, is far drier.

Certainly the Keys must have been incomparably finer before the great causeway was built which joins Key West to Miami with a 160-mile concrete ribbon. Nonetheless, we do like the Keys. The old section of Key West, the town at the southern end, still preserves the air of a town in the West Indies. One should see the house Ernest Hemingway owned and lived in through most of the 1930s; it is not only interesting to admirers of Hemingway (since he wrote most of his best-known books here) but also it has the proper West Indies flavour. Walk past the Audubon House, too, where Audubon lived while studying and painting the birds and animals of Florida; it is a fine example of old Key West architecture, although its furnishings these days are quite out of keeping with its past.

From Key West, as from the towns of Islamorada and Marathon along the Keys, one can go out on all-day deep-sea fishing expeditions, for tarpon and sailfish and marlin. The rates range from $6 to $20 a day per person, depending on the sort of boat and equipment.

About forty miles north of Key West is Bahia Honda Key, which has a splendid small state park. One can camp there, or simply stop for an hour or two to see its unique vegetation (some very rare trees and plants) or to swim from its fine beach. The rock-and-coral-edged Keys have very few beaches, so the one at Bahia Honda looks especially tempting.

Even more unusual is the John Pennekamp State Park on Key Largo, much closer to Miami. This is literally an underwater park, created to protect a coral reef. One can rent sailboats or paddleboats or motorboats and go out to the reef on one's own; there is snorkelling and diving equipment for hire too. For those who want to try a little snorkelling without the responsibility of their own boat, there are also organized boat trips out to the reef (reservations advised). Anyone who can swim, can snorkel, without any special training or experience; it's easy, and fun. Skin-diving, however, with air tanks and so forth, is something one must be taught to do. At the park they give a three-day course in skin-diving, and this would be a very good (and safe) place to learn, with good instructors. For the less adventurous, there are glass-bottom boat tours out to see the reef and its fish; reservations are strongly advised for these too. Summer is the time to go to John Pennekamp in order to be sure of calm and clear water, for the best viewing. But it is very hot there then, a veritable North African heat, and the sun is blistering.

New Orleans is the most fascinating city in the South, as San Francisco is the most exciting city in the West. San Francisco, perched on its steep hills overlooking the Pacific, is young and exhilarating, with a whiff of Oriental spice in its fresh sea breeze. New Orleans, on the other hand, seems mellow and sensual, a Mediterranean town transposed to the marshy delta of the Mississippi River. Much of Louisiana is every bit as 'southern' as the state of Mississippi across the river. But New Orleans and the region to the south-west of the city are different, the Franco-Spanish heritage plainly visible. There is a tradition of sophistication in New Orleans, a certain panache. It is not surprising that jazz should first have flowered there.

Spanish explorers were the first Europeans to penetrate the New Orleans region, but the French were first to claim it, coming down the Mississippi from their Canadian territories. The town itself was founded in 1717 and became the headquarters of the French colonial government in this area. Jesuits introduced the cultivation of sugar cane into Louisiana, and New Orleans grew rapidly as a port and a gathering place for the rich French planters. With Spanish territory on either side, in Florida and Texas, there must always have been a good many Spaniards in and about New Orleans, even in the days when it belonged to France. In any case, when the French empire in Canada dissolved, France gave up Louisiana as well, ceding it to Spain in 1762. But in 1803 Napoleon artfully got the Louisiana territory back from Spain, and then he promptly sold it to the United States for a price which with interest came to twenty-seven million dollars.

Since the signs of Franco-Spanish occupation linger on most vividly in Louisiana, and the arrangement was called 'the Louisiana Purchase', one tends to think of it as involving only that one state. However, the Louisiana territory actually included not only Louisiana but also the modern states of Arkansas, Missouri, Oklahoma, Iowa, Nebraska, Minnesota, North Dakota, South Dakota, and most of Kansas, Colorado, Wyoming, and Montana: the whole great Missouri-Mississippi River basin, in fact. It doubled the area of the United States at that time, and represented President Jefferson's greatest gamble.

The Louisiana Purchase opened up this territory to Anglo-American settlers from other parts of the United States, but in and around New Orleans the old French and Spanish families continued in control. Americans pushed on towards the West, and many strange types drifted through New Orleans, but on the whole the town changed them more than they changed the town. Frontier gamblers learned subtlety here, and for those who craved something more sophisticated than the usual shot of whisky, New Orleans invented the cocktail. And then there were the lovely quadroons, who made the demi-monde in New Orleans a thing of almost Parisian glitter.

All visitors to New Orleans today go first to the French Quarter, the heart of the old Franco-Spanish town and New Orleans' greatest tourist attraction. Some people are disillusioned there. Bourbon Street, once synonymous with jazz, is now principally devoted to girls, girls, girls in various stages of deshabille; this can be amusing at night, but in the daytime it only seems tawdry. On the whole, however, the French Quarter proves every bit as good as advertised, as long as one exercises a sensible reserve and resists the obvious tourist traps. For example, New Orleans is famous for its food; even the lowliest cafeteria will offer delicious crawfish bisque, superb oyster sandwiches. And some of the best restaurants are in the Quarter. There is still good jazz to be heard, too, if one knows where to look. For that, we suggest that you go first to the Jazz Museum, at the corner of Bourbon and Conti Streets. It is a great place, imaginatively organized, with fascinating jazz memorabilia, and listening booths in which one can hear Jelly Roll Morton and New Orleans' own Louis Armstrong and all the rest. It is also the place to find out where to go in New Orleans to hear good jazz today. Of course if you happen to be there at Mardi Gras time, when New Orleans puts on its greatest spectacle, you'll find jazz bands on every street corner.

One of the great charms of the French Quarter is its architecture, the wrought-iron gates and balustrades, the tiled roofs, the enclosed patios. When the wealthier people began to move out of this section after the Civil War, many of the old houses deteriorated, their lovely courtyards overgrown. Even twenty or thirty years ago, the Quarter was unfashionable enough so that one could rent a flat there for very little, and people who have known the Quarter over many years understandably mourn those good old days. However, the building and refurbishing that has gone on in the Quarter over the past few years has on the whole been well done. It is true that it is no longer as romantic a place as it once was; affluence is seldom romantic. But the more you walk around it, the deeper into it you penetrate, the more you can still sense its old flavour.

There are pamphlets which suggest specific routes for a walk through the French Quarter but it is pleasant enough just to wander about, peering through the gates at the patios, going down any passages which look interesting. Bourbon Street and Royal Street and Chartres Street are the principal thoroughfares, parallel to each other. (Unfortunately the streetcar named Desire no longer passes by; it has become a prosaic bus.) St Peter Street, which crosses these others to lead to Jackson Square, has some particularly attractive buildings. And at Jackson Square, formerly the Place des Armes, is the Cathedral, built in the late eighteenth century but greatly altered since, and the Cabildo building, seat of the French and Spanish governing councils. Beyond the Square, towards the wharves to the east, is the old French Market, where twenty-four hours a day one can get delicious New Orleans doughnuts and delicious New Orleans coffee.

The French Quarter is not the only interesting section of the city, however. The Garden District is charming in quite a different way. In the nineteenth century, while the old French families tended to keep to themselves in the Quarter, wealthy Anglo-American planters built houses on the opposite side of town, along the Mississippi. The French Quarter is now largely abandoned to tourists, but the Garden District remains the most fashionable part of New Orleans, its handsome Greek Revival houses still beautifully cared for. The centre of the Garden District lies along Prytania and Chestnut Streets, between Washington Street and Jackson Avenue; the last of the New Orleans streetcars take one there, out along St Charles Avenue.

Among New Orleans' more unusual attractions are the old burying grounds. These have only tombs, not graves, and many of the tombs are particularly lovely, now romantically overgrown with flowering tropical vines almost hiding the crumbling masonry. Two of these old French cemeteries are at the edge of the French Quarter, and one is in the Garden District, on Prytania Street between Conery and Sixth.

Good food is such an important part of life in New Orleans that we feel we must mention our favourite places. Like all tourists, and a good many New Orleanians, we do like 'breakfast' at Brennan's, an old Sunday morning tradition. Otherwise, of all the many famous restaurants in the Quarter we prefer Galatoire's: no fuss and superb food. For a much simpler meal, but a good one, go to Tujague's, opposite the French Market, and have Cajun or Creole cooking family-style. The most interesting restaurant in the Garden District is Corinne Dunbar's: traditional New Orleans haute cuisine in a handsome old house. One must book in advance. Then to discover how good New Orleans cooking is at all levels, go for lunch to the Pearl, on St Charles Street just off Canal; you can have just oysters at the bar, or wonderful soft shell crab or shrimp in crusty sandwiches or fixed some other simple but delicious way. New Orleans oysters are the best in the world, and another good place to sample them is Felix's Oyster Bar in the Quarter.

The Gulf of Mexico near New Orleans is rather uninteresting except for the giant oil rigs working away miles out at sea. If you have no car, you might like to take one of the bayou and river cruises which go every morning from New Orleans' Canal Street docks. But if you do have a car, or are willing to hire one, there are two fascinating trips to be made out of the city: to the old sugar plantations along the Mississippi River, or into the Cajun country. Since they lie in the same general direction, one could also combine the two, given two or three days for the trip.

At one time there were great plantations all along the Mississippi, and there are minor roads which run close to the river on either side above New Orleans, past many of these plantation houses. A few are open to the public, and others can be seen from the road. Anyone setting off to see them ought to be equipped with *The Pelican Guide to Plantation Homes of Louisiana*, to aid in identification: it's a local New Orleans publication.

Many of the finest plantation houses in Louisiana were built in the first half of the nineteenth century, in the Greek Revival style, with great white columns, often all the way round. They were built high, the living quarters well clear of the ground; malaria was rife all through Louisiana. Later ones were often 'steamboat Gothic', mock-Gothic with carved wooden fretwork.

A wonderful example of Louisiana steamboat Gothic is the house called 'San Francisco' on the east bank of the river, beyond Reserve on State Route 44. If you are careful to keep close to the river as you continue on beyond 'San Francisco', on State Route 30 just after the town of Burnside you will come to a splendid example of the Greek Revival style, Houmas House. It is still complete even to its garconnières, and it is open to the public and certainly worth visiting. Another fine Greek Revival house, also open to the public, is Ashland-Belle Hélène, six miles beyond the town of Darrow on this same side. From Darrow one can take a little ferry across the Mississippi to the west bank, and return to the city on State Route 18 past more fine plantation houses, including the lovely pink Oak Alley with its splendid avenue of live-oaks, and the beautiful Evergreen. The latter is not open to the public, but one can at least admire from the road the graceful curve of its exterior stairs and the garconnières which flank the house. We might also mention that one can eat (but not cheaply) at a fine old plantation house on the outskirts of New Orleans; it's called Elmwood, and it's on State Route 48 at Harahan on the east bank near the Huey Long Bridge.

The Cajun country is French Louisiana again, but these French settlers were totally unlike the wealthy sugar-cane planters. This is the region west of New Orleans, along the bayous of the Mississippi flood plain. The word 'Cajun' is a corruption of 'Acadian'. The Acadians were French Canadians driven out of Nova Scotia in 1755 by the British. Many of them found their way to New Orleans, where the French colony helped to resettle them in Louisiana. The rather questionable help consisted of giving them 'the land of trembling prairies', low and marshy delta country where the unpredictable Mississippi floods made farming impossible, and so the Cajuns took to fur-trapping and fishing and hunting alligators for the hide. Much of their region was inaccessible except by boat, and for almost two hundred years they led a lonely and isolated life. Recently, the growth of the shrimp industry and the discovery of oil in these parts have brought about a considerable change in their world; there are better roads now, and real schools. But twenty years ago, the man from whom you asked directions along the road would probably have spoken no English at all, only 'Cajun' French, which bears slight resemblance to the Parisian variety. Today the only way to see the Cajun country as it used to be is to go along the lesser bayous in a boat, hardly practicable for the average tourist. Yet this section of Louisiana is still very interesting; one can drive along Bayou Lafourche on State Route 308 and watch the shrimp boats unloading their catch, and get at least some idea of life on the bayou.

Farther to the west, the town of Franklin has some beautiful old houses, as does St Martinsville. At New Iberia, a very handsome house called Shadows on the Teche is open to the public. And one of the high points of any trip into this part of Louisiana is a stop at Avery Island, which is actually no more nor less an island than the rest of this swamp country. Avery Island was known originally for its vast salt mines, the most important in the South. Today this area specializes in growing hot peppers to be turned into a famous Louisiana condiment called Tabasco Sauce. The real attraction at Avery Island, however, is its bird sanctuary, part of an estate called Jungle Gardens. Particularly in the nesting season one can see thousands of snowy egrets, and there are also beautiful flowering shrubs, camellias and wisteria and azaleas.

The Mississippi River still has the power to stir the imagination. Anyone can see it in New Orleans merely for the price of a city bus fare, but to see it more or less as it looked in the days when Mark Twain was a riverboat pilot, one must see it upstream, well away from the city.

In the first half of the nineteenth century, the Mississippi was the only practicable route into the central portion of the American continent, and it was crowded with every imaginable sort of barge and boat. The young Abe Lincoln, for example, took a load of hogs from Illinois down the Mississippi on a flatboat. (It was in New Orleans that he first saw slaves sold. 'That sight was a continual torment to me,' he wrote to a friend a few years later, 'a thing which has and continually exercises the power to make me miserable.')

Travellers in a hurry today go north from New Orleans through the state of Mississippi on Interstate 55, but if you have the time, take instead U.S. 61, the highway which runs closest to the river. Most of the way you will not actually see the Mississippi, unless you stop to climb up on the levee. But Route 61 takes you through Natchez and Vicksburg, two river ports which were important stops for the great paddle-wheel steamers. The large and handsome Greek Revival houses in Natchez recall the days when the wealthy planters of this rich Delta cotton country moved into town every year for the 'season'. Route 61 will also take you through much poorer towns, where white and black alike drowse in the courthouse square. This is the country of William Faulkner's novels; Jackson, Mississippi, is supposedly the Jefferson of Faulkner's stories, and he himself spent much of his life in Oxford, Mississippi, farther north. You will be very conscious of the gulf between black and white in this region, but you should know that in these heavily black counties along the Mississippi River something is stirring these days: effective black political organization which has had an impact even on national politics.

The city of Memphis, just across the state border in Tennessee, is the unofficial capital of the Mississippi Delta country, the cotton market centre. Yet Tennessee as a whole is by no means uniformly 'old South'. Both Tennessee and the state of Kentucky to the north are called 'border' states for good reason. Not only are they along the border which separated South from North in the Civil War; they are also divided internally between an essentially southern-planter tradition and the much simpler world of the Appalachian Mountains region.

The earliest frontier settlements west of the Appalachian Mountains were along the rivers in Kentucky and Tennessee and Ohio. The settlers there in the first third of the nineteenth century lived an incredibly rough, primitive life, menaced by Indians and bears, disease and crippling accident, and, perhaps worst of all, loneliness. Out of this world there came legendary frontier heroes like Daniel Boone and Davy Crockett, and also rough-hewn political leaders like Andrew Jackson and Abraham Lincoln.

Andrew Jackson was the first President from the new lands of the West, and his two tempestuous terms had lasting effects on the United States government. The Hermitage, where he lived with his beloved wife, Rachel, whenever he was not in Washington, is still standing and open to the public, a few miles east of Nashville, Tennessee. (Nashville itself is split between two traditions: on the one hand it is genteel 'old South', but on the other hand there is 'the Nashville sound', which denotes Nashville's importance as a recording centre for country music.)

Abraham Lincoln was born in a log cabin near Hodgenville, Kentucky; his father later moved the family to an even meaner existence in Indiana, and finally Illinois. The cabin in which Lincoln was born is still there, now part of a National Historic Site, but completely encased in a kind of mausoleum, as depressing a sight as ever was. Yet much of the country in this central part of Kentucky has scarcely changed at all in the past hundred years, and driving along Route 31E, it is easy to imagine the Lincoln family here.

Mammoth Cave is about fifty miles south-west of Hodgenville; advertisements for it adorn every road in Kentucky. A series of limestone caverns, it is a great tourist attraction; Mammoth Cave and the Carlsbad Caverns in New Mexico are the two largest caves in the United States. The main part of Mammoth Cave system is now protected within a small National Park, but the rest of the area, including several other caves, is individually owned and hideously commercial.

North-east of Hodgenville, around Bardstown, are several of the leading bourbon whisky distilleries, and then, after a stretch of poor hill country, one comes to the rolling blue-grass region around Lexington, Kentucky, where many of the finest American racehorses have been bred. Many of the big horse farms here allow visitors to see the stables and watch the horses being exercised. Lexington, like Louisville, along the Ohio River farther north, was an oasis of refinement in Kentucky's frontier days; these are both still attractive cities. Every spring Louisville has the Kentucky Derby, America's most important flat race.

We have already made reference to the Shaker movement, in our New England chapter. In the early nineteenth century Shaker communities were also established in what was then the frontier country of Ohio and Kentucky. At Pleasant Hill in Kentucky, about twenty miles south-west of Lexington along Route 68, one can see the most extensive Shaker community still standing. Making it a particularly interesting place to stop is the fact that one can spend the night there in one of the original Pleasant Hill 'family houses', and eat in the old Trustees House.

About thirty miles south-west of Pleasant Hill, just off Interstate 75, there is another equally tempting place to spend a night or have a meal: Berea, where there is a celebrated college which draws most of its students from the Appalachian Mountains region. This rugged mountain country of eastern Kentucky and Tennessee, West Virginia, and the western sections of Virginia and North Carolina, was settled in the eighteenth and early nineteenth centuries by pioneers of English and Scottish stock. Scratching a bare living from the soil, their descendants remained largely cut off from the rest of America. They clung to the Bible, and to old crafts, and square-dancing, and old ballads. In parts of this country, coal mining provided a limited amount of work, but the people still remained very poor. Recently, moreover, as underground mines have been largely abandoned in favour of surface strip-mining with enormous machines, the job possibilities have become even more limited and, particularly in Kentucky and West Virginia, parts of this once wild and beautiful country have been hideously disfigured. It is altogether a sad story.

Berea, however, is not at all a sad place. The students there help to support themselves through weaving and other crafts (there is a shop), and the college also runs a splendid hotel with delicious food, the old Boone Tavern.

In the Roosevelt era of the 1930s, the federal government developed a scheme to bring a better life to all of Kentucky and Tennessee: the Tennessee Valley Authority or T.V.A. Dams to generate electricity were constructed along the major rivers; the dams created many large lakes in both Kentucky and Tennessee, where it is pleasant to stop and swim or perhaps camp. The increased economic activity which did indeed result from the T.V.A. is especially apparent around Knoxville in Tennessee, the T.V.A. headquarters. Also near Knoxville is Oak Ridge, the oldest atomic research facility in the United States. The Atomic Energy Commission has an excellent museum there.

East of Knoxville are the Smoky Mountains, part of the Appalachian chain, and along the border between Tennessee and North Carolina is Greaty Smoky National Park, which encompasses an especially fine section of these mountains. The Appalachians are very old mountains, their contours softened by age, and the Smokies in particular are heavily timbered; their name comes from the soft blue haze that seems to hang over them. The only thing wrong with Great Smoky National Park is its enormous popularity; people flock there in spring to see the dogwood and the wild rhododendron, in summer to enjoy the fine vistas and the mountain coolness, in autumn for the spectacular colouring of the hardwood trees intermingled with spruce and fir. The glorious Blue Ridge Parkway, which runs from Great Smoky to Shenandoah National Park in Virginia, is sometimes over-full of cars, too, and even the hiking trails through Great Smoky and northwards along the Appalachian Trail are tending to attract too many people these days. The Park Service is beginning to limit the number of overnight hikers through a permit system. We do not recommend avoiding either Great Smoky or the Blue Ridge Parkway, but we do suggest going on weekdays rather than weekends, and getting off the main roads to explore the more remote sections. Do, however, see the pioneer settlement in the Park at Cade's Cove.

Just east of the Great Smoky Park there is a Cherokee Indian Reservation, The town of Cherokee is mostly full of souvenir stands and tourist traps, but the Oconaluftee Indian Village, the Museum of the Cherokee Indian, and the Qualla Indian Crafts Cooperative are all well worth visiting.

The attractive resort town of Asheville, North Carolina, serves as a sort of gateway to Great Smoky. Rich northerners discovered Asheville in the late nineteenth century, and the most sumptuous Vanderbilt mansion of them all is here: Biltmore, a latter-day Loire château. Mrs Vanderbilt became greatly interested in the folk culture of this region, and one should visit the crafts centre which she established, Biltmore Industries.

Interstate 40, which leads from Asheville towards Washington, D.C., passes the city of Winston-Salem in the North Carolina tobacco country. It is worth stopping there to see Old Salem, the restored section of town which was settled by industrious Moravians in the late eighteenth century. Several of the old buildings are open to the public.

We have talked about the old South but we have said very little about the new South, and we must close this chapter by paying tribute to the most shining example of the progressive new South, the city of Atlanta in Georgia. Atlanta's most celebrated product is Coca Cola, but it deserves to be known as well for its imaginative urban planning, which has made it one of the most attractive cities in America. It has spectacular new hotels, an underground street of shops and restaurants, an impressive Arts Center, and flowering shrubs and greenery everywhere. Even in racial matters, Atlanta is ahead of most of the country; it is hardly coincidental that Martin Luther King, Jr., should have come from

Atlanta. One can visit his father's church, the Ebeneezer Baptist, and his grave.

SPECIAL KNOWLEDGE

Just as you would hardly find a leisurely drive through the Rockies pleasantly relaxing in mid-winter, you would be unlikely to enjoy driving through the South in mid-summer, unless you had an air-conditioned car. Only the mountain regions of the South are really pleasant in summer. The low swampy areas are particularly bad, not only miserably hot but also plagued by swarms of mosquitoes. Thus we strongly advise against the Okefenokee and the Everglades in summer, and even New Orleans can be pretty bad. The perfect time for these areas is winter and early spring, and in the swamps there are many more birds to see then too. On the other hand, many motels and hotels along the Florida coast cut their rates in half from early May to Christmas, and of course all buildings are air-conditioned, so some people do like to go to the Florida beaches off-season. And as we have noted, summer is the best time there for snorkelling and skin-diving.

We don't want to scare anyone away from the South by talking too much about its mosquitoes; in parts of the North they can be a problem too in summer. But we do suggest that anyone going to the Everglades who is sensitive to mosquito bites should, even in winter, carry mosquito repellant and be prepared to use it particularly at dawn and dusk. Furthermore, campers should know that the mosquito menace is much worse at the Flamingo campsite than it is at the Royal Palm campsite; in the warmer months one should simply not camp at all at Flamingo. One useful thing to bear in mind about mosquitoes is that they are, as a Park naturalist put it, 'weak flyers'; they thus present no particular problem to anyone on a bicycle, in a moving boat, or on the Shark Valley Loop tram trip.

There is one other hazard at Everglades National Park. The Park Service does not itself run any of the lodges, restaurants, or organized boat or pack trips in the National Parks. These are all run by concessionaires, with Park Service rangers responsible only for naturalist walks and talks, and the protection of the Park's natural phenomena. At some Parks, Yosemite for example, the concessionaires seem to do a magnificent job. We were, however, not favourably impressed with the situation at Everglades; the lodge there is comfortable, but the food is mediocre at best, and the narration on the boat trip we took included too many bad jokes and too little accurate natural history. Perhaps at Everglades one ought to make a particular effort to get to one of the rangers' talks instead.

If you are driving to Florida without advance reservations, the Florida Welcome Station at Jennings on Interstate 75 will help you book a room. It's run by the state, without charge.

On busy days at the Kennedy Space Center, the tour buses vary their routes so that hundreds of visitors won't converge on the same spot; it is, after all, a working base. Thus if you are especially anxious to see some particular thing, like the flight crew training operation, make sure you are assigned to a bus which is going there.

The food in the South can be awful, but it can also be very good indeed. Places called 'Ye Olde Southern Tea Room' or the like are very apt to have good regional food, with delicious hot breads and desserts. There also seem to be many cafeterias in southern cities, and some, particularly the Morrison's chain, are really great: wonderful food at moderate prices. Finally, we must confess to an addiction to the pecan nut, and admit that we can never resist stopping at one of the omnipresent Stuckey's chain of roadside snack bars which specialize in pecans in various guises.

Abraham Lincoln Birthplace National Historic Site, Kentucky
3 miles south of Hodgenville on U.S. Route 31E. 1 September to 31 May 8–4.45; 1 June to 31 August 8–6.45. Closed 25 December. Free.

Asheville, North Carolina
BILTMORE HOUSE, 2 miles south on U.S. Route 25. 1 February to 15 December, daily 9–5. Closed Thanksgiving. Tour lasts 2 hours.
BILTMORE INDUSTRIES, off Macon Avenue. Appalachian Mountain Crafts. Monday to Friday 9–4.

Avery Island, Louisiana
JUNGLE GARDENS, off State Route 29. Summer, daily 8.30–5.30; winter, daily 8.30–5.

Beaufort, South Carolina
ST HELENA'S EPISCOPAL CHURCH, Church Street between King and North Streets.

Berea, Kentucky
BEREA COLLEGE, Monday to Friday 8.30–4.30, Saturday 8.30–11.30. Tours run by students leave Monday to Friday at 9.30 and 1.30, Saturday at 9.30.

Bulls Island, South Carolina
Bulls Island is part of Cape Romain National Wildlife Refuge. Information from Cape Romain National Wildlife Refuge, Route 1, Box 191, Awendaw, South Carolina 29429, or telephone (803) 928–3368. To reach the island turn off U.S. Route 17 about 13 miles north of Charleston and follow Sewee Road to Moore's Landing. Boat leaves daily at 8.30, returning from Bulls Island at 4.30. Free. Take picnic as no food available on the island. In November and December there are 3 one-week periods for controlled hunting, during which times the public may not go over.

Charleston, South Carolina
CHAMBER OF COMMERCE INFORMATION CENTER, on Lockwood Boulevard at the Municipal Marina. Daily 8.30–5.30. Useful tourist information.
CIRCULAR CONGREGATIONAL CHURCH, 136 Meeting Street.
CYPRESS GARDENS, 20 miles north, on U.S. Route 52, then 4 miles east. 15 February to 30 April, daily 8–6.
FIRST BAPTIST CHURCH, 61–63 Church Street. Daily 8.30–5.

FORT SUMTER can be reached by boat from the Municipal Yacht Basin at the west end of Broad Street. 2-hour tours leave daily, 15 June to 7 September at 9.30, 10.45, 12, 1.30, 2.30, 4; 16 March to 14 June and 8 September to 15 October at 10 and 2; 16 October to 28 February at 2.

MAGNOLIA GARDENS, north-west on State Route 61. 15 February to 1 May, daily 8–6.

MIDDLETON PLACE, north on State Route 61. Daily 8–5.

NATHANIEL RUSSELL HOUSE, 51 Meeting Street. Monday to Saturday 10–1 and 2–5, Sunday 2–5.

ST MICHAEL'S CHURCH, Broad and Meeting Streets. Daily 9–5.

Cherokee, North Carolina

MUSEUM OF THE CHEROKEE INDIAN, at the Information Center on U.S. Route 441. 1 June to 31 August, daily 8–7; 1 April to 31 May and 1 September to 30 November, daily 9–5.

OCONALUFTEE INDIAN VILLAGE, 20 May to 19 October, daily 9 a.m.–9.30 p.m.

QUALLA ARTS AND CRAFTS COOPERATIVE (Cherokee Indian), U.S. Routes 441 and 19 on the Cherokee Indian Reservation. Summer, daily 8–8; winter, daily 8–4.30.

Corkscrew Swamp Sanctuary, Florida

16 miles west of Immokalee on State Route 846. Daily 9–5.

Disney World, Florida

Near Orlando on U.S. Route 192, just west of 1A. Daily 10–6. Accommodation information from Walt Disney World Reservations, P.O. Box 78, Lake Buena Vista, Florida 32830. Telephone (305) 824–8000.

Everglades National Park, Florida

General and camping information from the Superintendent, Everglades National Park, Box 279, Homestead, Florida 33030. Accommodation is available at the Flamingo Inn or, more economical for families of 4 or 5, there are comfortable cottages where you can do your own cooking. There is a store that sells provisions. It is important to reserve accommodation at Flamingo well in advance during the winter season, which runs from mid-December to mid-April. Reservations may be obtained from the Everglades Park Co. Inc., 18494 South Federal Highway, Miami, Florida 33157. Telephone (305) 238–8771. Campgrounds are available at Flamingo and Long Pine Key on a first-come, first-served basis. Fibreglass boats with outboard motors can be rented for $16 per day; canoes $5 per day, plus a deposit; bicycles, hourly 50c or daily $2.50. Sightseeing boat trips lasting from 1 to 4 hours, daily 9–5, cost from $1.50 to $5. The Shark Valley Loop Trip, in a little open tram-train with sunshade roof, starts opposite the Miccosukee Restaurant on the Tamiami Trail on State Route 41. It runs 7 miles into the Park, 17 miles in all. Trips lasting 1½ hours start every 45 minutes from 9.30–4.15 in summer; in winter, every 30 minutes from 9.30–4.

Florida Cypress Gardens
5 miles south east of Winter Haven on State Route 540. Daily 8.30–5.

Florida State Parks
Reservation of campsites is possible if stay is between 4 and 14 days. For forms and further information write to the Florida Department of Natural Resources, Bureau of Education and Information, Room 664, Larson Building, Tallahassee, Florida 32304.

Great Smoky National Park, Tennessee and North Carolina
General information from the Superintendent, Great Smoky Mountains National Park, Gatlinburg, Tennessee 37738. The Administration Building is 2 miles south of Gatlinburg. There are many campsites in the Park, some with facilities and some more primitive. From 1 June to Labor Day there is a 7-day camping limit.

John Pennekamp State Park, Florida
For reservations for glass-bottom boat tours or snorkel tours, write to P.O. Box 140, Key Largo, Florida 33037 or telephone (305) 852–4300. Glass-Bottom Boat Tours, daily 10, 12.30 and 3; Snorkel Tours daily, lasting 2 hours, 9.30, 12.00, 2.15; lasting 3 hours, 9.30 and 1.30.

Kennedy Space Center, Florida
VISITOR INFORMATION CENTER on State Route 405, 6 miles east of U.S. Route 1. Daily, 8 to sunset. Closed 25 December. Free. Coach tours daily (except 25 December or rocket launching days) every 15 to 20 minutes from 8 until 2 hours before sunset. Tour lasts 2 hours.

Key West, Florida
AUDUBON HOUSE, Whitehead and Green Streets. Daily 9–12 and 1–5.
ERNEST HEMINGWAY HOME AND MUSEUM, 907 Whitehead Street. Daily 9–5.30.

Mammoth Cave National Park, Kentucky
10 miles west of Cave City. Tours leave from the Visitors Center and last $\frac{1}{2}$ to $4\frac{1}{2}$ hours. June to September, daily 7.30–4; October to June, daily 8–4.

Miami, Florida
FAIRCHILD TROPICAL GARDENS, 10901 Old Cutler Road (Coral Cables). Daily 10–5.

Nashville, Tennessee
THE HERMITAGE, 13 miles east off U.S. Route 70N. Daily 9–5. Closed 25 December.

New Bern, North Carolina
TRYON PALACE, George Street, between Eden and Metcalfe Streets. Tuesday to Saturday 9.30–4, Sunday 1.30–4. Closed 1 January, Easter and 24–26 December.

New Iberia, Louisiana
SHADOWS ON THE TÈCHE, Main and Weeks Streets. Daily 9–4.30.
Closed 25 December.

New Orleans, Louisiana
GREATER NEW ORLEANS TOURIST AND CONVENTION COMMISSION,
334 Royal Street.
THE CABILDO, Jackson Square, Wednesday to Sunday 9–5.
JAZZ MUSEUM, in the Royal Sonesta Hotel, on Bourbon and Conti Streets.
Monday to Saturday 10–5. Closed holidays.
MARK TWAIN BAYOU TRIP. Leaves Canal Street Docks at the end of Canal
Street daily at 11, returning at 4.

Oak Ridge, Tennessee
AMERICAN MUSEUM OF ATOMIC ENERGY, Oak Ridge Associated
University for the United States Atomic Energy Commission. Monday to
Saturday 9–5, Sunday 12.30–6.30. Closed 1 January, Thanksgiving and
25 December. Free.

Okefenoke Swamp and National Wildlife Refuge, Georgia
From the eastern entrance, 7 miles south-west of Folkston, Georgia, one
can take guided boat trips into the swamp. The prices range from $10
for 2 people for 2 hours to $25 for 2 people for 8 hours; proportionately
less if more people. Also from this entrance there is a boardwalk. At the
Stephen Foster State Park entrance, near Fargo, Georgia, there are cabins
and a campground. Information on the latter from the Refuge Manager,
Okefenokee National Wildlife Refuge, P.O. Box 117, Waycross, Georgia
31501.

Plantation Houses along the River Roads, near New Orleans
ASHLAND-BELLE HÉLÈNE, 6 miles above **Darrow**, off State Route 30.
Daily 9–4.
ELMWOOD, on State Route 48 at **Harahan**, near the Huey Long Bridge.
Restaurant reservations, telephone 732–6862. Closed Mardi Gras, 4 July,
Labor Day and 25 December.
HOUMAS HOUSE, on State Route 30 just above **Burnside**. Daily 10–4.
OAK ALLEY, 2½ miles west of **Vacherie** on State Route 18. Daily 9–5.
SAN FRANCISCO, 2 miles above **Reserve** on State Route 44. Daily 9–5.

Pleasant Hill Shaker Town, Kentucky
20 miles south-west of Lexington on U.S. Route 68. Daily 9.30–5.

St Augustine, Florida
SIGHTSEEING TRAINS start from 3 Cordova Street. Daily 8–6, summer
until 8.
CASTILLO DE SAN MARCO, just off Fort Marion Circle. Daily 8.30–5.30.
Closed 25 December.
MARINELAND OF FLORIDA, 18 miles south on State Route A1A. Daily

8–5.30. Shows and underwater feeding, daily 9.30, 11, 12.30, 2, 3.30 and 4.50.

OLDEST HOUSE, St Francis Street at Charlotte Street. Daily 9–6.

Sarasota, Florida

RINGLING MUSEUMS (including Asolo Theater and Museum of Art), 3 miles north on U.S. Route 41. Monday to Friday 9 a.m.–10 p.m., Saturday 9–5, Sunday 1–5.

SARASOTA JUNGLE GARDENS, 1½ miles north, west of U.S. Route 41, on Myrtle Street. 1 November to 31 May, daily 8 until sunset; 1 June to 31 October, daily 9 until sunset.

Savannah, Georgia

CHAMBER OF COMMERCE, Bay Street at the end of Drayton Street, for helpful information and maps.

HISTORIC SAVANNAH FOUNDATION has its own information desk in the De Soto Hilton Hotel, P.O. Box 8207. They also run 2-hour tours, Monday to Friday departing at 9.30 and 1.30.

BONAVENTURE CEMETERY, at the end of Bonaventure Avenue. Daily, sunrise to sunset.

DAVENPORT HOUSE, 324 East State Street at Habersham Street, facing Columbia Square. Monday to Saturday 10–5.

INDEPENDENT PRESBYTERIAN CHURCH, Bull Street at Oglethorpe Avenue. Monday to Friday 9–5, Saturday 9–12.

OWENS-THOMAS HOUSE, 124 Abercorn Street facing Oglethorpe Square. 1 October to 31 August, Tuesday to Saturday 10–5, Sunday and Monday 2–5.

7 · THE MIDWEST

When politicians give speeches in the Midwest, they usually start by saying what a pleasure it is to be in the real heartland of the United States. The mid-westerner is supposed to be the quintessential American; Thomas Edison, Mark Twain, Henry Ford, Walt Disney, and Dwight D. Eisenhower are good examples, all raised in small mid-western towns in a day when the Midwest was predominantly rural and agricultural. Today there is also the industrial Midwest, equally significant. It is chiefly concentrated in a broad band stretching west through Ohio (Cleveland, Canton, Akron, Toledo, Dayton) and southern Michigan (Detroit and its satellite towns) and Indiana (South Bend, Gary, Indianapolis) to Chicago, in Illinois.

The mid-western states of North and South Dakota, Nebraska, Kansas, Missouri, Iowa, Minnesota, Wisconsin, and even southern Illinois and Indiana, are still mainly agricultural. Of course 'agricultural' in America these days does not mean the same sort of 'small' family farm of one hundred acres or so which was characteristic fifty years ago. Even dairy farms are now considerably bigger than that, and in the wheat-growing region of the Great Plains, and in the corn (maize) belt, mechanization has now made farms five or ten times larger more nearly the rule. This has meant the death of many small towns, but the medium-sized towns in the agricultural states retain a flavour of the old Midwest. The supermarket and the Sears store and the J. C. Penney store may have replaced the old general store, but there will still be a Main Street, and the tree-shaded residential streets are still lined with houses made of wood and painted white.

Moreover, the whole of the Midwest, agricultural and industrial, is still very plainly melting-pot America. Many of the large industrial cities have distinct 'ethnic' sections, in which the children and grandchildren of Bohemian, Greek, Polish, Serbian, Italian immigrants still cluster together; and more and more today one also finds sections largely populated by southern black Americans, and also clusters of southern white Americans from the poor Appalachian regions. In the agricultural areas, one can discern patterns of settlement by Norwegians, or Swedes, or Germans, or Finns, or Swiss, in addition to the old 'Yankee' mix.

In this chapter we are covering an enormous area of the United States, and we must therefore be highly selective. Since the federally-subsidized interstate super-highway system makes it possible these days to by-pass almost every major city as one drives across America, we will do just that ourselves. Most midwestern cities are rather similar, and not especially interesting; we will mention only those which are in some way unique, or which are relevant for our chief area of concentration, the best of the rural Midwest. Nonetheless we urge anyone who does visit one of the major industrial cities to be sure not only to see what industrial tours might be available, but also to investigate the city's cultural resources. There are some extremely good art museums, symphony orchestras, and repertory theatres in many of these cities. Cleveland's orchestra, for example, is one of the best in America; Cleveland, Toledo, and Kansas City all have particularly interesting art museums; and so forth.

The two most important cities of the industrial Midwest, and the only ones we will discuss in any detail, are Detroit and Chicago.

Just as 'Wall Street' stands for high finance, so 'Detroit' means assembly-line production, especially in relation to the automobile industry. And in one way or another, all the chief sights of Detroit are connected with the automobile. First and foremost, there are tours of automobile assembly plants. Several different automobile companies offer free tours, but the best known and the most complete is the tour of Ford's River Rouge works in Dearborn, just outside Detroit. This tour is deservedly popular, and our only warning is that, like all the Detroit automobile works, Ford shuts down in summer for six weeks or two months, in order to re-tool for the next year's models. Usually this happens in early August and continues until sometime in September.

However, if you should arrive in Detroit only to find all the automobile works closed to the public, bear in mind that there are also interesting tours of the General Motors Technical Center which one can do only in summer. The Technical Center, itself a Saarinen design, is the General Motors research facility; it is situated in Warren, about twelve miles north of midtown Detroit.

Also in Dearborn, only a short city bus ride from the Ford Visitors Reception Center where the River Rouge works tours begin, there are two enormously popular tourist attractions, the Henry Ford Museum and Greenfield Village. These were both creations of the first Henry Ford, who compensated for his limited schooling with a determination which led not only to the development of the Ford car but which also made him an indefatigable collector. As one might expect, he loved machinery of every sort. He also had an almost superstitious reverence for history. Thus he was equally avid to acquire the chair in which Lincoln was sitting when he was assassinated, and the first model of the gramophone. The results might have been appalling had Henry Ford not been fortunate in his curators. As it is, however, the museum is great fun. The collection naturally includes a superb array of old cars and engines, but it also includes silver and furniture and chronometers and covered wagons and a 'street' of old shops, all housed in an immense reproduction of Philadelphia's Independence Hall. The admission fee is hardly minimal, but one does get one's money's worth; it takes several hours to see the museum properly.

Greenfield Village adjoins the museum, but has a separate admission fee. Like the museum, Greenfield Village is a wild mixture, for Henry Ford ended by collecting buildings, one hundred of them all-told. There is Wilbur and Orville Wright's bicycle shop, where those young men first began to work on a flying machine; Thomas Edison's laboratory, moved intact from Menlo Park in New Jersey, with even the old rubbish heap at the back carefully put into sacks and brought here for greater authenticity; early American houses of every sort; and eccentric additions like a Cotswold cottage. The buildings are grouped together to form a mock-village which is pure surrealism but, like the Museum, great fun.

In the summer one can wander at will in Greenfield Village, but for the rest of the year one can only go through on a guided tour. In winter there is a two-hour walking tour; for an extra charge one can instead make a forty-five minute trip around the Village in a horse-drawn omnibus, stopping to see four or five of the chief buildings. (When there is enough snow, the omnibus is replaced by a horse-drawn sleigh.) In summer the omnibus tour still runs, but one can also then have a ride in a pony cart or a Ford Model T car, or on a steamboat or a steam train.

Detroit itself is no uglier than any other industrial city, but like most large American cities it has suffered a blight at the heart as those who could afford to do so moved out to the suburbs. However, there is a handsome group of civic buildings, including a spectacular auditorium, along the river in the business centre. Canada lies just across the river, opposite these new buildings; the international boundary is the middle of the bridge. Detroit is thus both a port of entry and an important stop on the St Lawrence Seaway, situated as it is between Lake Erie and Lake Huron. There are public beaches not far from the centre of Detroit and an elaborate recreation area on Belle Isle in the river.

Most visitors go to Detroit to see the attractions connected one way or another with the automobile industry, but there are other interesting places nearby. For example, north of the city, in the attractive little town of Bloomfield Hills, there is the educational complex collectively known as 'Cranbrook'. Cranbrook is several separate institutions with a common aim: 'to inculcate an appreciation of art and nature . . . with a passion for public service.' There is a boys' school, a girls' school, and a school for small children; an academy of art, a science museum, and a handsome church. Eliel Saarinen designed many of the buildings, and his equally famous architect son, Eero Saarinen, used Cranbrook as his headquarters. There are innumerable examples of Milles sculpture dotted about the handsome grounds, the art galleries are open to the public daily during the summer and at weekends in the winter, and the science museum, although comparatively small, is extremely well done.

About thirty-five miles from Detroit in the opposite direction is the Enrico Fermi Atomic Power Plant near Monroe, which has special films and exhibits for visitors. And in Battle Creek, Michigan, to go from one extreme to the other, you can tour the Kellogg cereal factory.

Detroit is a modern industrial city, very American to be sure, but with resemblances to other modern industrial cities all over the world. Chicago is far more complex. In the first place, it is bigger.

Chicago is America's second largest city, and it stretches interminably across the prairie. Moreover, except for New York, no city in America was built of so many diverse foreign elements, and while older cities absorbed their immigrants, moulding them to established patterns, Chicago was apparently still too raw and impressionable herself to do this. Thus the concentration of immigrants there in the late nineteenth century, with their inbred hatred of the police and authority and their gratitude towards anyone who would take their part, led first to the rise of a political 'machine' in control of the city government, and later to organized crime and the gangster. Other cities produced gangsters, to be sure, but if one wanted a really splendid all-purpose model, one had to turn to Chicago.

Today the gangsters are largely gone, or at least not readily visible. Since the city is much favoured as a business convention centre, there is every sort of nightclub, but on the whole the picture Chicago presents to the world these days is that of a reformed rake. Handsome new skyscrapers rise throughout the central portion of the city, and there is much emphasis on clean streets and general tidiness in those parts of town seen by most visitors. Most of the affluent businessmen commute too, to attractive suburbs where one need not worry about city problems.

Yet away from the centre of town this melting-pot city continues to boil and bubble. As one drives through the west side of the city today or through parts of the north side, it is still possible to trace the waves of European immigration. For a few blocks the shop names and signs will combine English with Polish, and then comes a district where German predominates, or Czech or Polish. You cross a street and you have crossed a border. People who know the city well can point to little restaurants away from the centre of the town where the food is pure Budapest or Cracow or Dubrovnik. And near the quiet parks on the far west side where elderly men sit reading foreign newspapers, one finds onion-domed churches. Yet with immigration now drastically reduced, this Old World flavour must inevitably fade. And coming on to take its place there is a burgeoning black culture. The 1970 census showed that Chicago's population is now more than a third Negro, concentrated mostly on the city's south side. Chicago, which has always had a strong black middle class, is now becoming the headquarters for several major new black business enterprises.

The heart of modern Chicago is also the site of the earliest settlement, where the Chicago River meets Lake Michigan. There on the south bank of the river is the Loop, so called because the elevated trams make a circle round it. Within the square mile of the Loop are the big shops and the theatres; at its western edge, farthest from the lake, lies the financial district, mostly along La Salle Street. Across the river on the north bank is the section known as the Near North Side, with the Michigan Avenue Bridge the most important link between the Loop and the Near North Side; Michigan Avenue is to Chicago what Fifth Avenue is to New York. (Its nearness to the lake, however, means that walking along Michigan Avenue in the winter can leave one absolutely numbed with cold. As the driving snow whips around you, it is all too clear why Chicago is called 'the Windy City'.)

Chicago may have her faults, but she has done better by her lake shore than any other mid-western city. Between Michigan Avenue and the lake there are either parks or handsome skyscrapers and blocks of apartments, and along the very edge of the lake runs the Outer Drive, which makes it possible to get from one end of Chicago to the other without contending with midtown traffic. Also along the lake shore are many public beaches and man-made harbours for small boats.

The Loop is the section most visitors to Chicago see, but it is really rather drab nowadays, suffering from competition with the new suburban shopping centres. However, you might still like to visit Marshall Field's, the enormous department store which sells everything one could ever possibly want. For generations now its toy department has represented every mid-western child's Christmas dream.

You can go underground if you like from Marshall Field's all the way to the new Civic Center at the corner of Randolph and Dearborn Streets; there are two good reasons to go there, above-ground or below. First is the fact that at the Tourist Council information desk on the main floor of this handsome new building there sits a splendid lady who has an inexhaustible fund of information about her city and all manner of useful brochures and maps and guides to ease one's visit to Chicago. Secondly, in the plaza to the south of the building you can see the giant metal sculpture which Picasso did for Chicago. (And the next building to the west is the City-County building, the seat of all power and authority in Chicago.)

Chicago is rich in architectural landmarks too, and many of

them are in the Loop. For example, instead of going to the Civic Center direct from Marshall Field's, you might walk south along State Street to Madison Street, to see the Carson Pirie Scott building. Carson Pirie Scott is another good department store, but the building is notable because it was designed by Louis Sullivan, Chicago's influential late nineteenth-century architectural pioneer. Notice particularly the magnificent iron work on the façade. (And if you can find a way to get inside that other celebrated Sullivan building, the Auditorium Theater, by all means see that too.)

If you are going to the financial district, you might zig-zag from Carson Pirie Scott west on Monroe Street to Dearborn, south on Dearborn, and then west again along Jackson Street to La Salle Street. You would thus pass several early Chicago skyscrapers, as well as the new Inland Steel Building (corner of Monroe and Dearborn: Skidmore Owings and Merrill) and the new Federal Center (Dearborn between Adams and Jackson: Mies van der Rohe). The chief tourist sight in Chicago's financial district is 'the pits', the commodities exchange in the Board of Trade building, where Jackson Street crosses La Salle Street; from the visitors gallery one can watch frenzied trading in everything from wheat to silver. At 209 South La Salle Street, a block north of the Board of Trade, is the Rookery, a late-nineteenth-century building notable for its open use of structural iron work; walk into its inner court. And two blocks west of the Rookery, at Quincy and Franklin, you can see Chicago's newest skyscraper, the Sears Tower, designed by Skidmore Owings and Merrill; it will be the world's tallest (109 floors) when it is completed.

For a good cross-section of Chicago, however, one must also go to the Near North Side. It is only a short ride from the Loop on a bus; as you cross the river, to the west you can see along the river's edge the striking Marina Towers, tall round buildings in which each apartment is a pie-shaped wedge, and the lower floors form a parking ramp for the residents. Just across the Michigan Avenue bridge on the right-hand side is the Tribune Tower, the home of *The Chicago Tribune*, that newspaper which was for years the great trumpeter of Midwest isolationism and of both anti-British and anti-Communist sentiment. With the death of Colonel McCormick, its oracular publisher, the *Tribune*'s tone softened somewhat, but it is still very firm about its likes and dislikes and still a significant force in the Midwest.

The Water Tower, on Michigan Avenue at Chicago Avenue, is

one of Chicago's most famous landmarks, one of the few buildings to have survived the Chicago fire of 1871. A turreted mock-castle built of the coarse yellow stone characteristic of nineteenth-century Chicago, it embodies all the provincial ugliness of that era in a most endearing manner. Near the Water Tower along Michigan Avenue are the smartest shops, and between Michigan Avenue and the lake there are many expensive blocks of flats; the most celebrated are the two stark black metal and glass buildings designed in the 1950s by Mies van der Rohe, which stand on the lake front at Oak Street. The most dramatic new building along Michigan Avenue itself is the John Hancock Center. It has shops at the street level, parking ramps and business offices up to the fortieth floor, then fifty floors of apartments, then an expensive restaurant, and, finally, on the hundredth floor, an 'observatory'. One can pay to go up to the observatory, but it costs only slightly more to go instead for just a drink to the restaurant section.

It is enlightening to walk from the John Hancock Center west, from Michigan Avenue to Rush Street. For the Near North Side includes not only the expensive little galleries and boutiques that one finds along Michigan Avenue, but also the raucous nightclub district of Rush Street. And if one walks north along Rush Street and then continues north on State Street, ahead and on the side streets to the right are what remain of nineteenth century Chicago's grandest town houses, solid stone edifices not without a certain charm. Yet very near, off to the left, is one of Chicago's bleakest down-and-out districts. Together these two contrasting sections end in 'Old Town', a rehabilitated slum area now a cross between Greenwich Village and the Istanbul bazaar. There are many pseudo-colourful places to eat in Old Town, and some which are both fun and good value. (Knowledgeable Chicagoans say that for less touristy browsing and eating, one must press on beyond Old Town to the next district to the north, one of the old 'ethnic' neighbourhoods now known as 'New Town'.)

In the late nineteenth century, the American Baedeker urged all Chicago visitors to see the Stockyards, but the Chicago Stockyards, rendered obsolete by advances in refrigeration, are now shut down. In their stead, Chicago offers visitors a steadily improving cultural scene. The Chicago Symphony, long consider-ed one of the top five American orchestras (with New York, Boston, Philadelphia, and Cleveland) is today thought by some critics to be the very best of all. In summer, when its regular season is over, the Chicago Symphony plays at the open-air Ravinia Festival on Chicago's affluent North Shore; the Festival also includes chamber music and jazz and folk-rock, and special buses are run from Chicago for the concerts. In the autumn, Chicago's Lyric Opera has a fine three-month season. And Chicago also has some excellent museums. The Art Institute is probably the finest museum of art in the Midwest, particularly celebrated for its remarkable collection of French Impressionists. We are especially fond too of one of its minor treasures: 'Mrs Thorne's rooms', fifty-odd miniature rooms which illustrate decorative styles in Europe and America over the past four centuries. Some of the furniture is genuinely old, cabinet makers' samples or pieces made long ago for dolls' houses; the remaining things are meticulous copies, and there are tiny *petit-point* carpets, and exquisite miniature chandeliers and sconces. Seeing the rooms is like gazing into little sunlit corners of history; young and old alike are fascinated.

Out on the lake shore, there are three more museums grouped together: the Field Museum of Natural History, and an aquarium and a planetarium. All of these institutions are really splendid examples of their kind. The Field Museum is particularly noted for its natural-habitat groupings of African animals, but it also has a fine American Indian section and other good anthropological exhibits. And the Shedd Aquarium grows more exciting every year. Quite a distance south of the centre of Chicago, near that area of depressing dilapidation which harbours the University of Chicago, is the Museum of Science and Industry. It has a captured German U-boat, a simulated coal-mine trip, and a plethora of scientific and mathematical exhibits which can be activated by the push of a button. While many of the exhibits have been arranged by business firms, giving part of the museum the appearance of a trade fair, everyone seems to enjoy it.

If you come into Chicago from the East at night, you will see the sky filled with flames from the hearths of the steel mills at Gary, Indiana. This region just to the south-east of Chicago rivals Pittsburgh in the production of steel; there is nothing pretty about it in the daytime, but at night it has its own strange beauty. Indeed Chicago altogether may surprise you. If you happen to stay in a hotel room which looks out on to the lake, Chicago at dawn is a wonderful experience.

.   .   .   .   .

Most mid-western cities differ very little one from the other. Belching out industrial smoke or processing the products of mid-western agriculture, they have not yet found time for much beyond business, although here and there one is pleasantly surprised. Most of them are relatively young, lacking distinctive history and character. The exceptions to all this are some of the cities and towns along the Ohio River and the Mississippi. The rivers were the first highways into this heavily wooded wilderness; the first white settlements were made along their banks. The city of Cincinnati, in Ohio, for example, dates its founding to 1788; it was the first real town in what is now called the Midwest, and at one time no foreign visitor thought his trip to the States complete until he had seen Cincinnati. Everyone admired its situation, on the hills above *la belle rivière*, the loveliest river in America; and everyone described it as the one genuine cultural oasis of the rough American frontier.

The contrast with the rest of the Midwest is hardly so pronounced today, yet Cincinnati does seem to deserve special mention. Its situation is still handsome; the views are lovely from some of the more expensive residential sections, where innovative building has made good use of the terrain. Perhaps because nineteenth-century Cincinnati attracted many German and German-Jewish and French settlers, it has better restaurants than most mid-western cities, and it also has particularly good music. Everyone should see the striking modern auditoriums at the Cincinnati College-Conservatory of Music, and in summer enjoy the celebrated Cincinnati summer opera season. Our favourite Cincinnati museum is the Taft, a highly personal collection of art comparable to the Frick in New York. The Taft family is an eminent one in Ohio, and the museum building is the fine Greek Revival house in which Charles and Annie Taft lived and accumulated their treasures.

However, our chief excuse for mentioning Cincinnati is its situation on the Ohio River. If one has no chance of seeing the Ohio farther from civilization, one might take a short river trip on a reproduction of an old stern-wheeler from Covington, Kentucky, just across from Cincinnati. But anyone with time to spare should consider driving along the Ohio on one of the old river roads. The Ohio forms the border between the states of Ohio and Indiana on the one hand and West Virginia and Kentucky on the other, and almost the entire length is interesting to drive along, rich in scenery, and highly evocative of nineteenth-century America. Perhaps this is because the people hereabouts do still on the whole lead a simple life; in some places there are only ferries to cross the river, or perilously swinging foot bridges.

Not only the country along the river, but most of southern Ohio and southern Indiana is handsome rolling country, much more attractive than the flatter northern parts of those states. And there are four places in southern Indiana which warrant special mention. One is the extraordinary town of Columbus (not to be confused with the much larger Columbus in Ohio). Thanks to the munificence of one of its richest citizens, Columbus is a paradise for anyone interested in contemporary architecture. Every major building in town, the schools, the banks, the post office, the public library, and so forth, has been designed by one of America's leading architects. It has to be seen to be believed. Particularly satisfying, too, is the way in which the best of the old buildings have been preserved and integrated into the whole.

South-west of Columbus, along the Wabash River, is the old territorial capital of Vincennes. It has many nice old buildings, and there is a fine nineteenth-century feel to the place. And then along the Wabash River below Vincennes, in the south-western-most corner of Indiana, there is New Harmony. New Harmony began in 1814 as a communitarian settlement, established by a fervent German millenarian named George Rapp. When in 1824 the Rappites decided this frontier wilderness was not right for them, they sold the land and their buildings to Robert Owen, the Welsh mill-owner and social reformer who was eager at that point to put his Utopian ideas into practice in the New World. All things considered, the Owen experiment was a disaster, but the sort of things that were tried there, what New Harmony symbolized in the history of the American frontier and of social reform, make it a fascinating place. It is just the right size for walking around, and there is just enough to see, including several of the old buildings, the symbolic Rappite labyrinth, and a lovely modern 'roofless' church designed by Philip Johnson.

The fourth place one might stop in southern Indiana is at Bloomington, to see the University of Indiana. There are other mid-western universities which figure more prominently in the world of academic scholarship, but if one wants a good typical example of a large mid-western state university, one cannot do better than Indiana. It is very attractive: tree-shaded buildings, and typically mid-western undergraduates strolling about. It includes an exceptionally good music school, with the most ambitious opera programs of any American university; it has also given to the world the Kinsey reports.

We regret that we haven't space to talk about some of the attractive small towns in Ohio. There is no single cluster there with the historical interest of the ones we have mentioned in southern Indiana, but many are rich in Victorian wooden houses with splendidly carved decorative details. Many early-nineteenth-century Ohio settlers came from New York State, and architectural historians like to point to the way in which they brought architectural influences along with them. Few states appear so dull as Ohio when seen only from its superhighways, yet few are as rewarding as Ohio if one takes time to explore its out-of-the-way corners. Some of its small college towns, for example, Gambier or Granville, are lovely.

As white civilization spread over Ohio and Indiana in the early nineteenth century, the territory of Illinois became the new frontier. It was thus to Illinois that Abraham Lincoln's frontiersman father moved his family after first trying Kentucky and then Indiana. Many places along the way claim some relic of the Lincoln family's wandering, but the place most worth visiting today is that to which the young Abe Lincoln went to find work in the 1830s: New Salem, a few miles north of Springfield, in Illinois. It was there that Lincoln began to teach himself law, poring over Blackstone at night, and it was as New Salem's representative that he was elected to the Illinois legislature, his first political victory. New Salem was only a small village in Lincoln's time; all of the Illinois territory was then a sparsely populated wilderness. After Lincoln's day New Salem almost disappeared entirely, abandoned in favour of more promising towns, but now it has been restored and reconstructed so that it looks as it did in the 1830s: a group of log cabins and rough board buildings in wooded country on the bank of the peaceful little Sangamon River, a very satisfactory place for anyone curious about Abraham Lincoln or the life of the American frontier.

Anyone seriously interested in Lincoln ought to go to Springfield too. Springfield, the capital of Illinois, is a rather unprepossessing industrial town, but the old legislative building in which Lincoln served is still there, used today as the Sangamon County Courthouse. And the house in which Lincoln lived with

9. Mormon Temple
and Tabernacle (*left*)
Salt Lake City, Utah

10a. Air Force Academy Chapel, Colorado. Designed by Skidmore, Owings and Merrill

10b. Ice Rink, Yale University. Designed by Eero Saarinen

his wife and growing family, from 1844 until he left for Washington in 1861 to be inaugurated as President, is still standing, near the centre of town; it is open to the public. Finally, two miles north of town is his tomb; after the assassination, the funeral train brought Lincoln back to Springfield.

As we have said, the pattern of early settlement followed the rivers. New Salem was on the little Sangamon River, and Chicago began as a fortified trading post where the Chicago River meets Lake Michigan. Along the Mississippi, as one might expect, towns grew up even earlier. The largest today is St Louis, situated at the confluence of the Mississippi River and the Missouri River; it began in 1764, when a Frenchman from New Orleans settled there. For years it remained a minor French outpost, of interest only to trappers and river boatmen. But then the United States acquired the vast Louisiana Purchase territory, and in 1804 President Jefferson dispatched Merriwether Lewis and William Clark to start from St Louis and see if they could find a river route all the way to the Pacific Ocean. When Lewis and Clark returned to St Louis two and a half years later, with their maps and journals and reports about the buffalo and the shining plains and mountains to the west, St Louis almost immediately began to prosper, as the jumping-off point for westward expansion. Today its French heritage seems largely buried under a later German influx, and industrialization has blurred the whole, but St Louis nonetheless has many cosmopolitan aspects. We especially like both its art museum and its zoo.

Both up and down the Mississippi from St Louis today, one can still find ferries to take instead of bridges to cross the big river. Some of the ferries are quite primitive, and for a brief moment one is back in the nineteenth century. And about one hundred miles north of St Louis, on the Missouri side, there is a town which takes one back to nineteenth-century life along the Mississippi: Mark Twain's Hannibal, where Tom Sawyer and Huck Finn grew up. We recommend Hannibal. One of the pleasantest things one can do there is to picnic at Riverview Park, on the bluffs above the river. But one can also visit Mark Tain's boyhood home, and go out on a paddle-wheel excursion boat.

Another sixty miles or so farther up the Mississippi, on the Illinois side, there is another interesting old river town: Nauvoo. In 1839, Joseph Smith, the Mormon prophet, settled at Nauvoo with a large band of followers; they had tried to settle at Kirtland,

Ohio, but they had been driven away from there. There was hostility at Nauvoo too; in 1844, Smith himself was killed by a hostile mob, and two years later Brigham Young led most of the Nauvoo Mormons on to Utah. However, many of the Mormon-period buildings have survived, along the river bank below modern Nauvoo, and others are now being reconstructed by the Mormon-supported Nauvoo Restoration, Inc. For most of the buildings, the Mormons ask no admission fees of visitors, and Mormon volunteers also guide tours. The old Hotel Nauvoo (1840) is a pleasant place to stop too.

If you continue on up the river from Nauvoo, the next good stopping place might be Galena, Illinois, which is actually not on the Mississippi but a short distance up a tributary, the little Galena River. Galena was a booming lead-mining town in the early nineteenth century, long before most of this region was settled; it continued prosperous throughout most of the century, and then abruptly died. General Grant's father had a harness shop here, and after the Civil War the citizens of Galena presented a handsome house to the victorious leader of the Union forces. Grant and his wife lived in the house for several years, and Mrs Grant seems to have had wonderful taste; it's almost the only Victorian house we've ever wanted to move right into, horsehair furniture and all. But Galena altogether has considerable charm, with its steep streets and handsome old buildings.

In the south-western corner of Wisconsin, above Galena, there is another picturesque old lead-mining town, Mineral Point. Most of the early-nineteenth-century miners here were Cornish; their little granite cottages can still be seen along Shake Rag Street. The early mining settlements hereabouts were nowhere near as colourful as those farther west, where gold and silver were the prize. But they nonetheless retain a character not quite like other mid-western towns.

If you were to swing away from the Mississippi to see Mineral Point, you might go on to New Glarus, which was entirely settled by Swiss families from the canton of Glarus. New Glarus today makes much of its Swiss heritage, and one can have delicious fondues in its restaurants. Moreover, many Amish families have now bought farms around New Glarus, and one frequently meets Amish buggies on the back roads west of the town. In this same general region, near the town of Spring Green along the Wisconsin River, is Taliesen, Frank Lloyd Wright's house and architectural school; it is open to visitors in summer. This is all beautiful country, and it gives one an idea of the great variety of nationalities represented in the upper Midwest. Nearer to Madison, the capital of Wisconsin and a handsomely situated city surrounded by lakes, there are also several predominantly Norwegian towns. And Wisconsin's largest city, Milwaukee, reveals its German heritage as the beer-brewing centre of the United States.

On the Mississippi at Cassville in Wisconsin, some twenty miles above the Wisconsin–Illinois border, there is a reconstructed nineteenth-century farming village called Stonefield. Run by the Wisconsin State Historical Society, it is very well done, and fun to visit; in addition, there is a pleasant state park on the bluffs above it. The next sizeable town up-river is Prairie du Chien, originally a fur trappers station. The Villa Louis, the suprisingly grand house of John Jacob Astor's fur-buying agent here, is open to the public. Short river cruises go from Prairie du Chien too, on a reproduction of a paddle-wheel steamboat.

We might also note that across the river from Prairie du Chien, at McGregor, Iowa, one can rent a houseboat for a few days or a week and go on one's own river trip. This is becoming a very popular sort of holiday in America, and there are several places along the Mississippi with houseboats for hire. We mention McGregor simply because this seems a good place to start from, and we know the rates here are moderate. Furthermore, McGregor has another attraction; the Effigy Mounds National Monument at McGregor represents a unique preservation of the ritual burial barrows of the Moundbuilders, the chief Indian inhabitants of the Midwest in the centuries before Columbus. At McGregor, the principal mound is in the shape of a bear, but there are also other animals, and great birds. (There are remarkable mound sites in southern Ohio, too, but Effigy Mounds has the advantage of a particularly lovely setting above the Mississippi.)

At its southern end, the Mississippi flows through a flat flood plain; the farther one goes upstream, the higher rise the bluffs on either bank. The drive from Prairie du Chien to Minneapolis along the Wisconsin side of the river is lovely, and especially so in autumn when the foliage along the way turns brilliant colours. Minneapolis, reached at last, proves to be a handsome city with a strong Swedish tradition, a revitalized city centre with striking new buildings and walk-ways, and some interesting things to do and see, including the Tyrone Guthrie Repertory Theater and two good art galleries, the Walker and the Institute of Arts. And one might press on beyond Minneapolis; the North Woods of Minnesota and Wisconsin and the upper peninsula of Michigan are especially popular with campers and fishermen because of all the lakes. The biggest lake of all, of course, is Lake Superior, the second largest in the world. It is too cold for swimming, but it is beautiful to see, a deep blue made even more dramatic by the bronze and gold bluffs along much of its shoreline, and the dark pines. This is stark country, the chief industries fishing and copper-mining. The summers are brief, the winters long and very cold. But here again the autumn colours, especially as one drives along Lake Superior, are beautiful; and the air is exhilarating.

We realize that comparatively few people have time for a leisurely exploration of the Ohio River valley and a leisurely drive up the Mississippi. Driving straight across the continent is more likely, and so we will turn now to the major mid-western east-west routes which cross that vast area between the Mississippi River and the Rocky Mountains. (We will discuss them going from east to west; anyone coming the opposite direction must simply take our descriptions in reverse order.) First of all, however, we must stress the fact that this is indeed a vast area, hundreds of miles with little change of scenery. We will single out places where one might like to stop, but there are not a great many of them. Over the longest stretches, one must just keep reminding oneself that it was a lot worse in a covered wagon.

Heading for the Southwest, most Americans would probably take Interstate 44 from St Louis, which cuts diagonally across the state of Missouri. In the south-western corner of Missouri, this route goes along the upper edge of the Ozark Mountains region, which extends into Arkansas as well. The Ozarks are heavily wooded, covered in spring with dogwood and redbud bloom, and colourful in the autumn too. Like eastern Kentucky and Tennessee, these steep hills and valleys were settled originally by gun-toting, Bible-quoting English and Scotch–Irish frontier families, and until quite recently the people of the Ozarks remained isolated and poor. Thus this region too was rich in old lore and ballads, and in Ozark mountain resort towns like Eureka Springs in Arkansas one can sometimes still find good local crafts, wood-working or patchwork quilts perhaps, in amongst the standard tourist wares.

After skirting the Ozarks, Interstate 44 sweeps on into Oklahoma and thus out of this chapter. But we would like in any case to suggest an alternative route to the Southwest, one that we have found more attractive. We suggest going from St Louis to Topeka in Kansas on Interstate 70, then taking Interstate 35 (the Kansas Turnpike) through the Flint Hills region to Wichita, then west across Kansas to Colorado, and finally down from Colorado into New Mexico. In other words, we suggest beginning just as if one were going to Denver; for Denver, one would take Interstate 70 all the way.

Just before Kansas City on this route, one goes through Independence, Missouri, which was the starting point for most of the wagon trains. There is not much left in Independence from those early days; the chief attraction there now is the Harry Truman Library and Museum, containing the documents and memorabilia of that presidential administration. It seems customary now to assemble each president's papers in the town in which he was born or grew up; thus the Truman Library is at Independence, and the Eisenhower Library is about one hundred and fifty miles farther west along Interstate 70, in Abilene, Kansas. Abilene was not always so respectable, however. From 1867 to 1871, Abilene was known as the wildest town in the West. It was a station on the new railroad, only then reaching this part of America, and the railroad gave Texas ranchers at last a practical way to ship live cattle east to market. (Men had been raising cattle in Texas since the early part of the century, but until the coming of the railroad they could only hope to salt the beef and ship it by sea.) When cowboys arrived at Abilene, having driven huge herds all the way from their Texas ranges, many long weeks on the trail, they were ready to explode. In the hope of maintaining a vestige of law and order, Abilene hired Wild Bill Hickok as Marshal.

Meanwhile, however, Kansas was rapidly filling up with permanent settlers, farmers who hated the cattle drives and the cowboys, and tried to fence them out. The conflicts became so bitter that the cattle drives were forced to finish farther west, and Abilene's wild days came to an abrupt end. Its reputation and the men who had made it moved on to Dodge City, in the western part of the state; Dodge City is where Wyatt Earp and Bat Masterson first achieved fame. One would go through Abilene on Interstate 70 on the way to Denver, and one could go through

Dodge City on our suggested route to the Southwest. Dodge City is still fun to see, for enterprising townspeople have restored the old Front Street saloon area and fitted up a stagecoach for tourists to ride in.

Anyone who is driving across Kansas for the first time may wonder why we have not warned about the flatness, the monotony. The answer is that most of the alternatives are even less satisfactory; one must just learn to admire the sight of a great grain elevator rearing up fifty miles ahead, and not demand more in the way of scenery or sights. The mid-western states just to the west of the Mississippi River (Missouri and Iowa and Minnesota) are relatively varied in terrain, but the higher and dryer Great Plains which stretch beyond towards the Rockies are, as the name implies, flat and treeless. Kansas is actually the most pleasant of these Great Plains states, the most nearly verdant.

On its way west across the continent to San Francisco, Interstate 80 goes from Illinois through Iowa and Nebraska. Iowa is rich farming country, as anyone driving through can plainly see; the chief crops are corn (maize) and hogs. Just west of Iowa City it is pleasant to diverge from Interstate 80 to see the Amana Colonies, a group of inter-related villages settled in the 1850s by still another German religious sect. Originally life in the Amana Colonies was both communal and strict. Today many of the old ways have been abandoned, but the villages are organized into a joint stock company which makes refrigerators and air-conditioners as well as rhubarb wine and locally crafted furniture, and also runs the restaurants and bakeries to which tourists now flock. One can tour the wineries and manufacturing works, and one can also eat delicious food; we can particularly recommend the Ronneburg Restaurant at Amana. At Homestead, another of the villages, one can stay the night at a pleasant and inexpensive inn, Die Heimat. Then if one wanted to make another stop in Iowa, at Des Moines, the state capital, there is an attractive Saarinen-designed Art Center.

Nebraska, the next state, is a sort of prototype of the Great Plains. The winters here are bitterly cold, with blizzards; it is muddy in the spring, miserably hot in summer, and dusty in the autumn. They grow wheat in Nebraska, and the farmers who own the enormous wheat farms generally do well today. But you might not guess this from the look of the smaller towns, most of which seem never to have recovered from the depression period of the 1930s when much of Nebraska was a 'dust bowl'.

Nebraska was largely settled by 'homesteaders' to whom the government gave 160 acres on condition that they would stay on the land for at least five years. Many of these homesteaders were immigrants, from Bohemia and Germany and Finland and other corners of northern Europe; a surprising number of them managed somehow to stick it out, despite the appalling loneliness which seems to have been the worst hardship. There are two tourist attractions in Nebraska which do a good job of commemorating this era. One is the Pioneer Village at Minden, south of Kearney. It may sound like a tourist trap, and it is undeniably something of a jumble; but it has brought together many typical old pioneer Nebraska buildings, such as a sod house of the sort in which most pioneer families lived in the early days when there was neither timber nor stone to be had. The other interesting place, the Stuhr Museum of the Prairie Pioneer at Grand Island, is a more sophisticated commemoration. It includes a re-created pioneer community, but its main museum building is an impressive structure designed by Edward Durrell Stone and set in an artificial lake. How the early pioneers would have welcomed that view of water!

Americans driving from Chicago to the Northwest would probably take Interstate 90 all the way. It goes through the rolling dairy-farming country of Wisconsin, where circus enthusiasts might like to stop at Baraboo to see the Circus World Museum, an elaborate and lively evocation of the great travelling tent-circuses which criss-crossed America in the days before films and television. Next the route leads on through the farming country of Minnesota, and then crosses the Missouri River in the midst of the South Dakota plains.

There are several Indian reservations in South Dakota. When the homesteaders came into the northern plains region, they were displacing the natural owners, the Plains Indians. These were the Indians one sees in western films, wearing feather head-dresses and beaded buckskin clothing, hunting from horseback. Over the past hundred years theirs has been a grim lot; herded on to reservations, thousands died of malnutrition and tuberculosis, and even today they suffer from too little education and scant chance to make a decent living in what were once their ancestral lands. Visiting these reservations can be rather a chilling experience, but since tourist-money is better than no money at all, we might note that there are Indian crafts shops open in summer on the two large reservations south of Interstate 90, Rosebud and Pine Ridge. The Pine Ridge Reservation also includes the site of the Wounded Knee massacre, where in 1890 the United States Cavalry killed more than two hundred Sioux men, women, and children in one of the last and ugliest episodes connected with westward expansion.

North of the Pine Ridge Reservation is Badlands National Monument, one hundred and fifty square miles of strangely eroded country, 'Hell with the fires burnt out'. At sunset the colours are astonishingly beautiful. And then north-west of these Badlands there is another very different sort of landscape: rugged, pine-wooded mountains, a dramatic contrast to the terrain before and beyond. These are the Black Hills, a holy place to the Sioux, and now prime tourist country. Rapid City is the principal town of the Black Hills region, and the principal tourist attraction is Mount Rushmore, where a sculptor named Gutzon Borglum spent twenty years carving sixty-foot portrait heads of Washington, Jefferson, Lincoln, and Theodore Roosevelt on the sheer granite cliff-face. Illuminated at night, they are eerily impressive. But there is more to see than that. In Rapid City itself there is a Sioux Indian Museum and Crafts Center. Nearby are the old gold-mining towns of Deadwood and Lead; the Homestake Mine at Lead is still being worked and can be visited. One can camp in Custer State Park, a rugged wilderness area with a large buffalo herd and Rocky Mountain sheep and deer and elk. And adjoining it on the south there is Wind Cave National Park, which encompasses rolling prairie uplands, with more buffalo and also with colonies of one of our favourite western creatures, the prairie dog. You should drive the scenic Needles Highway, which goes in part through Custer State Park. And train fanciers should take the narrow-gauge railway trip which begins at Hill City. One must choose one's sights with some care, but if you avoid the obvious tourist traps, the Black Hills can be a splendid place to spend a few days.

The most northerly east-west route is Interstate 94. In Minnesota this goes through the North Woods lake country, where Indians in canoes harvest the valuable and delicious wild rice. By the time one reaches Bismarck, half-way across North Dakota, one should be eager to pause, and so we will note that in summer there is an Indian Crafts Cooperative shop in the State Capitol building at Bismarck, and if one drives five miles south of the city, one can see the Mary College buildings designed by Marcel Breuer. The only considerable tourist attraction in North Dakota, however, is another Badlands, at the western edge of the state. These Badlands are not quite so forbidding as those in South Dakota. In fact Theodore Roosevelt, who owned a ranch here in the late nineteenth century, found them beautiful; they contributed to his conviction that a major effort needed to be made to preserve the American wilderness, and this became one of his chief goals when he was elected President. It is fitting that park areas here in the North Dakota Badlands bear his name.

This western part of the Great Plains is cattle country, much more western than mid-western in feel. And our last 'sight' for this chapter is a relic of the early days of cattle ranching hereabouts. The great challenge then, as we suggested earlier, was to find better ways to turn a profit from cattle. In the 1880s, an eccentric Frenchman, the Marquis de Morès, decided the answer was to slaughter the cattle on the spot, chill the meat, and then ship it east. At Medora in the North Dakota Badlands he built huge ice-houses, and a splendid house for himself. He was nearly a century ahead of his time, of course, and the enterprise was a failure. His ice-houses long ago burned down; but his 'château' is still there, still furnished virtually as he left it, a memorial to one more dream shattered on the Great Plains.

SPECIAL KNOWLEDGE

There are Gray Line tours from **Detroit** which include the Henry Ford Museum, Greenfield Village, and the Ford River Rouge works. But if you are planning to visit Detroit simply as a tourist, you might prefer actually to stay at Dearborn, near those major tourist attractions; Dearborn has a wide range of accommodations. Wherever you plan to stay, beware of the fact that in summer Michigan, alone of the mid-western states, does not observe Daylight Saving Time.

The **Ohio and Indiana Turnpikes** (Interstate 80–90) are heavily travelled, and the motels along the way all seem alike. We do, however, know of one exception: the Homestead Inn Motel at the Milan exit of the Ohio Turnpike, midway between Cleveland and Toledo. It's run in conjunction with a good restaurant in a nice old house; Milan itself, the pleasant little town in which Thomas Edison grew up, also has a charming old inn.

In **Chicago**, we generally prefer to stay at a hotel on the Near North Side, but some of the hotels in the Loop which cater principally for businessmen try to increase their weekend business by offering bargain rates then; it's worth inquiring. Our favourite Chicago restaurant is Biggs, but it is moderately expensive; there are several good 'ethnic' restaurants which are less costly. One can eat, expensively, ninety-five floors up in the John Hancock Center; there is also the Top of the Rock, in the Prudential building, and the Pinnacle Restaurant, which revolves, thirty-three floors high, at the top of the Holiday Inn on the lakefront at Ontario Street. For guided architectural walking tours of Chicago, see our listings at the end of this chapter. But there is also an excellent self-guiding brochure issued free by Chicago's First National Bank; inquire at the Tourist Council information desk at the Civic Center.

One pleasing aspect of travel in the Midwest is its cost; in the rural Midwest, motel rooms and meals are on the average considerably less expensive than in the East. Moreover, near most of the places we have mentioned along the **Ohio and Mississippi Rivers**, you will find pleasant state parks in which to picnic or camp; Indiana, Illinois, Missouri, Wisconsin, and Minnesota all have excellent state park systems. That part of the Midwest is also a good place to sample a 'tourist home', the American version of bed and breakfast. However, as one heads west into the Great Plains region, the country becomes less congenial. There are places to camp there, but except in the Black Hills they are generally much less tempting; one hot summer's day we drove a long way from the super-highway to get to a lake in Nebraska, only to find it about ten inches deep and covered in green slime. It's not all that bad, but that may just be the region in which to sample a big motel.

As a general rule, Anglicize any French place-names you encounter; Prairie du Chien is Prairie du 'sheen', Des Moines is 'da moyn'. And Sioux is 'soo'.

For a picture of Mississippi River life in the nineteenth century, there is no one better than Mark Twain. But the Great Plains region has also inspired some American classics. For a picture of the hard and lonely life of the pioneers, read Willa Cather's *My Antonia* or Mari Sandoz's *Old Jules*; for the equally lonely life in an isolated mid-western town, read Sinclair Lewis's *Main Street*. And then to learn all the ugly facts about what westward expansion meant to the American Indian, read Dee Brown's *Bury My Heart at Wounded Knee*, a recent book readily available in paperback.

Abilene, Kansas
EISENHOWER CENTER, on State Route 15 (South East 4th Street). Daily 9–4.45. Closed 1 January, Thanksgiving and 25 December.

Badlands, South Dakota
BADLANDS NATIONAL MONUMENT, on U.S. Route 16A off U.S. Route 90. The Visitor Center is open all the year round. Nature walks are taken by ranger-naturalists daily during the summer. For accommodation information see **Black Hills**.

Battle Creek, Michigan

KELLOGG CEREAL FACTORY. Conducted tours Monday to Friday 9–4. Closed holidays. Free.

Bismarck, North Dakota

AMERICAN INDIANS CRAFTS COOPERATIVE, State Capitol Building. Summer 1–5.

Black Hills, South Dakota

BLACK HILLS AND BADLAND ACCOMMODATION. For information write to The Black Hills, Badlands and Lakes Association, P.O. Box 539, Sturgis, South Dakota.

CUSTER STATE PARK, 5 miles east of Custer on U.S. Route 16A. The museum, food facilities and camping facilities are open 15 May to 30 September.

WIND CAVE NATIONAL PARK, 7 miles east of Pringle on U.S. Route 385. General information from the Superintendent, Wind Cave National Park, Hot Springs, South Dakota 57747. The cave is open 1 April to 31 October. Tours last 1 to 1½ hours; ask at the Visitor Center for times.

Bloomfield Hills, Michigan

CRANBROOK INSTITUTIONS, 20 miles north-west of Detroit off U.S. Route 10.

ART GALLERIES. Tuesday to Sunday 1–5. Closed major holidays.
SCIENCE MUSEUM. Monday to Friday 10–5, Saturday and Sunday 1–5. Closed major holidays.
GARDENS AND PARK. 1 May to 31 October, daily 1–5.

Cassville, Wisconsin

STONEFIELD STATE FARM, an open-air museum, 1½ miles north-west on County VV, in the Nelson Dewey Memorial State Park. 1 May to 1 November, daily 9–5.

Chicago, Illinois

TOURIST COUNCIL INFORMATION DESK, Civic Center, Dearborn and Randolph Streets. Monday to Friday 9–1.15 and 2.15–5. Telephone 321–8896.

'CHICAGO SCHOOL' ARCHITECTURAL TOURS. Guided walking tours of significant Chicago buildings. Tours begin from the steps of the Chicago Public Library at Randolph Street and Michigan Avenue, Tuesday, Thursday and Saturday 10 a.m., Sunday 2 p.m. $1 contribution. Further information from Glessner House, telephone 326–1393.

COMMODITIES EXCHANGE, Board of Trade Building, 141 West Jackson Boulevard at La Salle Street. Weekdays 9.30–1.15. Free.

FIELD MUSEUM OF NATURAL HISTORY, ADLER PLANETARIUM AND SHEDD AQUARIUM, Grant Park, Lake Shore Drive at Roosevelt Road.

FIELD MUSEUM OF NATURAL HISTORY. 1 May to Labor Day, Monday,

Tuesday, Thursday 9–6, Wednesday, Friday, Saturday, Sunday 9–9; September, October, March, April, daily 9–5, Friday until 9, Saturday, Sunday until 5. Closed 1 January and 25 December. Friday free.

ADLER PLANETARIUM. 1 June to 30 August, daily 9.30–9.30, Monday until 5; rest of the year, daily 9.30–4.30, Tuesday, Friday until 9.30.

SHEDD AQUARIUM. 1 May to 31 August, daily 9–5; 1 November to 28 February, daily 10–4; rest of the year, daily 10–5.

HANCOCK CENTER, 875 North Michigan Avenue. Daily 9 a.m.–midnight.

MUSEUM OF SCIENCE AND INDUSTRY, Lake Shore Drive and 57th Street. Monday to Saturday 9.30–5.30, Sunday and holidays 10–6. Closed 25 December.

RAVINIA FESTIVAL. Mid-June to mid-September. For information write to 22 West Monroe Street, Chicago 60603 or telephone 782–9696.

Cincinnati, Ohio

TAFT MUSEUM, 316 Pike Stret. Monday to Saturday 10–5, Sunday and holidays 2–5. Free.

Cleveland, Ohio

MUSEUM OF ART, 11150 East Boulevard. Tuesday, Thursday, Friday 10–6, Wednesday 10–10, Sunday 1–6. Closed 1 January, 4 July, Thanksgiving and 25 December. Free.

Covington, Kentucky

MARK TWAIN SCENIC CRUISES, leave from Greenup Street Dock. 1 June to 31 August, 2½ hour cruises Tuesday and Wednesday, 3 hour cruises Sunday and holidays, leaving at 2.

Dearborn, Michigan

FORD VISITOR RECEPTION CENTER, East Concourse, Central Office Building, Michigan Avenue (U.S. Route 12) at Southfield Road. Tours leave every half-hour, Monday to Friday 9–2.30. Closed holidays, including Good Friday and 2 weeks from a week before Christmas to the day after New Year's Day and for 6 to 8 weeks in the summer, when the assembly line is shut.

GREENFIELD VILLAGE, off Michigan Avenue (U.S. Route 12). Daily summer, 9–6; winter 9–5. Closed 1 January, Thanksgiving and 25 December.

HENRY FORD MUSEUM, in Greenfield Village. Daily summer 9–6; winter 9–5. Closed 1 January, Thanksgiving and 25 December.

Detroit, Michigan

DETROIT CONVENTION AND TOURIST BUREAU. 626 Washington Boulevard at Grand River Avenue, Detroit 26, Michigan.

GENERAL MOTORS TECHNICAL CENTER, 12 Mile Road and Mound Road in Warren. Tours run from 1 June to Labor Day, Monday to Saturday 10–4, Sunday 12–4.

Dodge City, Kansas

OLD FRONT STREET at the foot of Boot Hill. Daily summer 7.30 a.m. to 10 p.m., winter 8–6.

Effigy Mounds National Monument, Iowa

On State Route 76 near McGregor. Daily, summer 8–7, winter 8–5.

Galena, Illinois

GENERAL GRANT'S HOUSE, Bouthillier Street. Daily 9–5. Closed 1 January, Thanksgiving, and 25 December. Free.

Grand Island, Nebraska

STUHR MUSEUM OF THE PRAIRIE PIONEER, at the junction of U.S. Routes 34 and 281. 30 May to Labor Day, Monday to Saturday 9–7, Sunday 1–7; Labor Day to 29 May, Monday to Saturday 9–5, Sunday 1–5. Closed 1 January, Thanksgiving and 25 December.

Hannibal, Missouri

EXCURSION BOAT, leaves from the foot of Center Street. 1 May to Labor Day, Tuesday to Sunday, 5 departures between 11 and 7; 1- and 2-hour trips.

MARK TWAIN'S HOUSE, 206 Hill Street. 1 June to 30 September, daily 8–8; 1 October to 30 April daily 8–5. Closed 1 January, Thanksgiving and 25 December. Free.

Hill City, South Dakota

1880 TRAIN runs between Hill City and Keystone, leaving from 2 blocks east of U.S. Route 16 and 385. 11 June to 31 August, Monday to Saturday 8.15, 10.30, 1, 3.30, Sunday 10.30, 1, 3.30. Longer trips on Saturday for which reservations are required: reservations from W. B. Heckman, Black Hills Railroad, Hill City, South Dakota 57745.

Independence, Missouri

HARRY TRUMAN LIBRARY AND MUSEUM, north-west on U.S. Route 24. Monday to Saturday 9–5; 16 May to 15 September Sunday 10–5; 16 September to 15 May, Sunday 2–5. Closed 1 January, Thanksgiving and 25 December.

Kansas City, Missouri

WILLIAM ROCKHILL NELSON GALLERY OF ART, 45th Terrace and Oak Street. Tuesday to Saturday 10–5, Sunday 2–6. Closed major holidays. Saturday and Sunday free.

Lead, South Dakota

HOMESTAKE MINE, on U.S. Route 14A and 85. 1 June to 31 August, Monday to Saturday 8–5, Sunday 8–4; May, September, October, Monday to Saturday 8–3.30. Closed holidays.

McGregor, Iowa

BOATELS INC., rents houseboats for prices ranging from $150 to $400 a week.

Minden, Nebraska

HAROLD WARP PIONEER VILLAGE, on U.S. Routes 6, 34 and State Route 1D. Daily 8–7.

Minneapolis, Minnesota

MINNEAPOLIS INSTITUTE OF ARTS at 201 East 24th Street. Tuesday 10–10, Wednesday to Saturday 10–5, Sunday 1–5. Closed 25 December. Free.

WALKER ART CENTER, Hennepin Avenue and Vineland Place. 1 April to 31 October, Tuesday and Thursday 10–10, Wednesday, Friday, Saturday 10–5, Sunday 12–6; 1 November to 31 March, Tuesday 10–9, Wednesday to Saturday 10–5, Sunday 12–6. Closed holidays. Free.

Monroe, Michigan

ENRICO FERMI ATOMIC POWER PLANT, 7 miles north off Old Dixie Highway. Tuesday to Saturday 10–4.

Nauvoo Restoration Inc., Illinois

INFORMATION CENTER, Mulholland Street.

JOSEPH SMITH PROPERTIES (includes several of the original buildings), 3 blocks west of State Route 96 along the Mississippi River. 1 June to 15 September, daily 8–6; 16 September to 31 May, daily 8.30–5.

New Harmony, Indiana

VISITORS INFORMATION CENTER on U.S. Route 460, for brochures and walking guides.

NEW HARMONY STATE MEMORIAL. Open 1 May to 31 October. This includes the Rappite Labyrinth, Number Two Dormitory and Fauntleroy House.

ROOFLESS CHURCH, at North and Main Streets. Daily 8 a.m.–10 p.m.

WORKING MEN'S INSTITUTE, 1 May to 31 October, Tuesday to Saturday 10–4, Sunday 2–5.

New Salem, Illinois

LINCOLN'S NEW SALEM STATE PARK, on State Routes 97 and 123. Buildings open 15 April to 15 October, daily 8.30–5.

Pine Ridge Reservation, South Dakota

ARTS AND CRAFTS SHOP, U.S. Route 18 and State Route 87. Daily 9–12 and 1–5.

Prairie du Chien, Wisconsin

RIVER CRUISES, depart from the Villa Louis Landing, 30 May to Labor

Day, daily at 1, 2.15, 3.30, 6.30. Some cruises operate earlier and later in the year; check schedule locally.

VILLA LOUIS, north-west on Villa Louis Road. 1 May to 1 November, daily 9–5.

Rapid City, South Dakota

SIOUX INDIAN MUSEUM AND CRAFTS CENTER, 1002 St Joe Street, in Halley Park. Winter, Tuesday to Saturday 9–12, 1–4.30, Sunday 1–4.30; summer, Monday to Saturday 8–5, Sunday 1–5.

Rosebud Reservation, South Dakota

LAKOTA ARTS AND CRAFTS, at Rosebud, west of Mission, 12 miles south-west of U.S. Route 18. Daily 8–12 and 1–5.

St Louis, Missouri

ST LOUIS ART MUSEUM, in Forest Park. Wednesday to Sunday 10–5, Tuesday 2.30–9.30. Closed 1 January and 25 December. Free.

ST LOUIS ZOO, in Forest Park, 15 February to 30 November, daily 9–5; 1 December to 14 February, daily 9–4.30. Mid-May to late September, animal shows daily.

Springfield, Illinois

LINCOLN'S HOUSE, 8th and Jackson Streets. Daily 9–5. Closed 1 January, Thanksgiving and 25 December.

Spring Green, Wisconsin

TALIESEN, 2 miles east on U.S. Route 14, then 2 miles south on State Route 23. Tours of the school are from mid-June to Labor Day, Monday to Saturday 9–5, Sunday 12–5. Tours may be temporarily suspended without notice.

Toledo, Ohio

TOLEDO MUSEUM OF ART, Monroe Street at Scottwood Avenue. Tuesday to Saturday 9–5, Sunday, Monday and Holidays 1–5. Free.

8 · THE ROCKIES

We are including in this chapter the states of Montana, Idaho, Wyoming, most of Colorado, and the northern half of Utah. Approaching this region from the east, one climbs almost imperceptibly across the high plains country where first the buffalo roamed and then the longhorn steer. Then at about the longitude of Denver, the Rockies rear up like a wall, and from there on westwards one is in the midst of mountains. In the heart of this mountainous section there are four splendid National Parks.

Cynics may tell you that the West today is only synthetically colourful, the cattle-and-cowboy world now altered beyond recognition and the National Parks overrun with tourists. Let the cynics stay at home. One day, going along some side road in Colorado or Wyoming or Montana, you will come upon two or three cowboys jogging along behind some cattle, and you will know that the West is still all right. Or you will climb to the top of a high pass, perhaps in one of the National Parks, and be staggered by the rugged, towering mass of the Rockies around you, the continent stretching away to the east until the visible curve of the earth hides it from your sight. Then you will know that the West is not merely all right; it is still magnificent.

Most of the territory described in this chapter was not settled until the last third of the nineteenth century, and once one has seen the Rockies, it is easy to understand why settlement was so long delayed. Driving east or west through Colorado, for example, you have your choice of several passes over the Continental Divide, that invisible line along the spine of the Rockies which separates the eastern watershed in America from the western. One pass is Monarch, at 11,302 feet; another is Loveland, 11,992 feet; Wolf Creek Pass, 10,857 feet, is comparatively tame, but Independence Pass is over 12,000 feet, and quite terrifying. It is little wonder that wagon trains, which began crossing the continent to California as early as 1841, generally avoided Colorado. Some of them used the Santa Fe Trail and the California Trail south of Colorado. Others took the Oregon Trail through South Pass in Wyoming, the one gap in the wall of the Rockies in these parts.

The only white men who were familiar with this area in the early years were the 'mountain men', the trappers and hunters who ranged far and wide through the Rockies in search of beaver. From the time the Lewis and Clark expedition in 1804 revealed the possibilities of the West until civilization finally overtook it, the Rockies belonged to the mountain men. Most of them were Americans for whom the East was now too settled, but many were French–Canadian, some English, some Irish. Their custom was to gather at a trading post once a year to sell their furs and hear news of the outside world; the rest of the year each man moved through the wilderness alone, or at most with an Indian woman to keep him company.

When parties of settlers bound for California began to come through the Rockies, a mountain man was sometimes persuaded to act as guide. He was invaluable of course, knowing the terrain and the Indians as he did. But in this manner men like Jim Bridger and 'Broken Hand' Fitzpatrick, helping to map the trails and ease the crossings, were actually contributing to the destruction of their own way of life. There is a fascinating book called *A Lady's Life in the Rocky Mountains*, written by an intrepid Englishwoman, Isabella Bird, the first woman ever elected a Fellow of the Royal Geographical Society. She spent the year 1873 in the Colorado Rockies entirely on her own, and the most unforgettable character she encountered there was one Mountain Jim, a strange and romantic figure who was to be quite literally killed by encroaching civilization. At that, he had already outlasted most of his breed.

The mountain men vanished, but their mountains are still the basic fact of this part of the West. There are other things to draw one here, of course: cowboys, and deserted mining towns, and Mormon settlements. But over everything tower the Rockies.

Since four of the finest sections of the Rockies have been made

National Parks, visiting these National Parks is the most popular way to sample what the Rockies have to offer. People with a great deal of mountain experience in the West may go instead to more primitive regions where there are no marked trails at all and one can be completely on one's own, fifty miles from any other human being. But even in the most popular National Parks there are still vast unspoiled areas for those willing to go some distance from the roads and the information centres. Moreover, anyone unfamiliar with the Rockies will find that the maps and brochures and advice available in the National Parks add greatly to one's enjoyment and understanding of this region.

In Chapter 1, we discussed ways of getting information about the National Parks. In addition to camping facilities, there are accommodations at almost all the major Parks, but, as we indicated, the type and character vary considerably from one Park to the next, since concessionaires and not the Park Service actually run the lodges and the places to eat or buy food. The Park Service itself concentrates on protecting the flora and fauna, and also protecting tourists from their own inadequacies. Park regulations are extremely strict about disturbing the vegetation, harming the animals, and being careless with cigarettes and fires. Fire is the chief menace to these mountains, for even when things look green this is dry country, and forest fires can and do spread with horrifying speed. Thus there are firm regulations about camping, and permits are usually necessary for camp-fires.

The most famous National Park is Yellowstone, which was also the very first. It is the biggest too: more than sixty miles long and fifty miles wide. Most of it is in Wyoming, in the north-west corner of that state, but a bit overlaps into the neighbouring states of Idaho and Montana. Well-to-do travellers were going to Yellowstone even before the turn of the century, to marvel at the geysers and the falls and to exclaim at the grandeur of the vistas; it was very much the fashionable thing. These days it may not be so fashionable, but it is immensely popular. Especially in July and August, tourists pour into Yellowstone in overpowering waves, every available bed is booked weeks in advance, and would-be campers arrive at dawn at the established campsites, hoping to get a place as someone else leaves. (Campsites cannot be reserved ahead.)

Ideally, one should plan one's trip to Yellowstone for June or September, to avoid the tourist crush; in June the days are longer and the waterfalls are also at their most spectacular, and in September the Rockies have a mellow glow. These are the best months, too, to see the elk and moose and other animals; in midsummer they tend to disappear off into the higher reaches of the mountains. If you must see Yellowstone in July or August, you might consider staying outside the Park, in one of the small towns around the edge; or plan to camp not in the Park but in one of the nearby National Forest areas. (We will say more about the National Forests later in this chapter.) Another interesting alternative for campers would be the Bighorn National Recreation Area about one hundred miles east of Yellowstone, in Montana but just north of Lovell, Wyoming; it has a magnificent canyon, a new lake, interesting Indian remains, and great numbers of animals. (And a hundred miles is no distance in the American West!)

In any event, whenever you come to Yellowstone, do not simply concentrate on the geysers. They are certainly Yellowstone's most unusual feature; only in New Zealand is there anything even faintly comparable, and Yellowstone's relics of extraordinary volcanic activity are even more unusual and dramatic. But one should not think of Yellowstone only in terms of geysers and beggar bears, its other most celebrated feature. (One is warned not to feed the bears, but people do, and so they prowl around every campsite and even come to stand at car windows, hoping for a hand-out.) If you expect a National Park in the Rockies to be dramatically ringed by towering mountain peaks, then you will prefer one of the other three to Yellowstone; the Yellowstone region is already so high itself that the effect of the peaks around it is somewhat muted. But Yellowstone has great stands of pine trees, and carpets of wild flowers on its upland meadows, a splendid lake, a remarkable canyon, and beautiful waterfalls. If you can't 'back-pack' off into the more remote areas at least take as long a nature-trail hike as possible. At Yellowstone, as at all National Parks, there are excellent free brochures about the trails, and one can also buy all manner of books and booklets about the natural history of the region.

Yellowstone is 'open' all year, in the sense that if you can get there you can get in, at least through the north entrance at Gardiner, Montana. But the facilities, bus service to it, and the lodges and eating places, only begin to function in late May, and start closing down again by October. You need not ask why once you have seen the snow poles along the edges of the Park roads; six feet high, they are to indicate to the men who drive snow-ploughs where they may expect to find a road beneath the drifts. When there is no snow problem, you can get into Yellowstone at any of five entrances. The approach to the north-east entrance, by way of Red Lodge, Montana, is reputed to be the most dramatic.

Just below Yellowstone is a much newer National Park, Grand Teton, which includes most of what is known as Jackson Hole, a valley almost completely surrounded by high mountains. In the early nineteenth century, Jackson Hole and the Tetons above it were the favourite hunting-grounds of the mountain men; later the valley became notorious as a hideout for cattle rustlers and outlaws. But once this part of the West became better known, the hapless inhabitants of Jackson Hole had honesty and prosperity thrust upon them; the area was simply too choice to waste on ne'er-do-wells.

The Tetons are a spectacular range of the Rockies, with majestic snow-crowned peaks, and beautiful lakes along the base of the mountains. The effect is most striking if you come to Grand Teton by car, and approach the Park from the east on U.S. Route 26-287. After the desolation of the eroded Wind River country, beautiful in its way but bare and stark, you climb over a pass and suddenly there are the Tetons, with Jackson Lake a vast reflecting pool below.

Like most National Parks, Grand Teton is best explored on foot or on a horse. Only that way can one reach the high alpine meadows and the glaciers, or hope to see moose and elk at their best. The Park has the largest elk herd in the United States. (We had better interject here that the American 'elk' is known to Europeans as the wapiti or red deer, whereas the American 'moose' corresponds to the European elk.)

The big Jackson Lake Lodge at Grand Teton enjoys a spectacular view over Jackson Lake towards the towering Tetons, and it can be reached during the season by various combinations of plane or train and bus, making it an ideal destination for someone without a car. From the Lodge one can then do 'float trips' down the Snake River or pack-trips on horseback, not to mention bus tours of Yellowstone. It is an expensive place to stay, however, like many places in this Jackson Hole area. Most of the dude ranches near here are expensive too; on the surface everything seems very simple and 'Western', but it often proves to be a costly simplicity. Nonetheless, one can certainly visit Grand Teton without spending a fortune. There are various sorts of cabin-style accommodations within the Park, all of which can be booked ahead; they range from luxurious cottages with private baths to the crudest sort of log-and-canvas shelters with only bunks for beds. And there are superb camping sites as well.

The Tetons offer fine climbing, and there is a celebrated climbing school at Jackson, the town just south of the Park. There is also a spectacular aerial tramway, built for skiers but in operation year-round. Jackson itself has become rather self-conscious in recent years, and it has attracted a bizarre assortment of residents: eccentrics both rich and poor, solid ranchers, ski instructors, emigrée countesses, writers, wilderness guides, artists. Actually altogether they rather enhance its frontier flavour.

Far to the north of Yellowstone and Grand Teton, on the border between Montana and the Canadian province of Alberta, is Glacier National Park, third largest of the National Parks. Since its situation is relatively isolated, it is never as heavily visited as Yellowstone or Yosemite, yet you can quite easily get to Glacier by train or bus; there are convenient connections with trans-continental services, and the concessionaire who runs the hotels at Glacier also offers tours within the Park, by bus, boat, and horse. Some of the tours include a visit to Waterton Park, Glacier's Canadian twin.

One can also have a remarkable view of Glacier just in one day simply by driving through it in a car, taking the spectacular Going-to-the-Sun road which twists and turns for fifty miles from one side of the Park to the other, across the very heart of it, up over passes and down into valleys. It may seem sacrilege to spend so little time in such a magnificent place, but it's certainly better than not seeing Glacier at all, and one could at least stop from time to time to take one of the trails suggested in the Park brochure.

Glacier has glaciers. The Park is bisected north to south by the Continental Divide, and for ages ice has flowed down either slope of the Rockies here, scouring and digging at the flanks of the mountains. Thus there are hollows filled with sparkling blue mountain lakes, and alpine meadows covered with wildflowers. In cold mountain streams the trout fishing is superb.

There are three traditional Alpine-style hotels within the Park, but there are also lodges with more moderate prices. And one of

Glacier's great features is its system of simple chalets high up among the peaks; since they offer food and beds, they make it possible to go on splendid hikes without any camping equipment. There are more primitive overnight cabins up high too, but for those one needs one's own bedding and cooking gear.

At Browning, in the Blackfeet Indian Reservation just east of Glacier Park, there is an excellent museum devoted to the history and customs of the Plains Indians, those various Indian tribes which lived between the Mississippi River and the Rockies. Few other Indians were as wedded to the horse as the Plains tribes. Their distinctive, semi-nomadic culture centred around the hunting of the buffalo (bison), which furnished them with meat and warm robes, and with hides from which to fashion their other garments and their tepees. Unfortunately, the white man too discovered the buffalo's worth, and in the 1860s and '70s uncounted thousands of buffalo were shot, stripped of their hides, and left to rot on the plains. In no time at all the buffalo was practically extinct. Naturally the Indians retaliated by attacking the white man even more ferociously than before, and the white man's government responded in turn by ordering the Indians on to newly created reservations. The most famous encounter between the enraged and desperate Plains Indians and the United States Army was 'Custer's last stand', in 1876. In the north-west corner of what is now the Crow Indian Reservation near Billings, Montana, General Custer and 262 men were trapped and completely wiped out by a combined force of Cheyenne and Sious. But the Battle of the Little Big Horn was not only a last stand for General Custer; it proved to be the last stand of the Plains Indians too. After that, the United States Government made very sure the Indians stayed on their reservations; there were still sporadic outbursts for another twenty or thirty years, but never again any big battles. Most of the Plains Indians who are left today live poorly on their reservations in remote corners of their old lands; it is, as we suggested in the preceding chapter, a miserable story.

You might like to visit a Plains Indian crafts shop, however, and there are at least four others in Montana in addition to the one open in summer in conjunction with the museum at Browning. One is the Blackfeet Crafts Association at St Mary, at the eastern end of the Going-to-the-Sun road across Glacier. Two others are farther east in Montana, along U.S. 2: the Chippewa-Cree Craft Shop at Havre, and Ka-Eyta, a combined tribes' co-operative, at Harlem. South-east of Billings, and south of Interstate 94, at Lame Deer on U.S. 212 in the heart of the Northern Cheyenne Reservation, there is a Northern Cheyenne Craft Center. We are told that one can also rent a tepee at Lame Deer, and spend a night on the reservation. Furthermore, you can stay on at least one reservation in modern motel style, complete with colour television and a swimming pool; the Crow tribe has developed a small resort complex on their reservation, very near the site of Custer's last stand. It's called Sun Lodge, and it's at Crow Agency, Montana, on Interstate 90 sixteen miles south of Hardin. There's a reconstructed Crow Indian village nearby, and the Crows put on ceremonials and rodeos throughout the summer.

The main road going south from Glacier towards Missoula, Montana, passes the National Bison Range, where a large buffalo herd is carefully protected. One can go on a self-guided tour in one's car (buffalo are unpredictable) from the Refuge headquarters at Moiese. Missoula, below, is on the route of the Lewis and Clark expedition, which came through this unknown country in the first decade of the nineteenth century; the journals of the expedition make note of camping very near the site of the present town. The University of Montana is at Missoula, but the town also has a far more unusual institution: the United States Forest Service's fire-jumping school. Since forest fires are a constant danger in the West, the Forest Service has developed a corps of trained fire-fighters who can be dropped by parachute into inaccessible mountain regions at the first hint of a fire. If you happen to go through Missoula early in the summer, when the new fire-fighters are taking their practice jumps, you can watch.

The fourth of the great National Parks in the Rockies is called simply Rocky Mountain National Park, but it was once known as Estes Park. Isabella Bird, that intrepid Englishwoman we mentioned earlier, thought Estes Park the most beautiful mountain valley she had ever seen:

. . . an irregular basin, lighted up by the bright waters of the rushing Thompson (River), guarded by sentinel mountains of fantastic shape and monstrous size, with Long's Peak rising above them all in unapproachable grandeur, while the Snowy Range, with its outlying spurs heavily timbered, comes down upon the park slashed by stupendous canyons lying deep in the purple gloom.

Rocky Mountain National Park has only limited accommodation within the Park itself, unless you wish to camp. There are, however, many inns and motels in the village of Estes Park at the eastern entrance, or one can simply come out for the day from Denver by car or on a bus tour.

All the tour buses are sure to go through the Park along the Trail Ridge Road, which runs for fifteen miles at a height of more than 11,000 feet, passing over the barren tundra slopes overlooking the snow-covered peaks all around, with the valleys beneath stretching away to the eastern plains. For those who have time to stay at the Park for a few days, Rocky Mountain is a paradise for climbers. Horses can also be hired there. Or you might go on one of the organized nature walks with a ranger, and learn where you are most likely to see the big-horn sheep for which the Park is famous. Like most National Parks, Rocky Mountain schedules group walks, and has talks given by the rangers in the evening, but there are always maps available with which the visitor can make his own independent explorations.

In the West one not only finds National Parks but also, even more frequently, areas designated as National Forests. The National Forests were created to keep fine timber areas from being over-cut and certain lands from being over-grazed; despite the name, National Forests are not always covered with trees. They were not originally intended to double as recreation areas, but more and more today they are doing just that. One can ride and hike through them, so long as one observes the posted regulations, and many National Forests now also offer fine camping sites.

A rugged and beautiful state with no National Parks but magnificent National Forests is Idaho. It is a state rich in contrasts. In addition to the forest regions, there are high mountain ranges; the first really popular skiing resort in the United States was Sun Valley, in the Sawtooth Mountains of south central Idaho. East of Sun Valley is a strange volcanic region, fittingly called the Craters of the Moon, which has been made a National Monument. Equally forbidding but completely different is that wasteland which lies along Interstate Route 15 as it goes from Idaho Falls north to Dillon, Montana; it begins as mile after mile of flat and featureless desolation, and then near the Montana border the road climbs into great gaunt brown mountains as bleak as one's image of Central Asia. Yet just below Idaho Falls, where the Snake River flows westward across the southern part of the state, lies some of the richest farming land in the West.

We will say more about river expeditions in the next chapter, and we have already mentioned the possibility of doing a float trip as part of a Grand Tetons holiday. But we should note here that several river-expedition organizers run trips on the Salmon River in the rugged wilderness areas of central Idaho. We list the name of one reliable firm at the end of this chapter, and USTS or one of the other sources we suggest in Chapter 1 can supply additional names. These float trips use large rubber pontoon boats; one can go on trips which run a great many rapids, or trips which provide only moderate thrills. In either case, one camps at night in the wilderness by the river's edge, and the outfitter provides meals and everything else. With one of the major firms, the least expensive Salmon River trip currently costs $240 for six days, per person, all-in. (This is less expensive than the Grand Canyon runs, but more expensive than float trips through the rugged Utah desert country.) Obviously this is not a cheap holiday, but more and more people are eagerly trying it.

The most spectacular sight in Idaho used to be Hell's Canyon, where the Snake River runs through the deepest gorge on the North American continent, along the Idaho–Washington state border. Since dams have now been built on this part of the Snake, despite the anguished objections of conservationists, Hell's Canyon is no longer the unspoiled wonder it used to be. But one can still go on a rather terrifying drive along the canyon rim on a narrow, twisting road in the vicinity of Cuprum, Idaho, and there are also boat trips from Lewiston and one or two other points.

Historically, the settlement of the Rockies region divides roughly into four parts, beginning with the mountain men. The next to arrive were the Mormons, who came to what is now Utah in 1847 in search of an isolated refuge. By crossing the Continental Divide into the dry, unpromising Utah basin, they hoped at last to be safe from the outside world.

The Mormons considered themselves a chosen people, singled out by God to establish a new Jerusalem; their own name for their sect was not 'Mormon' but 'Church of Jesus Christ of the Latter-Day Saints'. 'Mormon' refers to one of their testaments, the Book of Mormon. Joseph Smith, the founder of the sect, said the Book of Mormon was a lost Book of the Bible; he had a series of revelations in 1830, and in the course of them he discovered the Book of Mormon inscribed upon golden tablets on a hill near Rochester, New York. From the very beginning Joseph Smith attracted a large and fervent following; by the time the nucleus of the membership set out for Utah, there were already thousands of converts in Great Britain in addition to the many thousands in America. In fact some English Mormons were probably among those first Utah pioneers, since many of them had emigrated in the 1840s to join their brethren in the United States.

Leading his growing band, Joseph Smith had tried to settle in New York, in Ohio, in Missouri, and in Illinois, but everywhere the Saints had trouble with the unbelievers. The worst trouble came in Illinois, when Joseph Smith was attacked and killed by a mob. After that it was obvious that the Saints must find sanctuary in the wilderness, and so they set off towards the West, with their new leader, the redoubtable Brigham Young. It was Brigham Young who led the first group of Mormon pioneers to what is now Salt Lake City, after a trek across the plains and the Rockies that was remarkable for its orderliness and planning although it was scarcely an easy trip. (Those who could not afford a horse and wagon pushed their possessions that incredible distance in wheel-barrows.) It was Brigham Young who told his people they must make the desert bloom, and they did; there are no harder-working farmers anywhere than the Mormons, as the neat and prosperous farms of Utah and southern Idaho still prove today. Brigham Young also told them where and how to build temples and tabernacles; the Tabernacle in Salt Lake City, with its vast dome and exceptional acoustics, is an extraordinary building for an isolated, agricultural community in the mid-nineteenth century, and so is the great Temple.

The success of the Mormon settlements did not act as a magnet for non-Mormon settlers. The country around the Rockies was lacking in rain and not particularly fertile; it was known that the Mormons had to work terribly hard for their living. Then too the Mormons themselves were most unenthusiastic about unbelievers settling anywhere near them. They were solving the population problem unaided; by now many Mormon families were poly-gamous, following the example of Brigham Young, who ulti-mately had seventeen wives. Outsiders refused to understand them, but then the Mormons considered most outsiders shiftless and dishonest anyway. As the years passed, however, more and more outsiders came through Utah, and there began to be unpleasant incidents. There was even one dreadful massacre, when a band of Mormons and allied Indians fell upon a peaceful wagon train *en route* to California and killed everyone except the very smallest children. Finally federal troops were sent into Utah, and for years the territory was under virtual armed guard. Not until the very end of the nineteenth century was Utah admitted to the Union as a state; by then Brigham Young was dead, and the Mormon elders agreed to accept civil law and abandon polygamy.

Mormons today continue to dominate Utah and much of Idaho; because of them these states are much less flamboyant than most of the other western states. On the street Mormons look just like everyone else; there is nothing unusual about their dress. But their lives are still centred around their religion; every Mormon must be prepared to drop everything at any stage in his life and rush off across the world at the behest of the Church elders. Moreover, strict Mormons do not drink or smoke or even allow themselves coffee and tea, and in the little towns of Utah and Idaho you will sense that you are in a temperance area. You will also notice the tidiness everywhere; Mormons are as uncompromising about dirt and waste and disorder as they are about spirits and sin.

Salt Lake City is still the capital of Utah and about forty per cent of its population is still Mormon; Temple Square is the spiritual centre of Salt Lake City. The Temple and the Tabernacle are there; visitors are very welcome at the Tabernacle, but only Latter-Day Saints are allowed into the Temple. Brigham Young's house, known as the Beehive House, is nearby, and open to the public. It is a very handsome house, extremely interesting to visit; like the official Mormon tour of Temple Square and the Tabernacle, it should not be missed. These tours are free. They are conducted by Mormon volunteers, who are naturally anxious to present their religion in a favourable light but are scrupulously non-aggressive about it.

If you happen to be in Salt Lake City on a Sunday, or on a Thursday evening, you can hear the celebrated Mormon Tabernacle choir, and every day promptly at noon one can also hear the great Tabernacle organ played. In addition, particularly if you are planning to see more of Utah, we suggest you also go to the state-run Visitors Information Center in Council Hall at the top of State Street, opposite the capitol building. Council Hall was built by the Mormons in 1866 and once served as the territorial capitol; it's a fine building and the Information Center is a good one, with all sorts of information about the National Parks in Utah and river float trips and so forth. We suggest too that you consider staying in Salt Lake City at the Hotel Utah, a gloriously ornate, old-fashioned and comfortable hotel, run by the Mormon Church and overlooking Temple Square. One gets the Book of Mormon on one's bedside table, and from the dining room on the top floor there is a fine view of the Wasatch Mountains.

Knowledgeable skiers now flock to Salt Lake City in winter, since it is even closer than Denver to superb skiing runs. Alta is the most famous of these, with reputedly the most challenging runs in America, but there are several other fine places too, all within twenty-five miles of Salt Lake City. Some of them are centred around picturesque little mining towns, for this is copper-mining country.

Just west of Salt Lake City is the Great Salt Lake, and it really is salt, like the Dead Sea. Elsewhere in Utah there are several little towns which figured prominently in Mormon history. But outside of the Salt Lake City region, Utah's main attraction for visitors is its remarkable rugged desert scenery to the south. This, however, belongs in our next chapter.

A student doing lessons about the Rocky Mountains with a map to colour, could now fill in Utah and Idaho. The time is 1858, just before the Civil War; Utah and Idaho are hardly overflowing with people, but they have enough settlers for their future character to be already determined. Colorado, Wyoming, and Montana, on the other hand, are still blank; now their turn is coming.

In 1858 along Cherry Creek in Colorado, on land that is today in the middle of the city of Denver, a prospector found traces of gold. The great Colorado gold and silver rush was on. It was almost ten years after the California gold excitement had begun; during those ten years many men on their way to or from California had poked around in the Rockies to see what they could find, and now someone had met with luck. The Cherry Creek strike itself proved insignificant, but prospectors spread through the Colorado mountains to the west, over every pass, up every valley, panning, washing, hoping, and there was one fantastic strike after another. Mining towns appeared everywhere in the Colorado Rockies, some at formidable heights: the town of Leadville, for example, was more than 10,000 feet up. The excitement lasted for about thirty years. Then the price of silver dropped sharply, and at the same time most of the gold mines which were not already played out came to be controlled by large, impersonal corporations; the day of the wide open mining camp, every man for himself, was gone. Leadville, which had reached an official population of 30,000 at one point, dwindled to a mere 4,000, and smaller towns disappeared altogether.

Today, the 'ghost' mining towns are among the chief tourist attractions in Colorado: biggish places like Leadville, Central City, Cripple Creek, Georgetown, Fairplay, Silverton, and also countless tiny mining settlements which boomed for a year or two and then were abandoned, leaving only a handful of lonely, crumbling cabins at the top of a mountain. The ghost town easiest to reach from Denver is Central City; it was the first of the important mining centres and in its day a serious rival to Denver, although this is hard to believe when you see the two places now. All the old mining towns in Colorado or Montana are somewhat alike: crudely-made timber buildings showing little evidence of paint, several saloons, a rococo hotel, and in the bigger towns 'opera houses' which in their time purveyed operettas, plays, music hall, talks – usually almost everything but genuine opera. The remarkable thing about Central City these days is that its Opera House now does boast a season of real opera each summer. The operas usually alternate with plays and musical comedies; whatever is done seems especially charming in the Victorian-Western setting. Most of the mining towns in Colorado have the advantage of a magnificent situation, high up in the Rockies. Central City is not as spectacularly situated as some of the others, but it is at the head of a narrow valley and is an excellent example of its kind.

The wildest mining town in Colorado was Leadville. It is situated in what must once have been a lovely and peaceful alpine meadow high in the Rockies, one hundred miles south-west of Denver. After silver was discovered in Leadville in 1875, thousands of men rushed there to crowd into hastily erected hotels and boarding houses and cabins and tents. Each of them hoped to make his fortune; of those who succeeded, none had a more dramatic story than one Horace Tabor.

Tabor had come to Colorado from New England with his wife Augusta and a small son. He had tried prospecting, without success, and in the 1870s he was running a shop in Leadville and also acting as postmaster. Actually Augusta Tabor did most of the work; her husband was amiable but not noted for his acumen or industry. Nonetheless, one day he 'grub-staked' two prospectors in return for a share of their future discoveries, and they promptly went out and uncovered a fantastic silver lode. From then on Tabor's luck seemed boundless; with the profits from his first lode he invested in another exploration, and then another, and in no time at all he had accumulated a fortune of $9,000,000, with more money coming in every day. In 1883 he divorced Augusta and married a beautiful young blonde girl known as 'Baby Doe' who had come to Leadville determined to find a rich husband. Two daughters were born: Tabor named them Elizabeth Pearl and Silver Dollar, and he showered luxuries on them and on his young wife. Then in 1893 silver was demonetized, and Tabor was ruined; he died penniless six years later in Denver. But the story is more than the usual rise-and-fall cliché, because of Baby Doe. Everyone assumed she would leave Tabor when his fortune evaporated, but she stood by him, selling her jewels and her finery, struggling to get food for the family, darning and patching and apparently never complaining. Just before Horace Tabor died he told Baby Doe she must never abandon the Matchless, his richest mine; someday silver prices would rise again and the mine would once more be valuable. So Baby Doe went back to Leadville with her little girls and there she stayed, living in a mean cabin at the entrance to the mine, dressed in rags, ekeing out a pitiful existence for almost forty years; her own death did not come until 1936.

The story has been told in one of the most interesting contemporary American operas, *The Ballad of Baby Doe*, which had its premier, appropriately, in the old miners' Opera House at Central City. Tourists in Leadville go to see Baby Doe Tabor's cabin at the Matchless Mine, and the house Tabor lived in during the lean years with Augusta, and the Opera House he built for Leadville, which was once called the Tabor but is now called the Elks Opera House. In its day the Opera House offered the Leadville miners every sort of extravagant entertainment, from spectacles with real elephants to Oscar Wilde talking on 'The Practical Application of the Aesthetic Theory to Exterior and Interior House Decoration, with Observations on Dress and Personal Ornament'.

Montana had its wild mining days too. The most famous strike in Montana was at Virginia City, which is often confused with another Virginia City in Nevada; both were mining boom towns. But the Virginia City in Montana was more wicked, really wicked. In its early days it had a sheriff named Henry Plummer who was the original of all the crooked sheriffs in Western films. He had a gang who robbed stagecoaches and ore wagons, and he pocketed the loot while he pretended to be on the trail of the thieves. Sheriff Plummer flourished for quite a while in this manner, but finally some of the local men organized a Vigilantes Committee. There had been more than a hundred unexplained, unpunished killings; now there were twenty-four hangings, and a crude peace settled over the Montana mountains. Today Virginia City is a bustling tourist attraction.

Western Montana is still mining country, and the city of Butte is quite as extraordinary as any ghost town. It is set right in the middle of an enormous open-pit copper mine; one feels like an ant trapped at the bottom of a giant red basin. The city sprawls all over the bowl's interior, with steep streets and ramshackle buildings; it is all thoroughly picturesque. Authenticity is carried to such lengths that even food in Butte seems every bit as bad as it was in the nineteenth-century mining camps; the only gastronomic treat is the saffron buns sold in the bakeries as a dim memento of the Cornish miners who must once have been here. Shooting is discouraged in Butte these days, and the last battle was fought long ago in the War of the Copper Kings, which determined the financial control of the mining, and ultimately of Montana itself. But the citizens of Butte still manage to keep in fighting trim by driving up and down the precipitous streets and right through traffic signals at fifty and sixty miles an hour; even now, this is no place for the faint of heart.

The dusty, grey-green cattle country lies east of the Rockies. It is monotonous, without trees, a great billowing sea which rolls from Texas up through Colorado and Wyoming and Montana all the way to Canada. It is high, with dry, clear air, and you can see for miles. When you drive across it, the mountains in the distance seem a mirage, always there, never any nearer; it must have been agonizing for the people in the wagon trains, the tantalizing visibility. This is one part of the Great Plains which has hardly changed at all: still a lonely infinity of pale rough grass and sagebrush. Topping a rise along a road in eastern Wyoming or Montana, you half expect to come upon a band of Indians camped in the hollow, or a herd of buffalo grazing.

We have described the early cattle drives, from Texas up to the rail-head towns of Kansas; that was the first half of the cattle boom, and it lasted for about twenty years. The second half was quite different, and for a time much more lucrative. Trying different trails to get their cattle to the railways, Texas cattlemen discovered these vast unclaimed grasslands. In no time at all, cattle 'spreads' were staked out all over northern Colorado and Wyoming and Montana where so recently the buffalo had thundered by.

The chief town of the cattlemen was Cheyenne, Wyoming, which still has a fine cowboy air about it; studying the saddles and boots in the shop windows there is an endless source of delight. Moreover, the little Wyoming State Museum in Cheyenne has a collection of branding irons and a few other scraps of Western memorabilia, the more endearing because so few and so ingenuous. But unhappily the building one would most like to see is gone; the old Cheyenne Club was torn down several years ago. It had been built in 1880: 'Some of our rich bachelors have associated themselves with a few married men for the purpose of forming an English club', reported the Cheyenne *Daily Leader* on 25 July of that year. One learns with surprise that many of the cattlemen in this second phase of the cattle boom were not weather-beaten ranchers at all. Men in England and Scotland had been attracted by the splendid combination of profit and romance in the cattle business; they invested heavily, either in syndicates or as individuals. By 1886 the English and Scottish companies between them controlled about twenty million acres of grazing land; 'controlled' did not precisely mean 'owned', but at the time it seemed quite good enough.

Many of these investors went West in person, or sent sons and nephews to settle out there at least temporarily. One of the most flamboyant was Moreton Frewen, a charming English plunger who acquired a huge spread in the Powder River region of northern Wyoming. He went 'Western' with a vengeance and was a tremendous hit on his annual trips back to London; on one of those trips he wooed and won the beautiful and talented Clara Jerome, and thus became the uncle of little Winston Churchill. Unfortunately young Mrs Frewen never learned to share her

11a. The Three Tetons and Mt St John, Grand Teton National Park, Wyoming

11b. Grand Canyon of the Colorado River

12a. Zuni Indians with their pottery

12b. Cowboys watering their herd

husband's passion for her own American West, despite the piano and the carpets and the weekly order of flowers Frewen had shipped from the East. It was perhaps just as well that within a few years he over-extended himself and had to sell out.

The Cheyenne newspaper rejoiced at Moreton Frewen's departure; a strong anti-British feeling was building up in the territory. There were many reasons for it; most of them can be discovered in the memoir of John Clay, a dour Scot who was sent out to manage some of the Scottish holdings in Wyoming and ended by staying on there until his death.

> The men who came from the other side of the Atlantic were young, mostly worthless in a business way, many of them dissolute, and when you rounded them up a very moderate lot. Very few of them survived the ordeal of hard winters, over-stocked ranges and other vicissitudes. . . .

Mr Clay clearly wrote from bitter personal experience. But then too Mr Clay was a hard man. The ordeals which drove so many of his compatriots out of the West were hardly negligible.

The first crisis came during the winters of 1886 and 1887, when the blizzards were so bad, the snow so deep, the cold so intense that horrifying numbers of cattle starved to death or were frozen on the open plains. Until then everyone had managed to squeak by without winter feeding, relying on the tough range cattle's ability to survive, disregarding all warning about the Wyoming climate. Now, however, there was a fearful outcry, and many British investors pulled out.

The second crisis was perhaps Mr Clay's 'other vicissitudes', a superb understatement for a life and death struggle which has provided meat for Western stories and films for eighty years now. The high – or low – point of the struggle is known as 'the Johnson County War'. To understand it, two things must be borne in mind. First, a man with a Wyoming cattle spread in the 1880s did not actually *own* much land. All he needed to buy was enough acreage for a few buildings and for enclosures in which he could bunch his cattle together once or twice a year for branding and counting and culling; the rest of the time the cattle ranged free on government land which no one else had yet claimed. Secondly, cattle rustling was always a serious problem in the West because the cattle did roam far and wide. Branding helped, but brands could be altered, and calves born late in the spring were

H

not branded until autumn. On the other hand, what looked like rustling might be no more than someone exercising his right to claim an ownerless animal, a maverick which had somehow escaped the branding iron.

These two facts became particularly important in the years right after the two hard winters, when settlers began to appear in the cattle country to stake out a homestead, 160 acres of unclaimed government land. At the same time the big spreads, having suffered severe losses, were beginning to be acutely sensitive about their herd-count and their grazing land. A few unscrupulous cattlemen tried to scare the settlers off; there were ugly instances of violence, defenceless homesteaders shot in the back by hired gunfighters. And when the homesteaders tried to market cattle, the Wyoming Stock Growers Association in Cheyenne refused to recognize their brands and simply impounded the cattle. Under the circumstances, it is reasonable to assume that some of those on the settlers' side had felt few qualms if a cattleman's stray steer ended up in some settler's herd, but the cattlemen did not help matters by calling all settlers 'rustlers'.

One spring day in 1892 the feud reached its climax. More than fifty men, half of them hired Texas gunfighters but the other half eminently respectable leading cattlemen, set out for northern Wyoming 'to teach some of the rustlers a lesson'. Some said the scheme was devised by John Clay, although he was back in Scotland on business when the invasion actually took place. In any event, he was president of the Stock Growers Association at that time, and he later said that he was proud to call the Invaders his friends. It is not surprising; due process had few supporters on the frontier.

The Invaders' first objective was the town of Buffalo in Johnson County, where they planned to begin by teaching a lesson to one 'Red' Angus, a Scot of another stripe who was the Sheriff there and who persisted in taking the settlers' side. On the way, however, the Invaders stopped at a cabin which had been part of Moreton Frewen's spread, there to besiege and kill two cowboys who had turned homesteader and become leaders among the settler group. Unfortunately for the Invaders, one of their victims was just the sort of hero Hollywood – and everyone else – loves: brave and handsome and just in all his dealings. He even had a ringing name, Nate Champion, and during the siege this paragon kept a running account:

Me and Nick was getting breakfast . . . Boys there is bullets
coming in like hail . . . They are shooting from the stable and
river and back of the house . . . Nick [his friend] is dead, he
died about 9 o'clock . . . Boys I feel pretty lonesome just now.
I wish there was someone here with me so we could watch all
sides at once . . . I shot at the men in the stable just now; don't
know if I got any or not . . . It don't look as if there is much
show of my getting away . . . I guess they are going to fire the
house . . . Good-bye boys if I never see you again.

All alone Nate Champion held off fifty men for nine hours before
they finally killed him.

The invaders' first action was their last; someone got word to
Sheriff Angus, every homesteader in the county rose up, and the
next day the Invaders themselves were besieged at the ranch
where they were planning their next move. Only Sheriff Angus's
regard for law and justice, and the intervention of the United
States Army, saved the Invaders from massacre. The trial which
followed was a mockery, for it was held in Cheyenne, the Invaders'
own bailiwick, and the Invaders were powerful men with friends
in high places. Yet in the end they found they had won all the
battles but lost the war. Juries now refused to convict any rustlers,
no matter how guilty, and life became intolerable in so many
ways for the big cattlemen that even more now left for good. It
was the end of an era.

None of this violence, however, tarnished the image of the
cowboy. The first great cowboy novel was Owen Wister's *The
Virginian*, published in 1902; its hero was the sort of cowboy
who has remained standard ever since in films and on television
(or at least until the 'new realism' with its anti-heroes came along),
an uncomplicated man, tall in the saddle. The cowboy world
still has such appeal that today all farmers in the West call themselves ranchers, and a recent Episcopalian Bishop of Montana
delighted his flock by having his clericals cut cowboy-fashion
and wearing black cowboy boots and a black cowboy hat.

Some of the cattle country, in Wyoming as in Texas, has now
been taken over by oil interests; for miles around Casper, Wyoming, the oil rigs go up and down in an endless minuet. But
towns like Cheyenne and Buffalo in Wyoming, and Miles City in
Montana, are still cowboy towns. You know it when you see the
breakfasts listed on the café menus: a steak, six ranch eggs, a

quarter of a pound of bacon, a pound of spuds (potatoes), a sack
of hot cakes and half a gallon of java (coffee) all for one person.
We have spoken of the museum at Cheyenne with its collection of
cattle-country memorabilia; you would also enjoy the Montana
Historical Society Museum and Galleries at Helena.

The owners of some of the big ranches are quite willing to
allow visitors to look over them, although this is interesting
chiefly for someone who cares about pure-bred beef cattle. Cattle
in the West are still branded, cowboys continue to look like cowboys, but these days the round-ups are likely to be for doling out
vitamins; ranches are now thoroughly business-like places. There
are frequent rodeos during the summer in the West, however,
with important ones during Cheyenne's Frontier Days at the end
of July, at the Montana State Fair at Great Falls at the beginning
of August, and at the Colorado State Fair at the end of August at
Pueblo. And we spoke in Chapter 1 of the many dude ranches
throughout the West which take paying guests.

For anyone with time for only one Rocky Mountain state,
Colorado would probably be the obvious choice and Denver the
obvious centre. Colorado has more high mountains (fifty-one over
14,000 feet), more breathtaking passes, more remarkable canyons
than any of the other four. Within its borders you can taste both
the alpine beauties of the northern Rockies and the golden Gothic
splendours of the arid Southwest, and in one corner of the state
there is Mesa Verde, a National Park which protects the finest
ancient Indian cliff dwellings in the country. All that Colorado
lacks is pre-eminence in the great cattle and cowboy period; there
Wyoming and Montana have the edge. But Colorado has cowboys
and cattle enough to suit most people, and there are the old mining
towns as an added bonus.

The simplest way to describe the delights of Colorado is in the
form of a circular, thousand-mile trip from Denver, moving in a
counter-clockwise direction. No one bus tour includes all the
places we mention, nor would one want to crowd everything into
a single trip, even with a car. But this hypothetical circular tour
will give some idea of the variety in this one state.

We have already described Rocky Mountain National Park.
Let us begin by going there, passing through the town of Boulder
on the way. Boulder is built around the University of Colorado,
an attractive university in the shadow of the Rockies, with

homogeneous buildings made of the red stone of the region, and skiing-runs only minutes away. After Rocky Mountain Park, you would head for Loveland Pass; by taking a minor road south from the Park you could fit in Central City on the way.

Driving towards Loveland Pass on Interstate 70, you go right past one of the most charming of the old mining towns, Georgetown, precariously perched in a narrow gorge. Georgetown has a special quality unique among the ghost towns of Colorado. For one thing, Georgetown never suffered a severe fire; most of these mining towns with their crudely-built frame houses were burnt down and rebuilt several times in the course of their boom days. But Georgetown is almost perfectly preserved in its original state, with several delightful Victorian-gingerbread buildings and a handsome house complete with Cornish-looking granite out-buildings, the property of one of the early mine-owners. It is only regrettable that the Hotel de Paris here has stopped being a hostelry and become a museum instead; it would have been so pleasant to stay there. The Hotel de Paris is surely the 'good hotel declivitously situated' which Isabella Bird described in 1873, 'at the end of a narrow, piled-up irregular street, crowded with miners standing in groups, or drinking and gaming under the veranda'. Miss Bird did not mention the food, but the Hotel de Paris was run by a Frenchman who was considered an amusing eccentric because he fretted about the excellence of his table.

Not far beyond Georgetown, Interstate 70 takes you past the turn-offs for Breckenridge and Vail, two of Colorado's best-known skiing places. The turn-off for Leadville is in between the two. Then comes the magnificent Glenwood Canyon, where for perhaps twenty miles the road goes between golden-red rock walls.

After Glenwood Canyon, the first sizeable town is Glenwood Springs, and fifty miles south of Glenwood Springs, in a valley difficult to reach from any other direction, is Aspen. This was once just another ghost town with abandoned silver mines, but at the end of the Second World War a Chicago industrialist, who admired the way culture and history and scenery were often combined at summer festivals in Europe, decided to see what he could do with Aspen. The result is fascinating. In the winter Aspen is one of the most attractive skiing resorts in the United States, with a strong international flavour because so many of the skiing instructors are Europeans, now happily settled there. In the summer,

Aspen has a superb music festival, with programmes at least three times a week from mid-June to mid-August, and rehearsals open to the public. One does not need to book ahead; the concerts have open seating, and there seems always to be room for everyone who comes.

Most of the artists who appear in the concerts also teach in the Aspen summer music school. The group varies from year to year but it unfailingly includes some of the best musicians in America, who delight in Aspen because there they can play what they like in relaxed and congenial surroundings. Moreover music is not Aspen's only summer attraction. There are also the mountains, to be explored on a hired horse or one's own two feet. There are any number of places to stay in Aspen, ranging from the Victorian splendours of the Hotel Jerome to stunning contemporary lodges and simpler motels.

Aspen is at the head of the Roaring Fork River valley, a handsome valley which looks just as valleys in the Rockies ought to look; along the rivers there are pale green cottonwood trees, with the darker green of spruce and pine on the slopes of the mountains on either side, and here and there, high up, stands of shivering silvery aspen trees. There are ranches along the Roaring Fork and some of its tributary valleys, and usually some photogenic cowboys about.

In western Colorado, well beyond Glenwood Springs, is Colorado National Monument, with slashing canyons and grotesque eroded rock formations. More unusual is Dinosaur National Monument, in the north-west corner of Colorado, quite a distance to the north of our circular tour. Dinosaur National Monument is a protected area because more dinosaur skeletons have been found there than anywhere in the Western Hemisphere; geologists are still hard at work chipping away at the rock strata to expose more remains. As one might expect, the best skeletons have been taken to various museums, but some examples have been left embedded in the rock for visitors to see. We will say more about Dinosaur National Monument in the next chapter, in connection with float trips in the Southwest. Its scenery is almost as remarkable as its fossils.

Heading south from the Colorado National Monument, one goes for some seventy miles through barren but beautiful high desert country to the Black Canyon of the Gunnison, another National Monument, deep and dark and forbidding, as the name implies. Traversing it is a feat only experienced rock climbers should attempt, with the advice and consent of the rangers there; for most people, simply looking down into it is enough. Our proposed circular tour passes the Black Canyon and heads deeper into the precipitous country of south-western Colorado; here once again you are very near the Continental Divide.

Going southward along U.S. 550 you come to Ouray, a little mining town already 7,000 feet up but surrounded by mountains twice that height. The road continuing south from Ouray is called the Million Dollar Highway because it cost that to blast a way up and over these forbidding mountains. Until the road was completed, many of the little towns south of Ouray could be reached only on the narrow-gauge railways built in the boom-days to carry ore from the mines. There was once an entire network of narrow-gauge lines through these mountains; normal operations have now long since ceased, but several lines have been resuscitated for tourists. At some places, like Central City, one is offered only a very brief ride along the old tracks in open-side observation coaches behind an engine which, while old and steam-powered, may not be native to these parts. However, from Durango, south of Ouray, there is a delightful day-long trip one can take, riding behind a proper old Colorado narrow-gauge steam engine in authentic Victorian coaches. The run is from Durango to Silverton and back, climbing 3,000 feet through beautiful gorges and groves of aspen trees. There is frequently a mock hold-up along the way, and more colourful goings-on at Silverton, where one has lunch. Silverton itself is a photogenic old mining town; both Silverton and the train have been used in countless films. We heartily recommend the trip, but warn that reservations are vital. (If you can't get reservations on the Durango–Silverton run, you might like to know that there is one other day-long narrow-gauge railway trip, in the southern Colorado mountains between Antonito, Colorado, and Chama, New Mexico. It runs on alternate days from each, and takes six hours; the coaches are not quite authentic but the engine is, and the trip includes some spectacular scenery.)

Durango is not far from Mesa Verde National Park, and it makes a good overnight stopping place for this region. One can also stay at Mesa Verde itself, however, and certainly no one who is in this part of Colorado should miss seeing Mesa Verde and its remarkable thirteenth-century Indian cliff dwellings. We will say more about it in the next chapter, when we discuss the other cliff dwellings of the Southwest.

To drive from Durango or perhaps Mesa Verde back towards Denver without retracing your steps, you would go east along U.S. 160 over Wolf Creek Pass and then north on U.S. 285, which leads to Denver by way of Fairplay, another old mining town. Alternatively one might cut east again off U.S. 285 on either U.S. 50 (over the Royal Gorge) or U.S. 24; that way you could end at Colorado Springs, diverging en route on a minor road to see Cripple Creek.

Cripple Creek was the last of the wide-open mining towns; its boom came with the discovery of gold there in the 1890s, when the silver mining towns were already dying. Some of the mines at Cripple Creek are still worked, and one of them runs trips for visitors down the shafts. But most of Cripple Creek is now a highly satisfactory ghost town, with a miners' museum, melodramas staged in the bar of the old hotel during the summer, and a four-mile narrow-gauge railway run.

The Cripple Creek route would, as we have said, lead one to Colorado Springs, a resort centre popular for nearly a century. Among the more interesting of the attractions so consistently advertised there is the cog-railway trip to the tip of Pike's Peak, 14,110 feet high. And not far north of Colorado Springs, along the main road to Denver, is the United States Air Force Academy. Visitors are welcome to look over the grounds and admire the striking buildings; designed by Skidmore, Owings and Merrill, they include a particularly beautiful modern chapel with magnificent glass.

One reason one might elect to take the Fairplay route instead of the route through Cripple Creek and Colorado Springs is that it is rather more fun to come upon Denver from above, dropping down from the Rockies. With all its smart new buildings and its crisp business-like air, Denver's chief fault these days is a lack of romance; there is almost nothing to remind you of its colourful frontier days. You must therefore help things along, by approaching Denver either from the mountains above it to the west, or from the east, so that the city appears against the backdrop of the snow-peaked Rockies after hundreds of miles of dusty, monotonous plains.

One does still sense a heady optimism and prosperity in Denver, however. You can go up into the dome of the State Capitol, which is covered with gold leaf, and have a splendid sweeping view of the Rockies. You can tour the United States Mint. Once the gold and silver poured out of the mountains into Denver as through a funnel, to emerge as coin of the realm; today there are no gold coins, but the Denver mint continues busy, producing half the United States coinage. For a light-hearted evocation of Denver's past, in a restored section of the old part of town, go to Larimer Square; it has tempting shops and lively restaurants. If you can afford it, stay at the Brown-Palace Hotel, Denver's traditional hotel in the heart of town. There are several museums in Denver too. The Colorado State Museum has delightful, instructive dioramas about every phase of Colorado history from the Mesa Verde cliff-dwellers to the mining and cowboy days; and on the top floor of this museum one can view a Western gun collection or shed a few tears at Baby Doe Tabor's satin slippers and Silver Dollar's lace christening dress. The Denver Natural History Museum has native birds and animals artfully arranged in their natural habitat, and a good mineralogy section. There is also an extraordinary new Denver Art Museum, where among many other treasures you will find a superb presentation of the life and art of the American Indian, one of the three or four best in the country. But you must not linger too long in Denver. You must get out of the town, into the mountains or across the plains.

SPECIAL KNOWLEDGE

Because of the heavy snows in this mountainous region, winter is hardly a sensible time to visit the Rockies, unless you are going there for the skiing. But, as we have suggested, it is also better if you can avoid the peak tourist season of July and August. Whenever you go, remember that anywhere in the Rockies you are likely to be a mile above sea level, and sometimes twice that. You must therefore be careful not to over-exert until you are acclimated, and you should bear in mind that even the hottest days (and the Rockies have almost perpetual sunshine in summer) are followed by cold nights. You will not need formal clothes; everyone in the West dresses casually. But you will want warm things, and stout shoes for hiking.

While some of the big hotels are expensive, on the whole anyone driving through the West will find **food and lodgings** considerably cheaper than in the East.

Butte is pronounced as if it were French. It is not only a town in Montana but also the term for a table or thumb of rock left rearing up above the surrounding plain after aeons of erosion. **Cheyenne** is pronounced Shy-enn; and **Glacier** is Glay-sher.

We have noted that it is possible to get to Grand Teton and Yellowstone and Glacier, in season, by plane or train or bus or a combination thereof. Managing without a car once one has arrived, however, really works well only at the two opposite ends of the economic scale. If you're going to rough it, camping, you can probably scrounge rides through the Parks as necessary, and some of the Parks are now developing more internal transport, if only to cut down on the indiscriminate clogging of Park roads with private cars. If you're planning to stay at one of the expensive lodges or Park hotels, the management can provide transport and tours; inquire about the possibilities when you make your reservations. Most people, however, find it best simply to fly to one of the larger towns near the National Park (Billings, Montana, for example); there one can hire a car, and also any camping supplies one might want.

From Denver, Continental Trailways runs 7-day bus tours to Mesa Verde, which include the Durango–Silverton narrow-gauge railway trip. Currently this tour cost $210 per person, double occupancy, covering everything but meals. Continental Trailways also offers a 7-day tour from Denver to Grand Teton and Yellowstone for around $238 per person, double occupancy. Obviously, this is not cheap; financially, two people could do better hiring a car on their own, provided they got a no-mileage-charge rate. Nonetheless, these tours are sometimes fully booked months ahead. In addition, Gray Line offers day-long tours from Denver, to Rocky Mountain National Park and to Central City and several other nearby places.

You can make a visit to one of the National Parks as tame or as strenuous as you like, but either way it is foolish not to read carefully the brochures you will be given as you enter. Each Park has some special regulations, some particular hazards. The most serious **hazard** in the Rockies area generally, however, is the autumn hunting season on small and large game. If you're driving through the upper Great Plains or the Rockies around October, and see a disproportionate number of men carrying rifles and probably wearing red lumber-jackets and caps, make a few inquiries before you head jauntily off into some wilderness area. You might just be mistaken for an elk. Finally, if you plan to do a lot of hiking in the Rockies, you might like to know that the U.S. Geological Survey Office at Denver can supply proper contour maps.

Antonito, Colorado

CHAMA RAILWAY. For reservations write to The Cumbres and Toltec Scenic Railroad, P.O. Box 789, Chama, N. Mex. 87520. Telephone (505) 756–6411. The train runs from the end of May to the beginning of October on Saturday and Sunday; in July, August and September also on Monday and Tuesday. On Saturday and Monday it leaves from Chama at 10 a.m., arriving at Antonito at 4 p.m. The round-trip is made by taking a coach from Antonito at 8 a.m. and returning by train, or by taking the train from Chama and returning by coach from Antonito at 4 p.m. On Sunday and Tuesday the train leaves from Antonito and the coaches from Chama, at the same times.

Aspen, Colorado

ASPEN MUSIC FESTIVAL. For information and bookings write to Box AA,

Aspen, Colorado. Box office telephone (303) 925-2423. Festival runs from mid-June to mid-August. Advance reservations usually not necessary.

Billings, Montana
For information about ranches throughout the Rockies area write to The Dude Ranchers' Association, Box 1363, Billings, Montana 59101.

Browning, Montana
MUSEUM OF THE PLAINS INDIAN CRAFT SHOP, ½ mile west of Browning. 1 June to 30 September. Open daily 8–8 except for the first and last fortnights of the season when it closes at 5 p.m. Free.

Central City, Colorado
CENTRAL CITY OPERA HOUSE ASSOCIATION. For opera and theatre reservations and information write to Central City Festival, Central City Opera House Association, 910 Sixteenth Street, Denver, Colorado. Telephone (303) 623-7167.

COLORADO CENTRAL NARROW-GAUGE RAILWAY. Operates from early May to October at weekends; from early June to Labor Day, daily 10.30–6.

Cheyenne, Wyoming
WYOMING STATE MUSEUM, Central Avenue at 23rd Street. Monday to Friday 8.30–5, Sunday 12–5; 1 June to 31 August also Saturday 8.30–5. Closed 1 January and 25 December. Free.

Colorado Springs, Colorado
AIR FORCE ACADEMY, 10 miles north on I-25. Grounds open during daylight hours. Museum and Visitor Center at south entrance, open daily 8–5. Free.

PIKE'S PEAK COG RAILWAY, from Manitou Springs to summit. Mid-May to mid-October, 2 trips daily at 9 and 2; early spring and late autumn, 1 afternoon trip daily; July and August, a third, sunset trip at 5.15.

Cripple Creek, Colorado
CRIPPLE CREEK AND VICTOR NARROW-GAUGE RAILWAY. Operates from Cripple Creek Museum, Bennett Avenue. Late May to first weekend in October, daily, every 45 minutes from 10 a.m. The ride lasts 35 minutes.

CRIPPLE CREEK DISTRICT MUSEUM. 30 May to 1 October, daily 9.30–5.15.

GOLD BAR ROOM in Imperial Hotel for old-time melodrama, mid-June to mid-September, Tuesday to Sunday.

Crow Agency, Montana
CROW INDIAN RESERVATION SUN LODGE (motel), Interstate Route 90 south of Hardin. For reservations write, or telephone (800) 228-9450.

CROW INDIAN HERITAGE VILLAGE, Interstate Route 90. Annual Crow Fair and Rodeo held the third week in August.

Denver, Colorado

COLORADO VISITORS' BUREAU, 225 West Colfax Avenue, Denver, Colorado 80202. Telephone (303) 892–1112.

COLORADO STATE MUSEUM, 14th Avenue and Sherman Street. Monday to Friday 9–5; Saturday, Sunday and holidays 10–5. Free.

DENVER ART MUSEUM, West 14th Avenue at Acoma Street at the south end of the Civic Center. Tuesday to Saturday 9–5, and Wednesday evening 6–9, Sunday 1–5. Closed Monday and holidays. Free.

DENVER NATURAL HISTORY MUSEUM, in City Park off Colorado Boulevard. Summer, Monday to Friday 9–5; rest of the year, Monday to Saturday 9–4.30; Sunday and holidays 12–5 all year.

GRAY LINE OF DENVER, P.O. Box 1977, Denver, Colorado 80201, for information on tours from Denver to Rocky Mountain Park, Central City, Georgetown, Pike's Peak and the Air Force Academy, Colorado Springs.

STATE CAPITOL, between Colfax and 14th Avenues facing Broadway. 31 May to Labor Day, guided tours every half-hour, daily 9–3; rest of the year, tour by appointment only.

U.S. MINT, Colfax Avenue and Cherokee Street. Conducted tours Labor Day to 1 June, Monday to Friday 9–11 and 1–2.30; 1 July to Labor Day, Monday to Friday 8–11 and 12.30–3. Closed holidays. Reservations must be made in advance.

Durango, Colorado

DENVER AND RIO GRANDE WESTERN RAILWAY. Late May to 1 October, departs daily 8.30 a.m. For reservations write to the Agent, Denver and Rio Grande Western Railway, Rio Grande Depot, Durango, Colorado 81301. Telephone (303) 247–2733.

Georgetown, Colorado

HAMILL HOUSE. 1 October to 30 April, Tuesday to Sunday 9.30–6; 1 May to 30 September, daily 9.30–6.

HOTEL DE PARIS, 6th Street. 15 June to 15 September, daily 9–6; 15 September to 15 October, open Saturday and Sunday only.

Havre, Montana (on U.S. Route 2)

CHIPPEWA CREE CRAFT SHOP, 529 First Street. Usually open 11–8.

Harlem, Montana (on U.S. Route 2)

KA-EYTA INC. (Gros Ventre and Assiniboine Craftsmen's Cooperative). Usually open 10–5.

Helena, Montana

MONTANA HISTORICAL SOCIETY MUSEUM, 225 North Roberts Street. 30 May to Labor Day, daily 8–8; rest of the year, Monday to Friday 8–5, Saturday, Sunday and holidays 12–5. Closed 1 January, Thanksgiving and 25 December. Free.

Leadville, Colorado

AUGUSTA TABOR CABIN, 116 East 5th Street. Daily 8–8.

MATCHLESS CABIN, where Baby Doe Tabor spent her last 30 years. 1 mile east of Leadville, continuing on East 7th Street. 30 May to Labor Day, daily 9–5.

OPERA HOUSE. 30 May to 1 October. Guided tours Sunday to Friday.

Lame Deer, Montana

NORTHERN CHEYENNE ARTS AND CRAFTS ASSOCIATION, U.S. Route 212 and State Route 315, on Northern Cheyenne Reservation. Summer 8–8; winter hours irregular.

Missoula, Montana

FOREST SERVICE FIRE-JUMPING SCHOOL, Ariel Fire Depot, Missoula County Airport. Monday to Friday 8–5. Daily tours from 4 July to Labor Day.

National Parks and Monuments

BLACK CANYON OF THE GUNNISON NATIONAL MONUMENT, COLORADO

NORTH RIM may be reached by 14-mile gravel road from State Route 92, east of Crawford. Closed by snow November to April.

SOUTH RIM may be reached by State Route 347 from U.S. Route 50, 6 miles east of Montrose.

Campsites on both rims open May to October.

COLORADO NATIONAL MONUMENT, COLORADO. Approach on State Route 340 and Rim Rock Drive from Fruita and Grand Junction. Camping facilities only. Visitor Center near west entrance, open daily 8–5; 1 June to 31 August, daily 8–8. Free.

DINOSAUR NATIONAL MONUMENT, UTAH AND COLORADO, 7 miles north-east of Jensen on State Route 149. General and camping information from the Superintendent, Dinosaur, Colorado 81610. Dinosaur Quarry Visitor Center near the western entrance north-east of Jensen for history and examples of dinosaur skeletons; early June to 1 September, daily 7 a.m. to 9 p.m.; rest of the year 8–5. Monument headquarters are 1½ miles east of Dinosaur. 1 April to 31 October, daily 8–5; 1 November to 31 March, Monday to Friday 8–5. For information on float trips see **National Parks** in listings for Chapter 9.

GLACIER NATIONAL PARK, MONTANA. General and camping information from Superintendent, Glacier National Park, Montana 59936. Accommodation available from 15 June to 15 September. Hotel, motel and cabin reservations from Glacier Park, Inc., East Glacier Park, Montana 59434. Telephone (406) 226–4841. Their winter (September to June) office is at 1735 East Fort Lowell, P.O. Box 4340, Tucson, Arizona 85717. Telephone (602) 795–0377. Park Headquarters are at West Glacier entrance.

GRAND TETON NATIONAL PARK, WYOMING. General and camping information from the Superintendent, Grand Teton National Park, Moose, Wyoming 83012. Accommodation available from 1 June to 1

October (a few of the lodges shut by 15 September). For further information, write to the Grand Teton Lodge Company, Jackson, Wyoming 83001. Their winter (October to June) office is at 209 Post Street, San Francisco, California. Visitors Center is at Park Headquarters in Moose; summer daily 8–7; rest of the year daily 8–5.

ROCKY MOUNTAIN NATIONAL PARK, COLORADO. General and camping information from the Superintendent, Rocky Mountain National Park, Estes Park, Colorado 80517. Park headquarters are near the eastern entrance. There are motels and inns near the eastern entrance of Estes Park and near the western entrance at Grand Lake.

YELLOWSTONE NATIONAL PARK, WYOMING. General and camping information from the Superintendent, Yellowstone National Park, Wyoming 82190. Various types of accomodation available from late May until the end of October. For further information, write to the Reservations Department, Yellowstone Park Company, Yellowstone Park, Wyoming 82190. Park Headquarters are at Mammoth Hot Springs near the north entrance.

Salmon River Boat Trips, Idaho
Information and bookings from Jack Currey's Western River Expeditions, P.O. Box 6339, Salt Lake City, Utah 84106. Telephone (801) 486–2323.

Salt Lake City, Utah
UTAH TRAVEL COUNCIL INFORMATION OFFICE, Council Hall, 2nd North and State Streets.

BEEHIVE HOUSE, State Street at Temple Street. Monday to Saturday 9–5. Free.

TEMPLE SQUARE TOURS start from the Bureau of Information in Temple Square.

St Mary, Montana
BLACKFEET CRAFTS ASSOCIATION SALES SHOP, U.S. Route 89. 15 June to 15 September. Daily 8.30–8.30.

Virginia City, Montana
VIRGINIA CITY OPERA HOUSE presents melodramas and mystery plays as performed by nineteenth-century touring companies; end of June to Labor Day, daily 8 p.m. Many other restored buildings are open during this period.

9 · THE SOUTHWEST

'It seemed to me the oldest country I had ever seen, the real antique land, first cousin to the moon . . . Man had been here such a little time that his arrival had not yet been acknowledged . . . The giant saguaro cactus, standing like a sentinel on every knoll, was not on the lookout for us, had not heard of us yet, still waiting for trampling dinosaurs . . . This country is geology by day and astronomy by night.'

It is J. B. Priestley speaking about southern Arizona, in a book called *Midnight in the Desert* which he wrote in the 1930s. No visitor to this part of America has written more perceptively about it; with Jacquetta Hawkes, he went on to do another superb book about a different section of the Southwest twenty years later, *Journey Down A Rainbow*. There is no other region of the United States as fascinating to foreign visitors as the Southwest. It is not pretty, nor pleasant, nor even immediately attractive; it is a harsh, stark, arid land. But it has qualities not to be found anywhere else in the world.

The Southwest, however, covers an enormous area, with striking internal variations. It includes the rolling plains of the cowboy and oil country of Texas and Oklahoma, the low desert regions of southern Arizona and southern New Mexico, and the high desert country, seamed with mountain ranges and deep canyons, which runs from southern Colorado and northern New Mexico west through Arizona and Utah into Nevada. This huge area varies enormously in tradition and 'feel' from one section to the next; the only sure common denominator is a dry sunny climate, and perhaps a predilection for Mexican food.

The scenery of course was there first, and the Grand Canyon is still the Southwest's most celebrated attraction. It is the most remarkable feature of that high country of which we have just spoken, along the top of Arizona. The Grand Canyon was carved out of this plateau by the Colorado River, the one great river of this generally river-less region.

No picture can do justice to the Grand Canyon, any more than a picture can reproduce the vastness of the Pacific Ocean. To quote J. B. Priestly once more, 'I have heard rumours of visitors who were disappointed. The same people will be disappointed at the Day of Judgment.' And yet even the Grand Canyon needs to be treated with proper respect, not rushed, and not seen only in the midst of a crowd from a tour bus. It is at its best at sunset and sunrise, watched quietly, and even more dramatic than the view from the rim is the view from below. Ideally then one should take time there to go on the day-long mule trip down to the river, or even the two-day trip which allows for a night at the Phantom Ranch lodge at the bottom. (Advance reservations are vital for either of these trips.) Or even better, do a float trip of several days down the Colorado; most of these float trips finish at the National Park section of the Grand Canyon, having started a long way upstream.

The extraordinary colours of the rugged walls of the great Canyon are its most dramatic feature, but its entire setting is magnificent. Driving to the South Rim portion of the National Park, one winds upwards from the town of Flagstaff through splendid pine forests. All of this makes the Canyon quite as spectacular in winter, with snow all around, as it is in summer. We can highly recommend it at Easter too; there is nothing else in the world quite like the Easter sunrise service at the rim of the Canyon. But we must warn that this year-round splendour also means year-round popularity; if you want to be sure of staying at the South Rim, at the Bright Angel Lodge or in one of its cabins, you really must make reservations well ahead. The North Rim is less heavily touristed, because it is harder to get to, but its tourist facilities shut down in winter.

Yet the Grand Canyon is by no means the only natural wonder in the Southwest. Poor in so many ways, the Southwest is rich in startling scenery. Sometimes it can seem chill and frightening, a moon landscape, and then again, early in the morning or at sunset when it is all suffused with a golden glow, the strange rocks and spires and escarpments are exceedingly beautiful. In southern Utah there is Zion National Park, and Bryce Canyon National Park. They are close to each other, and not far from the Grand Canyon, but they are each quite distinct and special. One could do worse than simply go from one National Park to another; there were good reasons for designating each one.

Zion National Park in its 94,000 acres encompasses a deep gorge on the Virgin River. After looking from above at the Grand Canyon, it is heady to plunge down into Zion. The towering cliffs on either side are a dark rose intermixed with a paler pink and mauve and orange; incredible colours, and in the spring and summer there are the varied greens of the trees as well.

At Bryce Canyon National Park, one stands on the rim and looks down again, but Bryce is as unlike the Grand Canyon as it is unlike Zion. Actually Bryce Canyon is less a canyon than a giant basin, its floor covered with grotesquely eroded rock formations which look like enormous pink stalagmites. As a Park, it is only about a third the size of Zion, and they complement each other.

From the end of May to the end of September there is a lodge open at both Bryce and Zion where one can stay more reasonably than at most of the better known Parks. There are also camping cabins available all the year round at Zion, and during the summer only at Bryce. At both Bryce and Zion, as at the North Rim of the Grand Canyon, there are horses for hire, and there are any number of good trails and walks and climbs; the rangers will supply maps and give advice.

These Parks are never as crowded as the more celebrated ones like Yellowstone and Yosemite, and either one would be a fascinating place to spend a few days' holiday in the West. If you are travelling by car, you can drop down to Bryce and Zion from Salt Lake City, or combine them handily with the North Rim of the Grand Canyon. Without a car the only way to get to Bryce and Zion is on a tour; tours run from Salt Lake City, and also from Cedar City, Utah, with connections to Salt Lake City.

Bryce Canyon and Zion encompass only a small part of the rugged and remarkable terrain of southern Utah; several other sections are also protected as National Parks and Monuments. For example, between Bryce Canyon and Zion there is Cedar Breaks National Monument, a great pink natural amphitheatre, with camping sites and a small lodge. And in south-eastern Utah there are three more special places: Capitol Reef National Monument, Canyonlands National Park, and Arches National Park. These latter three are not developed; they do not provide overnight lodging or food, or any amenities beyond simple camping sites. But each is remarkable in its own way, and although more people come to this region every year, one is not yet stumbling over hordes of tourists.

However, this is not territory to explore on one's own away from the few main roads; by and large there is no water and no protection from the sun, and a breakdown could be disastrous. If hiking, one should stick to the marked trails. And while you can drive across Capitol Reef on State Route 24, and along the edge of Arches National Park on U.S. 163, really to see this strange and wonderful eroded sandstone landscape one needs a four-wheel-drive car. Or a horse: only on horseback can you get to the extraordinary Indian petroglyphs in Canyonlands. Therefore to do it properly, you must go to Moab or Monticello, towns along U.S. 163, and put yourself into the hands of a knowledgeable guide. There are day-long trips available, and some much longer; we give the name of a reliable Moab firm in our listings at the end of this chapter.

Since Canyonlands National Park includes the confluence of the Colorado and Green Rivers, river trips are also one of the great attractions here. From about May 1 to October 15, there are daily two- and three-hour jet-boat trips into Canyonlands from Moab, and two-hour sound-and-light cruises at night; there is even a sternwheeler excursion boat. And there are proper float trips too, both day-long and longer ones, through Canyonlands on the Colorado River. We list two reliable firms which offer these.

One can do float trips elsewhere in Utah as well. For seeing this harsh, gaunt, but oddly beautiful world at its best, float trips are unquestionably a splendid invention. In Chapter 8 we have already mentioned Dinosaur National Monument; starting from within Dinosaur, one can do one- to five-day trips on the Green River. And then, the *ne plus ultra*, there are float trips varying in length from five to ten days down the Colorado River into the Grand Canyon. These are the most spectacular of all, but also the most expensive. Currently it costs $140 per person all-in to spend five days 'floating' from Dinosaur, and almost $300 for the same amount of time down through the Grand Canyon, with the same outfitter. (The least expensive organized river expedition through any of this exotic canyon country seems to be a nine-day canoeing trip through Canyonlands: $86.50 per person, but one must supply and cook one's own main meals.)

The Spanish explorers who came to the Southwest in the sixteenth century were not looking for natural wonders but for treasure. There were rumours about Seven Cities of Gold somewhere in these parts, and in 1540 Coronado brought a great army to spend two years fruitlessly searching. Yet there really were golden cities, which had probably been the basis for the rumours. And Coronado saw them too, but he dismissed them, for while they were golden in the sunlight they held no treasure to be looted. They were ancient Indian cliff dwellings, and three or four hundred years before Coronado came, they had been the centres of a flourishing civilization.

In fact, a thousand years ago the Four Corners region, where Utah, Colorado, Arizona, and New Mexico meet, was the most populous section of what is today the United States. To the north and east there were only nomad bands of Indians; here the Indians were a settled agricultural people, with a comparatively high standard of comfort and culture. They never reached the level of the Aztecs and the Mayas in Central America, but they were nonetheless respectable country cousins, with at least some of the same refinements. They lived in great blocks of flats which made use of and enlarged upon the natural caves in canyon walls; usually they also built free-standing apartment buildings, precursors of the modern pueblos. Why and how they left these cities, what became of them, no one knows with certainty. The usual assumption is that a drought of unusual severity drove them away. It has been established that there was such a drought, lasting twenty-three years, at the end of the thirteenth century. Or this entire area, appreciably greener and more fertile when they built their communities, may have been steadily growing dryer and dryer for several generations. At any rate there is no discernible sign of violence; they seem simply to have gone away, leaving all sorts of traces to delight future generations of anthropologists. Some of the modern Indians in the Southwest must be descended from cliff dwellers, but no one is quite sure which and how. Certainly the cultural level had dropped by the time the Spaniards came.

Three of the best groups of cliff dwellings are to be found at Mesa Verde in south-western Colorado, at Chaco Canyon north-east of Gallup, New Mexico, and at Canyon de Chelly in the heart of the Navajo Reservation. There are also several smaller 'cities', like that at Bandelier near Santa Fe. All the important cliff dwellings are now either part of a National Park, like Mesa Verde, or protected as National Monuments. Most of them have good small museums in the grounds, with exhibits and dioramas that make the Indian history of the Southwest much clearer. Mesa Verde, the best known, is a beautiful place quite apart from the remarkable cliff dwellings; it is, as its name suggests, a high mesa, and green with spruce and juniper and the aromatic piñon. The views from the road up to it are magnificent too, the landscape below splashed with golden aspen and cottonwood trees. The air is so clear that one can see the San Juan Mountains nearly a hundred miles away. And Mesa Verde is a fully developed National Park, with lodges and cabins, and walks and talks conducted by the Park rangers. Go to Mesa Verde if you possibly can.

The Southwest is not only notable for its evidences of an Indian past. It also has much the largest concentration in the United States of modern Indians. The Indians of the Southwest are the only ones in the United States who succeeded in holding on to a sizeable portion of their old land. Discriminated against and neglected, like all Indians, they were nonetheless better off in some ways because at least they had room enough to be themselves, in country ancestrally dear to them. No one else seemed to want their forbidding desert territory.

There are two major divisions of Southwest Indians, with sub-divisions: the nomad tribes (the Navajo and the Apache) and the Pueblo or village groups (the Zuni, the Hopi, and the Indians of the pueblos along the Rio Grande near Albuquerque and Santa Fe).

The Apaches now live mainly on two reservations in Arizona and two in New Mexico. In their day, the Apaches had an awesome reputation as the fiercest Indians of them all; they did go on fighting the white man longer than any other tribe. Actually, however, the Navajos were once just as predatory, as other Indian tribes could have borne angry witness; the Navajos simply adjusted sooner to the new shape of things. Today the Apaches, together with the Zunis, have become famous as firefighters. When a fire rages out of control in the western mountain timber country, fire-fighters are dropped into the area from planes; the Apaches and the Zunis have made a specialty of this dangerous work.

The Navajo are much the most numerous of the Southwest Indian groups. There are now about 120,000 of them, and the tribe is growing all the time. This is one of their great problems, for no matter how well they administer their lands they cannot adequately support so many people. They depend mainly on sheep for their livelihood, and they lead a hardy, independent life in the manner of sheep-herders the world over. The Navajo do not have villages. Each family has its own hogan or group of hogans; 'hogan' means dwelling place, and a hogan may be a crude temporary affair of brush, or a cabin of mud-plastered logs, or a little house. If you simply drive through the Navajo Reservation, you are not likely to see many Navajos at any one time, unless perhaps you go to the capital of the reservation at Window Rock, almost on the Arizona–New Mexico border. The great annual tribal fair is held at Window Rock in September, and the Tribal Council meets here. Also at Window Rock is the Navajo Arts and Crafts Guild centre, the best possible place to buy Navajo work or simply to learn about it. The Navajos run their own affairs in an exemplary manner, skilfully blending progress with tradition.

The Navajo Reservation is enormous: about the size of Ceylon, twice the size of Belgium. It encompasses some scenery quite as spectacular as that of the southern Utah region we have just described. Four specifically protected sections within the reservation are Navajo National Monument, Monument Valley Tribal Park, Canyon de Chelly National Monument (cliff dwellings), and Painted Desert National Monument. As more and more of the roads through the reservation are graded and paved, it becomes easier all the time to get to these places. But this is still somewhat forbidding territory, not entirely accessible by car, and there are also two good ways to see it properly guided. The Navajo Tribal Council now offers five- and six-day tours, starting at Window Rock with the Navajo Tribal Museum. The entire operation is Navajo-run, but the stops at night are at quite luxurious motels; the five-day tours currently cost $168 per person double-occupancy. (Shorter tours can be specially arranged.) The other alternative would be to spend a night or two at Goulding's Trading Post and Lodge in Monument Valley, the heart of the reservation, and do one of the day-long four-wheel-drive-vehicle tours which the lodge offers. To get to Goulding's, one would need one's own car; for the Navajo tours, one can fly into Gallup and be collected there.

As the development of these tours indicates, the Indians of the Southwest are today trying to expand their economic base. The Apaches, with several separate reservations in the mountainous regions of New Mexico and Arizona, are busily building lodges and camping facilities and ski areas for tourists. And almost all the Southwest Indians are also trying hard to keep old skills going as well, and to turn them to a profit.

Weaving and silverwork are the crafts for which the Navajo is celebrated. Good Navajo rugs, which are lovely, and not cheap, show variation in design, but traditionally the best rugs use only wool that has been dyed with vegetable colours. Navajo silver jewellery is impressive too. Once the Navajos used only turquoise and coral and shells and claws for their jewellery, but then they learned about metal-working from the white man and they took to combining the turquoise with intricately worked silver. Many trading posts not only have new jewellery to sell, but also collections of 'pawn': old family jewellery pawned by its Indian owners. Pawn can be particularly beautiful, rougher and heavier than modern pieces, but often more eloquent. Really good old Navajo pieces, however, are getting harder to find and more expensive all the time.

We should warn that 'trading post' is a word used very loosely in the Southwest. Early trading posts were simply shops in the middle of nowhere which sold anything and everything, and were willing to barter as well. At the trading posts on the Indian reservations, the Indians could trade things they made for whatever they needed from outside, and this they still do. There were trading posts in the towns too, and there still are, in Gallup and in and around Taos, for example. But these days every roadside curio shop calls itself a trading post. Even a genuine old trading post may now carry cheap souvenirs, and what looks like a second-rate curio shop may really be an historic and eminently reputable place. One simply has to develop an instinct for the true and the false. Moreover, the Southwest is flooded with machine-made copies of every kind of Indian object. Sometimes the copy is all that you want, but if there is any appreciable amount of money involved, it is always well to check the label to see whether what you are considering was actually made *by hand by Indians* and if so, what tribe. The laws of New Mexico and Arizona are rightly strict about the labelling.

Entirely enclosed within the Navajo Reservation there is another, smaller reservation, that of the Hopi Indians, a Pueblo tribe. One of the Hopi pueblos here, Oraibi, is exceedingly old; a roof timber in a dwelling there has been dated to 1370. Although they speak different languages, the Hopi and the Zuni and the Rio Grande Pueblo Indians are all related to a degree. Their religious ceremonies and dress are similar, they all live in the same sort of villages, and almost all of them make handsome pottery. But the totems of the Hopi and the Zuni, their kachina figures, are especially interesting; perhaps because they have been less touched by Christianity than any of the other Indian tribes of this region, their culture gives the impression of a particular strength. In the spring there have traditionally been ceremonial dances at some of the Hopi pueblos which visitors could watch; unfortunately, some recent visitors have behaved so badly that it now seems the dances may no longer be held.

However, just to the south-east of the Navajo and Hopi country in the town of Gallup, a four-day Indian Inter-Tribal Ceremonial is held every year in mid-August. Since August is the peak tourist month, one cannot expect the Inter-Tribal Ceremonial to be pure and austere, but the Indians themselves do come in great numbers, together with the white spectators, and there are Indian dances and contests and all sorts of colourful activities.

Quite as famous as the Inter-Tribal Ceremonial, but completely different, is the ceremony known as the Shalako at the Zuni pueblo south of Gallup. The Shalako is held every year a month or so before Christmas, and outsiders are allowed to go and watch, quietly. Much of it takes place at night and the spectators get very cold, as Jacquetta Hawkes attests in *Journey Down A Rainbow*. With its dramatically masked performers, the Shalako is exciting and a little frightening. The Zunis are a very interesting Pueblo group. With only one community, far from the Hopi and the Rio Grande pueblos, they are widely known for such diverse things as the Shalako, their skill as fire-fighters, their fine pottery, and the fact that they are the only Pueblo Indians who produce distinctive jewellery. Once you have seen Zuni jewellery, you can never mistake it: intricate channel-inlay work, with tiny turquoise stones in delicate silver settings, quite unlike the larger-scale Navajo style.

The rest of the Pueblo Indians live farther east in New Mexico. Most of their pueblos are between Albuquerque and Taos, which means that Santa Fe, in the middle, is a good headquarters for visiting them. But there are two, Acoma and Laguna, which are loosely connected with the Rio Grande Pueblos but are by themselves, midway between Gallup and Albuquerque. Laguna, near the highway, is not interesting to visitors except for its mission church, which has a wealth of delightful, innocent trimmings and a splendid herringbone ceiling. Acoma has a celebrated mission church too, but the situation of the pueblo alone would make it famous even if the church were not there. The Acoma pueblo, 'the city in the sky', is perched on the very top of a steep, forbidding butte or mesa, at the end of fifteen miles of very rough dirt road. ('Impassable in bad weather', the maps warn, and they mean it.) The Indians at Acoma are certainly not the friendly, outgoing sort, and the climb up to their pueblo is in itself quite an experience, but once you have been there you are unlikely ever to forget it. Acoma is extremely old, perhaps as old as Oraibi in the Hopi country, and you are very conscious of its antiquity. Here more than anywhere else in the Southwest you have a sense of what the country was like when the Spaniards came, and how mad they were to think that they could tame the land or its people. The massive, echoing nave of Acoma's church, with its vivid, primitive decoration and fine reredos, is powerfully impressive.

The fifteen or sixteen pueblos between Albuquerque and Taos are called the Rio Grande pueblos because they are along that river. The Taos pueblo, two miles north of the town of Taos, is the largest, best known, and the most photogenic. Here as at many of the pueblos there is a fee for entering and another fee for taking pictures; it seems only fair when one considers what an invasion of privacy visitors represent. Most pueblos also charge a fee for sketching, but there are some which allow no sketching at all at any price, and no photography either. One should never, never try to take pictures of an Indian or Indian things without asking permission. All of the pueblos are also more or less sensitive about visitors going near their kivas. Kivas are the sacred place, commonly a small separate building, round or square, with an entrance at the top; usually one can distinguish the kiva by looking for a ladder poking out of the top of a dome or cube. The men of the pueblos use the kiva as both club and temple, and the pueblo ceremonies centre around it.

Unfortunately, with the exception of San Felipe, which allows visitors into its church only between the hours of 8 and 10 on Sunday mornings, none of these Rio Grande pueblos have particularly old or interesting mission churches, nothing comparable to Acoma or Laguna. But the pueblos of San Ildefonso and Santa Clara, between Santa Fe and Taos near Española, are celebrated for their distinctive black pottery. Most of the other pueblos produce pottery with geometric patterns in colour on a white or biscuit ground, but at San Ildefonso and Santa Clara the specialty is either solid burnished black or else a pattern of black on black, part burnished and part mat, and sometimes with the pattern deeply incised. Pueblo pottery is very hard and dense, with a fine timbre; the black pots give an especially rich effect. Of these two pueblos, San Ildefonso is the more renowned because it is the pueblo of Maria, whose pots long ago began to attract international attention. Her son subsequently became a celebrated potter too, and there is a shop at the San Ildefonso pueblo which features their work. San Ildefonso is also noted for its particularly striking kiva, right in the middle of the plaza.

The Santa Clara pueblo now has a shop too, but in most pueblos you need only indicate the slightest interest in pottery in order to be surrounded by women opening up bundles of their artefacts. It may or may not be cheaper than buying from a recognized trader; that depends on the bargaining. At any rate it is more fun.

In the colder months you will be greeted at every pueblo with the delicious odour of burning piñon wood, warming the dwellings and heating the outdoor ovens. The piñon tree also bears a tiny and delicious nut, but it is the smell of burning piñon that lingers in the memory when one knows and loves the Southwest.

The very best place to learn about the Indians of the Southwest is at Santa Fe, one of the most interesting towns in America. At Sante Fe there is the superb Museum of Navajo Ceremonial Art, and in the old Palace of the Governors on the Plaza, now part of the multi-building Museum of New Mexico, there is an excellent section devoted to the Pueblo Indians.

Santa Fe was the Spanish provincial capital of this region. The fortune in gold and precious jewels found in Central America and Mexico having whetted Spanish appetites, Coronado's expedition was only the first of several attempts to find gold hereabouts. (Along the main road from Santa Fe to Taos, a notice informs passers-by that part of Coronado's army passed this way in 1540 to reach the great Taos pueblo; it gives one pause to reflect that in the last years of the reign of Henry VIII, fortune-hunting conquistadors in clanking armour were riding through this mountain valley on the other side of the world.) The dream of gold of course proved illusory, and Spain had to content herself with establishing military outposts and opening up the lands for Spanish settlement. Eventually there were big landowners here, with handsome ranch houses and luxuries brought from Spain and Mexico, fine orchards and vineyards, and many peons, both Spanish and Indian. There were also poorer Spanish settlers, who colonized the hills above the Rio Grande valley.

And there were missionaries. The indefatigable Spanish missionaries established countless missions in the Southwest; if the Spanish could not find gold, they could at least save souls. And in fact most of the Indians did accept Christianity to some degree. However, in 1680 there was a great and bloody Indian revolt against Spanish rule, and thereafter the missionaries never really succeeded in re-penetrating the Hopi and Zuni pueblos. Furthermore, in general they had to accept the fact that the Indians would adopt only so much of the new faith and ritual, blending it with their own strong traditions. It is this blending which underlies the special charm of the mission churches at Acoma and Laguna.

When Mexico seceded from Spain in the early nineteenth century, the change made little difference in this region. The Mexican government seemed almost as remote as Spain, and Santa Fe continued to be the centre of this isolated world, a sleepy, pleasant little town. There were a few Spanish–Mexican settlements in Texas too, but virtually none in Arizona, and California, almost a thousand miles away, had its own separate administration. Even after 1846, when Mexico was forced to abandon this territory and the United States absorbed it, there were few dramatic changes. Most of the important landowners around Santa Fe seemed content with the shift in government. To be sure, there were bitter fights over land grants from time to time, and some of the Anglo-American settlers who now arrived were inclined to look down upon the poorer Spanish-Americans. But on the whole the transition was not too painful, and today all of New Mexico happily capitalizes on her Spanish past. Buildings are done in the Spanish style, and every other restaurant advertises Spanish – or Mexican – food.

In Albuquerque, New Mexico's largest city and mostly very new, this Spanish-ness can seem rather artificial, even though a considerable proportion of the population is indeed of Spanish or Mexican ancestry. The adobe buildings of the University of New Mexico are attractive, and the 'Old Town' section of the city is reasonably quaint, with many tempting shops and restaurants. But in general Albuquerque is a disappointment to anyone expecting something picturesque: too big, lacking distinctive character.

Santa Fe, however, is something else. It is certainly not what it once was, but it is still a very special place, combining its Spanish past with a cosmopolitan present. Its population today is a zesty mixture of artists, writers, Spanish-Americans, the idle rich, and scientists from the neighbouring atomic research station at Los Alamos. The old Plaza in Santa Fe continues to be a gathering place, with Indians under the arches selling beads back to the white man, and the old La Fonda Hotel on the Plaza still a traditional meeting point. Even new things in Santa Fe are old. The place to go now to find Santa Fe's most interesting artists' galleries and shops and restaurants is Canyon Road. But Canyon Road is itself one of Santa Fe's old winding thoroughfares.

We have already mentioned the Museum of Navajo Ceremonial Art and the Pueblo Indian section of the Palace of the Governors at Santa Fe. The Palace of the Governors also includes a fine section devoted to the Spanish past of this region. In addition there is another segment of the multi-partite Museum of New Mexico which one definitely should not miss: the exciting Folk Art Museum, high up on the edge of town next to the Navajo Museum. And, finally, there is an unusual school at Santa Fe, the Institute of American Indian Arts. It draws Indian students interested in an arts education from all over the United States, to work both traditionally and in new directions. One can get an idea of what goes on there by going to its public sales gallery.

Santa Fe has good opera in the summer, too, out of doors in an amphitheatre a few miles north of the town. The repertoire combines the standard favourites with more contemporary opera; Stravinsky conducted his own works there. It is all splendid under the stars, but we must warn that the audience needs warm clothing. It cannot be stressed too often that at these high altitudes (Santa Fe is almost 7,000 feet up) a hot summer's day can turn virtually to frost at night; even in the daytime one can be cold in the shade.

Santa Fe has a good early Spanish parish church, the Church of San Miguel, between the Plaza and Canyon Road; it has a fine reredos and ceiling, and a great bell. But if you want really to glimpse the Spanish past of this region, you must take the 'high road' to Taos. The low road, along the highway, is much the quickest route, and it sufficed for Coronado's men and any number of other celebrated travellers. But the high road is picturesque, and one could go to Taos one way and return the other. We have mentioned little colonies of Spanish settlers in the hills above the Rio Grande valley; the high road goes through several of the oldest villages. The people in these villages have always been poor, and until quite recently they lived almost untouched by the rest of the world, like the Anglo-Americans of the Kentucky and North Carolina mountains. Like those other mountain settlers, these Spanish-Americans have always been deeply religious. Here in New Mexico the religion of course was Roman Catholicism, and it took an extreme form up in the hills. This is the region of the Penitentes, who practised flagellation and perhaps even crucifixion during Easter Week. Some of the practices continue to this day, and no outsider really knows much about them. The Church itself has been almost powerless; these villages became virtually schismatic, with a proper Roman Catholic church and then a separate Penitente chapel. It is kept strictly secret, of course, and one certainly does not make inquiries in the villages, but you can sometimes guess which is the Penitente chapel. If you see a gloomy little building, obviously not a house, with blind windows and no external ornament whatsoever with the possible exception of a bell, that may be it.

To reach these villages you leave the main road from Santa Fe to Taos at Pojoaque or Española, where the 'high road' goes off to the east; it is State Route 76 much of the way. The road leads up into the Sangre de Cristo Mountains, and the views are magnificent. The hills are a background of pink earth dotted with the little dark juniper and piñon trees. It is primitive country, where men still use hand ploughs; deer, jack-rabbits, wild turkey, pheasant and quail abound and there are plenty of trout in the rivers. The old tile roofs of the village houses are gradually being replaced with ugly tin ones, but bright strings of chili still festoon the walls in the autumn. You come to the first notable Spanish church before you have climbed to the really primitive part. It is at Chimayo, a place also famous for its weaving; there is a little shop in the village which sells the local handicrafts; and there is a splendid outdoor restaurant called Rancho de Chimayo. The church is called El Sanctuario, and it is altogether gaudy and beautiful. After Chimayo the road goes steadily up, to the village of Truchas. On the way you pass a road going off to the right to Cordova, a village with excellent wood carvers, as the statues in the church testify. Truchas has a Penitente chapel on the left as you enter the village, but nothing else of note. At Trampas, however, the next village, there is another splendid little Spanish church, mostly eighteenth century. Beyond Trampas are Penasco and Vadito, two more villages with a Penitente tradition, and then you reach State Route 3 and head down to join the main road into Taos once again.

Taos, fifty years ago much more isolated and simple than Santa Fe, is no longer what it was when D. H. Lawrence came to live there. It still draws artists and writers in abundance; it must have a higher ratio of galleries to people than any other small town in the world. (The Stables Gallery is the best.) But in the winter it now draws skiers as well; there are some very good runs on the mountains nearby, and some very attractive (albeit not inexpensive) skiing lodges. Furthermore, several communes have been established in the country around Taos, so that in the old square one now finds Indians from the nearby Taos pueblo in their blankets intermingled with commune-dwellers in theirs.

One should see Taos for any number of reasons, but we particularly recommend two of its 'sights'. One is a relic of the days when this was a frontier town on the road which ran between the Anglo-American world to the north and the Spanish-American world to the south. Kit Carson was one of the legendary figures of that period; he had begun as a mountain man and trapper in the Rockies, and later guided two epic expeditions seeking to map a passable trail to California. In between adventures he lived in Taos with his New Mexican wife, and his little house still stands there, a fine evocation of those early days. The other 'sight' is a superb museum which was established by one of Taos's more recent residents and admirers. It is called the Millicent Rogers Foundation, and it is some distance north of the town but worth every mile of the way; its collection of Southwest treasures of all sorts is quite extraordinary, and beautifully displayed.

One would of course go to the Taos pueblo too, and then on

the way back to Santa Fe one should stop to see the church at
Ranchos de Taos. It has a striking exterior, strong and solid, and
the interior is just as fine. There is something about this country
which one either loves or hates; the little St Francis with a grey
wool cloak and a skull in his hand in the church at Ranchos de
Taos may just sum it up. At any rate the contrasts hereabouts
endlessly fascinate. It is only a short drive from Santa Fe to Los
Alamos, where the bulk of the work on the first atomic bomb was
done, and where neutron physics, fusion, and laser beams are now
major preoccupations. From the excellent nuclear energy museum
there, and the twenty-first century, one can drop back seven
centuries in about as many miles, to see the pre-Columbian cliff
dwellings at Bandelier National Monument.

Many of the skiers who flock to Taos in winter fly in from the
oil-rich cities of Texas and Oklahoma. It is really not very far, by
American standards, but it is certainly a totally different world.
Texas and Oklahoma are much lower in altitude, and generally
characterized by rolling plains, very different from the canyon
and mountain country we have been discussing up to this point.
According to an 1847 guidebook to the United States, these
rolling plains were 'covered with a luxuriant native grass . . .
amply supplied with timber . . . [with] vast herds of buffalo and
wild horses wandering over the prairie, and abundant game and
deer'. It is not quite so idyllic today, but it would not be fair to say
that only a Texan could love Texas.

It is true that western Texas is not beautiful, except perhaps to
a cow or a cowboy or an oilman. It is mostly flat and dusty, cold
in winter and miserably hot in summer. The newly rich oil towns
there are all exactly alike; and every road goes on for ever. But in
the far south-west corner there is a National Park, Big Bend,
which is exciting in part for the very reason that it is so remote, as
well as wild and unspoiled. You feel sure bands of outlaws are
still hiding back in its rugged hills. Much too hot to visit comfortably in summer, it would nonetheless be a fine National Park
to choose in the dead of winter, when most of the other major
parks are covered in snow. And it is truly beautiful in spring, full
of wild flowers.

Far to the east of Big Bend is San Antonio, the only genuinely
colourful city in Texas. The little San Antonio River wanders
casually right through the middle of the city and makes San

Antonio seem still pleasantly informal. At night there are lights along the river, and you can walk down to the water's edge, and hear someone somewhere plucking at a Spanish guitar. Little water-taxis run along the river too, and there is a theatre there, and open-air restaurants and shops.

San Antonio has a special place in the affections of all loyal Texans, for it was here that the Republic of Texas had her baptism of blood. Texas, like New Mexico and Arizona and California, originally belonged to Spain and then became Mexican territory when Mexico seceded from Spain. But in the early nineteenth century Texas began to attract Anglo-American settlers. At the start, Mexico was perfectly willing for these new settlers to come since the region was underpopulated in any case, but disillusionment set in on both sides fairly soon, and the Anglo–American Texans proceeded to revolt against Mexican rule. The first serious engagement of the rebellion took place at San Antonio when a band of one hundred and eighty Texans barricaded themselves in a building known as the Alamo. (Presumably the name came from the overhanging cottonwood trees, *los alamos*.) The Texans were surrounded by four thousand Mexican soldiers under the personal command of Santa Anna, the military dictator of Mexico. Hopelessly outnumbered, they nonetheless refused to surrender, and to a man they died, among them Davy Crockett, the Tennessee frontier hero, and Jim Bowie, the soldier of fortune from New Orleans. Those who were not killed in the fighting were overpowered and slaughtered when the Mexicans broke into the makeshift fort. A month later, crying 'Remember the Alamo', an enraged, inspired army of Texans routed the Mexican forces at the Battle of San Jacinto near Houston, and the Republic of Texas was born. Mexico had learned too late that it is a tactical error to create martyrs.

Texas continued as an independent republic for nine years, and Texans will never let you forget it. They themselves seem sometimes to forget that they finally did join the United States; their cries of pain are terrible whenever they think their sovereign rights are being infringed upon by the federal government.

The Alamo is, of course, the chief tourist attraction in San Antonio. It is a peculiar building, originally a Spanish mission church and then part of a crude fortress, but it has considerable charm. San Antonio has done very well by its old buildings, skilfully preserving and restoring them. The Spanish Governor's

Palace, on Military Plaza not far from the Alamo, is a fine example of San Antonio's colonial past.

In the eighteenth century San Antonio was singularly rich in missions. It is hard to see why there should have been quite so many in one small area, but in addition to the one which became famous as the Alamo there are four more close together along the river at the edge of the town. The road which one takes to see them is called Mission Road, and the second mission along that road is the jewel of the four: the Mission of San José. Its church is very handsome, with splendid baroque ornamentation, and many of the outbuildings can also still be seen. In New Mexico, the mission churches were built merely as part of pueblos which were already there, and many of the old California mission are now stripped down to church and cloister, but at San José one can see all that an active mission once included. They were self-supporting villages, little theocratic city-states, with housing for the Indians and quarters for a military guard, as well as a school and the central religious buildings.

Texas is of course much too big for us to discuss in detail, but we might just say that much of the population in the southern part in particular is Mexican-American, and there is a considerable amount of poverty in amongst the Texas affluence. We should also note that Texans love spectacle, and in addition to rodeos everywhere, you will find a wealth of mock-Disneylands and historic panoramas and African safari-lands. But Texas has many less synthetic attractions too, including a magnificent hundred-mile stretch of unspoiled off-shore beach and sand dunes along the south-eastern coast: Padre Island National Seashore.

As befits the largest city of Texas, Houston has attractions on a very grand scale. Its big Museum of Fine Arts has some very good things, 'Western' and Indian as well as traditional, and a handsome wing designed by Mies van der Rohe. There is an extremely good collection of American furniture and decorative styles in Houston, the Hogg Collection, housed at 'Bayou Bend'. There is a dramatic new church, too: the interdenominational Rothko Chapel. Mark Rothko did the sombre paintings which line its stark octagonal brick walls, and a soaring steel sculpture by Barnett Newman is reflected in the pool at the entrance.

But most Texans seem to crave something larger than life-size, and for them Houston's prime attractions are the NASA Manned-Spacecraft Center, which oversees America's moon

13a. Thirteenth-century Indian cliff dwellings at Mesa Verde, Colorado

13b. Monument Valley, Utah

14a. El Santuario, a mission church near Chimayo, New Mexico

14b. Mission San Xavier del Bac, near Tucson, Arizona. The building was completed in 1797

flights, and the Astrodome, Houston's fantastic indoor sports arena, big enough for baseball and football games. Texans are mad sports fans altogether; anyone driving through the Texas–Oklahoma region in the autumn football season should try to see a local college football game. But then football is a special passion from Texas all the way up into the Great Plains region; you would also do well to look for a game in, say, Nebraska or Kansas.

Despite Houston's greater size, one feels that the real centre of Texas is the Dallas–Fort Worth area. The region around Houston is atypically green and wet, almost like the neighbouring state of Louisiana. At Dallas and Fort Worth, however, the new skyscrapers rear up out of properly hot, dry Texas plains. Only thirty miles apart, Dallas and Fort Worth are traditional rivals, and very different in tone, but each reflects elements basic to Texas today. Fort Worth, as every sign proclaims, is 'where the West begins'. Dallas, on the other hand, wants to be thought of as polished and cosmopolitan, and is pleased that one of its most famous attractions is the elegant Nieman-Marcus department store. Like Houston, Dallas has given generous support to Texas universities, some of which are now exceptionally good. Dallas has a Theater Center designed by Frank Lloyd Wright, and an opera season notable for having been the first to get Joan Sutherland to America and the only American opera company ever really to please Maria Callas. Nonetheless, our favourite cultural attraction in this area is the Amon Carter Museum of Western Art at Fort Worth. Housed in a breathtaking building by Philip Johnson, it can make even the most dedicated cowboy-hater love cowboy art. And the very newest of Texas's superb new museums is also at Fort Worth: the Kimball Art Museum, designed by Louis Kahn.

Despite the tall tales, cities like Dallas aren't really full of weather-beaten ranchers in cowboy hats driving Rolls-Royces. The money is there all right, and the high living, but it seems generally to be kept discreetly hidden within the handsome houses set in charming gardens which one finds in the smart residential sections. But one senses the wealth in subtle ways. Ordinary restaurants in Texas offer steak, in portions ranging from king-size on up but without any nonense about peripheral refinements. Here and there in the largest cities, however, one discovers astonishingly good expensive restaurants; one notable Texas billionaire was reputed to pay the salary of a very costly

French chef at the local hotel so that he could be sure of a good meal whenever he felt like dropping in.

Oklahoma is like Texas in this way; we have had two of the best meals of our lives in Tulsa. And while we don't really have space to say much about Oklahoma, we should note that Tulsa too has a superb museum of 'Western' art, the Gilcrease Institute. Oklahoma is also interesting country with respect to its Indian population, past and present. Here at least some American Indians have had the last laugh. Several tribes from the eastern part of the United States, including most of the Cherokee, were shunted off to the Oklahoma territory in the nineteenth century and given land nobody else then wanted. And then in the twentieth century oil was discovered on this land. Thus today at least some of the Indians in Oklahoma do very well. The old Cherokee capital is Tahlequah, east of Tulsa, at the edge of the Ozark Mountains near the Arkansas border. Several interesting old buildings are still standing, there is an outdoor pageant nightly in summer, and a crafts shop. Another major Indian centre is the town of Andarko, south-west of Oklahoma City. There is an excellent museum at Andarko, the Museum of the Southern Plains Indians; it has a crafts shop as well. Also at Andarko is 'Indian City', a very good recreation of a Plains Indian village, done in cooperation with University of Oklahoma anthropologists. South of Andarko at Lawton, old Fort Sill, the chief military outpost in the Oklahoma territory, still has enough of its nineteenth-century buildings left to give one a good picture of life on the Oklahoma frontier. And there is also a natural monument to those days in the form of a wildlife refuge: the Witchita Mountains Wildlife Refuge, west of Lawton along U.S. 62. It has large herds of both buffalo and longhorn cattle, as well as deer and elk, and handsomely eroded hills for background.

It is forty years now since J. B. Priestley wrote the description of southern Arizona with which we began this chapter, and surely he would be distressed by some of the changes which have taken place in that remarkable part of the Southwest. The section we discussed at the start of the chapter, the high plateau country of the upper Southwest, seems for many centuries to have been the only section with any appreciable amount of population. Next, the Texas and Oklahoma plains were settled. But only in this century has southern Arizona attracted large numbers of people, chiefly since the Second World War. Now it seems dangerously near to attracting too many.

The largest city in Arizona is Phoenix, and the very name indicates its newness. Obviously it is neither an Indian nor a Spanish name, and in fact Phoenix could never have existed at all until our own day; it has risen not from ashes but from nothing at all. This part of Arizona was so arid that few Indians lived here, and the Spaniards hardly bothered with it. Only in our century has it been made to bloom, with vast irrigation projects which have turned the Salt River Valley in which Phoenix lies into a fertile oasis. There are great groves of oranges and grapefruit and dates, and Phoenix is a prosperous city with more than half a million people.

The prosperity is not entirely agricultural, either. The climate here in the winter is very attractive, and Phoenix is ringed by resort towns and 'retirement communities'. Since 'retirement communities' seem to be a unique American institution, visitors to Phoenix ought really to see the most celebrated one in the United States, Sun City, about twenty miles north of Phoenix. One must be fifty years old to buy a house there, and many of the residents are of course considerably older, but there are golf courses and swimming pools and 'leisure activities' enough to keep everyone constantly on the move. It is a veritable Shangri-la, in fact, and one can spend a happy, frivolous hour or two touring the 'model homes', samples of new Sun City houses would-be residents can buy.

If it seems odd to begin a description of one city with talk about another, our justification is that Phoenix is unlike most cities in any case. In some ways it bears a resemblance to Los Angeles; it merges into the surrounding communities in an unplanned and unlovable urban sprawl across a huge area whose original configurations are now lost to view. Both cities have naturally dry and sunny climates; one could once have said that Phoenix did not have the smog problem Los Angeles suffers from, but unfortunately this is no longer quite true. Both cities are also perhaps at their best seen at night from above. At Phoenix, one of the nicest things one can do is to take a picnic to the peaks of South Mountain Park, a fine unspoiled area south of the city, and watch the sunset and then the lights coming on all over the great valley below. And if one does go to South Mountain, one can see on the way another one of the characteristics Phoenix shares with

Los Angeles; given enough water, everything grows luxuriantly here. Along Baseline Road, at the foot of South Mountain Park, there are miles of commercial flower gardens, a lovely sight in the late-winter peak blooming season.

Of course Phoenix is not nearly so large and international a city as Los Angeles, and the attractions it offers visitors are quite different. We like the Heard Museum; it is not an enormous collection, but it has some good Spanish colonial and Southwest Indian things. And we heartily recommend the Desert Botanical Garden; it might not seem very tempting in summer, when Phoenix is incredibly hot, but on a spring (or autumn or winter) morning it is lovely to wander through this splendidly arranged garden and learn about the remarkable desert plants of this region. For southern Arizona, wherever people have not crowded it out, still does have an extraordinary range of desert vegetation: enormous cacti like the saguaro, lovely desert shrubs like the ocotillo, and giant yuccas, and the flowering Joshua tree.

The most fashionable residential sections of the greater Phoenix region are to the north-east, and we recommend driving there, to Scottsdale, an affluent and attractive town with some very tempting shops with good Mexican and Indian things along its Fifth Avenue. Twenty or thirty miles north of Scottsdale, there is a newer, much smaller, explosion of affluence in the midst of very handsome mountain-and-desert scenery. It is two connected settlements, Cave Creek and Carefree; driving up there for lunch through a fine desert landscape not only is a pleasant excursion but would also give one a good idea of the sort of life people with money can lead hereabouts.

Not nearly so far north of Scottsdale, there are also two exceptionally interesting architectural centres to visit. One is Taliesen West, the winter home of Frank Lloyd Wright's architectural school and fellowship. Built long before Phoenix assumed its present proportions, it once seemed a remote and exotic flowering in the desert, its buildings one of the first significant attempts to come to terms architecturally with this kind of country. It still repays a visit; Wright's architectural fellowship is so far still continuing, and there are visiting hours. A much newer architectural centre is that of Paolo Soleri, the Italian city-planning visionary. *The New York Times* has admiringly called him 'the prophet in the desert'; his 'arcology' concept is revolutionary, and we strongly recommend a visit to his Cosanti Foundation.

The buildings there give one some idea of his approach, and there are large models of his projected cities of the future. Furthermore, it's a warm and cheerful place.

If Soleri can ever assemble enough money, he will someday have created a real city-of-the-future, Arcosanti, in central Arizona. Indeed by the time this book is published, there may at least be enough built at Arcosanti so that visitors will be allowed; work goes on steadily there. But one ought in any case to see that portion of Arizona, where the lower desert merges into the canyon country. One might combine a visit to Jerome with Oak Creek Canyon, perhaps spending a night at Sedona, a handsomely situated little town. Jerome is an old mining town with the most spectacular situation of them all, well worth the climb up to it. Oak Creek Canyon winds from Sedona in the valley below Jerome up towards Flagstaff and the Grand Canyon; driving through it is a glorious experience at almost any time of the year. (We recommend, too, the dramatic Chapel of the Holy Cross, built on an escarpment at the edge of Sedona.) In this same area, depending on which route one takes, one can also see two fine examples of pre-Columbian Indian settlements. One is Montezuma Castle National Monument, a cliff dwelling, and the other is Tuzigoot National Monument, an abandoned pueblo of the twelfth century which rears up above a lovely valley with a river shaded by cottonwood trees.

There is also another large city in Arizona which deserves mention: Tucson, south of Phoenix and not very far from Mexico. (If one is staying at Tucson, it is an easy trip to drive to Nogales, across the border, for the day; and Nogales is one of the better Mexican border towns.) Tucson is only half the size of Phoenix, but unlike Phoenix it does have some history. There were never great numbers of Spaniards around here, but there were missionaries, and the mission church of San Xavier del Bac near Tucson may well be the loveliest mission church of them all. Built in the late eighteenth century, it is much more ornate and rococo on the exterior than most of the mission churches one finds in the United States. It resembles neither the California examples nor those of New Mexico; people say that it is like the best old churches in Mexico itself. The inside of the church is beautiful too, richly decorated long ago by the mission Indians directed by the Franciscan builders.

Tucson is a simpler place altogether than Phoenix, although it too is beginning to suffer grievously from urban sprawl. We like Tucson best as a centre for exploring the desert, preferably by staying at a ranch and riding into the hills. (We will list our favourite Tucson ranch at the end of the chapter.) But in addition to the mission of San Xavier del Bac, there are things to see in and around Tucson. The Arizona State Museum in the grounds of the University of Arizona there has graphic, illuminating exhibits about many aspects of life in the Southwest. There is a good desert-botanic garden, the Arizona-Sonora Desert Museum, with desert animals as well as plants. And near this Desert Museum, west of Tucson proper, there is 'Old Tucson', a recreation of Arizona's frontier days which does double duty as tourist attraction and film set. A great many major films are indeed made there; it has sound stages too, and it is really great fun to visit, especially if they happen to be shooting a film when one goes.

Then too from Tucson you can go to Tombstone, one of those Western mining towns which bloomed overnight like a desert cactus and was equally spikey. Countless films have been made about Wyatt Earp's adventures as Marshal of Tombstone, and some of the famous landmarks of its wicked past have been carefully preserved. The mining here remained profitable for only a short time, but Tombstone is not entirely a ghost town, since it is not too far from Tucson and the address is irresistible to devotees of the old West.

There are other National Monuments in Arizona too: some, like Chiricahua, notable for their unusual rock formations, others, like Saguaro National Monument, for their vegetation. But we should not leave this lower desert country without mentioning two natural phenomena which are actually not in Arizona, but in southern New Mexico, a considerable distance to the east of Tucson. One is the White Sands National Monument, a sand desert which really does, as everyone says, look exactly like great billows and drifts of snow. The other is Carlsbad Caverns, a National Park area which protects America's most vast and dazzling underground world. There is an added attraction at Carlsbad Caverns too: great colonies of bats live in the recesses of the cave and emerge by the thousands every night, flying in formation.

We have left to the last the one area which is still noticeably underpopulated, the state of Nevada. Strictly speaking, it is not really part of the Southwest, but its look and climate make it seem to fit logically into this chapter.

Nevada is barren, with no major rivers and virtually no rainfall at all. In the West one soon becomes conscious of 'eastern slope' versus 'western slope' as a crucial climatic distinction. Nevada lies on the eastern slope of the towering Sierra Nevada range, which means that any moisture the clouds have carried from the Pacific has already been jolted out of them by those mountains before the clouds reach Nevada. Bare blue sky above, bare dry land below is all one sees. It goes without saying that Nevada is hardly a rich farming state, but there are a few fertile valleys and even in the most barren parts some cattle and sheep. Where vegetation is so sparse, one may need a grazing area of a hundred acres, two hundred acres, even more, for every animal one owns, so you may not actually see any animals at all. But they are there, the sheep up in the hills in the summer, often with Basque shepherds especially imported for the lonely life.

There are only two real population centres in Nevada, one around Reno, half-way down the western border of the state, and the other in the south-western corner, at Las Vegas. Both Las Vegas and Reno are wide-open gambling towns, lighting up the desert at night with their spectacular neon signs. Las Vegas is of course the more famous, simply because no other place anywhere has so many flamboyant casinos and hotels. Nowhere else will you find such galaxies of stars; up and down the Strip the big names flash on and off in an effort to lure you to this casino or that with the prospect of being entertained by the inimitable so-and-so before or after you pause at the tables. It works, of course; Las Vegas is well-nigh irresistible. But there does come the moment when all the dazzle begins to seem a bit much, and even the added novelty of being able to gamble before breakfast, gamble by the swimming pool, and gamble in the supermarket begins to pall. And then you realize that Las Vegas hasn't anything else to offer. One can of course go to see Hoover Dam, only thirty miles away; when it was built in the 1930s it was the engineering marvel of the world, and it is still the largest if not the highest dam in the United States. There are tours down inside it, and one can also go to swim or take a boat ride on the enormous lake it has created, Lake Mead. But after that there is nothing to do but go back to the tables again, tempting perhaps if you're having a run of luck, but not so good if your reserves are shrinking.

Reno is different, because Reno is situated in much more interesting country. Reno is quite high: 4,491 feet up, with mountains nearby. Its casinos are downright bourgeois compared to the splendour at Las Vegas, but they are certainly adequate. At Reno too, as everywhere in Nevada, you encounter 'slot machines' in every spare corner waiting to swallow your loose silver. But when at Reno you run out of gambling money, there are other things to do and see. You can, for example, see what must be the only town library with reflecting pools and fountains in amongst the books. And you can go to see surely the most remarkable museum of antique cars anywhere in the world, Harrah's Automobile Collection. (You can even get to it from the centre of town in an antique bus.) Its founder also owns Reno's fanciest casino; it is a consolation to know that one's losings go to such a noble cause. For Harrah's Automobile Collection really is magnificent: vast barns full of treasures, every possible sort of rare vintage car lovingly restored and tended. (One can watch men at work on restoration in the outbuildings on the grounds.) Presumably you could also go to see Reno's courthouse, which yields up more divorces than any other courthouse in America, although now that other states have relaxed their divorce laws not so many people come to Reno for that. And you can hunt out restaurants which offer Basque food: the influence of the Basque sheep-herders who have been imported into this part of Nevada.

Moreover, when you have exhausted the possibilities of the town itself, there are good excursions one can make from Reno. The first is one not many people make, and this would seem a pity except that it helps to keep it relatively unspoiled. The attraction in question is Pyramid Lake, thirty miles or so north of Reno, on State Route 33. Driving up to Pyramid Lake one goes through bare mountainous country like pale elephant hide, and then suddenly around a bend one sees ahead and below a great clear lake of a startling dark blue, set into a pink and mauve mountainous background. With any luck, there may not even be anyone else around; there are a few camping sites at Pyramid Lake, and in the summer some fishing and water-skiing, but much of the year it is virtually deserted. You can sit at the pull-off above the lake, observing the subtle colour changes as the sun moves across, and perhaps eating the picnic you have cleverly supplied yourself with. The casinos of Reno will seem a very long way away.

Alternatively, one can go south from Reno, to Virginia City.

We have talked before about old mining towns, and we will encounter them again in California, but Nevada's Virginia City was the most fabulous mining town of them all. This is the site of the Comstock Lode, the richest strike in the history of the West, almost four hundred million dollars in gold and silver yielded up in less than twenty years. At its peak period, in the 1870s, trains were leaving Virginia City at the rate of two an hour to carry off the ore. The great fortunes here were made by coalitions of shrewd entrepreneurs from San Francisco, mostly men who had started off in life not as struggling miners but as struggling shop-keepers and money-lenders. Many of the Comstock Lode million-aires were the very prototypes of the villainous mineowners in standard Western films, busily cheating their partners and the general public. But some of them at least were lavish with their riches, building mansions at Virginia City fitted with marble and gold, dressing their wives in Paris velvets, importing entire opera companies for one evening's entertainment. The ordinary Virginia City miner, who earned high wages for his man-killing work, had extravagant pleasures too; for once, no Hollywood version could possibly be an exaggeration. In addition to the usual girls and the cold-eyed gamblers, there were the most famous entertainers in the world, actors and singers and public speakers; Virginia City paid well, and in any case everyone was curious to see it. The local newspaper, *The Territorial Enterprise*, even had the sort of witty, courageous editor films like to attribute to all Western towns, and Mark Twain, after a brief and catastrophic try at mining, did his first successful writing for this paper. Virginia City today is a tourist attraction because of its past; many of the old buildings remain. We recommend beginning with the slide-show at the Visitors Bureau. But go too to the graveyard on the hill and contemplate the crumbling tombstones of all the hapless miners who came to these mountains from the far corners of the earth: 'native of Bavaria', 'native of France', 'native of Cornwall', 'native of Wales'.

The drive itself to Virginia City is quite beautiful, winding up into the mountains, and afterwards one can head for Carson City on State Route 80, past Gold Hill and Silver City with their little miners cabins still straggling up the mountainsides. Carson City is the capital of Nevada, the smallest of all the state capitals, and it is also on the the way to Lake Tahoe, a very large alpine lake set in the Sierra Nevadas. Lake Tahoe too is a remarkable blue in colour, but it is surrounded not by bare rock but by pine forests, which enhance the colour of the water in a completely different way. There are state parks on both sides of Lake Tahoe, with camping sites; they seem very peaceful and remote from the world. But Lake Tahoe is half in Nevada and half in California, and this means that along its southern shore there are now great gaudy gambling casinos right up to the California state line. Tahoe now almost rivals Las Vegas in the glitter of the star-attractions at its casinos, although it is not nearly so big. In any case, it all seems a very long way from the lonely saguaro sentinel in the desert with which we began this chapter.

SPECIAL KNOWLEDGE

No other region which we have described has so varied a **climate** as the Southwest. The season of the year should thus be one's first consideration when planning a trip there. We have stressed the fact that the northern section is generally high, which means cold and snow in winter and cold nights even in summer, when the days can get very hot indeed. The southern half, however, is mostly low, and since there is virtually perpetual sunshine, one finds a glorious autumn, winter, and spring, but summer heat like Anatolia. (In Nevada, even though it is considerably farther north, roughly the same distinction applies; Reno has the high-altitude desert climate, and Las Vegas the low.) This does not mean that one should not go to the northern parts at all in winter, or to the southern section in summer. The only entire area you should really rule out in winter is the southern Utah canyon country; there simply isn't enough population in that region to warrant keeping the roads clear of snow. But many people have a particular fondness for the high country from Santa Fe to the Grand Canyon in winter. You would probably be unable to do much back-country exploring there then; much of the Navajo Reservation, for example, would become inaccessible. The main highways, however, the road to the Grand Canyon, and towns like Santa Fe and Taos, would all be fine. The southern desert country presents the reverse situation. Summer is terribly hot around Phoenix and Tucson, yet many people go there then and enjoy it immensely. The rates at every motel and dude ranch drop noticeably, which is tempting. Everything is air-conditioned, and one simply plans hikes or horseback rides for the early morning, and afterwards leaps into a swimming pool.

If you are **driving** on back roads in the Southwest after a rain in spring or summer or during a sudden thaw in winter, you must beware of flash floods. So many of the river beds are dry so much of the year that many minor roads pass right down into and across them without bridges. When there is a sudden rush of water from one of the infrequent rains, many roads become temporarily impassable. Another sound driving warning for the Southwest is never to let your petrol tank get too low; petrol stations are not all that frequent in the less populated areas. Moreover a relatively full tank is a good idea altogether in extremely hot or cold climates. If you are driving in very hot weather (and perhaps climbing through rugged terrain) you are warned in the West always to check your water and tires every morning before setting off, and then to watch lest your car over-heat. If it seems to be doing just that, simply pull up and wait for it to cool down, opening the bonnet for better circulation but not removing the radiator cap until everything is cool. Many people also advise carrying extra water when driving through the desert, and if it is really hot you might drive at night and spend the day at a motel with a swimming pool.

One can get to the South Rim (the chief Park section) of the **Grand Canyon** by transcontinental train; special buses run from the station at Williams, Arizona. There is also bus service three times a day from Flagstaff, Arizona, which one can reach on Greyhound and Continental Trailways buses. There are several possible ways to fly to the Grand Canyon as well. Within the Park itself, sightseeing buses run along the South Rim, collecting and depositing passengers at the lodges.

Anyone considering a **float trip** should ask how many boats and people will be involved; it is far pleasanter to be part of a relatively small expedition. We have also been told that May and September are the best months for float trips on the Colorado River, which flows through deep caverns that can get very hot in summer.

The Utah Travel Council publishes an excellent brochure, *Utah: Discovery Country*, which they will happily mail free of charge. It is the best possible source for information about float trips and National Parks tours and organized camping expeditions anywhere in Utah. (See listings.)

One is confronted by a great many strange and new things when one visits the Southwest for the first time, and we would hope that anyone planning a trip there would try to do a little homework in advance. But one can of course buy excellent books and booklets once one has arrived; the shops at the Grand Canyon, at Santa Fe and Taos, and in Scottsdale, are particularly good sources.

At Santa Fe one can find out about any **Pueblo Indian** festivals which might be going on during one's stay; there seem to be festivals at one pueblo or another almost year-round, but the dates change every year. Furthermore, there are now six-day **tours** of the Rio Grande pueblos, run as a combined Pueblo Indian enterprise. Since one does not face any special problem with terrain or transport in this region, a tour might seem unnecessary. Yet the pueblos tour involves a deep look into Pueblo Indian life, spending time with Indian families, and it can thus not fail to be interesting. (See listings.)

We wax very enthusiastic over the **food** in the Santa Fe region. All over the Southwest one finds Mexican restaurants and quick-snack places, and some are very good. But around Santa Fe one gets not only the standard Mexican specialties but also echoes of the older Spanish tradition, and in the very best restaurants innovative variations on both. We particularly recommend The Shed in Santa Fe (lunch only), El Farol and Three Cities of Spain on Santa Fe's Canyon Road (the latter is a combined restaurant and coffee house, with classic films some nights as well), Rancho de Chimayo on the high road to Taos, and La Cocina de Taos at Taos itself. And do try sopaipillas with honey.

Apache is pronounced 'apatchy', Navajo is 'navaho', Canyon de Chelly is 'canyon de shay', Albuquerque is 'albukerky', saguaro is 'suwarro'; pronounce Houston as in Euston, for Tucson say 'tooson' and for Taos 'tah-os'. An *arroyo* is a river bed or water course, usually dry. A *mesa* or *butte* is a projection of table-land or plateau above a surrounding plain.

National Parks and Monuments

All the following National Parks and Monuments are open daily unless otherwise stated.

ARCHES NATIONAL MONUMENT, UTAH. For information write to the Superintendent, Canyonlands National Park, Moab, Utah 84532. There is a modern campground, but campsites cannot be reserved.

BANDELIER NATIONAL MONUMENT, NEW MEXICO. 28 May to 5 September, daily 8–7.30; 6 September to 27 May, daily 8–5.

BIG BEND NATIONAL PARK, TEXAS. General information from the Superintendent, Big Bend National Park, Texas 79834. The administrative building at Panther Junction is open daily 8–5. Most of the petrol stations in the park close at 6 p.m.

BRYCE CANYON NATIONAL PARK, UTAH. For general and camping information write to the Superintendent, Bryce Canyon National Park, Bryce Canyon, Utah 84717. Camping facilities are available from 1 May to 15 November; no reservations. The inn with cabins is open from early May to early October and the lodge also with cabins, from 10 June to Labor Day; for reservations write to Utah Parks Co., Cedar City, Utah 84720.

CANYON DE CHELLY NATIONAL MONUMENT, ARIZONA. The Visitor Center is open daily; summer 8–7; winter 8–5. Campground facilities only. Half- or whole-day jeep trips are available from mid-May to mid-October. Cost for a whole-day tour, including lunch, is $15; a 2-hour tour is $3. Horses can also be hired.

CANYONLANDS NATIONAL PARK, UTAH. Information from the Superintendent, Canyonlands National Park, Moab, Utah 84532. Camping facilities. For tours into Canyonlands in four-wheel-drive vehicles, write to Mitch Williams Tag-A-Long-Tours, 452 North Main Street, Moab, Utah 84532. Telephone (801) 253-4346. Approximate cost $20 to $25 per person per day. For float trips, see under separate heading.

CAPITOL REEF NATIONAL MONUMENT, UTAH. General and camping information from the Superintendent, Torrey, Utah 84775. Camping facilities.

CARLSBAD CAVERNS NATIONAL PARK, NEW MEXICO. 27 miles southwest of Carlsbad on U.S. Routes 62 and 180, turning off on State Route 7. There is a bus service from Carlsbad and El Paso. Complete tour is 3 miles and takes 3½ hours, allowing 40 minutes for lunch. A shorter trip joins the tour by elevator in the lunch room. Tours leave at frequent intervals.

CEDAR BREAKS NATIONAL MONUMENT, UTAH. For general and camping information write to the Superintendent, Cedar Breaks National Monument, Box 749, Cedar City, Utah 84720. Camp season extends from early June to late October. The Lodge is open June to Labor Day; for reservations write to Utah Parks Co., Cedar City, Utah 84720.

CHACO CANYON NATIONAL MONUMENT, NEW MEXICO. Visitor Center and Museum, 29 May to 4 September, daily 8 a.m.–9 p.m.; 5 September to 28 May, daily 8–5. Free. Campground facilities only.

CHIRICAHUA NATIONAL MONUMENT, ARIZONA. 36 miles south-east of Wilcox on State Route 186. Visitor Center is open 1 September to 31 May, daily 8–5; 1 June to 31 August, daily 8–6. Camping information from Visitor Center. Horses may be hired from Faraway Ranch near the entrance.

GRAND CANYON NATIONAL PARK, ARIZONA. General and camping information from the Superintendent, Grand Canyon National Park, Grand Canyon, Arizona 86023.

SOUTH RIM: Reservations for accommodation and mule trips are advisable at any time of the year, but are essential from 1 May to 31 October. For reservations write to Fred Harvey, Grand Canyon, Arizona 86023. A Park bus runs from Flagstaff to the South Rim and back, 3 times daily in summer, and once daily in winter. There is also a train from Williams in the summer. For float trips see under separate heading.

NORTH RIM: Accommodation is open from June to Labor Day. There is a Park bus which operates from Cedar City from mid-June to 31 August. For reservations write to Utah Parks Co., Cedar City, Utah 84720.

MESA VERDE NATIONAL PARK, COLORADO. For general and camping information write to the Superintendent, Mesa Verde National Park, Colorado 81330. Museum with tour information is open mid-June to Labor Day, daily 7.45–7.30; rest of the year, daily 8–5. Free. For accommodation reservations write to Mesa Verde Co., Mesa Verde National Park, Box 277, Mancos, Colorado 81328. Accommodation is only available from early May to mid-October.

MONTEZUMA CASTLE NATIONAL MONUMENT, ARIZONA. Entrance is on State Route 79, 5 miles north of Camp Verde. Summer daily 7.30 a.m.–7 p.m.; rest of the year 8–5. The 'Castle' can only be seen from the outside.

MONUMENT VALLEY NAVAJO TRIBAL PARK, ARIZONA. Visitor Center, 4 miles south-east of U.S. Route 163, is open daily from 1 March to 31 October. Campground facilities only. For information on Goulding's Valley Tours into Navajo Country, see Monument Valley.

SAGUARO NATIONAL MONUMENT, ARIZONA. Saguaro is divided into 2 parts. The Rincon Mountain section is 17 miles east of Tucson, going out on East Broadway. The Tucson Mountain District is 15 miles west on Speedway Boulevard and Anklam Road.

TUZIGOOT NATIONAL MONUMENT, ARIZONA. 2 miles east of Clarkdale. 1 June to 8 August, daily 7–6; 9 August to 31 May, daily 8–5.

WHITE SANDS NATIONAL MONUMENT, NEW MEXICO. 15 miles south-west of Alamogordo on U.S. Route 82. 30 May to Labor Day, daily 7 a.m.–10 p.m.; April, May, September and October, daily 8–8; rest of the year, daily 8–6. Visitor Center open 30 May to Labor Day, daily 8–8; April, May, September and October, daily 8–7; rest of the year, daily 8–6.

ZION NATIONAL PARK, UTAH. For information write to the Superintendent, Springdale, Utah 84767. Campgrounds are open all the year with no reservations. Zion Inn is open mid-May to 30 September; and Zion Lodge from early June to Labor Day. Write for reservations to The Utah Parks Co., Cedar City, Utah 84720.

Float Trips in the National Parks

FLOAT TRIPS on the Colorado River through Canyonlands and the Grand Canyon, and on the Yampa and Green Rivers through Dinosaur. For information write to Grand Canyon/Canyonlands Expeditions, P.O. Box O, Kanab, Utah 84741; telephone (801) 644-2691. Or Jack Currey's Western River Expeditions, P.O. Box 6339, Salt Lake City, Utah 84106; telephone (801) 486-2323. Cost per person $150 to $200 per 5 days. Also, Mitch Williams, Tag-Along-Tours; see Canyonlands.

CANOEING TRIPS through Canyonlands on the Colorado River. For information on organized trips, cooking your own meals but with canoeing equipment and lunches supplied, write to Tex's Tour Center, P.O. Box 67, Moab, Utah 84532; telephone (801) 253-2312. Cost per person is $86.50 approx.

Tours to the National Parks

CEDAR CITY, UTAH. Tours leave from here to Bryce Canyon and Zion, and also longer ones which include the Grand Canyon; reservations from Utah Parks Company, P.O. Box 400, Cedar City, Utah 84720; telephone (801) 586-9476. The 3-day 2-night tour without meals costs approximately $44.50 per person.

Acoma, New Mexico

ACOMA PUEBLO is 3 miles south-west on State Route 23, which is a gravel road and may be impassable in bad weather, and then a steep climb up to the top of the mesa. The Pueblo is open daily 1 hour before sunrise to 1 hour after sunset. An admission fee is charged.

Andarko, Oklahoma

INDIAN CITY is 2½ miles south on State Route 8. 1 June to 6 September, daily 9-6; 7 September to 31 May, daily 9-5. Closed 23 November and 25 December.

MUSEUM OF THE SOUTHERN PLAINS INDIANS, east on U.S. Route 62. 1 June to 30 September, Monday to Saturday 9-4.30, Sunday 1-5; 1 October to 31 May, Tuesday to Saturday 9-4.30, Sunday 1-5. Closed 1 January, 25 November and 25 December. Free.

Dallas, Texas

DALLAS THEATER CENTER, 3636 Turtle Creek Boulevard. Tours Monday to Friday 1-1.30, Saturday 11-2, Sunday 2-4. Closed 16 August to 1 September and holidays.

Fort Worth, Texas

AMON CARTER MUSEUM OF WESTERN ART, 3501 Camp Bowie Boulevard, 2½ miles west. 1 June to 31 August, Monday to Saturday 10-5,

Sunday and holidays 1–5.30; 1 September to 31 May, Tuesday to Saturday 10–5, Sunday and holidays 1–5.30. Closed 1 January and 25 December. Free.

KIMBELL ART MUSEUM, Will Rogers Road West (opposite Will Rogers Coliseum). Tuesday to Saturday 10–5, Sunday 2–5. Closed 1 January, 4 July, Thanksgiving and 25 December.

Gallup, New Mexico

INDIAN INTER-TRIBAL CEREMONIAL lasting 4 days, takes place in mid-August.

Hoover Dam, Nevada, Arizona

Just east of Boulder City on U.S. Routes 93 and 466. A guided tour decends by elevator and lasts 35 minutes. End of May to Labor Day, daily 7 a.m.– 8 p.m.; rest of the year, daily 8–5.

Hopi Reservation, Arizona

HOPI SILVERCRAFT ARTS AND CRAFTS COOPERATIVE GUILD, on State Route 264 at Second Mesa. Daily 8–6.

Houston, Texas

ALLEY THEATRE, 612 Texas Street, is an innovative repertory theatre and an architecturally interesting building. Monday to Friday, conducted tours at 12.45.

ASTRODOME is just off Kirby Drive, near the junction with the South Loop Road. Guided tours daily at 11, 1 and 3; 1 June to 31 August, an additional tour at 5. Tours do not take place when the arena is in use.

HOGG COLLECTION is at Bayou Bend, 1 Westcott Street. 2-hour tours leave every 15 minutes. Tuesday 1.15–2.30, Wednesday to Friday 10–11.15 and 1.15–2.30, Saturday 10–11.15. Families with children under 17 only admitted on the second Sunday in every month. Closed August and national holidays.

MUSEUM OF FINE ARTS, South Main Street and Montrose Boulevard. Tuesday to Saturday 9.30–5, Sunday 12–6. Free.

NASA-MANNED SPACECRAFT CENTER, 22 miles south-east on U.S. Route 45, then 2½ miles east on NASA Road 1. Several buildings are open daily 9–4. Closed holidays. Advance reservations for guided tours from Special Events Office, AP5 NASA-Manned Spacecraft Center, Houston, Texas 77058. Telephone (713) 483-4321.

ROTHKO CHAPEL, 1401 Sul Ross, near the corner of Alabama and Montrose Streets. Daily 12–8.

Indian Arts and Crafts Centres

APACHE SUMMIT CAFÉ, LODGE AND SHOP, Mescalero, Mescalero Apache Indian Reservation, New Mexico; on U.S. Route 70, ten miles west of Ruidoso.

CHEROKEE INDIAN ARTS AND CRAFTS CENTRE, see under Talequah Oklahoma.

HOOKSTONE, see under Santa Fe.

HOPI SILVERCRAFT COOPERATIVE, see under Hopi Reservation.

JICARILLA ARTS AND CRAFTS SHOP, on State Route 17 at Dulce, New Mexico, on the edge of the Jicarilla Indian Reservation.

ZUNI CRAFTSMEN COOPERATIVE, see under Zuni Pueblo.

Indian Festivals

FLAGSTAFF, ARIZONA. Pow-wow 1–4 July.

GALLUP, NEW MEXICO. Four-day Inter-Tribal Ceremonial, mid-August.

WINDOW ROCK, ARIZONA. Navajo Fair, mid-September.

ZUNI PUEBLO, NEW MEXICO. Shalako Ceremony, November or December.

Lawton, Oklahoma

FORT SILL MUSEUM, in Fort Sill Military Reservation, 5 miles north on U.S. Route 62 and 281. Daily 8.30–4.30. Closed 1 and 2 January, 24 and 25 December.

WICHITA MOUNTAINS WILDLIFE REFUGE, 12 miles west on U.S. Route 62 to Cache and then north. Camping facilities only.

Monument Valley, Utah

Tours in four-wheel-drive station wagons to various parts of Monument Valley leave daily at 9. Independent tours may be arranged in advance. For information write to Goulding's Valley Tours, Goulding's Monument Valley Lodge, P.O. Box 1, Monument Valley, Utah 84536.

Phoenix, Arizona

COSANTI FOUNDATION, 6433 Doubletree Road, Scottsdale. Visitors are welcome to walk through the grounds and view the buildings and watch the soleri windbells being cast.

DESERT BOTANICAL GARDEN, 5800 East Van Buren Street, in Papago Park. Daily 9–5.

HEARD MUSEUM, 22 E. Monte Vista Road, Monday to Saturday 10–5, Sunday 1–5.

TALIESEN WEST, off Shea Boulevard on Titel Road. 1 October to 30 June, Monday to Saturday 10–4, Sunday 12–4. Guided tours every half-hour. No tours when it rains. Check for summer hours.

Ranchos de Taos, New Mexico

CHURCH OF ST FRANCIS OF ASSISI, on the Plaza. Summer daily 6–6. It may also be open sometimes during the rest of the year.

Reno, Nevada

HARRAH'S AUTOMOBILE COLLECTION, on Dermody Way, off Glendale Road, 3½ miles east of Reno. Daily 9–6; open till 10 p.m. in summer. Free bus from Harrah's, Reno.

Salt Lake City, Utah

SALT LAKE CITY. Gray Line run tours, 4 to 5 nights, to Monument Valley, Dinosaur, Mesa Verde, Durango-Silverton; also 4 to 5 nights to Capitol

Reef, Bryce Canyon, Zion Cedar Breaks and the North Rim of Grand Canyon. Approximate cost with meals $208 per person. Reservations from The Gray Line, 29 West South Temple, Salt Lake City, Utah 84101; telephone (801) 521–2150.

San Antonio, Texas

THE ALAMO, on Houston Street, near the junction with Avenue E. Monday to Saturday 9–5.30, Sunday 10–5.30. Closed 24 and 25 December.

GOVERNOR'S PALACE, on Military Plaza. Monday to Saturday 9–5, Sunday and holidays 10–5.

SAN JOSE MISSION, 6539 San Jose Drive, 6¼ miles south on U.S. Route 281. 1 April to 30 September, daily 9–8; 1 October to 31 March, daily 9–6.

Santa Fé, New Mexico

CHURCH OF SAN MIGUEL, on Old Santa Fé Trail and E. de Vargas Street. Daily 8.30–11.30 and 1–5.30.

HOOKSTONE (the students' sale shop) at the Institute of American Indian Arts, on State Routes 85 and 64, and Interstate 25. During the school year, Saturday and Sunday 10–5, weekdays by appointment.

MUSEUM OF INTERNATIONAL FOLK ART, Old Santa Fé Trail, on the edge of the town. 16 May to 15 September, Monday to Saturday 9–5, Sunday and holidays 2–5; 16 September to 15 May, same hours but closed on Monday. Free.

MUSEUM OF NAVAJO CEREMONIAL ART, Old Santa Fé Trail, on the edge of the town. 16 May to 15 September, Monday to Saturday 9–5, Sunday and holidays 2–5; 16 September to 15 May, same hours, but closed on Monday. Free.

PALACE OF THE GOVERNORS, on the Plaza. 16 May to 15 September, Tuesday to Saturday 9–5, Sunday and holidays 2–5; 16 September to 15 May, same hours but closed on Monday. Free.

PUEBLO TOURS. For information, write to Eight Northern Pueblos Enterprise Inc., Tour Division, Box 580, Santa Fé, New Mexico 87501. Inclusive cost, $260 per person for 6 days.

Sedona, Arizona

CHAPEL OF THE HOLY CROSS, near Sedona on State Route 179. Daily 8–5.

Taos, New Mexico

KIT CARSON HOUSE AND MUSEUM, on U.S. Route 64, east of the Plaza. Summer daily 7 a.m.–7.30 p.m.; winter daily 8–5. Closed 1 January, Thanksgiving and 25 December.

MILLICENT ROGERS FOUNDATION, 4 miles north off State Route 3. 16 March to 14 October, Monday to Saturday 9–5, Sunday 1–5; 15 October to 15 March, Monday to Saturday 10–4.

PUEBLO DE TAOS, 2½ miles north. Open during daylight.

THE STABLES GALLERY, two blocks north of the Plaza. 1 May to 10 November, daily 9–5; rest of the year, 9–4.

Talequah, Oklahoma

CHEROKEE INDIAN ARTS AND CRAFTS CENTER, on Route 2.

'TRAIL OF TEARS' PAGEANT is performed from the end of June to the end of August, Tuesday to Sunday at 8.30 p.m.

Tucson, Arizona

ARIZONA STATE MUSEUM, on the University campus, near E. 3rd Street. Monday to Saturday 10–5, Sunday 2–5. Closed holidays. Free.

ARIZONA-SONORA DESERT MUSEUM, 14 miles west in Tucson Mountain Park. Daily 9 until sunset.

OLD TUCSON, 12 miles west on Tucson Mountain Park Road. Daily 9 until sunset.

SAN XAVIER DEL BAC MISSION, 9 miles south-west on the Mission Road. Conducted tours by the Brothers every half hour, daily 9.30–4.30.

TANQUE VERDE RANCH, P.O. Box 515 Route 8, Tucson, Arizona 85710. Telephone (602) 296–6275. 19 miles east going out on Speedway Road. Free transportation from the airport; swimming pools, whirlpool, tennis; slow, medium and fast rides are organized with quiet or spirited horses to suit your pace; reservations advisable; from $24 to $35 per person per day, lower rates 1 May to 15 December.

Tulsa, Oklahoma

GILCREASE INSTITUTE, 2½ miles north-west at 2500 W. Newton Street. Monday to Friday 9–5, Saturday, Sunday and holidays 1–5. Closed 25 December. Free.

Window Rock, Arizona

NAVAJO ARTS AND CRAFTS GUILD, east of the junction of Navajo Routes 12 and 3. Summer daily 8–8; rest of the year, Monday to Friday 8–6, Saturday 9–5, Sunday 1–4.

NAVAJO SCENIC TOURS organize a 5-day tour leaving on Mondays, and a 6-day tour leaving on Fridays from 1 May to 31 October. 5-day tours cost $168; 6-day tours cost $207; this includes accommodation but not meals. Shorter tours can be arranged.

NAVAJO TRIBAL MUSEUM, Navajo Tribal Fairgrounds. Daily 8–5. Free. The Navajo Fair takes place in mid-September.

Zuni Pueblo, New Mexico

ZUNI is 39 miles south of Gallup on State Route 53, on the Zuni Indian Reservation. The Shalako Ceremony is held about a month before Christmas.

ZUNI CRAFTSMEN COOPERATIVE. Daily 8–5.

10 · THE WEST COAST

The astonishing thing about the Pacific coast is that everything there is larger than life. One is led to expect certain impressive features, the sequoia and redwood trees perhaps, and snow-peaked mountains, and San Francisco Bay. But no one prepares you for the fact that these are not isolated rarities, that the West Coast altogether is on a Brobdingnagian scale. One may go there sceptical about the wonders only to end by protesting that there is not nearly enough talk about the magnificence of it all.

The city of Seattle and its corner of the state of Washington are a case in point. Although more than a hundred miles from open sea, Seattle is a major port. Ships pass through the Strait of Juan de Fuca, between the Olympic Peninsula on the American side and the Canadian island of Vancouver, and then steer south-ward between the islands of Puget Sound. Reached at last, Seattle itself seems almost an island, squeezed between the salty Sound and the freshwater Lake Washington; from any vantage point in the city one can see water. But this is not Seattle's only charm. On a clear day the great snow-crowned dome of Mount Rainier is also visible, fifty miles away to the south-east. Everywhere on the West Coast there is this sense of the outdoors, luring one off to the mountains or the sea. It is the supreme attraction of life there.

There are not a great many conventional tourist sights in Seattle, nor yet any really notable buildings. Its chief charm is its situation, sprawling up and down over hills with water on every side. Thus what one chiefly wants in Seattle is an overall view. This is one city in which one would do well to take a sightseeing tour by bus; one can get maps for a self-guided tour in one's own car from the Visitors Bureau, but we prefer first to become oriented without having to think about the driving. Moreover, these tours give one a very good idea of what it is like to live in Seattle. They swing you by the University of Washington, for example, where the football stadium on the lake has docks so that spectators can come to the games in their own boats – a vivid illustration of the way everyone in Seattle takes to the water on every possible occasion. For orientation combined with something else, one can also go to one of the hotel bars or restaurants up on high. The most popular over-all view, however, is from the top of the Space Needle, a souvenir of Seattle's World Fair of 1962. One can take a monorail from the centre of town to the Space Needle; the ride itself is fun. And then one can go either to an observation platform at the top, or eat in the (expensive) revolving restaurant.

There are three museums in Seattle which have collections particularly appropriate for this region. Seattle's most important industry, responsible for most of the city's growth over the past thirty or forty years, is Boeing Aircraft; the Museum of History and Industry devotes particular attention to aeronautical developments. The Seattle Art Museum in Volunteer Park is not especially big, but it does have a very good collection of Far Eastern porcelains and jade, which makes one very conscious of Seattle's links to the Orient. It also has a representative sampling of the work of two of Seattle's most interesting modern painters, Mark Tobey and Morris Graves. And at the University of Washington, the Burke Museum has a superb section devoted to Northwest Coast Indian culture and artefacts. The Indians of this north-west coast of the United States and Canada had perhaps the most distinctive culture of any North American Indians; these are the Indians who carved the great totem poles and made enormous sea-going dugout canoes from the giant trees of the region. One should not miss this opportunity to learn something about them. And you might then also go to the University of Washington Arboretum, where there is a fine Japanese Tea Garden.

One of the most beautiful sights in Seattle, however, is something much more humble; it is the Pike Place Market along the waterfront, where stall after stall proffers the most glorious array imaginable of fruit and vegetables. There are all sorts of strange and wonderful varieties, but the stalls are so lovingly ordered, the produce so glistening and fresh, that even the lowly carrots are exciting. All over the West Coast one encounters magnificent fruit and vegetables and the markets are full of tempting things, but this particular one overflows with them. It has fish stalls too, offering the salmon and crabs and oysters for which the Pacific coast is famous. Moreover, one can eat cheaply and quite well there in the cafeterias which the stall-owners themselves patronize.

Not very far from the Pike Place Market is the old heart of Seattle, the Pioneer Square area. Caught up in the preservation fever now endemic in America, Pioneer Square is currently enjoying a great revival of interest; its old buildings are filling up with art galleries and unusual little shops. To see some of these, you might walk from the waterfront up Main Street to Occidental Avenue South, and then go to the right for a block along Occidental. Two unusual restaurants here are the Prague and Das Gasthaus. (We should note, however, that one can eat very well, and frequently very inexpensively, at all sorts of interesting restaurants in Seattle; it's a good place for sampling Chinese food, for example, and Mexican food too.) Seattle's most unusual tour also starts from the Pioneer Square area: a two-hour walking tour of Seattle's old waterfront district, lost to sight underground after the street levels were raised in the 1890s. The tour is fun, and very well done; wear stout shoes and try it.

But no one will want to linger long in the city in fine weather. There are too many fascinating excursions to be made. Mount Rainier, for example, gleaming in the distance in the midst of the Cascade Mountains, is a justly popular National Park area. Like many of the mountains on the West Coast, Rainier is an extinct volcano. The peak of its cone collapsed aeons ago, but it is still 14,410 feet tall, its crater filled with ice, and glaciers flowing down its sides. The Park includes hundreds of trails one can take in summer through the forests on the lower slopes and the alpine meadows covered with wild flowers. Moreover, it is easy to get to Mount Rainier even without a car; from late June to early September there is a regular bus service to the Park from Seattle in addition to day-long bus tours. There are lodges at the main visitors' centres within the Park, and there are also many camping sites, and shelter cabins for hikers.

Another splendid trip one can do from Seattle, all in one day if time is tight, is to the San Juan Islands. The San Juans are a lovely chain of islands in the straits which lie between Seattle and

Vancouver, British Columbia. The boat trip through them has been called the most beautiful water trip in America, and we tend to agree. There is an almost classic harmony between island and water and vegetation and light and colour as one sails through the San Juans; there are echoes of western Scotland, of Japan, of Norway or Tasmania or the American state of Maine on the other side of the continent; but the San Juans finally are simply themselves, and quite special. Ferries run to them from Anacortes, a little more than an hour and a half's drive north of Seattle. One could take the ferry all the way through the islands to Sidney in Canada, and then back again. Or, if one got off to a very early start in order to get to Anacortes for the first ferry, there would be time instead to take one's car off at Orcas to explore that loveliest of the islands before catching one of the late ferries back. (A fine place for lunch on Orcas is the Outlook Inn; it seems a pleasantly inexpensive place to stay, too, but there are more luxurious lodgings on the island as well.) We should say a word here about these ferries too. The Washington State Ferry System seems to be run with exceptional efficiency, and these are surely the only ferries in the United States one positively enjoys eating on. (It's easy to see why Seattle commuters who take the ferries which criss-cross Puget Sound seem to wait to have breakfast until they're aboard!) However, one cannot make reservations, even on the San Juans run. We are told that during the heavy tourist season extra ferries are put on as necessary, but one should probably anticipate some difficulty if one times one's departure too fine.

Anyone planning to go from Anacortes north towards Canada instead of back to Seattle might like to take a side-trip to the Lummi Indian Reservation north-west of Bellingham. The Lummi Indians make heavy, hand-knitted, raw-wool jerseys of a distinctive pattern, and they also do weaving. We know of no better souvenirs of the Northwest. One can get the jerseys in Seattle (see listings) as well, but we have not seen the woven goods there.

West of Seattle, on the Olympic peninsula, there is a unique National Park. It is Olympic National Park and it is divided into two separate sections, the main Park and the Olympic Ocean Strip. It is much farther from Seattle than Mount Rainier; one would need three days even to scratch the surface, for just the journey out to the first entrance takes half a day. Yet one is amply repaid for the time it takes to see it all. The mountainous spine of the Olympic peninsula is part of the coastal range which borders the Pacific deep into California; these mountains are not as towering as the Cascades and the Sierra Nevadas farther inland, but they are quite high enough. Mount Olympus, the tallest, is about 8,000 feet, and since it and its sisters virtually rear up from the sea, they make a dramatic effect. But the most remarkable feature of the Olympic peninsula is its rain forest. The western flank of these mountains often gets as much as 150 inches of rain a year, and this in combination with the mild coastal climate has resulted in a completely exotic growth of trees. The trees are mainly Sitka spruce, western hemlock, western red cedar, and Douglas fir, most of them staggeringly tall, sometimes 200 feet and more, with tremendous trunks. These trees are found elsewhere along the West Coast, but the specimens in the Olympic rain forest include the very biggest, and nowhere else do they crowd together so densely. The floor of the forest beneath is covered with soft moss and ferns, and the whole is suffused with a pale green, luminous light. There are few places so glorious.

The Olympic Ocean Strip is also fine. It is a primitive and beautiful stretch of shore which stays that way because it is rather troublesome to get to. The northern part, perhaps the best, can be reached by footpaths which start three miles inland at Lake Ozette. Alternatively, one can walk along the shore from the town of La Push. Anyone who likes icy water is presumably free to bathe, but the chief attraction of this ocean strip is the variety of sea life to be found in the tidal pools, and the splendid sea birds and the seals, and the occasional deer or bear. Agate-hunters, too, do well all around the shore of the peninsula, both here and along the northern coast. There are also some Indian settlements along the ocean strip. They are a remnant of the old coastal tribes, and University of Washington anthropologists have a dig under way at the point on the shore at which the Lake Ozette trail ends. Informal tours of the dig are given for visitors two or three times a day.

To see the best of the Olympic Peninsula, drive first to the mountainous section of the National Park, going in from the northern entrance up the Heart o' the Hills Road to Hurricane Ridge. The views are spectacular. At the visitors' centre on the way in, one can get information about hiking trails, short and long, as well as campsites. After seeing this mountainous section of the Park, we recommend returning to Port Angeles, the town at the base, and then continuing west along State Route 112, less heavily travelled than U.S. 101. (Whatever route one takes, all along the way one passes the stumps of gigantic trees and encounters gigantic logging trucks; it is part of the startling effect of this entire region.) Then cut over towards the Coastal Strip section of the Park, heading either for Lake Ozette or for the more populous La Push. (There is no big hotel within the Olympic National Park, but there are simple motels and lodges and camping sites all around the peninsula.) The main road into the third section of the Park, the rain forest, veers off U.S. 101 south of the La Push turn-off; it leads to the other main visitors centre and to the Hoh River Trail, the chief trail into the rain forest. It is possible to see the rain forest from other points, however. There is a very comfortable lodge, the Lake Quinault Lodge, near Quinault and just south of the lower edge of the Park; one can go on fine rain forest explorations using it as a base, although one would not then have the advantage of Park naturalist talks and so on. In any case, after seeing the rain forest one can either head back to Seattle or continue on south to the coast of Oregon. But we should add that if there is time to spare, U.S. 101 along the eastern edge of the peninsula, along the Hood Canal (an old misnomer for 'channel') makes a beautiful drive, particularly in May when the rhododendron is in bloom.

The great river of the Pacific Northwest is the Columbia, which begins in Canada, winds a snake-like path southwards across the eastern part of the state of Washington, and then turns west to flow to the Pacific, forming the border between Washington and the state of Oregon. The Columbia is a mighty river, whose energy has been dramatically harnessed with dams like the Grand Coulee. It is also an historic river. It was the path along which Lewis and Clark penetrated this region in 1805, the first white Americans to come overland to the Pacific Ocean. The Columbia is also a beautiful river, and Portland, Oregon's leading city, owes much of its special charm to its setting, locked in between the Columbia and one of its tributaries, the Willamette River, with mountains also pressing close on the north and east. In Portland one should be sure to go to Washington Park; from the elevation on which the park stands there is a wonderful view across the city to Mount Hood, 11,245 feet high and always covered in snow. Washington Park is a fine place in any case, with experimental rose gardens (Portland is famous for its roses) and handsome Japanese gardens as well.

One trip which everyone who visits Portland should make is a drive eastward along the Columbia River Gorge. One might take the upper-level Scenic Highway one way and Interstate 80N, down along the river, the other. The views are splendid, and Multnomah Falls is only one of the fine falls one sees. Moreover, if it is the right time in autumn or spring, one can watch the salmon using fish ladders to get around Bonneville Dam, some forty miles east of Portland. For a longer trip, we suggest turning south off Interstate 80N at the town of Hood River, and going on the Mount Hood Loop Highway up the slopes of Mount Hood to the snow-line.

One soon runs out of superlatives in the Northwest; everything is on such a massive scale, especially the natural wonders and the effect they make. Furthermore, we have not space enough to deal adequately with inland Washington or Oregon. But we should say that one of the newest National Parks, North Cascades in Washington, along the Canadian border, is the newest favourite of true wilderness lovers. State Route 20 goes through it, and there are some fine lake trips one can take there, but the Park at this point is still largely undeveloped and offers good rugged hiking through its glacial highlands.

Eastern Washington and Oregon resemble parts of Idaho and Montana and even Wyoming. There are mountainous sections, but there is also cattle country. And while Oregon may seem very green indeed around Portland, the central and south-eastern parts of the state are quite arid.

In summer, if one were taking Interstate 5 from Portland to California through southern Oregon, it would be good to take a brief break from natural wonders and go to the Shakespeare Festival at Ashland. It is the oldest Shakespeare Festival in the United States; the productions are staged in a reproduction of the Elizabethan Fortune Theatre, and we hear they are very interesting. In this same region, inland in southern Oregon, there is Crater Lake National Park. As its name suggests, Crater Lake lies within the cone of an extinct volcano, part of that Cascade Range to which Mount Rainier also belongs. The lake is six miles across, set deep within the cone, and the water is superlatively dark blue.

It is the deepest lake in the United States, nearly 2,000 feet to the bottom, which must have something to do with the colour. There are patches of fir trees massed along the rocky rim, and here and there the surface of the lake is broken by strange little volcanic islands, cones within cones. The Indians regarded this as a sacred and fearsome place, forbidden to ordinary mortals, and it is easy to understand their awe. Nowadays, however, there is a lodge, and camping sites. And in winter, Crater Lake has become a popular skiing centre; there are heavy snows, which begin early in the autumn and have been known to keep the Crater Lake Rim Drive closed until July. The lowland climate of the American Pacific Coast is much milder than that of the same latitude on the Atlantic Coast, but in the mountains the combination of altitude and heavy coastal moisture results in very heavy snows.

But most people go to Oregon to see the Oregon coast. It is wild and craggy, with sheer cliffs and few safe harbours. Many of the beaches both there and along the northern California coast are tempting because they are almost deserted and very beautiful, but the bathing is often extremely dangerous. U.S. 101, as scenic a highway as ever there was, goes through Oregon along the coast and then into California, passing superb and lonely stretches of cliff and beach. The route begins in the extreme north-western corner of Oregon at the town of Astoria, near the spot at which Lewis and Clark camped for Christmas in 1805. Astoria is a very old town by Oregon standards; it began in the early nineteenth century as Fort Astor, the westernmost link in the chain of John Jacob Astor's fur stations, the American counterpart of the Hudson's Bay Company.

There are a great many state parks along U.S. 101, for camping and picnicking and sometimes even swimming. One can make reservations for campsites at some of these state parks, and in our listing at the end of the chapter we tell how to go about it; it's a matter of some importance since too many people are now discovering the beauties of this coast, and camping space can fill up quickly. The greatest concentration of parks and tourist accommodations in general is between Depoe Bay and Florence. At Depoe Bay one can watch fishing boats slip into the rocky harbour between the cliffs, and at Neskowen, twenty miles farther on, there is unusually safe swimming. Newport is a good place to pause, part commercial fishing town and part resort; one can hunt for agate on the beaches to the north of the town, and even do some surfing if you can bear the temperature of the water. South of Yachats one can take a lift down through the cliffs to see the sea lion caves and rookery; this is the only mainland sea lion rookery in the United States.

The distances in this part of the world are appalling. It is three hundred and eighty miles from the Oregon–California border to San Francisco, by the shortest route, on which one first eases into California over the mountains and then drops down into the Sacramento Valley. Taking this route, one passes marked evidence of volcanic activity where the Cascade Range merges with the Sierra Nevada Mountains. Towering, glacier-capped Mount Shasta is obviously dormant, but Lassen Peak, one of several volcanic mountains in Lassen Volcanic National Park, erupted as recently as 1917.

The longer, coastal route to San Francisco, U.S. 101, is very different. It runs between giant redwood trees for so many miles that claustrophobic travellers may find that awe eventually becomes something akin to desperation. About half the distance down, at the town of Leggett, the coastal route splits into two, and one can either continue south on U.S. 101, the quicker alternative, or stay right along the coast on State Route 1. The latter does take a long time to drive, but it is undeniably scenic. There are some fine state parks and lonely beaches along it, a splendid inn at Little River (called Heritage House), and at Fort Ross one can see an old Russian chapel and stockade. From 1812 to 1841, Russia maintained a garrison and trading post on this isolated coast while the Russians were hunting the northern California sea otter to virtual extinction.

One enters an entirely different world as one nears San Francisco. True, there are thick fogs along the rocky coast in the winter and many of the natural features continue to suggest the country farther north; one could never mistake this region for southern California. But it does lie within the boundaries of the old Spanish territory, and it represents a unique blend of many diverse California elements. Within a hundred miles of San Francisco there are landmarks illustrating every important stage in the history of the state.

Spanish explorers discovered California in the early sixteenth century and claimed it for Spain, but no one stayed to settle. In 1579, Sir Francis Drake sailed along the coast. He missed the narrow entrance to San Francisco Bay, but he did drop anchor in what is now called Drake's Bay, a few miles farther north. For two centuries after that, however, no one paid any attention to California. Then in the late eighteenth century Great Britain began to show signs of pushing her claims southward along the western edge of the continent, and Russia, too, already firmly entrenched in Alaska, became a threat. Hastily Spain dispatched her usual combination of soldiers and missionaries to establish outposts in the California territory, and soon afterwards groups of settlers arrived. Many Spaniards amassed large ranch holdings, where they led a delightfully relaxed and pleasant life. They were a long way from real civilization, but they were blessed with an agreeable climate and a generous supply of Indian peons. Like many a newcomer since then, they became ardent 'Californios' almost overnight.

In fact they became such ardent Californios that they bitterly resented the stupidities of the colonial administration, and evinced little loyalty either towards Spain or towards Mexico, which established its independence of Madrid in 1821. In defiance of the authorities, they welcomed the trickle of Americans coming into California in the second quarter of the nineteenth century, and thus they themselves brought their pleasant way of life to an end, for the ambitious, impatient Americans were not the sort to appreciate the genial anarchy of Spanish California. The Americans promptly got together, and first declared California an independent republic and then asked the United States to admit it to the Union. The Spanish Californios raised an army and fought for a few months, but then, assured of their lands, they surrendered, and Mexico formally signed California over to the United States in 1847. It is said that the British, who had once hoped to take over California themselves, lost their chance because of a woman. There was a British agent on the scene before most of the Americans arrived, and he was popular with the Californios, and making progress. Then he shot himself over a disappointment in love, and that was the end of that.

The original Spanish settlements extended from southernmost California all the way to Sonoma, forty or fifty miles north of San Francisco. At Sonoma there was a Franciscan mission, the northernmost of nineteen such missions which today comprise the most interesting remains of the colonial period. The Sonoma mission is not as impressive as some of those farther south, but

Sonoma itself has remained a sleepy little town basking in the California sunshine, and the fact that the mission is still an integral part of its square, not merely an isolated curiosity, gives it a special charm. Moreover, about a mile west of the town is the ranch house of Mariano Vallejo, a great landowner hereabouts in the early nineteenth century, military governor of northern California in its Mexican period, and one of the most attractive figures in all of California's history. His house at Sonoma is not grand by European standards, but it represented power and wealth in the colonial period of California, and it reflects the complex personality of the fascinating Vallejo.

Some sixty miles east of Sonoma is Sacramento, today the capital of the state of California but once the site of Sutter's Fort. Johann Augustus Sutter was a Swiss–German who had come to America to seek his fortune, and then drifted west to California when that territory was still solidly Spanish. He was given permission to build a trading post where Sacramento now stands, and the trading post soon became the centre of an almost feudal empire. It was the goal of many of the first American settlers who came over the mountains into California; Sutter helped them to establish themselves up and down the Sacramento Valley. His industry was to be his own undoing, however. In 1847, he sent a company of men east of Sutter's Fort to build a mill on the American River, and the men discovered gold there. In the gold rush which followed, poor Johann Sutter was ruined, for everyone took to the hills in search of easy money and all of his enterprises collapsed for lack of labour. The state of California has now reconstructed Sutter's Fort, and it too is open to the public, in the heart of the modern city.

If you were driving to San Francisco from the north on U.S. 101, you could diverge to do a loop southward which would take you through Sonoma but still bring you into San Francisco over the Golden Gate Bridge, surely the proper way to approach that city. And you would make the happy discovery that this loop also takes you through the California wine country. There are vineyards near U.S. 101 too, including Korbel, which makes one of the best California champagnes. But it is really the Napa Valley that one should see. Coming from the north, you would therefore turn off U.S. 101 on to State Route 128, which merges with State Route 29, along which one finds most of the Napa Valley wineries. (If you were to come to the Napa Valley from San Francisco, the most pleasant route is over the Golden Gate Bridge to State Route 37, and then State Route 121 to Sonoma and on up.)

Most of the vineyards offer tours and tasting, and some even have picnic grounds. There are also little state parks and other pleasant picnic places in the region, and we stress the fact because this region is wonderful picnic country. The delicious fruits, San Francisco sourdough bread, Monterey Jack cheese and good local Italian sausage, all put together with a bottle of California wine: it is what we dream of in the long winters far from California.

Almost any of the vineyards are pleasant to visit, but in the Napa Valley we particularly recommend Inglenook (very picturesque, and good wine), Louis Martini (not picturesque, but one of the very best California winemakers), and Charles Krug and Robert Mondavi. Both of the latter also offer an added attraction in summer; the Mondavi vineyard has delightful Sunday evening concerts in July, and Charles Krug has concerts on Saturday nights in August.

The marketing centre for this region is St Helena, an attractive town too. And near Sonoma there is another notable vineyard, Buena Vista, with nice old buildings; it was the first of all of these wineries, established here in the mid-nineteenth century by a refugee Hungarian count. Finally, we should say that the most famous of the winery concert series is Paul Masson's 'Music at the Vineyards'. Paul Masson, however, is south of San Francisco in Santa Clara County, not so interesting a region to visit otherwise.

California changed dramatically with the gold rush. In the 1840s, it had taken wagon trains four months to come from Missouri to California. Now the Overland Stage began to make regular runs from St Joseph, Missouri, to Sacramento in only twenty-one days, and a little village called Yerba Buena at the entrance to San Francisco Bay finally came into its own as the port nearest the gold camps. For a booming town, Yerba Buena was a cumbersome name; the citizens decided to change it, to San Francisco.

The city of San Francisco has been an exciting place ever since its re-christening. The original settlement had been started in 1776, with a mission and a small garrison, the usual *presidio*. Yet it never amounted to much until the excitement over gold brought thousands of men swarming through town. San Francisco then became the logical place to spend your money if you had had a lucky strike, and also the logical place to drown your sorrows if you had been ruined.

The section along the waterfront was known as the Barbary Coast in the gold-rush days. It was a den of thieves, a haven for every vice, and a likely place for a man to be shanghaied. However, San Francisco is built on steep hills which rise straight up from the water's edge, and it was simple for those men who were becoming millionaires overnight to shield their families from the unpleasantness along the docks. They simply put their great houses on the heights: hence 'Nob' Hill.

Most of the early San Francisco fortunes were built on California gold. Later there were the even more profitable gold and silver strikes around Virginia City, Nevada, just across the California border, and more millions to be made in California land sales, both honest and dishonest, and additional millions to be accumulated from shipping and railroads and banking. One of the interesting things about San Francisco is the way in which all of this pyramiding wealth was firmly controlled by a mere handful of men who began with nothing, and ended with a financial empire. In fact there were really only four men, Collis Huntington, Leland Stanford, Mark Hopkins, and Charles Crocker, and you still encounter their names everywhere in California. Alternating Machiavellian skill and crude force, they managed to keep almost everything in their own hands. Only when stricter federal regulations began to be applied to business dealings was their iron grip on San Francisco and most of California finally loosened. For that matter, San Francisco does still have the air of being a neat, containable, private world. The core of it is not very big, really; when you have been there a day, you feel very much a part of it.

There is a freshness and excitement in San Francisco, and the mood is perhaps heightened by the time-difference for anyone coming from the East; one finds oneself leaping out of bed to greet San Francisco's dawn. (The wretched California stockbrokers have to leap out of bed even before dawn in order to be at their desks when the Stock Exchange opens in New York City.) Tourists in San Francisco also show an alarming tendency to forget they are tourists, so in keeping with the spirit of the place we have only a limited amount of proper sightseeing to suggest; after that our readers are on their own. We will assume that they will be staying at a hotel near Union Square, at the heart of everything. There are both expensive and inexpensive hotels in that region and the Convention and Visitors Bureau can supply a list; we might note, however, that the only San Francisco hotel with real character is the splendid old Palace, now the Sheraton-Palace.

The first thing to do in San Francisco is to take a cable car to Fisherman's Wharf, for a boat tour of the harbour. We suggest that you go there first, in the morning, because San Francisco viewed from the Bay is then at its best, with the sun shining towards the city and the Golden Gate Bridge. The cable cars are of course one of the great delights of San Francisco too; they are not merely tourist attractions but a vital part of the city transport system. Fisherman's Wharf, on the other hand, is now very touristy. One can hardly see the fishing boats for the souvenir shops, and the restaurants there are also very touristy. Nonetheless, it is a good centre to begin from, in addition to offering harbour tours. You might like to look over the fine array of old ships and nautical mementoes in the Maritime State Historic Park section along the Hyde Street pier. And you will also want to see The Cannery and Ghirardelli Square, two prime examples of the way in which San Franciscans these days are putting their old buildings and districts to use. Along the waterfront here, there were large warehouses and factory buildings which were no longer being used. Instead of tearing them down, however, someone had the brilliant notion of converting them into two very different sorts of multi-level structures for little shops and restaurants. The result in each case is striking, and eminently successful. Moreover, both the shops and the restaurants are tempting. (Do buy some of the Ghirardelli chocolate; but don't feel you must see the film at Ghirardelli Square.)

After you've seen the Fisherman's Wharf area, take a cable car back up the hill and ask to be let off at California Street. You can then walk two blocks down California Street to Grant Avenue, to see Chinatown. Other American cities have a Chinatown; New York, for example, has one, and Los Angeles too has a Chinese section. But San Francisco's Chinatown is deservedly the most famous. It is certainly not what it was in the late nineteenth century, when one went, with Chinese guides, to see 'gorgeously costumed' Chinese theatre and 'gambling dens' and 'opium cellars'. But it is nonetheless a fascinating place for simply strolling around, or for eating in one of the myriad tea parlours or restaurants. San Francisco's Chinese community is large (perhaps 75,000

15. San Francisco with Coit Tower atop Telegraph Hill in the centre and the Bay Bridge in the background

16a. Redwoods in
Muir Woods National
Monument, California

16b. On the Monterey
Peninsula, California

today) and very diverse; many of its families have been a hundred years and more in San Francisco, but new Chinese immigrants also continue to arrive, these days even at an accelerated rate. Thus Chinatown unquestionably maintains its ethnic distinction and it is very colourful.

Everyone who visits San Francisco should see not only the view from the Bay but also the view from on high. The traditional place to go for a drink and the view used to be the Top of the Mark, at the Mark Hopkins Hotel on Nob Hill. Now four other towering hotels also have bars and restaurants aloft. But the Bank of America building, near Chinatown, has a very elegant place too, the Carnelian Room; it is open to the general public after five, for drinks or dinner, and its view is particularly fine. Do remember, however, that all of these bars and restaurants on high are enormously popular; if you want to be sure of a good table for seeing the Bay at sunset, you had better arrive a bit early.

In addition to the cable car route to Fisherman's Wharf, there is another run which goes along California Street, from Nob Hill down to the eastern section of the waterfront, past Chinatown and the Bank of America building to Embarcadero Plaza. The latter is the new trade centre, embellished by the monumental Vaillancourt Fountain. On the way down California Street you would cross Montgomery Street, and there just across from the Bank of America building is a delightful visitors' attraction, the Wells Fargo History Room. It is an adjunct of the Wells Fargo banking system which is still a significant force in California financial life. And at Embarcadero Plaza, at the foot of Market Street, San Francisco's financial centre, there is a ferry dock from which boats go across the Bay to Sausalito. We are very partial to Sausalito, a charming little town. Today it is hardly the undiscovered treasure it was twenty years ago, but it is still one of the nicest places around the Bay to visit. There are some good shops and waterfront restaurants, and if you walk east along the waterfront and then up Locust or Pine or Johnson Street, you will see what a delightful place it must be to live in.

Sausalito is also one place where the night life is still fun. The North Beach area, San Francisco's old Italian section, used to be a glorious place to spend an evening, but it is now dominated by an array of fleshpots, each one just like the other. North Beach is still a good place to go for delectable Italian sandwiches or other

K

Italian food, and to gather picnic supplies in its Italian grocery shops and bakeries. But for an evening on the town, with jazz or folk singing, we suggest Sausalito. Be sure to check with someone first, however, to find out when the last ferry or bus comes back!

With the cable cars and the Bay ferries, transport has always provided one of San Francisco's major tourist attractions. Now there is another element, BART. The new BART system (Bay Area Rapid Transit) uses the most advanced designs and concepts in equipment and stations, and makes it possible for people to whisk from the centre of San Francisco to the other side of the Bay in no time at all. You might like to take BART to Berkeley, in order to try out the new system and also to see the University of California, the most prestigious of the great American state universities.

We are not in favour of too much formal sightseeing in San Francisco. It is the sort of city in which one really wants just to wander around, with no pressures, savouring its disparate elements. San Francisco is a very sophisticated place, with interesting repertory theatre and contemporary art, and a good opera season. While there is a sense of freshness and youth in the air, it is also a very elegant city, as the shops around Union Square attest. One should explore that area a bit, if only to see Gump's, San Francisco's most celebrated shop, where San Francisco's ties to the Orient are tantalizingly reflected. Have tea or an ice cream confection, too, at Blum's on Union Square.

In the area around the classical-baroque Civic Center and the Opera House, San Francisco on a sunny day suddenly seems a very Mediterranean city. One gets this feeling a bit too in that part of San Francisco which lies beyond the central core, on the other side of its steep hills. There are streets of delightful houses there, gleaming white with Victorian gingerbread trim known here as 'carpenters' Gothic'. In what's called Cow Hollow, from the 1600 block of Union Street westwards, there are now a great many boutiques and antique shops. Cow Hollow is a fine place for leisurely browsing.

However, not everyone has the energy or time to explore independently, and we think a bus tour is not at all a bad idea in San Francisco. It can take you through these other parts of the city, and also show you places like the old Spanish mission church; the latter is worth seeing not only for itself but because it is still part of a predominantly Spanish or Mexican–American district. A tour would also take you through Golden Gate Park, splendidly old-fashioned in tone and full of every possible sort of San Franciscan, half of them on bicycles. (One can hire bicycles at the east and west entrances of the park.) However, anyone with any interest at all in the art of the Far East ought to take extra time for Golden Gate Park, for the De Young Museum there has the Avery Brundage Collection, in the Asian Art and Culture wing. The Brundage Collection is scarcely matched anywhere else in the world, and it is superbly displayed.

There really are no end of things to do in and around San Francisco. One can, for example, take ferries not only to Sausalito but also to another attractive little commuter's town, Tiburon, and to Angel Island State Park in the Bay, a fine place for picnics and bicycling. (One can hire bicycles there too.) But we have saved until the last the one expedition you ought to make, unless you have come into San Francisco from the north and have already seen it all. There is a beautiful grove of redwood trees only a short distance north of San Francisco, called Muir Woods. It is in Marin County, which is still surprisingly rural for an area so close to a large city. Even if you are not generally inclined to hire a car and set off, we urge that you get one in order to go over the Golden Gate Bridge to Muir Woods. You should also include on the trip both Mount Tamalpais and Point Reyes National Seashore, a bit farther to the north. If you then saw no more of the California coast, you would at least have a very good idea of how magnificent it is.

There are bus tours from San Francisco to Muir Woods as well. San Francisco is in fact a good centre for bus tours to all sorts of glorious places in California, and we will say more about them in our sections at the end of the chapter.

It is hard to leave San Francisco, however. Undeniably it has changed somewhat in recent years. Whereas once many of its old sections and customs seemed in imminent danger of disappearing, today everything traditional in San Francisco is so eagerly embraced and refurbished that some of the old casual spontaneity is gone. The sky-line too is certainly altered by all the new buildings. Nevertheless, San Francisco is still an enormously attractive place, and one is willing to leave it only because California also has so many more wonders to see.

There are mountains all along California's spine, the towering

Sierra Nevadas. With such peaks as Mount Whitney, 14,495 feet high, the Sierras represented the final formidable obstacle to wagon trains heading for California in the nineteenth century. The only feasible pass through these mountains in the northern part of California then was the one still used today for the super-highway from California to Nevada, Interstate 80 north of Lake Tahoe. (For Lake Tahoe, see Chapter 9.) It is called Donner Pass, after the Donner wagon train, which broke down trying to get through in winter snows and finally descended to murder and cannibalism.

These days the Sierras supply California with much of her recreation, and in the Sierras lies Yosemite National Park. Like everyone else on the West Coast, Californians are never indoors when they can be out, surfing at the beaches or climbing a mountain. For many of them, Yosemite is now an old story. They say, quite accurately, that Yosemite is full of people, and thus choose to go instead to Parks like Sequoia and King's Canyon. These are south of Yosemite and with somewhat similar, and magnificent, scenery; there are only the simpler sort of accommodations there and it is wonderful country for hiking and 'back-packing'. Or they might go to Lassen Volcanic National Park in the northern part of the state, where the Sierras merge with the Cascades and there is still ample sign of volcanic activity. There is fine hiking there too.

Yet for newcomers to the Sierras, Yosemite is still the noblest introduction: its core a deep and truly lovely valley, with grey granite walls rising sheer for 4,000 feet in some places, and in addition thousands of acres of wild and unspoiled high country.

An Englishman, James Hutchings, was the first to write about the Yosemite valley, in 1856. But more important to the future of the region was the proselytizing of the Scottish-born John Muir, America's most remarkable nineteenth-century naturalist, who became tremendously excited about California with its giant trees and majestic mountains. (Muir Woods, near San Francisco, was named in his honour, and there is a Muir Trail in Yosemite National Park.) Like all enthusiasts, John Muir wanted people to share his pleasures, and he urged everyone to go to Yosemite. He would doubtless be somwhat nonplussed to see the throngs who now take his advice every summer. Yet we cannot agree with those who regard this popularity as profanation. Furthermore, we have never seen large numbers of people handled so well, blended into the landscape so well, as they are at Yosemite by both the National Park Service and the Park concessionaire.

The National Park Service has made several parts of the Park accessible by car. One can drive straight across it to the Tuolumne Meadows section of the high country, or to Glacier Point, from which there is a breathtaking view of the entire valley and its waterfalls. And one can drive down into the heart of the valley, which is quite as beautiful as everyone says it is, although this also means that it is the section most crowded with people in high season. The most dramatic approach to the Park is from Merced, on the west, or from Fresno, to the south. From April to October, in addition to campsites there are all manner of accommodations at Yosemite. One can stay in a traditional and rather formal old hotel, the Ahwahnee, or in simple cabins, or in something in between. Our own preference as base is the Yosemite Lodge, which has both simple cabins and motel-like rooms. It looks up to the waterfalls, and it has an excellent cafeteria (delicious mountain trout) and even a bookshop full of tempting books about Yosemite and the West in general. From it or any of the other accommodation centres in the valley one can take a little shuttle bus to the Visitors Center and one can also arrange for pack trips or horseback rides. There are, they say, 700 miles of trails to walk or ride along.

The most remarkable stands of giant sequoia trees are to be found south of Yosemite, at Sequoia National Park, which protects another magnificent section of the Sierras. But Yosemite has three groves of sequoias too. The sequoia tree, also known as the Wellingtonia, is related to the redwoods of the coast, the trees in Muir Woods and along U.S. 101 in northern California. The Douglas fir and the Sitka spruce, the enormously tall trees of Washington and Oregon, are quite different, lusty specimens of 'normal' trees. Sequoias and redwoods, on the other hand, are a botanic curiosity, survivors of a prehistoric world like the cryptomeria of Japan. Logically, they should have disappeared with the brontosaurus, or have been ground to a pulp beneath the glaciers, never to rise again. Redwood trees are generally taller than sequoias; one redwood measures 368 feet, whereas sequoias usually stop just short of 300 feet. Sequoias, however, are thicker, 30 feet, or more across. Sequoias also live to a riper age; the unfortunate baby redwood can only look forward to a life span of 2,000 years or so, while his sequoia cousin may live twice as long.

In the winter, most of Yosemite closes down because of snow. There is skiing, however, and one can still go into the valley section by way of the Merced-Arched Rock entrance. Late spring is particularly lovely at Yosemite, for the spectacular waterfalls are then at their best and the Park is not yet too crowded. In the summer the accommodations are likely to be booked for weeks or months ahead, and every campsite is sure to be taken early in the day. Then in September the crowds disappear, the trees begin to turn red and gold, and Yosemite is once again not only beautiful but tranquil as well.

Anyone with time to spare could have a fine loop-trip from San Francisco, combining Yosemite with Lake Tahoe and the old gold-mining towns of the Forty-Niners. Many of the California gold camps were just tent colonies which disappeared without trace when the surface gold ran out. But many others were more permanently built, and they have become very popular places to visit. They are quite unlike the ghost mining towns high in the Rockies, and equally unlike Nevada's Virginia City, for the foothills of the Sierras hereabouts are far less harsh, almost pastoral. Indeed one of the real pleasures in driving through this 'Mother Lode' country comes from the nature of the scenery itself.

The appropriately named State Route 49 goes past many of these little mining towns, and most of the others are only a short detour away. To combine the Forty-Niner country with Yosemite, you might like to stay for a night at Sutter Creek, or Volcano, or Mokulumne Hill; all three offer lodgings tempting for one reason or another. The Hotel Léger at Mokulumne Hill is a proper old miners' hotel now delightfully done up in style, but not expensive, and 'Mok Hill' itself is attractively situated. The St George Hotel at Volcano is equally picturesque, and in a considerably wilder and more isolated section of this country. And at Sutter Creek, a somewhat bigger town whose picturesque old main street is now lined with antique shops, there is the Sutter Creek Inn; it is not an old miners' hotel but an old house, and an unusual and sybaritic place altogether. (If you'd like really bargain-rate lodgings, in an old miners' hotel so authentic that one still enters through the bar-room, try the National Hotel at Jackson, today the largest of these towns.) Wherever you plan to stop for the night, however, telephoning ahead for reservations would certainly be advisable. Moreover, you certainly ought also to see Columbia. The best preserved of all these towns, it is now a state historic park and run as a museum village, with no cars permitted within its boundaries. It is usually terribly full of sightseers, but one should go there nonetheless, and be sure to see its little museum. It puts the world of the Forty-Niners in the proper perspective.

The Monterey peninsula is a very special part of California, with a character all its own. It is a little over a hundred miles south of San Francisco. Fortunately for visitors without a car, Gray Line runs day-long bus tours to it from San Francisco.

Monterey was the Spanish capital of Alta California, and the town's importance continued right up to the moment when the American flag was raised over California, and even briefly afterwards; the first state constitutional convention was held there. But with the discovery of gold, San Francisco soon eclipsed Monterey, and it became little more than a peaceful fishing village. A good many people recognized its appeal, however. Robert Louis Stevenson, for example, spent part of 1879 living and writing at Monterey, and in the twentieth century retired Navy people in particular began to settle there in considerable numbers. Then in the 1930s the stories of John Steinbeck called additional attention to its indolent charm, and over the past forty years Monterey has gained so much in tourist popularity that it has undeniably lost something. It was inevitable, of course, but it remains a pleasant place to visit, with its Spanish colonial heritage carefully preserved in the area around the Friendly Plaza. The fishing-village aspect of Monterey, however, is now also gone forever. This too has been inevitable; the deep-sea fishing industry of the California coast has changed radically in recent years, partly in response to a radical change in the availability of its prime catch, the giant tuna. Thus the boats in Monterey's harbour are now mostly there simply to take out amateur deep-sea anglers, and the waterfront is given over to shops and seafood restaurants.

Along the peninsula beyond Monterey is Pacific Grove, a community with some mysterious appeal for Monarch butterflies, which winter there in vast numbers, covering the branches of the pine trees. And at Pacific Grove begins the '17-Mile Drive', a road which goes round the shore of the peninsula to Carmel. Robert Louis Stevenson called this peninsula 'the finest meeting place of land and water in existence'; if you take the 17-Mile

Drive on a perfect day, you may be inclined to agree. The great attraction of the peninsula is the Monterey cypress, which is found only in this area. It is a cypress tree of a special sort, and most specimens, clinging to the rocks along the coast here, have been so warped and twisted by the winds that they look like Japanese bonsai trees seen through the wrong end of a telescope. Most of the peninsula is privately owned; there are houses here and there among the trees, and three golf clubs. But there is also a small strip of open beach, a picnic area, and many viewpoints where one may park. Everything is left in its natural state, with no obtrusive organization or souvenir stands; a few spots are simply set aside so that the visitors themselves will be as unobtrusive as possible. There is a fee for taking the 17-Mile Drive, but it is well worth paying. The most spectacular part of the peninsula is unfortunately very private indeed, the purlieu of the Cypress Point Club. But there is a viewpoint nearby, with a telescope, so that one can see the westernmost rocks beyond the club grounds, where hundreds of sea lions gather to sun themselves, together with pelicans and black gulls and cormorants and handsome grey gulls with pink beaks. In the early morning, even deer can sometimes be seen going over the road and across the Cypress Point golf course. At the southern end of the 17-Mile Drive there is a splendid inn, the Del Monte Lodge; it is, of course, very expensive to stay at but one can stop there for a drink to enjoy the view. Next to it is the celebrated Pebble Beach Golf Links, where anyone willing to pay the fee can arrange to play; much of the course is along the sea.

Just south of the Monterey peninsula is Carmel, an extremely attractive little town. It is half retired Navy, half artists' colony, and expensively quaint; the citizens refuse to have any civic 'improvements' that would change the character of the place. There are any number of smart shops at Carmel where one can pay $20 for a gnarled piece of driftwood, but the Carmel Bach Festival in July is genuinely good, and Carmel would be a very pleasant place to spend a night at any time of the year. There are a great many inns and motels discreetly tucked away in the town and many of them are moderate in price. The Carmel beach is lovely: a curving strip of fine white sand shaded by Monterey cypresses and pines.

At Carmel there is one of the old Spanish mission churches, this one formally known as the Basilica of San Carlos Borromeo del Rio Carmelo. We think it the most interesting of all the California missions. It was the headquarters of Junipero Serra, the remarkable Franciscan who established the California mission system ; Father Serra's cell and study here have been restored, and he is buried in the sanctuary. Moreover, this is certainly one of the most beautiful missions, with a striking parabolic ceiling, a splendid altar and reredos in the main church, a lovely little side chapel, a cloister, and a fine garden and setting.

On the exterior, the California mission churches are not particularly impressive. One must not expect sophisticated architecture, the splendours of colonial Mexico or something like a medieval European abbey; these are comparatively primitive adobe structures, built by the local Indians to a stock design. Moreover, the California missions lack the purity of the earlier mission churches of New Mexico, where the strong and timeless utilitarian form sometimes sets one to thinking about eighth-century Ireland or le Corbusier at Ronchamps. Nonetheless, those of the California mission churches which have survived without too much alteration certainly warrant visiting, especially for their ingenuous and colourful interiors. Another good one to see in this region is San Juan Bautista, about twenty-five miles north-east of Monterey; there is something about its setting which is particularly nice.

San Juan Bautista is not directly on U.S. 101, but it is near it, and this is also true of most of the old missions. For U.S. 101 generally follows the old Camino Réal, the royal highway of the Spanish colonial period. It is one of several possible routes from San Francisco to Los Angeles. About half-way along it, one can stop to see still another fine old mission church, San Miguel.

The least direct but certainly the most scenic route to Los Angeles is State Route 1 along the coast. At Point Lobos, just south of Carmel, there is a state park, with more of the beautiful Monterey cypress trees, more sea lions, more birds. One cannot camp there, but it is a fine place for picnicking. South of it, one enters a region in which the road has literally had to be carved out of the cliffs above the ocean. It is not frightening to drive, because the engineering has been so skilful, but it is unquestionably spectacular. Part of it, the Big Sur region about thirty miles south of Carmel, is exceptionally rugged and craggy. The road goes inland here briefly, through a mountain valley which includes the Pfeiffer-Big Sur State Park, a fine wilderness area with camping sites. But the coast remains the principal attraction. It is much admired by writers and artists, and one passes houses clinging dramatically to the cliffs.

After Big Sur, it is another sixty or seventy miles to San Simeon, with spectacular vistas all along the way and only a few isolated houses. San Simeon itself is a village, but it is also the name of a fantastic mock-castle on the heights above, which was the creation of William Randolph Hearst, that most powerful and eccentric of American newspaper publishers. It is an incredible place, beautiful on the outside, with terraced gardens and pools and orange and lemon trees on a peak overlooking the Pacific and the mountains, and incredible inside in quite another way. On a fine day, with the sun sparkling on the ocean far below and the air heavy with the scent of the trees, San Simeon is entrancing.

San Simeon now belongs to the state, and one can see it on guided two-hour tours. The tours begin at the foot of the mountain; buses take groups up to the top at regular intervals, passing the little herds of zebras which are now all that is left of the San Simeon menagerie. Since the capacity of the bus is limited, the tour-groups are limited in size too, and in summer particularly it is necessary to reach San Simeon early in the day, or even the night before, in order to be sure of a place at all. Even then one may have to wait two or three hours for one's turn. The alternative is to write well in advance for a reservation; see our listings.

South of San Simeon the route flattens out and is much less dramatic. There are a few pretty bays, but there are also clusters of oil wells, and towns, and people. At San Luis Obispo, State Route 1 and U.S. 101 come briefly together. From that point on, one would presumably stick to U.S. 101, although just off State Route 1 at Lompoc there is a mission, La Purisma Concepcion, which is mostly a reconstruction but interesting and attractive nonetheless because of its outbuildings and its fine situation.

About the same distance to the north of the town of Santa Barbara, but to the east of U.S. 101, there is the unique little settlement of Solvang. As the name suggests, this is a Danish community; it was founded only in 1912. Solvang is thoroughly Danish in appearance, and it has an excellent Danish pastry shop, fine for tea. It also boasts a Spanish mission, once almost the only thing there. Called the Mission of Santa Ines, this is not one of the more famous ones, but the interior decorations have faded to a lovely pastel which gives it a quality all its own. Many of the Spanish missions were completely abandoned in the nineteenth century, and some almost crumbled away entirely. This was due not to the Americanization of California, but to a battle between the civil and religious authorities in California's Mexican period which ended in the secularization of the missions. For a time in the nineteenth century Santa Ines was used as a farmhouse, but the basic structure was not damaged and the Capuchins have since restored it.

The biggest and most famous of the coastal towns north of Los Angeles is Santa Barbara, long the favourite winter resort of rich conservative people from the East. It is beautifully situated between the mountains and the sea, and no expense has been spared to keep the Spanish sections Spanish and make the nice parts nicer. Santa Barbara also has the best preserved of all the missions, a large and impressive structure which is now the mother-house of the Franciscan Order in California. It lacks the intimate charm of San Carlos Borromeo or Santa Ines, but it has its own particular attractions, not the least of them the fact that the Franciscans themselves act as guides there.

As one comes to expect in California, Los Angeles is surrounded by some magnificent scenery. But in some other ways she certainly leaves something to be desired. Los Angeles has been described as fifty suburbs in search of a city, and this is painfully accurate. 'Downtown' Los Angeles is by no means as neglected today as it was even ten years ago, yet it remains, for most tourists, simply the place where all the freeways intersect, plaited over and under in a futuristic tangle. With the exception of Olvera Street with its colourful Mexican street market, and the handsome new multi-building Music Center, central Los Angeles does not include any of the sights most visitors come here to see. Moreover, it's a painfully long distance away from most of them.

However, before we plunge into the geography of the greater Los Angeles area, we must announce that the situation for visitors has been eased considerably by the ingenuity of RTD, the Los Angeles public transport system. There is a bus service to every corner of this vast area, and it is made readily comprehensible. We urge anyone planning to spend time there either to write ahead for the RTD transit information kit, or to equip oneself on arrival. There is even a brochure outlining '21 vest-pocket tours' which one can do on the buses, to see all the standard Los Angeles sights and more besides. The central bus station is in the downtown area, and one can get all the maps and brochures either there or at the Southern California Visitors' Council office, another very useful place for all manner of tourist questions. See our listings; and remember that RTD will also answer telephone inquiries about what bus to take where. There are also, of course, Gray Line tours.

The general improvement of the central area of Los Angeles has certainly made that district a more attractive place to stay. There are good hotels, and the region around Olvera Street also includes what is left of the old Spanish core of the town, centred around the old Plaza. It is pleasant to spend an hour or two there, and then one might eat good Mexican food along Olvera Street. If there were something tempting on at one of the Music Center theatres afterwards, so much the better.

One can of course see central Los Angeles without staying in it. The only problem is deciding which corner of the area to choose instead; whatever choice one makes, one will then be miles across town from something else one wants to see. For the greater Los Angeles area really is fifty miles from end to end, and Disneyland and Beverly Hills, for example, are at opposite ends. We ourselves have experimented with staying at Santa Monica, at Pasadena, in Beverly Hills, in central Los Angeles, near Disneyland, and once (in early ignorance) even within the confines of Hollywood. We have not emerged from all this experimentation much the wiser, except that we now know there are disadvantages to each.

The easiest way to convey the geography of Los Angeles and the location of its various points of interest is to pretend that the centre of the city is the centre point of a clock dial, with 12 o'clock due north. Santa Monica, the nearest attractive seaside community, is then at 9 o'clock, roughly twenty miles from the centre of town. Beverly Hills and Hollywood are closer in, at 10 o'clock and 11 o'clock respectively. At about 10.30, so to speak, and a bit closer in again than either Beverly Hills or Hollywood, there is a complex of attractions which one might make one's starting point for seeing the best of greater Los Angeles: the Los Angeles County Museum of Art, the La Brea tar pits, the Farmers Market, and CBS Television City.

The Museum of Art is actually three buildings, all new and striking, set around an open plaza where one can have lunch out of doors. The Ahmanson Gallery houses the permanent art collection, and it is decidedly worth visiting. Los Angeles may have started its collecting late, but it has benefited both from the most advanced ideas in museumship and from extraordinarily generous donors. (One finds here now most of the treasures bought in recent years at Sotheby's by the California industrialist, Norton Simon.) The museum is particularly strong in the art of the Post-impressionist period and after, but everything here seems perfect of its kind, and displayed to perfection as well.

The La Brea tar pits are right next to the Museum of Art, a study in bizarre contrast. They really are tar pits, still bubbling away; they are significant because they were also bubbling away in the Pleistocene period, and thus trapped an astonishing range of prehistoric animal life. There are markers around the pits describing it all; to see the actual specimens which were recovered, however, one must go to the Museum of Natural History in another part of town.

Across Wilshire Boulevard from the tar pits is a combined restaurant and art gallery which we heartily recommend to anyone looking for a good lunch in delightful surroundings: The Egg and the Eye. And yet we are torn, for we also are very fond of eating at the Farmers Market, and that too is only a short walk due north from here. The Farmers Market began simply as a fine place to buy the best California fruit and vegetables, but long ago it took to purveying exotic groceries of all kinds and everything else as well from Guatemalan blouses to Swedish Christmas-tree ornaments. It has restaurants too, and stalls which sell food to eat on the spot: Chinese, Mexican, Italian.

North of the Farmers Market, at Fairfax Avenue and Beverly Boulevard, is CBS Television City, one of the major American television studios. Television production has become more important to Los Angeles than film-making, particularly since so many films are now shot on location, far away. One is thus as likely to see a famous face at one of the major television studios as anywhere else in the Los Angeles area. There are tours of the studios of the three principal television networks, but CBS seems the best choice because it is close to other points of interest, a matter of some importance in Los Angeles.

The CBS studios are roughly equidistant from Hollywood, to the north-east, and Beverly Hills, due west. There is nothing much to see these days in Hollywood proper. Tourists still go to look at the stars' footsteps embedded in the pavement in front of the ornate old Grauman's Chinese Theater, but nothing else in the neighbourhood reflects any of the old glamour; rather the reverse. To see what remains of the movie-world glitter, one is best advised to go to Beverly Hills, where one may encounter someone famous in the smart shops along Wilshire Boulevard. (You can get to these smart shops simply by taking a bus along Wilshire Boulevard beyond the Art Museum; get off at the Beverly Wilshire Hotel and walk on from there. Investigate North Rodeo Street too.) Or you might eat dinner at one of the expensive restaurants along La Cienega Boulevard, also in Beverly Hills.

There is one film studio, Universal, which offers tours. Much of its production these days is devoted to television series, but its tour is fun nonetheless and it gives a fine over-all view of the inner workings of film production. To take the tour, which lasts four hours, you can either go directly to the studio by bus or car, or you can do it all through Gray Line.

Street vendors along Santa Monica Boulevard in Beverly Hills sell 'maps to the movie stars' homes', and anyone with a car could also investigate the glamorous life in that manner. The houses which are along the 'canyons' up above Beverly Hills and Bel Air, in the foothills which close Los Angeles in at the north, are very attractive no matter who the owners may be. Moreover, if you had a car and the time, you would find it worth driving up into these hills after dark some night, to see the breathtaking panorama of the lights of Los Angeles stretching away to the horizon.

The architecture and the life-style of the contemporary-minded affluent citizens of Los Angeles is far more sophisticated today; Hollywood flamboyance has largely disappeared. But some relics of the past remain to remind one of the old tone, and one of these is Forest Lawn Memorial Park, that fantastic cemetery which Evelyn Waugh described so pitilessly in *The Loved One*. It is at about 1 o'clock on our imaginary clock dial, north-east of Hollywood, and it is such a popular tourist attraction that Gray Line runs special tours there.

The Pasadena Freeway goes from the centre of Los Angeles towards 2 o'clock, according to our system. On its way to Pasadena it passes the turn-off for the Southwest Museum; not very many visitors seem to know about the Southwest Museum and yet it has one of the finest collections of American Indian art and culture to be found anywhere. And at Pasadena itself there is an even more remarkable place, the Huntington Library, Gallery, and Botanical Gardens. We are told that Pasadena suffers more from smog than almost any other part of the Los Angeles region, but when we saw the Huntington it seemed the ideal oasis to which to retreat on a hot Los Angeles day. It is a large estate, handsomely situated high up above the valley. The gardens are absolutely magnificent, and its various collections are worth every moment of the drive to Pasadena. The Library section is primarily a centre for scholarly research, but it too exhibits some of its rarest treasures.

Greater Los Angeles is of course an exotic blend of diverse elements, rich and poor, old and young, black and white and oriental and chicano (Mexican–American). The Watts district, at 6 o'clock on our imaginary dial, is now almost entirely a black section, but a poor Italian immigrant named Simon Rodia once lived there, and in the course of thirty years he created a labour of love which has become celebrated as 'the Watts towers'. A peregrinating art critic of *The Times* called them 'one of the oddest and most touching works of art in America, and one of the most remarkable works of folk art anywhere'. They are a soaring, intricate complex of broken bits of glass and tile and tin in a steel framework; the highest tower is nearly one hundred feet high, and the effect is indeed innocently beautiful. They are quite easy to get to, too, and we urge you to go.

The greatest tourist attraction in the Los Angeles area is Disneyland, Walt Disney's splendid fun-fair. It is farther from the centre of the city than any of the other places we have mentioned, in a south-easterly '4.30' direction. However, one can go there on an ordinary bus; a Disneyland Freeway Flyer starts at the main RTD station in Los Angeles. (There are also day-long Gray Line bus tours which include both Disneyland and Knott's Berry Farm.) If one cares about getting a turn on the various rides at Disneyland without long waits, it is wise to get there early in the day, particularly at weekends and in the summer. Note too that it is closed entirely on Monday and Tuesday in the autumn and winter months.

No matter how sophisticated one's tastes may be, everyone seems to love Disneyland. Even those who begin with a superior sniff are usually captivated sooner or later, even if only by the meticulous neatness and cleanliness. In fact the only real criticism we have heard came from one visitor who complained that Disneyland was positively antiseptic; she said she much preferred the casual disorder and confusion of Knott's Berry Farm nearby, where the main attraction is a rip-roaring simulation of the old West, with stagecoach rides and a chance to pan for gold. Perhaps in deference to Knott's Berry Farm, a much older enterprise, Disneyland rather neglects the world of the cowboys and the prospector, and concentrates instead on space (Tomorrowland) and the fairytale (Fantasyland) and the quainter aspects of nineteenth-century America (Main Street and Frontierland).

There is one last tourist attraction in the greater Los Angeles area which deserves to be mentioned: Marineland, on the coast west of Disneyland and almost forty miles from central Los Angeles. Marineland is essentially an elaborate aquarium combined with a porpoise circus like those in Florida. Like them, it is a fascinating place, and the Palos Verdes peninsula on which it is situated is also attractive, offering a lovely view of the Pacific from its hills. On the coast near Marineland there is a small church built entirely of glass, the Wayfarers' Chapel.

Going south from Los Angeles along the coast, you pass one beach resort after another, many of them rather unprepossessing. One of the best is Laguna, which is also an artists' colony. Five or six miles south of Laguna is a particularly famous mission, San Juan Capistrano. Most of it now lies in ruins, but they are highly romantic ruins, with white doves perched on the crumbling arches of the cloisters. And thirty miles farther on is still another mission, San Luis Rey. This last was one of the largest missions, and it is still in use, a handsome building with a delightful, gaudy interior. Near the missions, and in the inland valleys of this region, are countless orange and lemon groves. The industrious Spanish missionaries introduced the cultivation of these fruit trees to California in the eighteenth century, and they are now an important part of the economy.

The city of San Diego, almost at the Mexican border, is a year-round resort town where the temperature is almost the same in January as in June. With an excellent harbour, San Diego is an important naval base, and it has fine beaches too. All of this one might expect, but we should also mention that the San Diego zoo is celebrated throughout the country for its innovations in animal care and the excellence of its collection.

Los Angeles itself can be very hot in the summer, and anyone who is there then ought to sample one of the beaches. One might drive perhaps to Santa Monica and then turn north, to Malibu and beyond. If you have no car, you can nonetheless get to several different beaches by bus.

At certain times of the year, one can swim in the morning and ski in the afternoon; Los Angeles is that close to good mountains, and the coastal climate is that different from the climate further inland. But in winter many of the Los Angeles citizenry are inclined to long not for skiing but for a hotter sun, and so they go to the desert. Much of southern California is properly considered desert. Some of it, the Imperial Valley for example, has responded so luxuriantly to irrigation that it is now astonishingly rich agricultural land. Other areas, like the Mojave Desert, remain arid and desolate. There are also a few desert towns which have blossomed as resorts. The most famous of these is Palm Springs, a splendid oasis in the midst of date-growing country about one hundred miles south-east of Los Angeles. It has countless hotels and motels, and tempting shops; many film stars have houses there too.

The most remarkable desert in all of California, however, is Death Valley. It is not really near Los Angeles, nor any of the other places we have discussed in this chapter; it is along the Nevada border, not too far from Las Vegas. We would like to suggest combining Death Valley with Yosemite by driving along the spine of California, for we ourselves like that drive along U.S. 395. Unfortunately, however, Death Valley tends to become uninhabitable at the very moment in spring at which the eastern entrance to Yosemite becomes passable, and in the autumn the situation is reversed. Nonetheless, we urge that anyone who is driving through California during the cooler months of the year consider going to Death Valley. At any time between the beginning of November and the end of April it is a magnificent spot to spend a day or two. There is one expensive hotel and two simpler lodges, all of course with swimming pools; there are also campsites. In winter Death Valley is beautifully hot, in spring the mountain passes leading down into it are rich in flowering desert vegetation, and at all times of the year its canyons and craters are extraordinarily colourful, and there are wonderful corners to explore. It is fascinating to stand at the lowest point in the western hemisphere, 280 feet below sea level, with Mount Whitney at 14,495 feet on the horizon. But Death Valley is much more than a curiosity, and without any hesitation we will leave our readers there.

SPECIAL KNOWLEDGE

The **season** of the year makes a considerable difference to several of the regions we have discussed in this chapter. One could of course happily visit San Francisco or Los Angeles at any time. San Francisco is never either really hot or really cold, although it may be damp and foggy. Los Angeles is hot in summer and generally mild in winter: a considerably warmer climate than San Francisco's, with much more sun but sometimes also with bad smog. The Seattle and Portland regions are more seasonal in their appeal to visitors. It is never bitterly cold there, but they do get a great deal of rain. Since one would like bright clear weather for exploring the great outdoors around Seattle and Portland it is thus safest to go there in full summer, although May–June and September and early October can sometimes be fine too. Driving down the coast would not tempt most people in winter, but in summer, when California's lowland interior can get very hot indeed, the coast road between San Francisco and Los Angeles seems particularly attractive. We have warned that the eastern entrance to Yosemite is usually open only from May to October, although one can get in from the west all year round. We should also remind everyone that even in mid-summer it can get downright cold in the mountains, especially at night, so that one wants both stout shoes and a warm jacket for a place like Yosemite. On the other hand, the Forty-Niner country, which one might combine with Yosemite, is not nearly so high, and it therefore tends to be hot in summer. That is when most people go there, however, so that is when all its old miners hotels are sure to be open; the rest of the year some are shut except on weekends and some shut completely for a period in winter. (That, together with their limited capacity, is good reason for telephoning ahead.) But our most serious climate warning concerns Death Valley. We have said it is only a good place to go between early November and late April, and we do mean that; most of the facilities in Death Valley shut down for the long hot summer, and this includes the only garage, and the ranger patrols of the side roads. A breakdown in the desert heat there could then be a serious affair. We might also refer our readers back to our notes at the end of Chapter 9, for general advice about desert driving; there is more than one desert in southern California. And for summer driving throughout most of California, make sure that any car you hire has air-conditioning in good working order; it makes trips a lot more pleasant, and usually costs no more.

Desert driving is not one's only **driving** challenge in California. The Los Angeles freeways and San Francisco's hills present certain problems too. With the freeways, it is important to plan exactly which freeways and exits you will want before you set off; a good navigator sitting beside you is even better protection, for there is certainly no chance for the driver to pause and reflect once he has plunged into those streams of traffic. In San Francisco, where driving up and down the precipitous hills can be a real test of nerve, the law says that cable cars always have the right of way, and that anyone who parks on the hills must have the emergency brake full on and the car wheels turned into the curb. (You can also avoid the worst hills with a little judicious route-planning.) Despite all these strictures, we are very much in favour of everyone taking to the roads in order properly to explore the West Coast. The scale of this country may make for long distances between objectives, but it also means that only the roads near the biggest cities are ever crowded, and since the West Coast is even more car-oriented than the rest of America, one need never worry about a lack of petrol stations or motels. Moreover, as we have said before, if there are at least two people, it is almost always considerably cheaper to hire a car (with one of the free-mileage schemes) than it is to take an organized tour of some region.

Nevertheless, there is no lack of regional **tours** for the West Coast, in addition to the tours in and around the cities which Gray Line and other companies operate. One can, for example, do a tour through southern California from Los Angeles. There is also an excellent organization, California Parlour Car Tours, which runs bus tours along the California coast road between Los Angeles and San Francisco, and other tours from San Francisco to the Monterey peninsula, and to Yosemite, and to Lake Tahoe and Nevada's Virginia City and Reno. For Oregon, the Gray Line at Portland offers tours all the way to Crater Lake, and along the Oregon coast. Seattle is also a fine centre from which to circle out, to Mount Rainier and in other directions. One- and two-day Gray Line tours of the Olympic Peninsula start from Port Angeles, on the peninsula itself; you can make connections by taking an ordinary bus from Seattle to Port Angeles. (In summer, one can also get to Port Angeles from Victoria in British Columbia by ferry.) See our listings for all of these.

Organized tours are not one's only alternative to a car. You can get to Yosemite, and also to Lassen Volcanic National Park, by **bus**. For Yosemite, one goes first to Merced or Fresno in California by Greyhound bus or Continental Trailways (or even by plane) and then takes a Yosemite Park and Curry Co. bus into the Park itself. (The very best source of information about how to get to Yosemite is the Yosemite Park and Curry Co., which has offices in San Francisco, Los Angeles, Dallas, and Seattle; these offices can also make the necessary reservations both for their buses into the Park and for accommodations there.) To let you see a bit of Canada from Seattle, from May to October there is a ferry run between Seattle and Victoria, British Columbia, which allows for five hours at Victoria. By taking a connecting bus for part of the way, one can even go all the way from Seattle to the city of Vancouver in British Columbia by sea, stopping at Victoria. (The Canadian Pacific operates these two services.) And finally we might even note that inveterate gamblers have been known to fly from Los Angeles to Las Vegas in the evening just for a few hours at the gaming tables; the plane schedules make this possible, and it's not even prohibitively expensive.

We have said that one cannot make reservations for **camping** sites in the National Parks. One can make reservations, however, for both the Oregon and the California state park systems, and both of these states have magnificent parks which anyone camping in the West is sure to want to try. For each system there is a central mailing address to which one can write for general information about the parks and the reservation system, and there is alsa a central telephone number for each system. Through this number in Oregon one can find out which Oregon parks currently have space available and how to reserve it. The California system works a bit differently, since one must book and pay for one's reservation through a **Ticketron** office. One can telephone the central number for general information, but there are also regional Ticketron numbers one may call to learn the whereabouts of the nearest Ticketron booking office, and also to learn which parks have space available. You might note, however, that reservations in the California system must be made by the Monday preceding any given Friday-to-Thursday period; after that, no further reservations are accepted and camping space is awarded on a first-come, first-served basis. (See our listings for these addresses and telephone numbers.)

San Francisco has more than the usual number of **tourist information sources**, and we have included them all in our listings. International visitors who have any special questions or problems might like to get in touch with the International Hospitality Center, a very helpful organization which can also arrange for visitors to meet American families.

There are some excellent topical and regional paperback **guidebooks** for the West Coast, the *Sunset Travel Books*, published by a West Coast firm. Widely available there, and lively and accurate, they make indispensable companions for exploring such areas as the Forty-Niner country or the California coast and its parks.

The West Coast has superb **seafood**: the salmon of Washington and Oregon, Dungeness crab, Rex sole, sand dabs, California abalone, and the ineffable Olympia oyster. But the same warning we gave for New England applies here; unless you are sure you are in an exceptionally good restaurant, have your seafood as little tampered with as possible. Order the oysters without the 'cocktail' sauce, for example, and try to have the salmon poached; there is an ugly tendency in most West Coast seafood restaurants to overcook and to smother the natural glories with inferior embellishments. Along equally sybaritic lines, we must also mention I. Magnin's, a splendid chain of **women's clothing** shops. There is an I. Magnin's in all the major cities of the West Coast, the best possible source for elegant California fashions.

We are somewhat reluctant to recommend **hotels** we have not sampled ourselves, but everyone tells us that the Salishan Lodge is the most spectacular place to stay at along the Oregon coast; it's near the town of Glenadon Beach. The most luxurious of all the new American Indian resorts is also in Oregon, at Warm Springs in the rather arid but handsome north-central region; it's called Kah-nee-ta, and it has an enormous mineral water swimming pool, luxurious cottages, and camping tepees.

Since the great sport off the California beaches is **surfing**, we conclude by noting that Los Angeles provides a special service for surfers. To get the daily report on surfing and beach conditions at Malibu, telephone 457–9701; for South Bay-Redondo Beach, telephone 379–8471.

Ashland, Oregon

OREGON SHAKESPEAREAN FESTIVAL. Indoor and outdoor performances from early June to mid-September; mid-March to early May, indoor performances including modern plays. For information write to Shakespeare, P.O. Box 605, Ashland, Oregon 97520.

Carmel, California

BASILICA OF SAN CARLOS BORROMEO DEL RIO CARMELO. South of Carmel on Lasuen Drive. Monday to Saturday 9.30–5, Sunday and holidays 10.30–5. Closed Thanksgiving and 25 December.

Los Angeles, California

SOUTHERN CALIFORNIA VISITORS' COUNCIL, 705 West 7th Street at Hope Street, Los Angeles, California 90017; telephone 628–3101. Open weekdays.

TRANSPORTS AND TOURS

R.T.D. (public transport system). Information from the central bus station and information office, 6th Street at Los Angeles Street; telephone 747–4455. Written inquiries to R.T.D. Public Information, 1060 South Broadway, Los Angeles, California 90015.

C.B.S. TOURS. Tickets obtainable from C.B.S. Ticket Division, 7800 Beverly Boulevard, Los Angeles. It is usually possible to visit the studios without reservations on a first-come, first-served basis.

GRAY LINE TOURS, 1207 West 3rd Street, Los Angeles, California 90017; telephone (213) 481–2121.

UNIVERSAL STUDIOS TOUR, Hollywood Freeway at Lankershim Boulevard, Universal City. 8 June to 7 September, daily 9–5; rest of the year, Monday to Saturday 10–3.30, Sunday 10.30–3.30. Closed 1 January, Thanksgiving and 25 December. The tour lasts 4 hours.

DISNEYLAND, 1313 Harbor Boulevard, off the Santa Anna Freeway at Anaheim. Mid-June to mid-September daily 8 a.m. to 1 a.m.; rest of the year Wednesday to Friday 10–6, Saturday and Sunday 9–7. Over Christmas and Easter holiday periods, open daily. Besides the R.T.D. bus and the Gray Line bus tour there is transport by helicopter from the Los Angeles International Airport.

THE EGG AND THE EYE (restaurant and gallery-boutique), on Wilshire Boulevard opposite the County Museum of Art. Restaurant open Tuesday to Saturday 11–3.30 and 6–11; Sunday brunch 11–7.

FOREST LAWN MEMORIAL PARK, 1712 South Glendale Avenue, Glendale. Daily 8.30–5.30. Free.

THE HUNTINGTON LIBRARY, GALLERY AND BOTANICAL GARDENS, 1151 Oxford Road, San Marino. Tuesday to Sunday 1–4.30. Closed major holidays and October. Free.

KNOTT'S BERRY FARM, on Beach Boulevard off Santa Anna Freeway at Buena Vista. Summer, Sunday to Thursday 9 a.m.–11 p.m., Friday and Saturday 9 a.m.–midnight; rest of the year, Monday to Thursday 10–7, Friday and Saturday 10–10, Sunday 10–9. Closed 25 December.

LOS ANGELES COUNTY MUSEUM OF ART, 5905 Wilshire Boulevard. Tuesday to Friday 10–5, Saturday 10–6, Sunday 12–6. Closed Thanksgiving and 25 December.

MARINELAND, Palos Verdes Drive South at Long Point. Daily 10 to sunset. For feeding times and shows telephone 377–1571.

MUSIC CENTER FOR THE PERFORMING ARTS is in the Civic Center. Tours in summer, Monday, Tuesday, Thursday and Friday, 10–4; rest of the year Monday to Thursday 10–2; telephone 626–5781.

SOUTHWEST MUSEUM, 234 Museum Drive. A fine American Indian collection. Tuesday to Sunday 1–4.45. Closed major holidays and mid-August to mid-September. Free.

WATTS TOWERS, 1765 East 107 Street. Daily 10–5.

Lummi Indian Reservation, Washington

LUMMI INDIAN ARTS AND CRAFTS AND LUMMI INDIAN WEAVERS, on State Highway 540, 7 miles north-west of Bellingham. 1 June to 31 August, daily 8.30–6; 1 September to 31 May, daily 8.30–4.30.

Mokulumne Hill, California

HOTEL LÉGER, in Mokulumne Hill on State Route 49, telephone (209) 286–1312. Open from 1 May to mid-January; from mid-January to 30 April open from Wednesday to Sunday.

National Parks, State Parks, National Monuments

COLUMBIA STATE HISTORIC PARK, California. On State Route 49. The Museum is open daily 8–5. Closed Thanksgiving and 25 December.

CRATER LAKE NATIONAL PARK, Oregon. General information from the Superintendent, Crater Lake National Park, Box 7, Crater Lake, Oregon 97604. From 15 June to 15 September, overnight accommodation, meals and limited garage facilities are available. For accommodation reservations from 15 June to 15 September write to Crater Lake Lodge Inc., Crater Lake, Oregon 97604; rest of the year to Crater Lake Lodge Inc., P.O. Box 25160, Portland, Oregon 97225.

DEATH VALLEY NATIONAL MONUMENT, California. General information from the Superintendent, Death Valley National Monument, California 92328. Accommodation includes Furnace Creek Inn, telephone (714) 786–2361, Furnace Creek Ranch, telephone (714) 786–2345, open from November to mid-April, and Stove Pipe Wells Village, telephone Stove Pipe Wells 1 via San Bernardino, open all year. Reservations for the first two may be obtained from Los Angeles, telephone 776–5535.

FORT ROSS STATE HISTORIC PARK, California. Daily 9–5; summer until 6.

HEARST SAN SIMEON STATE HISTORIC PARK, California, off State Route 1, between San Francisco and Los Angeles. Tours leave every 20 to 30 minutes and last about 2 hours. The ticket office opens at 8 a.m., but tickets may be obtained in advance from the Hearst Reservation Office, Department of Parks and Recreation, Box 2390, Sacramento, California 95811. There is a reservation and a cancellation fee.

LA PURISMA MISSION STATE HISTORIC PARK, California. 4 miles north-east of Lompoc near State Route 1. Daily, summer 9–6; winter 8–5. Closed 1 January, Thanksgiving and 25 December.

LASSEN VOLCANIC NATIONAL PARK, California. Headquarters are $\frac{1}{2}$ mile west of Mineral on State Route 36. General information from the Superintendent, Lassen Volcanic National Park, Mineral, California 96063. Accommodation information from Lassen National Park Company, Manzanita Lake, California 96060. Accommodation is available from mid-June to mid-September and during this period there is a bus service from the Greyhound bus station at Redding, California, run by Lassen National Park Company buses. Some campgrounds open May to October.

MOUNT RAINIER NATIONAL PARK, Washington. For information, including accommodation, hotel and camping, write to the Superintendent, Mount Rainier National Park, Longmire, Washington 98399. *See also under* **Seattle** (Tours and Ferries).

OLYMPIC NATIONAL PARK, Washington. General information from the Superintendent, Olympic National Park, 600 Park Avenue, Port Angeles, Washington 98362.

Gray Line of the Olympics, 107 East Front Street, Port Angeles, runs tours into the Olympic National Park daily from 1 June to 10 September, subject to a minimum of 4 passengers. Port Angeles may be reached by Greyhound bus (telephone MA4-3456) or from Victoria, Canada, by ferry which runs from 18 June to 6 September.

OREGON STATE PARKS, Oregon. For information and reservations write to State Parks and Recreation Section, 300 State Highway Building, Salem, Oregon 97310; or telephone (800) 452-0294 (toll free).

SEQUOIA AND KING'S CANYON NATIONAL PARKS, California. For general information apply to the Superintendent, Sequoia and King's Canyon National Parks, Three Rivers, California 93271. Accommodation (cottage and tent cabins only) information from Sequoia and King's Canyon National Park Co., Sequoia National Park, California 93262. Accommodation available from mid-May to October. Camping and hiking supplies, and even a mule or a burro, can be hired within Sequoia at Giant Forest, near the Lodgepole Visitors' Center.

YOSEMITE NATIONAL PARK, California. General information from the Superintendent, Yosemite National Park, California 95389. The Visitor Center in Yosemite Village, open daily 8–6, will supply maps and information on hikes, riding, films and evening programmes and talks. The Yosemite Park and Curry Co., Yosemite National Park, California 95389, will supply information and reserve accommodation for longer hikes or riding trips and for the Yosemite Transport System which runs a daily bus service from Fresno and Merced. Reservations for the latter should be made for both inward and outward journeys, which take 2½ hours (altogether 5 hours from San Francisco). In summer it is essential to book accommodation and during the rest of the year advisable. This information is also available from the Yosemite Park and Curry Co., at 3075 Wilshire Boulevard, Los Angeles, telephone (213) 388–1151, or Russ Building, San Francisco, telephone (415) 434–0660. In Seattle the telephone number is (206) 682–1981, and in Dallas (214) 741–6814.

Portland, Oregon

WASHINGTON PARK, south-west of the city at the head of Park Avenue. Japanese Gardens are open 1 June to 31 August, Tuesday to Saturday, 10–6, Sunday 10–8; Labor Day to 31 October, Saturday and Sunday 12–5 (weather permitting).

Sacramento, California

SUTTER'S FORT, 28th and L Streets. Daily 10–5. Closed Thanksgiving and 25 December.

San Diego, California

SAN DIEGO ZOOLOGICAL GARDENS, Balboa Park off Park Boulevard. 1 July to Labor Day, daily 9–6; Labor Day to 31 October and 1 March to 30 June 9–5; 1 November to 28 February 9–4.

San Francisco, California

CONVENTION AND VISITORS BUREAU, Fox Plaza, San Francisco, California 94102. Telephone (415) 626–5500.

VISITORS INFORMATION CENTER (to open in 1973–74), Hallidie Plaza, Powell and Market Streets.

FREE TELEPHONE SERVICE for recorded announcement of daily special events and 'sightseeing trips': 391–2000.

A GRAY LINE BUS is parked at Union Square along Powell Street, where one can obtain general information on San Francisco.

INTERNATIONAL HOSPITALITY CENTER, 55 Grant Avenue, Monday to Friday 9–5; telephone 986–1388.

REDWOOD EMPIRE ASSOCIATION VISITORS' CENTER, 476 Post Street.

TOURS AND FERRIES

CALIFORNIA PARLOR CAR TOURS, 369 Market Street, San Francisco 94105. Excellent 3- 4- and 5-day tours along the coast to Los Angeles, Yosemite and other places of interest in California.

GRAY LINE TOURS, Gray Line Terminal, First and Mission Streets. Telephone 771–4000. Tours of San Francisco operate mornings and afternoons. There are also tours to Sausalito, Muir Woods and the Monterey Peninsula.

HARBOR TOURS INC., Pier 43½, Fisherman's Wharf. 1¼-hour boat tours on San Francisco Bay. Frequent daily departures from 10 a.m. Also operate passenger service to Tiburon and Angel Island from 13 March to 21 November, Saturday, Sunday and holidays; 1 June to 10 September to Angel Island daily. First boat leaves at 10 a.m., last one at 3.45 p.m. Telephone (415) 362–5415.

SAUSALITO FERRY leaves from the San Francisco Ferry Building at the foot of Market Street. Ferries leave fairly frequently.

THE CANNERY, at the end of Columbus Avenue on Beach Street. Shops are open Monday to Saturday 10–6, Sunday, 11–6. Open later between Thanksgiving and 25 December.

GHIRARDELLI SQUARE, between North Point, Larkin, Beach and Polk Streets. Shops are open normal shopping hours and Sunday afternoons, and some are open late on Friday and Saturday evenings.

MARITIME STATE HISTORIC PARK, at the foot of Hyde Street. 1 May to 15 September, daily 9 a.m.–10 p.m.; rest of the year 9–6.

MISSION SAN FRANCISCO DE ASIS (or MISSION DOLORES), Dolores Street near 16th Street. Daily, summer 9–5; winter 10–4.

WELLS FARGO HISTORY ROOM, in the Wells Fargo Bank, 420 Montgomery Street. Every banking day 10–3. Free.

M. H. de YOUNG MEMORIAL MUSEUM, in the Golden Gate Park, near the 8th Avenue and Fulton Street entrance. Daily 10–5.

San Juan Batista, California
MISSION SAN JUAN BATISTA is on the northern side of the Plaza. Daily, summer 9.30–5.30; winter 10–4.30. Closed 1 January, Thanksgiving, 25 December and during the fiesta in mid-July.

San Juan Capistrano, California
MISSION SAN JUAN CAPISTRANO. Daily 7–5.

San Luis Rey de Francia, California
MISSION SAN LUIS REY DE FRANCIA, 4 miles east of Oceanside on State Route 76. Daily 9–4.30. Closed Thanksgiving and 25 December.

San Miguel, California
MISSION SAN MIGUEL ARCANGEL, on U.S. Route 101. Daily 10–5. Closed 25 December.

Santa Barbara, California
MISSION SANTA BARBARA, Los Olivos and Laguna Streets. Monday to Saturday 9.30–5; Sunday 1–5.

Seattle, Washington
SEATTLE VISITORS BUREAU, 215 Columbia Street, Washington 98104.

TOURS AND FERRIES

CANADIAN PACIFIC RAIL FERRY SERVICES, Granville and Cordova, Vancouver 2, B.C. A ferry service runs from Seattle to Victoria and on by coach to Nanaimo and then again by ferry to Vancouver, from 30 April to 2 October, daily 8.30, arriving 5.45; before 25 June and after 11 September there is a 6-hour wait in Victoria, arriving Vancouver at 1.45 a.m. the following morning.

GRAY LINE TOUR: 'Discovery' bus tour of Seattle. These run daily, one in the winter, several in summer, and last 2 hours. For reservations telephone MU2–1234.

MOUNT RAINIER NATIONAL PARK SIGHTSEEING TOUR, operated by Mount Rainier National Park Hospitality Service, Government Services Inc., Western Tours Inc., 415 Seneca Street; telephone 682–5950.

BILL SPEIDEL UNDERGROUND TOUR, starts from Pioneer Square and takes 2 hours. Reservations required a day in advance: telephone MU2–4646. Monday to Saturday 9–5.

WASHINGTON STATE FERRIES: Seattle Terminal, Pier 52, foot of Marion Street; telephone 464–6400. Anacortes, Ferry Terminal, telephone 293–2188. Ferries from Seattle and Anacortes go to Orcas Island, and on to Sidney, B.C.

WESTERN TOURS: Coach and coach-and-boat tours. 1 June to Labor Day, daily, lasting 2¼ to 3½ hours. For reservations telephone MU2–5950.

THOMAS BURKE MEMORIAL STATE MUSEUM, University of Washington. Tuesday to Saturday 10–4.30, Sunday 1–4.30.

INDIAN CENTER CRAFTS, 1900 Boren Avenue (for Lummi Indian knit-wear). Monday to Friday 9.30–4.30, Saturday 10–3.

MUSEUM OF HISTORY AND INDUSTRY, McCurdy Park on Lake Washington, 2161 East Hamlin Street. Tuesday to Friday 11–5, Saturday 10–5, Sunday 12–5. Closed 1 January, 30 May, Thanksgiving and 25 December. Free.

SEATTLE ART MUSEUM, Volunteer Park. Tuesday to Saturday 10–5, Sunday and holidays 12–5, Thursday evenings 7–10. Free.

SPACE NEEDLE, in Seattle Center. The observation deck is open daily 7.30 a.m.–11 p.m.

Solvang, California

MISSION SANTA INES. Summer, daily 9–5.30; winter, Monday to Friday 9.30–4.30, Saturday and Sunday 9–5.

Sonoma, California

MISSION SAN FRANCISCO SOLANO DE SONOMA, at Spain and First Street East. Daily 10–5. Closed 1 January, Thanksgiving, 25 December.

VALLEJO'S RANCH HOUSE, about a mile west of The Plaza. Daily 10–5.

Wineries, California

NEAR U.S. ROUTE 101, NORTH OF SAN FRANCISCO

KORBEL, about 10 miles west of Healdsburg, near Guerneville. Daily 8.30–4.30. Tours 15 June to 15 September; telephone (707) 887–2294.

NAPA VALLEY AND SONOMA AREA

BUENA VISTA, Old Winery Road, 1 mile east of Sonoma Plaza. Daily 9–5. Tours by appointment. Telephone (707) 938–8504.

CHARLES KRUG, State Route 29, just north of St. Helena. Daily 10–4. Telephone (707) 963–2761.

INGLENOOK, State Route 29 at Rutherford. Monday to Friday 10–4. Telephone (707) 963–7182.

LOUIS MARTINI, State Route 29, ½ mile south of St. Helena. Daily 10–4.30. Telephone (707) 963–2736.

ROBERT MONDAVI, State Route 29, at Oakville. Daily 10–4.30. Telephone (707) 963–7156.

SOUTH OF SAN FRANCISCO, SANTA CLARA VALLEY

PAUL MASSON, near Saratoga, taking the Saratoga exit from Interstate Route 280. Daily 10–4. Telephone (408) 257–7800. 'Music at the Vineyards': tickets available only in advance, from 330 Jackson Street, San Francisco, California 94111.

INDEX